The Human Rights of Children

# Nijhoff Law Specials

VOLUME 105

The titles published in this series are listed at *brill.com/nlsp*

# The Human Rights of Children

*Selected Essays on Children's Rights*

*By*

Michael Freeman

BRILL
NIJHOFF

LEIDEN | BOSTON

Library of Congress Control Number: 2022933731

Typeface for the Latin, Greek, and Cyrillic scripts: "Brill". See and download: brill.com/brill-typeface.

ISSN: 0924-4549
ISBN 978-9004-21909-0 (paperback)
ISBN 978-9004-21910-6 (e-book)



This book is printed on acid-free paper and produced in a sustainable manner.

# Contents

# Preface

This collection of essays is a response to appeals I have received that I put together essays I have written and published on themes relating to children's rights over a period of more than 30 years.

I was one of the first legal scholars to write on children's rights, certainly to see the interdisciplinary nature of the issues. There are legal doctrinal questions, of course, but these presuppose that a case has been made for recognising that children have rights. This brings into the equation moral and political philosophy. Contributions can also be made by the historian, the psychologist, the anthropologist, the theologian. The list is endless. I do not pretend to command expertise in such a range of subject areas. And, as Alexander Pope reminded us " A little learning is a dangerous thing."

I am grateful to all who assisted with the preparation of the text, in particular my wife, Vivien, whose support is increasingly invaluable.

*Michael Freeman,*
June 2021

# Acknowledgements

The essays in this volume are reproduced with the kind permission of all copyright holders. The author is grateful for their support.

Chapter 1 "The Human Rights of Children", *Current Legal Problems*, Volume 63, 2010, Oxford University Press.

Chapter 2 "A Time to be Born and a Time to Die", *Current Legal Problems*, Volume 56, 2003, Oxford University Press.

Chapter 3 "Upholding the Dignity and Best Interests of Children: International Law and the Best Interests of Children", *Law and Contemporary Problems*, Volume 73, Number 2, Spring 2010, Duke University School of Law.

Chapter 4 "Whose Life is it Anyway?", *Medical Law Review*, 9, Autumn 2001, Oxford University Press.

Chapter 5 "The Morality of Cultural Pluralism", *The International Journal of Children's Rights*, 3: 1-17, 1995, Kluwer Academic Publishers.

Chapter 6 "Cleveland, Butler-Sloss and Beyond – How Are We to React to the Sexual Abuse of Children?", *Current Legal Problems*, 1989, Stevens and Sons Ltd, Law Publishers, London.

Chapter 7 "Does Surrogacy Have a Future after Brazier?", *Medical Law Review*, 7, Spring 1999, Oxford University Press.

Chapter 8 "Images of Child Welfare in Child Abduction Appeals", from *Ethnic Minorities, their Families and the Law*, J. Murphy, ed., 2000, Hart Publishing.

Chapter 9 "The Limits of Children's Rights", *The Ideologies of Children's Rights*, M. Freeman and P. Veerman, eds.,1992, Kluwer Academic Publishers.

CHAPTER 1

# The Human Rights of Children*

## Introduction

A few years ago *The Guardian* newspaper published an article by Julie Bindel entitled 'Six Weeks of Suffering'.[1] She argued that school holidays should be cut in half because the presence of children in her space – streets, parks, museums, public transport, restaurants – offends her. Let me quote her:

> I live in an area where kids (*sic*) are routinely taken to proper restaurants for lunch, but I was here before it became Nappy Valley... There seems to be no escape this summer. Ken Livingstone[2] has made it easier for the little monsters to follow me around London by giving school children free bus travel... There they are, in the museums when you least expect them.

Imagine *The Guardian*[3] publishing an article which objected to black people in restaurants or gays in museums! This article was written by the founder of 'Justice for Women'. You may find it telling that, espousing the position she does in relation to women, she could hold such views about children. You may also be discomforted by the publication of such an article in a liberal newspaper. But, of course, you may not. You may think, as the Canadian philosopher Harry Brighouse does,[4] that it is 'strange' to think of children as having rights. Or you may he concerned, as Bruce

* This paper is dedicated to the memory of Professor Neil MacCormick of Edinburgh University who died in 2009. He was a great friend of UCL and a member of the Editorial Board of Current Legal Problems. His article referred to in n 161 is seminal for understanding children's rights. I had the privilege to chair the paper which became that article. Neil will be sorely missed.

1 *The Guardian*, 18 August 2006, 35.

2 The Mayor of London at that time.

3 *The Daily Telegraph* famously attacked children's rights in a leading article entitled 'Scrap The Children Act' in 1996 (5 September). Its main concern was that the Act allowed children to 'divorce' their parents.

4 'What Rights (If Any) Do Children Have?' in D Archard and C Macleod (eds), *The Moral and Political Status of Children* (Oxford, 2002), 31-52, 31.

 | DOI:10.1163/9789004219106_002

Hafen puts it,[5] that we are 'abandoning' children to their rights. The majority opinion is still, as the most influential of writers of the last generation expressed it,[6] that the only right that children have is to autonomous parents.[7] But if, like me, you are appalled by the sentiments in Bindel's article, you may also ask why such attitudes are still prevalent, even predominant.[8] And you may have noticed the new Equality Act 2010.

## Equality Legislation

The Equality Act 2010 bans discrimination on more or less every conceivable ground, except discrimination against those under 18 years of age. The Discrimination Law Review in 2007 explained why children are excluded from the scope of the legislation.[9] Two paragraphs offer an attempt at justification. It argues that the 'basic principle of age discrimination legislation, that people should not be treated differently on the basis of their age, is... rarely appropriate to the treatment of children'.[10] We are nevertheless assured that there is commitment to ensuring that children have 'appropriate means of redress where they perceive they have been

5 He wrote of this in several places including 'Children's Liberation and the New Egalitarianism: Some Reservations about Abandoning Youth To Their Rights' (1976) *Brigham Young Law Review* 605-58.

6 Joseph Goldstein, Anna Freud, and Albert Solnit. They wrote a trilogy: *Beyond The Best Interests of the Child* (New York, 1973); *Before The Best Interests of the Child* (New York, 1980); *In The Best Interests* their thesis was put together in *The Best Interests of the Child* (New York, 1996). For the view that they are no longer seen as authoritative sources see JM Spinak, 'When Did Lawyers for Children Stop Reading Goldstein, Freud and Solnit?' (2007) 41 *Family Law Quarterly* 393.

7 See *The Best Interests of The Child,* op cit, n 6, 90. They also recognize the child's right to be represented by parents (*ibid,* 140), and to have parents who care (*ibid,* 148, 228). See M Freeman, 'The Best Interest of the Child? Is *The Best Interests of the Child* in the Best Interests of Children?' (1997) *Int J of Law, Policy and the Family* 360-88, 363-6.

8 A striking difference is UNICEF, *The State of The World's Children 2007* (New York, 2006), with its ringing call for equality, particularly its emphasis on the rights of women and children being 'mutually reinforcing' (p 1).

9 Department for Education and Skills, Department of Trade and Industry, Department for Work and Pensions, Ministry of Justice, Department for Communities and Local Government, *Discrimination Law Review – A Framework for Fairness: Proposals for a Single Equality Bill for Great Britain – A Consultation Paper* (London, June 2007).

10 *Ibid,* para 9.26.

treated unfairly'.[11] Indeed, we are told that the Commission for Equality and Human Rights 'will be considering the equality needs of children as part of its Strategic Plan'.[12] A year later the Government Equalities Office published a White Paper.[13] This states very clearly that 'it is wrong that people are treated in a discriminatory way because of their age'. And so, the Equality Act will 'enable us to make it unlawful to discriminate against someone because of their age when providing goods, facilities and services or carrying out public functions'.[14] Examples are given: a doctor who fails to investigate a health complaint raised by an older person or nor providing treatment simply because of their age. But it is not discrimination against children that is being addressed.

There was, of course, a consultation exercise. The case for including children was put, and nor just by children's rights organizations such as the Children's Commissioner and the Children's Rights Alliance for England, but also by the Equality and Human Rights Commission. The finding that 43 per cent of under-18-year-olds considered that they had been treated unfairly because of their age was cited.[15] Some of the examples of discrimination against children are quoted in the Government response. Although the list is illustrative, rather than exhaustive, it is worth quoting:

> [s]igns on shop doors saying 'no school children' or 'only two children at a time', difficulties experienced by teenagers in accessing mental health and child protection services, discriminatory treatment in leisure services such as cinemas and swimming pools, a lack of appropriate and safe seating in public transport for babies and younger children, the use of mosquito electronic devices, ASBOs, stop and search, curfews, dispersal zones and restrictions on the use of public space.[16]

In addition, local authorities cited concerns about restricted access to services for young people with learning disabilities as they leave chil-

---

11 *Ibid*, para 9.27.

12 *Ibid*.

13 *Framework for a Fairer Future – The Equality Bill*, Cm 7431, June 2008.

14 *Ibid*, 16.

15 *The Equality Bill – Government Response to the Consultation*, Cm 7454, July 2008, para 3.25.

16 *Ibid*. But ASBOs are to he abolished. See *The Guardian*, 4 August 2010.

dren's services and move into adult services.[17] The Government response was short (in length and shrift!):

> We have considered the arguments... for prohibiting age discrimination against children as well as adults. However, we continue to believe that age discrimination legislation is nor an appropriate way to ensure that children's needs are met.[18]

How are we to explain the way we think about children? There are a number of explanations one of which, that children are seen as property,[19] has had enough said about it already. I pause therefore to reflect on two other possible explanations. Both uncover over-articulated, but nevertheless useful, dichotomies. One asks about the relevance of the well-trodden public/private division to children and their lives; the second explores further the human beings/human becomings dualism.

### The Private World of Children

There· has been a lot of discussion of the implications of the public/private boundary in family law scholarship.[20] In my 'Inaugural' 25 years ago I explored this in relation to women.[21] I need not repeat what was said there, nor explore the ways that a burgeoning literature since has discussed the implications for women of seeing the home as a private space. But it has implications for children too, and this has been but little explored. This is not the place, nor is there the space, to ask theoretical questions about the public/private dichotomy: for example, to note the

---

17 *Ibid.*

18 *Ibid,* para 3.33.

19 I have discussed this in *The Rights and Wrongs of Children* (London, 1983); 'The Child in Family Law' in J Fionda (ed), *Legal Concepts of Childhood* (Oxford, 2001), 183-201, 187-8; and elsewhere. The classical source is Thomas Hobbes: parents may 'alienate' children, 'pawn them for hostages, kill them for rebellion, or sacrifice them for peace' (*The Elements of Law, Natural and Political* (1650) (Oxford, 1994), 23.8).

20 For example, K O'Donovan, *Social Division in Law* (London, 1976). See also E Gamarnikow *et al, The Public and the Private* (London, 1983); A Jaggar, *Feminist Politics and Human Nature* (Totowa, NJ, 1983}; and C Pateman, 'Feminist Critiques of the Public/Private Dichotomy' in A Phillips (ed), *Feminism and Equality* (Oxford, 1987), 103-26.

21 'Towards A Critical Theory of Family Law' (1985) 38 *Current Legal Problems* 153-85.

arbitrariness of the division[22] to discuss the ways the public inevitably defines what is private[23] to ask whether there is a space between the public and the private, an intermediary level perhaps.[24] But it is worth asking what the impact is on children of 'relegating' them to the 'private' realm. Rights are largely public coinage: it is thought that they are not as important in the private sphere. For children this is seen as a 'walled garden of "Happy, Safe, Protected, Innocent Childhood"'.[25]

Of course, this is the stuff of fairy tales, and, as a description of childhood, for many it is just plain wrong, with poverty, disease, exploitation, and abuse rife across the globe. The curtain of privacy hides all manner of evils: sexual abuse[26] forced marriages[27] female genital mutilation[28] religious indoctrination,[29] even slavery.[30] It also stifles the opportunities children might have to participate in the public arena, to communicate their views to decision-makers. And when they do communicate their opinions in public, they are deemed 'out of place', and met with patroni-

22 J Ribbens McCarthy and R Edwards, 'The Individual in the Public and Private: The Significance of Mothers and Children' in A Carling (ed), *Analysing Families* (London, 2002), 199-217.

23 See Freeman, *op cit*, n 21, and MDA Freeman, 'Rethinking Family Law' in MDA Freeman (ed), *State, Law and the Family – Critical Perspectives* (London, 1984), 1-6, 1.

24 See H Arendt, *The Human Condition* (Chicago, 1958); J Habermas, *The Structural Transformation of the Public Sphere: An Inquiry into a Category of Bourgeois Society* (Cambridge, MA, 1991).

25 J Holt, *Escape from Childhood* (Harmondsworth, 1975), 22-3. It is perhaps appropriate that the most famous collection of fairy tales is by the Brothers Grimm!

26 See M Freeman, 'The Sexual Abuse of Children' in B Brooks-Gordon, L Gelsthorpe, M Johnson, and A Bainham (eds), *Sexuality Repositioned* (Oxford, 2004), 317-38.

27 The Universal Declaration of Human Rights, Article 16(2) condemns the practice. So does Recommendation No 21 of the UN Committee on the Elimination of All Forms of Discrimination Against Women. Munby J has described forced marriage as 'an abomination', as much 'beyond the pale' as FGM and honour killings (*Singh v Entry Clearance Office, New Delhi* [2005] 1 FLR 308, para. 88). There is now legislation in the UK, the Forced Marriages (Civil Protection) Act 2007.

28 According to UNICEF, about 70 million women today have been subjected to this: UNICEF, 'Female Genital Cutting Must Stop' (2009). On its long-term problems see World Health Organization, 'Female Genital Mutilation and Obstetric Outcome' (2006) 367 *Lancet* 1835-41.

29 See JG Dwyer, 'Parents' Religion and Children's Welfare: Debunking The Doctrine of Parents' Rights' (1994) 82 *California Law Review* 1371-447. On schools see JG Dwyer, *Religious Schools* vs. *Children's Rights* (Ithaca, NY, 1998). See also I Narisetti, *Forced Into Faith: How Religion Abuses Children's Rights* (Amherst, NY, 2009). But *cf* J Lees and J Howarth (2009) 23 *Children and Society* 162-75.

30 Including bonded labour, sexual slavery. See 'Special Issue' of *Children and Society* vol 22 (3) (2008).

zation or simply ignored.[31] This is, of course, not to say that the position of the child is any stronger in the private sphere – the power imbalance ensures this.

The public/private divide may make more sense to men than to women.[32] It reflects their lives more than it does women's. Indeed, women may not see the two spheres as separable at all: they do not leave the 'private' behind when they enter the public realm of work. Women's experiences (their 'standpoint'[33]) tell us that the public/private divide is problematic and make us ask questions about their interrelationships. Less thought has been given to what the 'standpoint' of children might be on the private/public divide.[34] How do they perceive the 'school'? It is a focal place of childhood, a space where they naturally belong. Is it an extension of the family? It performs many – inevitably too many – of the same functions. But school is also a place where children learn about the world, about the place they will occupy in it, about power and inequality. Schooling is an imperative for economic development: as such it is a key investment, though not all education occurs at school. As far as children are concerned, the school may well be experienced as private, rather than public. Certainly, in so far as the language of rights has any meaning in the school setting, they inhere in parents, not their children. This is clear not only from domestic legislation,[35] but also from the UN Convention on the Rights of the Child (hereafter UNCRC)[36] and European jurispru-

---

31 See J Hine, *Children and Citizenship* (London, 2004).

32 This is explained well by DE Smith, *The Everyday World As Problematic: A Feminist Sociology* (Boston, Mass, 1987).

33 On 'standpoint' see KT Bartlett, 'Feminist Legal Methods' (1990) 103 *Harvard Law Review* 829.

34 Leena Alanen is one of the few to address this. See 'Gender and Generation: Feminism and the Child Question' in J Qvortrup, M Bardy, G Sgritta, and H Wintersberger (eds), *Childhood Matters: Social Theory, Practice and Politics* (Aldershot, 1994), 27-42.

35 See M Freeman, *Understanding Family Law* (London, 2007), 198-200. See also (the much earlier) M Freeman, 'Children's Education: A Test Case for Best Interests and Autonomy' in R Davie and D Galloway (eds), *Listening To Children in Education* (London, 1996), 29-48. It is worth adding that children also do not have duties to attend school.

36 This is despite Article 28 (and 29). It is worth examining Article 30 which emphasizes group rights, rather than child members of the group. Jane Fortin comments: 'Arguably these provisions [she cites others, as well] underline parents' rights in education, rather than children's rights' (*Children's Rights and the Developing Law* (London, 2009), 412).

dence[37] and the UK courts' interpretation of the European Convention on Human Rights. The *Williamson* case[38] is an egregious example: the case, to which further reference is made later, centred on Christian fundamentalist parents who believed their rights had been infringed by the legislative ban on corporal punishment in schools. The House of Lords rejected their claim, but only Baroness Hale saw it, and then only in a passing comment, as a question of children's rights to an education in a non-violent environment.[39]

Not all children are in school. Many – at least 20 per cent of the world's children – work,[40] many in 'hazardous forms of labour'.[41] Many more – no one knows how many – are engaged in low-status work in the home environment. This work is largely bidden within a private economy of care: it is not paid employment and there are no employment rights. For such children the 'heartless world' has been installed in the 'haven'.[42] Also hidden are the many 'young carers',[43] perhaps as many as 50,000 in Britain. Despite the NHS and Community Care Act 1990 and the Carers and Disabled Children Act 2000, there remains little recognition of the contribution that children make to informal care.

But perhaps the most interesting group of children to test the public/private binary are street children. They are not a category recognized

37 Early on in *Kjeldsen, Busk and Perimen v Denmark* (1976) EHHR 711, para. 52. See also *Valsamis v Greece* (1996) 24 EHRR 294. Ursula Kilkelly, *The Child and the European Convention on Human Rights* (Aldershot, 1999) discusses this case and many others.

38 [2005] UKHL 15; [2005] 2 AC 246.

39 *Ibid*, para 85. She was also the *only* member of the House of Lords to appreciate that a 14-year-old girl might have a different opinion from her parents on dress. See *R (on the application of Begum) v Head Teacher and Governors of Denbigh High School* (the *Begum* case) [2007) AC 100, para 93. She said: 'It is part of growing up.'

40 ILO, *The End of Child Labour* (Geneva, 2006). On the economics of child labour, see E Edmonds, *Child Labor* (Cambridge, Mass, 2007). See also M Liebel, *A Will of Their Own: Cross Cultural Perspectives on Working Children* (London, 2004), B Weston, *Child Labor and Human Rights* (Boulder, Co, 2007), and Y Noguchi, '20 Years of the Convention on the Rights of the Child and International Action Against Child Labour' (2010) 18 *International Journal of Children's Rights*, forthcoming. On India's woeful record in tackling child labour see R Blakely, 'The Abandoned Generations: How Child Labourers Suffer as India Ignores the Law', *The Times*, 15 October 2009, 35.

41 Now the target of the ILO. See ILO Convention No 182, Article 3, and G Nesi, L Nogler, and M Pertile, *Child Labour in a Globalized World* (Aldershot, 2008).

42 *Cf* C Lasch, *Haven In a Heartless World: The Family Besieged* (New York, 1977).

43 J Aldridge and S Becker, 'Children Who Care' in B Franklin (ed), *The New Handbook of Children's Rights* (London, 2002), 208-22.

as such by the UNCRC, though as children many of the articles of the Convention address their situation.[44] The street is 'a metaphor'[45] for the public sphere. Street children are 'out of place':[46] They don't belong on the street, which is adult territory. They should be at home, in the family. Instead, they are doing things on the street (sleeping, eating etc) which should be done in the privacy of the family. They are an anomaly, not really children and not quite 'human'. It is not surprising that in parts of the world, particularly Latin America and Brazil, they have been subjected to violence by state authorities.[47] It is, of course, only because children should be in the family that the category of the street child has been constructed.

Dickens describes 'street children' (though he does not call them this – the term is a modern one). Today we do not perceive of our children on the street as 'street children'. We may see them as truants (from school), as gangs, as nuisances 'hanging about on the streets', and perceive them as a threat. But they are not street children – they are to be found in Rio and Nairobi. However, because of the perceived threat, increasingly we control the public space of children, once more confirming that children are supposed to be in the private space of the family or quasi-private space of the school, but not roaming in adult territory. Curfews go back a long way. They were first used in North America in the late nineteenth century against children of immigrant families.[48] In England and Wales child cur few schemes were introduced in 1998.[49] In 2003 group dispersal powers were introduced and effectively replaced the curfew powers.[50] Under this law, a police officer can remove any child under 16, who is not under the effective control of a parent or other responsible person over 18, from any public place within the prohibited locality between the hours of 9 pm and 6 am, and take him/her home. The law is incompatible with several articles of the European Convention on Human Rights

44 J Ennew, 'Outside Childhood – Street Children's Rights' in *op cit*, n 43, 388-403. See also J Ennew, 'Why The Convention is not about Street Children' in D Fottrell (ed), *Revisiting Children's Rights* (The Hague, 2000), 169-82.

45 *Per* K Wells, *Childhood in a Global Perspective* (Cambridge, 2009), 29.

46 See *Childhood*, vol 3(2) (1996) 'Special Issue'.

47 On Brazil, in particular, see G Dinnenstein, *Brazil: War on Children* (London, 1991).

48 See GZ Chen, 'Youth Curfews and the Trilogy of Parent, Child and State Relations' (1997) 72 *New York University Law Review* 131-74.

49 Crime and Disorder Act 1998, s 14, amended by the Criminal Justice and Police Act 2001.

50 Anti-Social Behaviour Act 2003, s 30(6).

(Articles 5, 8, 11, and 14);[51] it also is in conflict with the UNCRC (including, most obviously, Article 15).[52] It sends out the message that children out of place are not entitled to adult rights. It is, incidentally, legislation which almost certainly has backfired. It antagonizes the young and arguably aggravates the behaviour against which it is targeted. But, more significantly, it curtails innocent activities and is particularly oppressive to those from poorer homes where there are limited facilities.[53] We now also have an ultrasonic device, the mosquito, which can be used to deter teenagers from congregating in public places – the noise emitted being uncomfortable for their ears but not mature ones.[54] This innovation – for which there is no statutory authority – is an outrage. We are told it is harmless but cannot know whether there are long-term harmful consequences. The UN Committee on the Rights of the Child has condemned the practice,[55] but this is unlikely to lead to its demise in the near future.

## Human Beings/Human Becomings

For many it was clear why children didn't have rights. They were not truly persons yet, but only on their way to achieving this. Onora O'Neill, the Kantian philosopher, will have spoken for many when, as recently as 1988, she wrote that a child's 'main remedy is to grow up'.[56] A child is an adult in the making. S/he is a future adult, rather than a young human being. The child lacks skills (is incompetent): the adult, by contrast, the finished product, has full competency. As Nick Lee stated, we were expected to make 'sense of childhood *through* adulthood... Children's lives and activities in the present are... envisaged... as preparation for the future'.[57] The child, on this view, underwent a journey that ended on attaining adulthood. This assumed, to quote Nick Lee again, 'adults' stability and

51 But see *R(W) v Metropolitan Police Commissioner and Another* [2006] 3 All ER 458 (a 14-year-old boy sought judicial review of the decision to exercise s 30(6) powers in a designated area of Richmond).

52 The UN Committee on the Rights of the Child in its 2008 report on the UK said group dispersal powers violated Article 15 of the Convention: see paras 34-35.

53 See, further, C Walsh, 'Curfews: No More Hanging Around ' (2002) 2 *Youth Justice* 70.

54 Apparently those over 25 do not hear it!

55 *Op cit*, n 52. See also C Walsh, 'The *Mosquito:* A Repellent Response' (2008) 8 *Youth Justice* 122.

56 O O'Neill, 'Children's Rights and Children's Lives' (1988) 98 *Ethics* 445-63.

57 N Lee, *Childhood and Society – Growing Up In an Age of Uncertainty* (Maidenhead, 2001), 8.

completeness... [that] allow them to act in society, to participate independently in serious activities like work and politics [while] children's instability and incompleteness mean that they are often understood only as dependent and passive recipients of adults' actions'.[58] This view of childhood was nurtured by a number of disciplines: in particular, developmental psychology[59] (the work of Piaget[60] being prominent), social anthropology,[61] and sociology (including Talcott Parsons[62]). As summarized by Allison James[63] this saw children as 'inadequate, incomplete and dependent'. Therefore, 'society must invest in their care, training and upbringing since it is children who represent the future of the social world. Within this conception of "the child" ... there was little room for any notion of the agentic child – the radically different model of the "child" that was to become a key feature of the "emergent paradigm" within the new sociology of childhood'.

This new sociology of childhood emerged in the 1970s and 1980s.[64] The result was a paradigm shift.[65] Instead of talking about children as 'becomings' the new framework concentrated on them as 'beings'. Why did this shift occur, and occur when it did? The child liberation movement, spearheaded by John Holt[66] and Richard Farson,[67] seems to have had little influence on the new sociologists of childhood. There was no interest then in the ideas of such early thinkers about children's rights as

---

58 *Ibid.*

59 On which see E Burman, *Deconstructing Developmental Psychology* (Hove, 2008).

60 *The Child's Construction of Reality* (London, 1955).

61 For example, M Mead, *Coming of Age In Samoa* (Harmondsworth, 1969) (originally published in 1928).

62 *The Social System* (London, 1951).

63 'Agency' in J Qvortrup, WA Corsaro, and M-S Honig, *The Palgrave Handbook of Childhood Studies* (Basingstoke, 2009), 34-45, 37.

64 See, for example, C Jenks, *Sociology of Childhood* (London, 1982); A James and A Prout, *Constructing and Reconstructing Childhood* (London, 1990). A good 'state of the art' volume is J Qvortrup, WA Corsaro, and M-S Honig, *The Palgrave Handbook of Childhood Studies* (Basingstoke, 2009). See also the journal *Childhood.*

65 On which see T Kuhn, *The Structure of Scientific Revolutions* (Chicago, 1970). Kuhn's model has been used to explain the revolution in Juvenile Justice in California: see E Lemert, *Social Action and Legal Change* (New York, 1970).

66 See his *Escape From Childhood* (Harmondsworth, 1975).

67 *Birthrights* (Harmondsworth, 1975).

Janusz Korczak[68] or Ellen Key.[69] It goes without saying that Piaget, Parsons, Mead etc had entirely ignored what they had to say. Korczak, in particular, had understood that children could be encouraged to be agents: he pioneered children's parliaments, children's juries, and children's newspapers in Poland in the 1920s. The first serious history of childhood was published (in English) in 1962: although this, Ariès's *Centuries of Childhood*,[70] has been shown to give a distorted picture[71] it was influential at the time. If, as Ariès claimed, the 'idea of childhood' only emerged in the seventeenth century, then perhaps it was a social construction.[72] By the 1970s we had become aware of the phenomenon of child abuse – though not as yet sexual abuse.[73] That children needed advocates was all too apparent after the Maria Colwell case.[74] It seems perverse now that children were thought to be adequately represented in child abuse cases by their abusers.

There had, of course, been initiatives by the League of Nations in 1924 and the United Nations in 1959. Each had formulated Declarations of the Rights of the Child.[75] The emphasis in both was on protection of the child: the clear image of the child which emerges is that of the child as a 'becoming'. The 1959 Declaration had little impact on thinking about chil-

---

68 On whom see G Eichsteller, 'Janusz Korczak – His Legacy and Its Relevance for Children's Rights Today' (2009) 17 *Int J of Children's Rights* 377-91. A flavour of his thoughts can be found in J Korczak, *Wisdom for Parents* (edited by S Joseph) (Chapel Hill, N Carolina, 2007). A brief comparison between Korczak and Eglantyne Jebb is drawn by B Milne, 'From Chattels to Citizens? Eighty Years of Eglantyne Jebb's Legacy to Children and Beyond' in A Invernizzi and J Williams (eds), *Children and Citizenship* (London, 2008), 44-54.

69 *The Century of The Child* (New York, 1909) (originally published in Swedish in 1900). And see W Koops and M Zuckerman, *Beyond The Century of the Child* (Philadelphia, 2003).

70 London, 1962.

71 See, for example, L Pollock, *Forgotten Children* (Cambridge, 1983).

72 See P Berger and T Luckmann, *The Social Construction of Reality* (Harmondsworth, 1967).

73 This barely surfaced until the Cleveland cases in 1987. See M Freeman, 'Cleveland, Butler-Sloss and Beyond: How Are We To React To The Sexual Abuse of Children?' (1989) 42 *Current Legal Problems* 85.

74 See DHSS, *Report of Committee of Inquiry into Care and Supervision of Maria Colwell* (London, 1974). See also J Howells, *Remember Maria* (London, 1974). The UN Committee on the Rights of the Child was still concerned about this in 1997: see its report on Nigeria (CRC/C/15/Add.61, para 40).

75 On which see P Veerman, *The Rights of the Child and the Changing Image of Childhood* (Dordrecht, 1992), 155-80. The book examines a large variety of other declarations, many of them hardly known today.

dren. Nor should too much significance be attached to the naming of 1979 as the International Year of the Child.[76] But this was the initiative which ultimately led to the UNCRC. Of course, there was initially no enthusiasm for this, and the drafting process was protracted.[77] The Convention itself recognizes the child as both 'becoming' and 'being', that children should be allowed to participate in decisions (see Article 12), whilst accepting the paternalism of the best interests principle (in Article 3).[78]

But we still haven't accounted for the paradigm shift. The disciplines which had nurtured the 'becoming' model were beginning to question received 'truths'. For example, Piaget's work was shown to be of limited value.[79] The thought and reasoning of young children was shown to be much more sophisticated than Piaget claimed. As Woodhead and Faulkner explained: 'what appears to be "faulty" reasoning actually indicates children's ingenious attempts to create sensible meanings for what are, to them, nonsensical situations and contexts'.[80] The structural functionalist agenda of Parsons was also critiqued. It placed too much emphasis on the role of social structures and institutions in shaping society and so left little space for the part that individuals (including children) could and did play in society. Wrong famously accused Parsons of having an over-socialized conception of man.[81] The structure-agency debate began to awaken an interest in children, on the part that children played in the growing-up process and in socialization.

And there were significant studies, some now classics. I would cite in particular Myrna Bluebond-Langner's *The Private Worlds of Dying Children.*[82] This reveals children as actors in the scripting of death on a cancer ward. It is an ethnographic study based in the Department of Pediatrics in a teaching hospital in the US. Her aim was to 'get as close as possible

76 M Freeman, 'The Rights of Children in the International Year of the Child' (1980) 33 *Current Legal Problems* 1-31.

77 On the controversies see D Johnson, 'Cultural and Regional Pluralism in the Drafting of the UNCRC' in M Freeman and P Veerman (eds), *The Ideologies of Children's Rights* (Dordrecht, 1992), 95-114.

78 See M Freeman, *A Commentary on the United Nation Convention on the Rights of the Child: Article 3 – The Best Interests of The Child* (Leiden, 2007).

79 See M Donaldson, *Children's Minds* (London, 1978).

80 M Woodhead and D Faulkner, 'Subjects, Objects or Participants? Dilemmas of Psychological Research with Children' in P Christensen and A James (eds), *Research with Children: Perspectives and Practices* (London, 2000), 9-35, 25.

81 D Wrong, 'The Oversocialized Conception of Man in Modern Sociology' (1961) 26 *American Sociologial Review* 183-93.

82 M Bluebond-Langner, *The Private Worlds of Dying Children* (Princeton, NJ, 1978).

... to their thoughts, their interactional strategies, and their structuring of the situation'.[83] And she was able to reveal children's role in the structuring of hospital life and the relations between parents and children. To quote one example:

> A five-year-old boy interprets his mother's crying as indicating that he is very sick. 'See my mommy's red nose, that's from me. Everybody cries when they see me. I'm pretty sick'. He also notes that he is getting more presents than his sister. 'I get more presents than when I had my tonsils out. My sister gets the same'. Finally, he has been behaving in ways that are ordinarily cause for reprimand and finds he is not reprimanded... He acts the sick role and claims his right on the basis that he is truly ill.[84]

By the late 1980s it was recognized that children were 'beings', social actors. This is reflected in the *Gillick* case of 1985,[85] in which Lord Scarman pronounced that a child's capacity to make her own decision depends on her having 'sufficient understanding and intelligence to make the decision' and not on 'any judicially fixed age limit'.[86] Two leading sociologists of childhood, writing in 1990, said:

> ... children are and must be seen as active in the construction of their own lives, the lives of those around them and of the societies in which they live. Children are not just passive subjects of social structures and processes.[87]

And Berry Mayall,[88] commenting some years later, confirmed that 'children are social actors... they take part in family relationships from the word go; they express their wishes, demonstrate strong attachments, jealousy and delight, seek justice'. There has since been much research done to demonstrate the agency of children in their families, in school settings

---

83 *Ibid*, xi.
84 *Ibid*, 9.
85 *Gillick v West Norfolk and Wisbech AHA* [1986] AC 112.
86 *Ibid*, 186.
87 A James and A Prout, *Constructing and Reconstructing Childhood* (Basingstoke, 1990).
88 B Mayall, *Towards A Sociology of Childhood* (Maidenhead, 2000), 21.

and in society generally: for example, how they negotiate their parents' divorce[89] and how they cope with an abusive environment.[90]

It is important to recognize that children are more than pre-adult becomings. But it is equally important to understand that appreciating that they are 'beings' does not preclude their being also 'becomings'. It is all too easy to assume children have to be one thing or the other. That the child is both a 'being' and a 'becoming' is often glossed over. Although not articulated in this conceptual form, English judges have recognized this. An example is Sir Thomas Bingham MR's statement in *Re S* in 1993 that 'children are human beings in their own right', but 'a child is, after all, a child'.[91] He noted 'a judicious balance'[92] had to be struck between these two considerations. But he was overcautious in making this balance. He held that to have 'social judgment' the child needed insight and imagination which only maturity and experience could bring.[93] So too the judges who decided – wrongly I have argued[94] – that though a child could consent to medical treatment, their refusal to do so could be overruled on a best interests test.[95] An example is *Re L (Medical Treatment: Gillick Competency)*:[96] a 14-year-old deeply religious Jehovah's Witness lacked, so the court said, 'the constructive formulation of an opinion which occurs with adult experience'.[97] I am not sure what that is, or how many adults have it, but I have no doubt that on the evidence of this case her understanding was comparable to that of most adults. She had, for example, taken the step of carrying an 'Advance Medical Directive/Release Form'. This case is particularly significant because the judge acknowledged that

89 C Smart, B Neale, and A Wade, *The Changing Experience of Childhood* (London, 2001).

90 J Mason and J Falloon 'Some Sydney Children Define Abuse: Some Implications for Agency in Childhood' in L Alanen and B Mayall, *Conceptualizing Child-Adult Relations* (London, 2001). See also B Saunders and C Goddard, 'Some Australian Children's Perceptions of Physical Punishment in Childhood' (2008) 22 *Children and Society* 405-17.

91 *Re S (A Minor) (Representation)* [1993] 2 FLR 437, 448.

92 *Ibid.*

93 *Ibid.* Another example is Coleridge J in *Re N (Contract: Minor Seeking Leave to Defend and Removal of Guardian)* [2003] 1 FLR 652. But these cases must now be read in the light of Thorpe LJ's judgment in *Mabon v Mabon* [2005] 2 FLR 1011.

94 'Rethinking Gillick' (2005) 13 *Int J of Children's Rights* 201-17.

95 Cases such as *Re R (A Minor) (Wardship: Consent to Treatment)* [1992] Fam 11 and *Re W (A Minor) (Medical Treatment: Court's jurisdiction)* [1993] Fam 64.

96 [1998] 2 FLR 810.

97 *Ibid*, 812.

she had not been given 'all the details which it would be right and appropriate to have in mind when making such a decision'.[98]

This conveniently leads us back to the becoming/being binary. The assumption is that adults are competent, and children are not. Competency is seen as an adult characteristic, something that children Jack and acquire the closer they get to adulthood. This we say is reached at

18 (it was 21 until relatively recently),[99] but we allow a 'child' to consent to medical treatment,[100] and to marry, at 16.[101] That it is arbitrary is not my point. This is rather that a moment's reflection will tell us of the many competencies that children have that adults Jack. My granddaughter at five painted 'Van Goghs'! Three-year-olds play the violin. Most children have computer skills which far exceed mine. Children have creative imaginations which adults may Jack. Many adults never exercise agency. Others are 'has beens', rather than 'beings', though only in extreme cases do we deprive them of agency as a result. But looking at children though the conventional binary is necessarily measuring children against adults. Lee grasps this. 'It is... hard to think of children changing over time without accepting the terms of the dominant framework... It seems hard to chart and to describe change unless one has a fixed finishing point, such as journey's end or standard, complete adulthood, to refer to.'[102] Why should we do this? Children may be able to create a better world than the one they were born into. And their children a better one still. The being/becoming binary ignores change, which is continuous. The metaphor of 'time as an arrow'[103] captures this well. It overlooks the fact that adults are also 'becomings' as well as beings. Children have many rights: one important one is the right to become adults. The Convention acknowledges

98 *Ibid*, 813.

99 1970. This was effected by the Family Law Reform Act 1969.

100 Family Law Reform Act 1969, *s* 8(1). 'Consent' does not extend to refusal: *Re W* [1993] Fam 64. Whether this can stand with the Mental Capacity Act 2005 may be doubted: see, for agreement, L Hagger, *The Child As Vulnerable Patient* (Farnham, 2009), 27.

101 Marriage Act 1949, s 2. There is little rhyme or reason to the hotchpotch of provisions setting out when a child can do various things: the current list is in J Claridge, *At What Age Can I? A Guide To Age-Based Legislation* (Colchester, 2008).

102 N Lee, *Childhood and Society* (Maidenhead, 2001), 136.

103 See P Coveney and R Highfield, *The Arrow of Time* (London, 1990). Martin Amis's brilliant novel, *Time's Arrow* (London, 1991), may also be consulted. E Uprichard, 'Children *As* "Being and Becomings": Children, Childhood and Temporality' (2008) 22 *Children and Society* 303-13 develops the theme well.

this when it emphasizes 'development' as a right.[104] It leaves open what development means.

The child is both a 'being' and a 'becoming'. Of course, putting it this way simply accepts the adult/child dualism: the being child will become an adult. It would take another paper to draw out the implications for a rights agenda of accepting that children are both 'beings' and 'becomings'. We would inevitably raise questions about work and education, about sexual activity, and health questions. But my excursion into the being/becoming debate was part of my exploration of why it is commonly thought children don't have rights, and it is not necessary to pursue these questions here.

We now need to investigate why children should have rights. Before doing so, I pause to ask why rights are important – for all of us.

## The Importance of Rights

Rights are about necessities, not luxuries.[105] They are important because they are inclusive: they are universal, available to all members of the human family. In the past, they have depended on gender and race. Women were non-persons. Black people were kept in subservience by policies which justified 'separate but equal' practices (or worse, by slavery). But, just as concepts of gender inequality have been key to understanding womanhood and women's social status, so 'the concept of generation is key to understanding childhood'.[106]

It has always been to the advantage of the powerful to keep others out. It is not, therefore, surprising that adults should want to do this to children: that they should wish to keep them in an often imposed and prolonged dependence which history and culture show to be neither inevitable nor essential. Think of the other side of inclusion, of exclusion and what this generates on the part of the excluders and their victims, the socially excluded. Note the way the powerful regulate space (social, po-

104 On Article 6, see further, M Nowak, *A Commentary on the United Nations Convention on the Rights of The Child – Article 6* (Leiden, 2005). Artide 6 should be read in conjunction with Article 29 (aims of education).

105 P Alderson, *Young Children's Rights* (London, 2008) also notes this at 19.

106 B Mayall, *Towards a Sociology of Childhood* (London, 2002), 120.

litical, geographical),[107] define participation,[108] marginalize significance, and hamper development.

Rights are indivisible and interdependent. Human rights include the whole range of civil, political, social, economic, and cultural rights. Denying certain rights undermines other rights as well. For example, if we do not put in place structures to tackle domestic violence,[109] we will not protect children from child abuse. And *mutatis mutandis.*

Rights are important because they recognize the respect the bearers are owed. To accord rights is to respect dignity:[110] to deny rights is to cast doubt on humanity and on integrity. Rights affirm the Kantian principle that we are ends in ourselves, and not means to the ends of others.[111]

It is, therefore, important that, as Ronald Dworkin so eloquently reminded us, we see rights as 'trumps'.[112] They cannot be displaced because it would be better for others, or even society as a whole, were these rights not to exist. Of course, for the powerful – and for children adults are always powerful – rights are an inconvenience. The powerful would find it easier if those below them lacked rights. It would be easier to rule, decision-making would be swifter, cheaper, more efficient, more certain. It is hardly surprising that we have had to fight for all the rights we have. As Patricia Williams explained:

> For the historically disempowered, the conferring of rights is symbolic of all the denied aspects of their humanity: rights imply a respect that places one in the referential range of self and others, that elevates one's status from human body to social being.[113]

107 SC Aitken, *Geographies of Young People: The Morally Contented Spaces of Identity* (London, 2001); C Ward, *The Child in the City* (London, 1978) (capturing it in pictures).

108 See J Boylan and J Dalrymple, *Understanding Advocacy for Children and Young People* (Maidenhead, 2009).

109 30 per cent of all applications under the Children Act 1989 include an allegation of domestic violence: see House of Commons Home Affairs Select Committee, *Domestic Violence, Forced Marriage, and Honour-Based Violence* (London, 2008).

110 'There is hardly any legal principle more difficult to fathom in law than that of human dignity' (*Omega Spielhallen* case [2004] ECR J-9609). An excellent introduction is Brenda Hale, 'Dignity' (2009) 31 *JSWFL* 101-8.

111 *Fundamental Principles of the Metaphysics of Ethics* (London, 1895) (originally published in 1785).

112 R Dworkin, *Taking Rights Seriously* (London, 1977).

113 P Williams, *The Alchemy of Race and Rights* (Cambridge, Mass, 1991), 163.

Those who criticize rights – Bentham[114] and Marx,[115] for example – are often blind to the privileged position from which they write. Rights may be more important for the weak – and this includes children – than to the powerful.

Rights are important because those who have them can exercise agency.[116] Agents are decision-makers: they are people who negotiate with others, who alter relationships or decisions, who can shift social assumptions and constraints. And there is now clear evidence that even the youngest can do this.[117] We won't believe this because we don't want to, and it is counter-intuitive. As agents, rights-bearers can participate. They can make their own lives, rather than having their lives made for them. And participation is a fundamental human right.[118] It enables us to demand rights. We are able to do so when there is freedom of speech[119] and orthodoxies can be challenged, freedom of association and other understandings can be nourished,[120] and freedom of information.

Rights are an important advocacy tool, a tool for change, a weapon to use in the battle to secure recognition. Giving people rights without access to those who can present those rights – without the right of representation[121] – is thus of limited value. But this is also to acknowledge that we must get beyond rhetoric. Rights without remedies are of symbolic importance, no more. And remedies themselves require the injection of resources, a commitment on behalf of all of us that we view rights with

114 'Nonsense Upon Stilts in Anarchical Fallacies' in J Bowring (ed), *The Works of Jeremy Bentham* (Edinburgh, 1838-1843), vol II, 489-534. And see LW Sumner, 'Rights Denaturalized' in RG Frey (ed), *Utility and Rights* (Oxford, 1985), 20-41.

115 *On The Jewish Question* in the *Marx-Engels Reader* (ed R Tucker) (New York, 1978). Both Bentham's essay and Marx's can be found in Jeremy Waldron, *Nonsense Upon Stilts* (London, 1989).

116 On agency and children see A James, 'Agency', *op cit,* n 63.

117 See P Alderson, J Hawthorne, and M Killen, 'The Participation Rights of Premature Babies' (2005) 13 *Int J of Children's Rights* 31-50. See also P Alderson, K Sutcliffe, and K Curtis, 'Children *As* Partners with Adults in their Medical Care' (2006) 91 *Archives of Diseases in Childhood* 300-3; and P Alderson, 'The Ethics of Space in Clinical Practice' (2007) 2 *Clinical Practice* 85-91.

118 On participation see N Thomas, 'Towards A Theory of Children's Participation (2007) 15 *Int J of Children's Rights* 199-218. See also the 'Special Issue' of the *IJCR* (2008) vol 16(3).

119 See JS Mill, *On Liberty* (London, 1859), ch 2.

120 And see UNCRC Article 15. In relation to which note group dispersal powers and ASBOs.

121 See UNCRC Article 12.2.

respect, that we want them to have an input into the Jives of all people, and not just the Jives of the powerful and the privileged.[122]

Rights offer legitimacy to campaigns, to pressure groups, to lobbies, to NGOs, to direct and indirect action, in particular to those who are disadvantaged or excluded. They offer a way in: they open doors.

Rights are also a resource: they offer a reasoned argument. They can put a moral case. Too often those who oppose rights can offer little in response.

Rights offer fora for action. Without rights the excluded can request, they can beg, they can rely on *noblesse oblige,* on others being nice or generous or co-operative or foresighted. But they cannot demand what is their due.[123] Without rights there is no entitlement.[124]

But the most fundamental of rights is the right to possess rights. Hannah Arendt expressed this better than anyone when she observed, à propos the Holocaust, that 'a condition of complete rightlessness was created before the right to live was challenged'.[125] Before the Nazis robbed the Jews of their lives, they robbed them of their humanity, just as generations had done with slaves. To quote Arendt again:

> Slavery's fundamental offence against human rights was not that it took liberty away... but that it excluded a certain category of people even from the possibility of fighting for freedom...[126]

## Why Rights for Children

In 1989 the UNCRC was adopted.[127] We have just celebrated its twentieth birthday.

---

122 See M Paulsen, 'Legal Protections Against Child Abuse' (1966) 13 *Children* 48.

123 B Bandman, 'Do Children Have Any Natural Rights? *Proceedings of the 29th Annual Meeting of Philosophy and Education Society,* 1973, 234 at 236.

124 See J Feinberg, 'Duties, Rights and Claims' (1966) 3(2) *American Philosophical Quarterly* I, 8.

125 H Arendt, *The Origins of Totalitarianism* (London, 1986), 296.

126 *Ibid,* 297.

127 A useful commentary is S Derrick, *A Commentary on the UN Convention on the Rights of the Child* (The Hague, 1999). There is now a huge literature on the UNCRC and particular states. Examples are C Banks, 'The Discourse of Children's Rights in Bangladesh' (2007) 15 *Int J of Children's Rights* 391-414; J Grugel and E Pemzzotti, 'Claiming Rights under Global Governance: Children's Rights in Argentina' (2007) 13 *Global Governance* 199-216; GO Odongo, 'The Domestication of International

It is a Convention *on*, not *of*, the Rights of the Child: perhaps – I am not sure – this was deliberate, because there are many ambiguities in the Convention and thus plenty of scope for governmental (and other) interpretation.

It may be noted also that it is about 'the child', and thus sets a global standard, and ignores the many different childhoods that exist in the world.[128] That this standard is Eurocentric is criticized by some,[129] but relativism is misplaced in human rights communications (or, at least, so I believe).[130]

Early on, in the drafting process, there was concern that the Convention might be 'just a sentimental, symbolic gesture on behalf of children'.[131] This has not proved to be the case. As is well-known, all states have ratified the UNCRC except Somalia and the United States. There are now two additional Protocols,[132] and a third is being spoken of.[133] I will have more to say about this later in this paper.[134]

The Convention is international law's response to the paradigm shift in thinking about children, identified earlier in this paper. And it recognizes the child both as 'being' and as 'becoming'.[135] It importantly gives the child a seat at the international law table. I argue later in this paper,[136] as I did first in 1991,[137] that it fails children by nor going further and giving them also a microphone.

---

Standards on the Rights of the Child: A Critical and Comparative Evaluation of the Kenyan Example' (2004) 12 *Int J of Children's Rights* 419-30.

128 See K Wells, *Childhood In A Global Perspective* (Cambridge, 2009), ch 1.

129 This is certainly Wells' view, *ibid.* She does not consider why the African Charter essentially reproduces the UN Convention.

130 See M Freeman, 'The Morality of Cultural Pluralism' (1995) *3 Int J of Children's Rights* 1-17; S Harris-Short, 'International Human Rights Law: Imperialist, Inept and Ineffective? Cultural Relativism and the UNCRC' (2003) 25 *Human Rights Quarterly* 130-80.

131 *Per* CP Cohen, SN Hart, and SM Kosloske, 'Monitoring the United Nations Convention on the Rights of the Child: The Challenge of Information Management (1996) 18 *Human Rights Quarterly* 438-71.

132 *On the Sale of Children, Child Prostitution and Child Pornography* (2007); and on the *Involvement of Children in Armed Conflict* (2002).

133 *On a Communications Procedure,* presented before the Human Rights Committee in June 2009.

134 *Infra,* 38-41.

135 See the discussion at *supra,* 9-15.

136 *Infra,* 38.

137 'The Limits of Children's Rights' in (eds) M Freeman and P Veerman, *The Ideologies of Children's Rights* (Dordrecht, 1992), 29-46, 42.

If children were only 'becomings', the Convention would have emphasized the importance of their best interests (as it does),[138] and concentrated on provision and protection rights exclusively: to life, survival and development;[139] to protection from violence, injury, abuse and neglect;[140] to the highest possible standard of health;[141] to education;[142] etc. But, because it accepts children are also 'beings', it gives them 'a voice'. It recognizes the dangers of wrapping them in silence. Thus, children are given the right to express views freely in all matters affecting them,[143] and the opportunity to be heard in judicial and administrative proceedings affecting them.[144] And there are other participation rights too: freedom of expression;[145] thought, conscience and religion;[146] freedom of association and of peaceful assembly.[147] And one of the aims of education, as laid down in the Convention, is the development of the child's personality, talents, and abilities to their fullest potential.[148]

The international community thus recognizes that children have rights. And nearly everyone concedes that children must have some rights at least, for example, the right nor to be tortured. Some on the extreme right seem to place greater emphasis on the rights of the unborn child than on the rights of children. And many can support protection rights, but nor participation rights. Martin Guggenheim, the American family lawyer, in the recent *What's Wrong With Children's Rights* – note there is no question mark – offers children but one right, to be raised by parents who are minimally fit and who are unlikely to make significant mistakes in judgement in their rearing of their children.[149] It is not that he does nor believe in rights: he is a passionate defender of parents' rights, even describing them as 'sacred'.[150]

But there are also those who can see no point or value in talking about children's rights. They cannot see that it can achieve anything positive for

138 In Article 3.
139 See Article 6.
140 Article 19.
141 Article 24.
142 Article 28 (and see also Article 29).
143 Article 12.1.
144 Article 12.2.
145 Article 13.
146 Article 14.
147 Article 15.
148 Article 29(1)(a).
149 M Guggenheim, *What's Wrong with Children's Rights* (Cambridge, Mass, 2005), 43.
150 *Ibid*, 71.

children. Where there are rights claims there is the opportunity for public challenge and scrutiny: without them it is all too easy to ride roughshod over lives. It may be that we can look to a time when virtue will prevail and there will be justice for all.[151] Perhaps when the lion lies down with the lamb (and Isaiah poignantly adds a little child shall lead them).[152] But until then we need to be able to think in terms of rights. Indeed, we are more likely to reach a position where rights are no longer necessary by taking them seriously now.

It is therefore imperative that we address some of the arguments posited by those who are critical of children's rights. Onora O'Neill's essay is a classic,[153] and I have addressed and criticized it before.[154] But on re reading I realize there are criticisms which can be made which I have not previously adduced. She claims that 'children's fundamental rights are best grounded by embedding them in a wider account of fundamental obligations, which can also be used to justify positive rights and obligations'.[155]

In her view 'taking rights as fundamental in ethical deliberation about children has neither theoretical nor political advantages',[156] and that a more 'perspicuous and complete view' of ethical aspects of children's lives 'can be obtained by taking obligations as fundamental'.[157]

She sees the dependency of children as 'very different'[158] from the dependency of other marginalized groups. I have argued elsewhere that these differences can be exaggerated.[159] She does not discuss what she considers the theoretical underpinning of rights to be, but her references to claiming and waiving suggest she is committed to the 'will theory' of rights.[160] But, as was convincingly shown by Neil MacCormick,[161] and this

151 On the relationship between rights and virtues see B Bandman, *Children's Right To Freedom, Care and Enlightenment* (New York, 1999), 11-15.

152 Isaiah, XI, 6.

153 'Children's Rights and Children's Lives' (1988) 98 *Ethics* 445-63.

154 'Taking Children's Rights More Seriously' in P Alston, S Parker, and J Seymour (eds), *Children, Rights and the Law* (Oxford, 1992), 52-71, 56-9.

155 *Supra,* n 153, 446.

156 *Ibid,* 447.

157 *Ibid.*

158 *Ibid,* 461.

159 *Supra,* n 154, 57-9.

160 I discuss this (and the interest theory) in MDA Freeman, *Lloyd's Introduction To Jurisprudence* (8th edn, London, 2008), 394-6. See also, in relation to children, MDA Freeman, *The Rights and Wrongs of Children* (London, 1983), 56-7.

161 'Children's Rights: A Test Case for Theories of Rights' (1976) 62 *ARSP* 305-16 (reprinted at eh 8 of *Legal Right and Social Democracy* (Oxford, 1982)).

à propos children's rights in particular, the interest theory is more coherent and has greater explanatory power. Children have interests to protect before they may have wills to assert (though there is now increasing evidence that they can do so even as babies),[162] and others can complain on behalf of younger children when these interests are trampled upon.[163] It is because children have moral rights – for example, to be educated – that correlative duties are imposed. That there may be enforcement problems says nothing about the moral right.

It cannot be right – Fortin, I note, calls it a 'counsel of despair'[164] – that a child's 'main remedy is to grow up'.[165] For abused and neglected children this is obviously no remedy. Some of them like 'Baby Peter'[166] will not grow up. Others will have their development stunted by inadequate parenting. O'Neill ignores the impact on adult life that parenting and socialization leave. But then she is, I think, implicitly adopting a model of good parenting, and it may be that the children who need rights most are the ones deprived of such experiences.

O'Neill's model of childhood is the conventional deficit one. As such, she underestimates the capacities and maturity of many children: for example, their ability to represent themselves and, indeed, other children. There is now evidence that this can promote resilience and positive self conception.[167] This is important to bear in mind if, as is hoped, children get the opportunity to challenge breaches of the UNCRC.[168] O'Neill also ignores the fact that we are prepared to impose criminal responsibility on

---

162 See P Alderson *et al*, 'The Participation Rights of Premature Babies' (2005) 13 *Int J of Children's Rights* 31-50. HLA Hart in 'Are There Any Natural Rights?' (1955) 63 *Philosophical Review* 175-91 contests this: 'If rights usage sanctions talk of the rights of... babies, it makes an idle use of the expression "a right" ...' (p 181).

163 See one attempt to explain this in H Cohen, *Equal Rights of Children* (Totowa, NJ, 1980). I comment upon his concept of the 'child agent' in *The Rights and Wrongs of Children, supra,* n 160, at 46-8.

164 In *Children's Rights and the Developing Law* (London, 2009), 14.

165 This is O'Neill's view: see *supra,* n 153, 463.

166 See Lord Laming, *The Protection of Children in England: A Program Report* (London, 2009).

167 See S Grover, 'Advocacy by Children as a Causal Factor in Promoting Resilience' (2005) 12 *Childhood* 527-38.

168 This is discussed *infra,* 38.

children as young as 10[169] (and younger if we consider civil sanctions):[170] often long before we are disposed to confer rights upon them.

O'Neill is not alone in adopting the conventional deficit model of childhood. This is at the root of much other contemporary philosophical writing about children. Thus, in the view of Harry Brighouse, 'the further an agent departs from the liberal model of the competent rational person, the less appropriate it seems to he to attribute rights'.[171] It hardly needs saying, but it was once thought inappropriate to attribute rights to women, who were considered to fall short of the so-called 'liberal model'. Brighouse does not have difficulty with seeing children as bearers of welfare rights (that is of provision and protection rights), but he has problems with agency rights, at least as far as young children are concerned. It is, of course, easier to justify welfare rights, and to defend some limitations on agency rights.[172] But welfare rights work better in a rights culture where agency, for example the opportunity to participate in decisions about oneself, is acknowledged. Children are best protected from abuse, for example, where they are recognized as rights-bearing persons whose dignity is upheld.[173] Brighouse is particularly critical of three agency rights, all of which are recognized in the UNCRC: to freedom of expression, to freedom of religion, and to enjoyment of one's own culture.[174] But why should children he deprived of these rights? Why – to take one of Brighouse's examples – should it be thought that the child's right to cultural identity 'jeopardizes the family as an institution'[175] (whatever this

169 In effect lowered to 10 by the abolition of the *doli incapax* principle in 1998: Crime and Disorder Act 1998, s34. Perhaps the worst example of this policy in practice is the conviction of two 10-year-old boys for the attempted rape of an 8-year-old girl. See *The Guardian*, 25 May 2010. Had the *doli incapax* presumption realized, I suspect this prosecution would not have taken place. Appeal against conviction has been rejected: see *The Times*, 28 July 2010.

170 In particular ASBOs, breach of which attract criminal sanctions. Children are now punished for what previous generations considered 'pranks' (like climbing a tree – see *The Observer*, 14 November 2009, 6).

171 *Supra*, n 4, 31.

172 As I have done in arguing for 'liberal paternalism': see Freeman, *supra*, n 160 (1983), 54-60.

173 See MDA Freeman 'Upholding the Dignity and Best Interests of Children: Inter national Law and the Corporal Punishment of Children' (2010) 73 *Law and Contemporary Problem*, 213-53.

174 Articles 13, 14, and 30.

175 *Supra*, n 4, 29. See also L Burrows (Mrs Gillick's sister!), *The Fight for the Family: The Adults Behind Children's Rights* (Oxford, 1998).

may mean)? Any more than manifestation of religion – for example, by dress – jeopardizes the school as an institution?

English courts have had to grapple with this issue three times recently,[176] not, of course, under the UNCRC, which is not part of English law, but invoking Article 9 of the ECHR. I will refer only to the *Begum* case.[177] The House of Lords held that a school was entitled to impose a dress code that prevented Shabina Begum from wearing the *jilbab,* which she believed she was required to wear by her religion. The Lords accepted that children had the right to manifest their religion under Article 9 of the European Convention on Human Rights (ECHR). The majority held there was no interference with her right to manifest her religious belief because she was free to go to another school where she could wear the *jilbab.* Unanimously, they agreed that even if there were a breach it could be justified to protect the freedoms of other pupils at the school (particularly the girls) who might otherwise feel pressurized into wearing the *jilbab.* This is not a case note on this case,[178] but the judgments reveal some interesting judicial attitudes to children and their rights, and these are worth drawing attention to. In particular, note Lord Hoffmann's concern that Begum was 'intent on enforcing her "rights"',[179] and note the way he put 'rights' into quotation marks.

Or Lord Bingham's narration of the facts of the case and his dear anger at Begum 'talking' of 'human rights' and legal proceedings to the assistant head of the school.[180] The history of rights is about seeking rights aggressively.[181] There is emphasis in the judgment also of the fact that Begum had worn the *shalwar kameeze* for two years prior to the onset of the dispute with the school over the dress code. Read the judgments and you get the impression that Begum is almost estopped from complaining because she had acquiesced in the school policy for some time. Only Bar-

176 See in addition to *Begum, supra,* n 39, *R(X) v Head Teacher and Governors of Y School* [2008] 1 All ER 249 and *R (Playfoot) v Governing Body of Millais School* [2007] EWHC 1698 (Admin) (a Christian pupil who wanted to wear a 'purity ring' – the school prohibited jewellery).

177 *R (on the Application of Begum) v Head Teacher and Governors of Denbigh High School* [2007] AC 100. See generally D McGoldrick, *Human Rights and Religion: The Islamic Headscarf Debate in Europe* (Oxford, 2006).

178 There are several: S Edwards (2007) 19 *CFLQ* 247; A Pimor (2006) 28 ]*SWFL* 323.

179 Para 52.

180 Para 10.

181 R Williams, 'Taking Rights Aggressively: The Perils and Promise of Critical Legal Theory for Peoples of Color' (1987) 5 *Law and Inequality* 103-34.

oness Hale,[182] and she briefly, acknowledges that in this period Begum had gone through the stages of puberty, that she had ceased to be a girl, and had become a young woman, that she was now a different person. She had good reasons for wanting to change the way she dressed.

Carol Brennan's essay on children's rights exhibits another common concern, that children will make mistakes.[183] Her main reason for refusing to acknowledge that children have autonomy is that 'often children do not choose well or wisely'.[184] She accepts that adults can also fail to make the right decisions. But, as Dworkin told us many years ago, it is fundamental to believing in rights that we accept that there is a right to do what we consider to be the wrong thing to do, to make mistakes, to let others do things we would not do.[185] To encourage children to be agents requires that we give scope to that agency. There are limits – I have written about these as long ago as 1983 in my hook *The Rights and Wrongs of Children.*[186] Space precludes further discussion of them in this paper. Suffice it to say that I recognize there are limits to children's agency. We would not allow children to take decisions which severely impair their ability to exercise autonomy in the future.

Other critics of rights for children take a different approach. Barbara Arneil argues that we have put too much faith in the power of rights and rights discourse, and this has had bad consequences for children.[187] She puts the case instead for an ethic of care,[188] which emphasizes responsibilities over rights. This, she says, offers a better way of answering children's needs than putting our faith in the ability of rights to achieve this. In her view, 'rights theories do not see children as children'[189] This is a criticism of substance, and one increasingly voiced. In effect it amounts to regarding children's rights as an oxymoron. Arneil's own vision sees

---

182 At para 93.

183 'Children's Choices or Children's Interests: Which Do Their Rights Protect?' in D Archard and C Macleod (eds), *The Moral and Political Status of Children* (Oxford, 2002), 53-69.

184 *Ibid,* 59.

185 *Taking Rights Seriously* (London, 1977).

186 See n 160.

187 'Becoming versus Being: A Critical Analysis of the Child in Liberal Theory' in D Archard and CM Macleod (eds), *The Moral and Political Status of Children* (Oxford, 2002), 70-94.

188 A concept first invoked by C Gilligan, *In a Different Voice* (Cambridge, Mass, 1982). On children and feminist ethics of care see T Cockburn, 'Children and the Feminist Ethics of Care' (2003) 10 *Childhood 71-89.*

189 *Supra,* n 187, 93.

the child's development in 'holistic terms, going beyond the capacity for rationality'.[190] Every child is included, and 'the state's role goes beyond both education to social welfare to a fully integrated set of services focused on the child's need for care and the parent's responsibility for caregiving'.[191] She envisions the child's growth to independent adulthood as 'an organic process that unfolds within the context of a multitude of interdependent relationships within both the family and society at large'.[192] She believes this vision embraces children as 'full beings'.[193]

There are a number of responses to this. It describes – rather it prescribes – a future so far from present realities that I doubt whether it is attainable in the foreseeable future. It envisions, as is so often the case, the child as an object of concern rather than a subject or participant. It over-simplifies the distinction between adults and children, perhaps neglecting even Carol Brennan's 'gradualist' model. It fails to see the importance of rights where relationships, for whatever reason, are poor: how would she deal with the 15-year-old who cannot discuss contraception with her parents – the classic *Gillick* scenario?[194] It above all underestimates the role that a rights agenda can play in forging relationships, and it overlooks the asymmetry of relationships where rights, and therefore power, is on one side only.

There are many other critiques of children's rights. Space precludes a consideration of all of them. But I must not ignore one to which no reference has yet been made. Children's rights, it is frequently asserted, can be used to the disadvantage of women.[195] Most obviously, children's rights could be used to control the Jives of women, in particular mothers. Debates about whether mothers should stay out of the employment market to look after children, the advantages and disadvantages of this, are endless, and I cannot pursue them here.[196] Fran Olsen's feminist cri-

190 *Ibid.*

191 *Ibid.*

192 *Ibid.*

193 *Ibid.*

194 *Gillick v West Norfolk and Wisbech AHA* [1986] AC 112.

195 For the view that the relationship between women's rights and children's rights is symbiotic see J Todres, 'Women's Rights and Children's Rights: A Partnership with Benefits for Both' (2003-2004) 10 *Cardozo Women's LJ* 603-24.

196 They are rooted in history: see J Lewis, *Women in England 1870-1950* (Brighton, 1984), 33-6.

tique of children's rights is the classic account.[197] It is striking how discussions of children's rights invariably take a gender-neutral approach, but then women's rights discourse is dominated by the experiences of adult women. Girls are thus doubly marginalized.[198] There is much in Olsen's critique that remains pertinent. Certainly, an examination of the UNCRC can reveal a concern with protecting the lives of boys rather than girls: she cites the targeting of child soldiers,[199] rather than of child marriage.[200] But she also accepts the important explicit prohibition of sex discrimination in Article 2 of the UN Convention.

Her article repays re-reading. I cannot go into her clever analysis of the different feminisms and their take on children's rights or on the Convention. I accept that children's rights can be used as a tool for controlling women as the main carers of children. But I am also fortified that what evidence there is finds that increases in the power of children have usually led to a corresponding improvement in that of their mothers.[201] The lesson may lie in forging alliances, so that groups which have, or continue, to experience discrimination and marginalization work together. An early feminist, Shulamith Firestone, recognized this. Those who worked for women's rights should also campaign for children's rights, she argued.[202] This is nota theme often taken up since, though there are now signs of a resurgence of interest in the interconnection.[203]

---

197 'Children's Rights: Some Feminist Approaches To the United Nations Convention on the Rights of the Child' in P Alston, S Parker, and J Seymour (eds), *Children, Rights and the Law* (Oxford, 1992), 192-220.

198 See N Taefi, 'The Synthesis of Age and Gender: Intersectionality, International Human Rights Law and the Marginalisation of the Girl-child' (2009) 17 *Int J of Children's Rights* 345-76.

199 *Supra,* n 197, 194.

200 But compare the African Charter on the Rights and Welfare of the Child 1990, Article 21 (2), and see DM Chirwa, 'The Merits and Demerits of the African Charter on the Rights and Welfare of the Child' (2002) 10 *Int J of Children's Rights* 157-77.

201 See M Hill, J Davis, A Prout, and K Tisdall, 'Moving The Participation Agenda Forward' (2004) 18 *Children and Society* 77-96.

202 *The Dialectic of Sex* (New York, 1975).

203 For example, E Burman, 'Beyond "Women vs. Children" or "Women and Children": Engendering Childhood and Reformulating Motherhood' (2008) 16 *Int J of Children's Rights* 177-94, and N Taefi, *supra,* n 198.

## Making Children's Rights Count

In the last part of this paper I look at six ways in which we can make children's rights count. We have to counter the criticisms, and we must accept that we may initially be flying in the face of public opinion. There is a concern that children's rights do not command public support. There is some evidence of this in Australasia. In 1999 there was a Senate Inquiry in Australia into the status of the UNCRC: 51 per cent of the submissions recommended withdrawal from the treaty: this was not, of course, done.[204] In 2009, New Zealand held a referendum on its law – the only one in the English-speaking world – making it unlawful to hit children: 87 per cent of those who voted wanted the law reversed: I understand there is no intention of changing the law as a result.[205] The media is not supportive either: children's portrayal there is largely negative. Sweden, I understand, has training days for the media, an example we might do well to follow. Parliament is at best equivocal. Often it responds to moral panics and reacts to folk devils (the boys who killed James Bulger,[206] or the families who killed Victoria Climbié[207] and Baby Peter[208]). It has a commitment to end child poverty: there is now a Child Poverty Act that puts the target to end child poverty by 2020 on to the statute book.[209] The Equality Act 2010 does not include children.[210] The attempt to make the UNCRC part of English law did not succeed.[211] And there is still no leg-

204 Parliament of the Commonwealth of Australia Joint Standing Committee on Treaties, *UN Convention on the Rights of the Child*, 17th report, August 1998. But see Chapter of Rights and Responsibilities Act 2006 (Victoria), ss 17, 23, 25 and 44.

205 Personal communication from Professor AB Smith, Children's Issues Centre, Otago University, Dunedin.

206 See M Freeman, *The Moral Status of Children* (The Hague, Kluwer, 1997), ch 12. This erupted again in 2010 when it was revealed that Jon Venables had been recalled to prison for breach of parole conditions.

207 See Lord Laming. *The Victoria Climbié Inquiry*, Cm 5730 (London, TSO, 2003).

208 See Lord Laming, *The Protection of Children in England: A Progress Report*, March 2009. For reaction see *Professional Social Work*, April 2009, 5.

209 Little progress has been made thus far – the commitment dates from 2000. See L Elliott, 'Up, Up, Up Child Poverty, Pensioner Poverty, Inequality', *The Guardian*, 11 June 2008, 1-2.

210 See *supra*, text to nn 9-18. See also C Davies, 'Discrimination "a daily fact of life for children"', *The Observer*, 19 March 2009, 14.

211 The Children's Rights Bill was moved in the House of Lords on 19 November 2009. It made no further progress.

islation making it unlawful to hit children.[212] There is some judicial support for children's rights.[213] This can he traced back to 1970[214] (and in the United States to Re *Gault*[215] in 1967). There is no more eloquent spokesperson for children's rights today than Baroness Hale of Richmond. Thus, in *Williamson* – the action brought by Christian fundamentalist parents (and teachers) to challenge the ban on corporal punishment in schools – she observed:

> This is, and always has been, a case about children, their rights and the rights of their parents and teachers. Yet there has been no one here... to speak on behalf of the children. The battle has been fought on ground selected by the adults.[216]

Her judgment, she said, was 'for the sake of the children'.[217] Anyone with an interest in why children's rights can so easily be marginalized would do well to read this case through each of its stages. It was fought on the question whether the state could legitimately undermine the religious rights of parents: children's rights did not get a look in.

We need a children's rights agenda, and I offer the following.

### (i) *Education*

As ever, any agenda for change needs to start with education. The majority of the population is totally unaware of the UNCRC. This is not surprising since it is unaware of most things of significance. One way of making the general public aware of children's rights is through the medium of the soap opera. This has worked with other issues like domestic violence. Decision-makers need to be trained: there could be children's rights aware-

---

212 The Government prevented discussion of a ban on hitting children during a debate on the Children and Young Persons Bill in October 2008, by prolonging debate on other issues.

213 Pre-eminently by Baroness Hale of Richmond.

214 *Hewer v Bryant* [1969] 3 All ER 578. Lord Denning MR said (*obiter*) that 'the legal right of a parent to custody of a child is a dwindling right which the courts hesitate to enforce against the wishes of the child, the older he is'.

215 387 US 1 (1967).

216 R (*on the Application of Williamson*) *v Secretary of State for Education and Employment* [2005] 2 FLR 374, 395.

217 *Ibid.* See also *Re E (A Child)* [2008] UKHL 66, para 6 ('With the best will in the world, there is a tendency to see confrontations... through adult eyes, and to forget these are not the eyes of children, who are simply the innocent victims of other people's quarrels').

ness days for judges, for social workers, for the police. And children also need to be taught that part of citizenship is the ability to exercise rights (and bear responsibilities). Rather than stifling participation by children and young people, we should be encouraging it. This involves giving them the vocabulary, debating with them, engaging, including, in fact recognizing, to return to an earlier theme of this paper, that they have a part in the public arena. If this creates a less quiescent, less complacent, more demanding society for the future, so much the better. The New Labour government came to power in 1997 with the slogan of 'Education, Education, Education'. This is the last thing it had in mind, but let us say we agree with them, and test out the slogan in this context.

### (ii) *A Children's Rights Ombudsman*

I first advocated an ombudsperson for children in 1987.[218] There was already one in Norway, established in 1981.[219] There were further calls for a 'children's rights commissioner', including a major report in 1991,[220] and the United Nations Committee on the Rights of the Child urged the creation of a Commissioner in its reports on the United Kingdom in 1995[221] and 2002.[222] The Government resisted, but after devolution Wales in 2001[223] and Scotland in 2003[224] went ahead, and Northern Ireland also created a Commissioner in 2003.[225] A Children's Commissioner for England was eventually established in 2004,[226] and the first Commissioner[227] started in post in March 2005.

---

218 'Taking Children's Rights Seriously' [1987] I *Children and Society* 315-16 (the 'Brian Jackson Memorial Lecture').

219 See M Flekkøy, *A Voice for Children: Speaking Out As Their Ombudsman* (London, 1991).

220 M Rosenbaum and P Newell, *Taking Children's Rights Seriously* (London, 1991). See also P Newell, *Taking Children Seriously* (London, 2000).

221 Committee on the Rights of the Child, *Concluding Observations: UK and Northern Ireland:* CRC/C/15/Add 34 (Geneva, 1995).

222 Committee on the Rights of the Child, *Concluding Observations: UK and Northern Ireland:* CRC/C/15/Add 188 (Geneva, 2002). See particularly para 19.

223 Children's Commissioner for Wales Act 2001. An evaluation in Nigel Thomas *et al*, 'Evaluating the Children's Commissioner for Wales' (2010) 18 *Int J of Children's Rights* 19-52.

224 Commissioner for Children and Young People (Scotland) Act 2003.

225 Commissioner for Children and Young People (Northern Ireland) Order 2003, SI 2003/439 (NI 11).

226 By the Children Act 2004.

227 Al Aynsley-Green (knighted shortly after his appointment). See *The Guardian* (Education Supplement), 3 November 2009, 1-2. His successor is Maggie Atkinson.

But what we have got is a Children's Commissioner, not a Children's Rights Commissioner. The Commissioner has a mandate to promote awareness of the views and interests of children. In particular to:

(a) encourage persons exercising functions or engaged in activities affecting children to take account of their views and interests;
(b) advise the Secretary of State on the views and interests of children;
(c) consider or research the operation of complaints procedures so far as relating to children;
(d) consider or research any other matter relating to the interests of children.[228]

This is a narrow remit. Other Commissioners in the United Kingdom are required to promote and safeguard the *rights* of children: the English Commissioner is only to promote awareness of their views and interests. Even though s 2(11) directs the Commissioner to have regard to the UNCRC (incidentally the only reference in the Act to children's rights[229]), it is of concern that the rather tame word 'interests' is substituted for rights in the general mandate. Even in s 2(11) the word 'rights' is avoided: reference is made instead to the 'interests of children'.

The Commissioner's hands are tied in other ways too. He may undertake an investigation on his own initiative, but he must first consult with the Secretary of State. He may also be directed by the Secretary of State to launch an investigation. In each case the trigger is a child, though he is not permitted to conduct an investigation into an individual child as such. The Scottish Commissioner is similarly constrained, but not so their counterparts in Wales and Northern Ireland.

The establishment of a Commissioner has to be seen as an opportunity lost.[230] Beverley Clucas is surely right to note that 'the excision of children's rights from the Act suggests a view that children are less-than-

Neither was particularly involved in children's rights prior to their appointment. Atkinson was, however, swiftly into action shortly after she took up her appointment condemning the low age of criminal responsibility. There is now (summer 2010) the possibility that the Commissioner will be scrapped as part of a cost-cutting exercise by the new Conservative-Liberal Democrat Coalition. See also *The Guardian* (Society Section), 4 August 2010, 3.

228 Children Act 2004, s 2(1).

229 Presumably because this was unavoidable!

230 J Williams, 'Effective Government Structures for Children?: The UK's Four Children's Commissioners' (2005) 17 *Child and Family Law Quarterly* 37.

full persons'.[231] To step back from a rights discussion to one where the emphasis is welfare is most regrettable. There is no evidence that the Commissioner has advanced children's rights, nor is any Commissioner likely to do so if the remit remains as it is. A Government committed to a rights agenda in 1998 (when the Human Rights Act was passed), by 2004 either had dropped this commitment or had decided that it did not apply to children.

We need a Children's Rights Ombudsman (I remain wedded to this, perhaps, esoteric title). We need an institution to which children can refer their complaints, most obviously breaches of the UNCRC. Articles 4 and 42 of the UNCRC require us to establish an institution to promote and protect children's rights, and thus far we have not clone so. We need an institution independent of government, not one tied in to a government programme (which lists indicators of child welfare, but ignores rights).[232]

### (iii) *Duty to Ensure Legislation's Compatibility with the UNCRC*

Since the implementation of the Human Rights Act 1998 it has become mandatory for all Bills to be certified as compatible with the ECHR. So much of our legislation falls short of complying with the UNCRC that an argument can be made for the introduction of a similar procedure as exists with the ECHR. Of course, the status of the Convention is different from that of the ECHR. This difference will go if another proposal on my agenda were to be implemented: of which more later.[233]

The UNCRC has a number of general principles.[234] Let us consider just one of these and its implications for the proposal. Article 3 contains the best interests principle. This states:

> In all actions concerning children, whether undertaken by public or private social welfare institutions, courts of law, administrative authorities or legislative bodies, the best interests of the child shall be a primary consideration.

231 'The Children's Commissioner for England: The Way Forward?' (2005) 35 *Family Law* 290.

232 *Every Child Matters*, Cm 5860 (London, 2003), and Children Act 2006.

233 *Infra*, 33.

234 See Articles 2, 3, 6, and 12.

All ratifying states have agreed to this provision. It may be argued that it now constitutes a norm of customary international law.[235] As L'Heureux-Dubé J of the Canadian Supreme Court explained in *Baker v Canada (Minister of Citizenship and Immigration)* 'the decision-maker should consider children's best interests as an important factor, give them substantial weight and be alert, alive and sensitive to them'.[236] This must be right because to do any less would undermine the best interests principle, and that would be inconsistent with the principles of interpretation of human rights treaties and the need to give effect to their object and purpose.[237]

The implications of this are considerable. Are our immigration laws compatible with the best interests of the child?[238] Is the age of criminal responsibility, which at 10 is one of the lowest in the developed world, defensible in terms of a best interests standard?[239] Is the law (s 58 of the Children Act 2004), which retains the reasonable chastisement defence to assaults on a child, acceptable when measured against Article 3 (and various other Articles, and other treaties)?[240] The UN Committee on the Rights of the Child has been critical of all these laws, and understandably so.[241]

### (iv) *Incorporate the UNCRC into UK Law*

The enforcement mechanism of the UNCRC is relatively weak.[242] Ratifying states provide periodic reports to the UN Committee on the Rights of the Child, and comments and recommendations are made. There is no

235 See, to like effect, Geraldine van Bueren, *Child Rights in Europe* (Strasbourg, 2007). But see J Eekelaar, 'Deciding For Children' (2006) 7 *Australian J of Professional and Applied Ethics* 66, 77.

236 [1999] 2 SCR 817, para 75.

237 Vienna Convention on the Law of Treaties, Art 34. And see *Loizidou v Turkey* (Preliminary Objections) (1995) 29 EHRR 99, para 72. See, further, Richard Gardiner, *Treaty Interpretation* (Oxford, 2008), 159-61.

238 See J McAdam, 'Seeking Asylum Under the Convention on the Rights of the Child' (2006) 14 *Int J of Children's Rights* 251-74. See, more generally, 'Special Issue' of *Children and Society* vol 21(4) (2007).

239 See D Cipriani, *Children's Rights and the Minimum Age of Criminal Responsibility* (Farnham, 2009).

240 See, more fully, MDA Freeman, *supra*, n 173.

241 Most recently in CRC/C/GBR/CO/4 (October 2008), paras 6 (a), 40-2, 70-1, 77-80.

242 It is contained in part II of the UNCRC: see Articles 42-45.

sense that the UK Government has been over-concerned at the criticisms it has received, or that it has done very much about it.[243]

In 1995 I proposed that the UNCRC be incorporated into UK law.[244] That was before the ECHR was so incorporated, and there was absolutely no possibility of its happening. In 1995 very few ratifying states had incorporated the UNCRC: many have now done so. Some have adopted constitutions which expressly recognize the rights of children. South Africa is an example: in the aftermath of apartheid it incorporated and made justiciable a number of UNCRC rights.[245] Section 39 of the South African Constitution requires courts to consider international law when deciding questions arising with respect to rights protected in the Constitution. Justice Sachs in *M v State* drew from this the conclusion that 'courts must function in a manner which at all times shows due respect for children's rights'.[246]

The UN Committee on the Rights of the Child has twice urged the UK Government to incorporate the UNCRC.[247] The Government is unlikely to take the initiative to do this. The response of the Joint Committee on Human Rights was to urge that at least some of the rights and principles in the Convention should be incorporated.[248] But which? Those with which the Government has little trouble? Those which are likely to cause it least trouble? Those which involve least expenditure of resources? And how would it justify such a piecemeal response? I think it's incorporation or nothing.

---

243 But it has (in 2008) withdrawn reservations to Articles 22 and 37(c) of the Convention. This was welcomed by the UN Committee: see *supra,* n 241, para 4(a).

244 'Children's Rights in a Land of Rites' in B Franklin (ed), *The Handhook of Children's Rights: Comparative Policy and Practice* (London, 1995), 70-83, 82-3.

245 On which see J Sloth-Nielsen and B Mezmur, '2+2 5? Exploring the Domestication of the CRC in South African Jurisprudence (2002-2006)' (2008) 16 *Int J of Children's Rights* 1-28. But they note 'the main beneficiaries of children's rights related cases were in fact adults who had sought to bolster their claims via children's rights based arguments', at 3.

246 *M v The State* CCT 53/06 [2007] Z ACC 18.

247 Committee on the Rights of the Child, *Concluding Observations on the UK and Northern Ireland,* CRC/C/15/Add. 188 (Geneva, 2002), paras 8-9; Committee on the Rights of the Child, *Concluding Observations on the UK and Northern Ireland, CRC/C/*GBR/CO/4 (Geneva, 2008), para 11.

248 Joint Committee on Human Rights, *The UN Convention on the Rights of the Child,* 10th report of Session 2002-2003, HL Paper 117/HC Paper 81, para 22.

The mood may have changed. There is now talk of a Bill of Rights and Responsibilities.[249] This would have to include a provision relating to children. Or so we assume. But including children in a Bill of Rights and Responsibilities, at least specifically, may not be necessary if incorporation of the UNCRC is effected. A Bill to do this was tabled in Parliament on the twentieth anniversary of UNCRC, on 20 November 2009. It was modelled on the Human Rights Act and would have incorporated the provisions of the UNCRC and the two Protocols as a Schedule.

It would not be the first time we had incorporated a children's convention into UK law. The Hague Convention on International Child Abduction was incorporated in 1985.[250] The answer cannot be that we have already incorporated the ECHR, because, as Baroness Hale frankly admitted recently, there is 'virtually nothing' in this about children.[251] The ECHR is anyway largely about civil and political rights. Whilst these are very important to children, so are social and economic rights, the right to health care and to freedom from poverty. The UNCRC recognizes the former (explicitly in Article 24); the latter can be found in the development provision in Article 6.2 – 'the overarching goal of the contemporary understanding of development is the *eradication* of poverty'.

The case for incorporation is convincing. True, this is not the conventional common law approach, but that is no argument against such an innovation now. We need to take a new approach to children's rights. We need a procedure to ensure that our laws comply with the provisions of the UNCRC: the reporting mechanism under the Convention is nota success, and the more overburdened the Committee gets the less successful the procedure will be. Our judges have become used to interpreting the provisions of the UNCRC and the ECHR. What they will do with conflicts between a general principle of English child law like the paramountcy principle[252] and Article 3 of the UNCRC remains to be seen. The Article in the UNCRC is wider in scope in that it applies to a range of institutions, but when it comes to courts' decision-making the UNCRC says the best interests of the child are a 'primary consideration', and the Children Act 1989 mandates they are 'the paramount consideration'.[253]

---

249 Joint Committee on Human Rights, *A Bill of Rights for the UK*, 29th report of Session 2007-2008, HL Paper 165-I, HC Paper 150-I (London, 2008), para 139.

250 Child Abduction and Custody Act 1985.

251 *Supra*, n 249, para 141.

252 Children Act 1989, *s* 1(1).

253 See Article 3(1) and s 1 (1) respectively.

The Bill failed to make progress. Since more attempts will be made, an appraisal of the Bill is called for.

I think the omission of the Preamble was a mistake. It offers interpretational guidance. I regret that the Bill reproduced some of the inconsistencies that are in the Convention. An obvious example is Article 5. This requires the State to respect the responsibilities, rights and duties of parents etc to provide, in a manner consistent with the evolving capacities of the child, appropriate direction and guidance in the exercise by the child of Convention rights. I have omitted the reference to members of the extended family or community as provided for by local custom, though the Bill did not do so. My concern is not with this concession to Africa, but with the conflict between Article 5 and the rather more significant Article 12. It is true that Article 12 can be interpreted paternalistically, but the Committee on the Rights of the Child has rightly, I believe, been critical of states which have so interpreted it.[254] It should not be forgotten also that the Convention reflects a number of compromises.[255] If we were starting from scratch we would not necessarily accept them.

It is one of the ironies of the UNCRC that, although it emphasizes participation by children in all matters affecting them, children had very little input into the Convention. How different a Convention in which the child's voice is heard would look is a matter of controversy. There is, however, nota little irony in having a Convention which emphasizes participatory rights, whilst foreclosing the participation of children in the formulation of the rights to be encoded. In 2000 I argued that the 'next Convention cannot afford to ignore the voice of children'.[256] The Children's Rights Bill is not the next Convention, but perhaps it is an opportunity lost to take note of children's views.

The Convention pays too little attention to certain groups of children.[257] A good example is the disabled child.[258] Of course, the non-discrimination principle in Article 2 applies to them and Article 23 requires us to recognize that a mentally or physically disabled child should enjoy

254 Including the UK. See *supra*, n 241, paras 32-3.

255 As discussed by D Johnson, 'Cultural and Regional Pluralism in the Drafting of the UN Convention on the Rights of the Child' in M Freeman and P Veerman (eds), *The Ideologies of Children's Rights* (Dordrecht, 1992), 95-114.

256 'The Future of Children's Rights' (2000) 14 *Children and Society* 277, 282.

257 See the discussion, *ibid*, 282-5.

258 See the discussion (in relation to education) by J Fortin, *Children's Rights and the Developing Law* (London, 2009), ch 12. See also the UN Committee report on the UK, *supra*, n 241, paras 52-3.

'a full and decent life, in conditions which ensure dignity, promote self-reliance, and facilitate the child's active participation in the community'. But this adopts a model of disability, where the emphasis is on discrimination, rather than inclusion.[259] By using the language of anti-discrimination rather than the principle of inclusion, it legitimates segregation. The article thus emphasizes welfare rather than rights. However, the UN Committee on the Rights of the Child has stressed that states recognize disabled children's rights to inclusion on regular schools, and has criticized states which provide only segregated education.[260] Its 2006 General Comment emphasizes that 'Inclusive education, should he the goal of educating children with disabilities'.[261] The Children's Rights Bill said that courts and tribunals must take concluding observations and a General Comment such as this one, into account.[262] That is significant, but what of education authorities? It is also significant that the UN Convention on the Rights of Persons with Disabilities does recognize the right of disabled persons to an 'inclusive education', and specifically requires states to ensure that they are 'not excluded from free and compulsory primary education, or from secondary education, on the basis of disability'. They should also have the support they need 'to facilitate their effective education'.[263] This Convention is thus more disabled child friendly. But the United Kingdom has not ratified it, and there is thus no suggestion that it will he incorporated into UK law.

Disabled children are but one example of children marginalized by the Convention. Space precludes discussion of others. But I may cite gay children.[264] Does Article 2 (the non-discrimination principle) extend to them? Only if 'other status' can be so stretched, and this is a clear reference to illegitimacy, not sexual orientation. The Convention does far too

259 See *supra*, n 256, 282. See also C Low, 'A Defence of Moderate Inclusion and the End of Ideology' in R Cigman, *Included or Excluded?: The Challenge of Mainstream for Some SEN Children* (London, 2007).

260 See the discussion in R Hodgkin and P Newell, *Implementation Handbook for the Convention on the Rights of the Child* (Geneva, 2007), 335-7.

261 Committee on the Rights of the Child, *General Comment No 9: The Rights of Children With Disabilities*, CRC/C/EC/9 (Geneva, 2006), para 66.

262 See clause 27.

263 United Nations Convention on the Rights of Persons with Disabilities, Article 24(1), (2)(d).

264 An early exploration of this is P Veerman *et al*, 'HIV Prevention, Children's Rights, and Homosexual Youth' (1999) 7 *Int J of Children's Rights* 83-9.

little to enhance the status of girls.[265] Our legislation already bans female genital mutilation[266] (though, I suspect, not very effectively[267]). Couldn't a Children's Rights Bill specifically give girls the right not to be subjected to this barbaric practice? Or would such a step open the can of worms that is male circumcision?[268] The Convention has no minimum age for marriage.[269] Isn't it about time we rethought the age of 16?[270] Shouldn't an incorporation bill have something to say about this? The Convention fails also refugee children: it employs an outdated definition of refugee, and imposes no duty on states to provide asylum.[271] It innovatively protects the rights of indigenous children,[272] but only does so negatively – they should not 'be denied the right' to enjoy their own language and culture. And what about children who break the law? The Convention says there should be a minimum age of criminal responsibility, but leaves it open to states to fix this age.[273]

When the Convention was formulated we could stretch this to 14 by reason of the *doli incapax* principle.[274] But that has gone,[275] and we now have one of the lowest minimum ages of criminal responsibility in the

265 For example, on education. See, in relation to Africa, L Mwambene, 'Implementing the Girl Child's Right To Education in Selected Countries in Africa' in J Sloth Nielsen (ed), *Children's Rights in Africa* (Aldershot, 2008), ch 13.

266 Female Genital Mutilation Act 2003. Legislation was first passed in 1985.

267 A different approach is described by N Ford, 'Communication for Abandonment of Female Genital Cutting: An approach Based on Human Rights Principles' (2005) 13 *Int J of Children's Rights* 183-99.

268 On the difference see Baroness Hale of Richmond in *R v Secretary of State for Home Department, Fornah v Secretary of State for Home Department* [2007] 1 AC 412, para 93.

269 The UN Committee on the Rights of the Child is frequently critical of states with low ages of marriage. Examples are Andorra (see CRC/C/15/Add.176, 2002), Benin (see CRC/C/15/Add.1 06, 1999), Cameroon (see CRC/C/15/Add.164, 2001), Chile (see CRC/C/15/Add.175, 2002), Madagascar (see CRC/C/15/Add. 218, 2003).

270 It was fixed at 16 in 1929.

271 See Article 22, and G Goodwin-Gill 'Unaccompanied Refugee Minors: The Role and Place of International Law in the Pursuit of Durable Solutions (1995) 3 *Int J of Children's Rights* 405-16.

272 See Article 30. See, further, R van Krieken, 'The Stolen Generation and Cultural Genocide: The Forced Removal of Australian Indigenous Children from their Families' (1999) 6 *Childhood* 297-311.

273 See Article 40.

274 This stretched back 800 years.

275 Crime and Disorder Act 1998, s 34. And see *DPP v P* [2007] 5 All ER 628. Valuable discussions are presented in D Ormerod (2008) *Criminal Law Review* 165 and 721.

developed world.[276] The Children's Rights Bill could have changed this, but as it merely was intended to incorporate the Convention, it is obviously unable to do so.

Of course, the Children's Rights Bill was progress, and is to be welcomed. But I feel rather as I did when I first saw the Human Rights Bill. We could do better than replicate what international institutions formulated a generation or more earlier.

### (v) *Giving Children the Right of Petition*

In 1990 (in Jerusalem on the eve of the first Gulf War) I asked: 'Why not a system whereby aggrieved children can complain and seek redress when their State, through a Party in the Convention, violate rights contained within it?'[277] A footnote (to the printed text) adds 'As under the European Convention on Human Rights'.[278] I responded: 'Perhaps these concepts are too ambitious for a nascent development like international children's rights', and added that this was a direction in which we must 'ultimately' look.[279] In 2000, I returned to this proposal and noted: 'The sight of children hauling their own states before an international court would be particularly gratifying.'[280] I had, you will note, surreptitiously moved from children complaining to the UN Committee to children being offered the opportunity to challenge state actions in some (as yet unconstructed) court. I referred in 2000 to the possibility of a Protocol allowing for, what I called, 'international petition'.[281] There was, I added, no reason to believe that we would see this in the near future.

This may still be right, but there is now a groundswell of opinion favouring what is now to be called 'a communications procedure'.[282] An Optional Protocol was proposed before the Human Rights Council on 17 June 2009. It has the support of 51 states. Unsurprisingly, these do not include the United Kingdom or the United States: rather more surprisingly neither Sweden nor Norway supports the proposal. The initiative seems to have come largely from Central and Eastern Europe, the draft reso-

---

276 See D Cipriani, *Children's Rights and the Minimum Age of Criminal Responsibility* (Farnham, 2009) for a comprehensive study of the issue.

277 See MDA Freeman, 'The Limits of Children's Rights' in M Freeman and P Veerman (eds), *The Ideologies of Children's Rights* (Dordrecht, 1992), 29-46, 42.

278 *Ibid*, 47, n 102.

279 *Ibid*, 42.

280 *Supra*, n 256.

281 *Ibid.*

282 As it is in other Conventions: see *infra*, nn 283-91.

lution being introduced by Slovakia. The 'communications procedure' is envisaged as complementary to the reporting procedure under the Convention. There is to be a debate on this proposal shortly. At the moment the details remain vague.

Is there a case for individual petition, for children in particular, but presumably also adults (their parents, for example) to make complaints and representations to the UN Committee on the Rights of the Child? Giving children the right to petition the Committee would operationalize Article 12 of the Convention, and show we are taking participation rights seriously. It would act as a constraint on states taking steps in clear breach of the Convention. Initially, at least petitions would achieve huge, world-wide publicity. Imagine the child hauling the UK before the Committee for introducing the 'mosquito'. It might deter: it might encourage change. It would give a greater profile to children's rights. The argument that the proposal is too radical can readily be countered by looking at existing precedents. The African Charter on the Rights and Welfare of the Child has a right of individual petition for all children:[283] it is, in fact, hardly used. There are procedures allowing for individual's communications in other core international human rights treaties:

- the International Covenant on Civil and Political Rights;[284]
- the International Covenant on Economic, Social and Cultural Rights;[285]
- the International Convention on the Elimination of All Forms of Racial Discrimination;[286]
- the Covenant on the Elimination of All Forms of Discrimination Against Women;[287]
- the Convention against Torture and other Cruel, Inhuman and Degrading Treatment or Punishment;[288]
- the International Convention on the Protection of the Rights of All Migrant Workers and Members of their Families;[289]
- the International Convention for the Protection of All Persons from Enforced Disappearances;[290] and
- the UN Convention on the Rights of Persons with Disabilities.[291]

283 Optional Protocol.
284 Optional Protocol.
285 Optional Protocol.
286 Optional Protocol.
287 Optional Protocol, part 3.
288 Article 20.
289 Article 2 of Optional Protocol.
290 Article 31.
291 Optional Protocol, Annex 2.

So, African children can petition (under the African Charter), girl children can petition (under CEDAW), and disabled children can use the Disabilities Convention. Is there any reason why the rights should not be extended to other children?

There is the concern that the Convention includes social and economic rights as well as civil and political ones. The former involve the outlay of resources. And, the argument goes, this could lead to a child challenging the way his/her government uses (or rather fails to use) its resources. This may be particularly pertinent with the new Child Poverty Act 2010. The Convention does not talk in terms of a right to be free from poverty, as such, but it obligates the state to ensure to the maximum extent possible the 'development of the child', and we know growing up in poverty obstructs this.[292] It also recognizes the child's right to enjoy an adequate standard of living, and the state's duty to provide parents with appropriate assistance, to the maximum extent of its resources.[293] The Government is aware of the need to tackle child poverty. There is a pledge to end it by 2020. A 'key outcome' of *Every Child Matters* is 'economic well-being'.[294] In 2007 a Child Poverty Unit was established.[295] There is a 10-year Children's Plan, part of which is that children should grow up 'free from the blight of child poverty'.[296] Child poverty is in decline, but it still affects nearly a quarter of UK children.[297] It is three times higher than in Denmark.[298] It is of some reassurance that it is coming down in the UK, though it is increasing in most of the rest of Europe.[299] But it remains an intractable problem. Is there any reason why a UK child shouldn't be able to use the right of petition to indict the Government? That the petition relates to resources is no answer. The African Charter, which contains a child's right of petition, embodies social and economic rights as well.

It is not clear what the nascent third Protocol will involve. If it is to be just a communications procedure, will it inform the Commit tee of

---

292 So, for example, poverty is a barrier to educational success, it damages children's health, poor children are more likely to experience unsafe environments. The right to development is in Article 6.2 of the UNCRC. See also n 104, *supra*.

293 See Articles 29.1 and 29.3.

294 HM Treasury, *Every Child Matters*, Cm 5860 (London, 2003), para 1.3.

295 This has a remit to develop policy on ending child poverty. In January 2009, it published *Ending Child Poverty: Making It Happen* (London, 2009).

296 *Op cit*, n 294, para 1.8.

297 See Child Poverty Action Group, *Ending Child Poverty -A Manifesto for Success* (London, 2009), 15.

298 *Ibid.*

299 *Ibid.* It is at its highest in Italy (see *Eurostat*).

much more than it knows already? It will offer a child's insight, children's experiences, but otherwise it may appear merely to reinforce what other organizations have already made known. My view is that more is required if the Convention is going to be made more effective. And it is to the model of the ECHR that I think we need to look. We must consider establishing an international court (or tribunal) to hear complaints by children against their governments for breaches of the UNCRC. This is far from an easy solution. One concern is that most of the child petitioners will be adults by the time their cases are heard. Geraldine van Bueren's proposal for binding interim measures is therefore attractive.[300] She cites precedent for this from the Indian Supreme Court.[301] Of course, I have been assuming the child's complaint is against the state. It may very well be against a parent. But even then it may relate to an aspect of parental responsibility which the state has conferred in breach of the Convention. An obvious example is the parent's right to hit a child, which English law allows[302] but the UNCRC does not.[303] A challenge on such a matter might prove the catalyst for change.

It will be interesting to follow the debate on the third Optional Protocol. It is unlikely to succeed immediately, and even if does there may be only a minority of ratifications. But I believe it will eventually be adopted. Pressure must then be brought in the UK government to ratify. I have never understood why Protocols should be optional.

### (vi) *Treating Children as Citizens*

As we saw earlier in this paper, children are never spared politics, that is, in its widest sense. In its narrow sense, they are. Most obviously, they are denied the vote. I intend to look briefly at the question whether children should have the vote. It was Patricia Williams who, in the context of racism, observed:

> ... if women enter environments where only men have been talking to men, the conversation is bound to change. If blacks enter spaces

300 So argued at lecture given at Garden Court Chambers on 'Children's Rights' at LSE on 24 September 2009.

301 *PUCL vs Union of India and Others*, Civil Writ Petition 196 of 2001.

302 Children Act 2004, s 58.

303 Article 19.

> where whites have only been talking to other whites, the conversation is bound to grow somewhat more encompassing.[304]

I would argue that this also applies if children are included in spaces and conversations hitherto the preserve of adults. Of course, as indicated earlier in this paper, children are thought to occupy only the 'private' space of home, family and school. To see children as citizens has been thought to see them as 'out of place'. But, as Jeremy Roche put it, 'the demand that children be included in citizenship is simply a request that children be seen as members of society too, with a legitimate and valuable voice and perspective'.[305] The demand that children be seen as citizens goes beyond the debate about the vote, but I will concentrate just on this.

It was a manifesto commitment of the Liberal Democrats in 2001 to lower the age of voting to 16, but the Electoral Commission in 2004 rejected such a reform.[306] In its view 16-year-olds had insufficient social responsibility and emotional maturity. The Commission feared that if the age at which people could vote was lowered, the percentage of those voting would also decrease.[307] Only 37 per cent of 18-24 year olds voted in the 2005 election, compared with 61 per cent of those aged between 35 and 44. But it is possible that encouraging 16-year-olds to vote might lead to more people voting as they become involved in the political process. It might have a knock-on effect, encouraging social responsibility and active citizenship.

One cannot fail to be struck by the similarity of arguments once used to deny the vote to labourers, women and, in the United States, to African-Americans.[308] The main reason why children are not given the vote is that they are thought to lack political competence. But so do a large number of adults who have the vote, and some of whom exercise it. Does this damage the well-being of democracy? I doubt it. The 'know-nothings'

---

304 P Williams, *The Rooster's Egg or The Persistence of Prejudice* (Cambridge, Mass, 1955), 93.

305 J Roche, 'Children: Rights, Participation and Citizenship' (1999) 6 *Childhood* 475-93, 479. See also T Cockburn, 'Children and Citizenship in Britain' (1995) 5 *Childhood* 99-117.

306 Electoral Commission, *Age of Electoral Majority: Report and Recommendations* (London, 2004).

307 *Ibid*, paras 3.16-3.28.

308 P van Parijs, 'The Disenfranchisement of the Elderly, and Other Attempts to Secure Intergenerational Justice' (1998) 27 *Philosophy and Public Affairs* 292-333 is a good discussion of the issues.

vote both ways sufficiently enough to cancel each other out. Voting as *The Sun* tells you to is much more dangerous to the health of democracy!

We allow children to marry at 16, to join the army at 16, we make them criminally responsible at 10. There is a case for tying the voting age to the age of criminal responsibility: why should we punish those who have no say in the making of the laws they have broken? The most widely-quoted empirical study of children and politics suggests:

> By the age of nine, much of the political language of adult life has been acquired. By eleven, many children have as good a working vocabulary for politics as many adults could claim, and a framework of ideas which, even if developed no further, will enable them to grasp the facts of current affairs, understand something of relationships between principles and issues in politics and make their choices at general elections.[309]

Because of the need for gradual change, I would support lowering the age for voting to 16. But I see no reason why there should be an age at all. In what way would democracy be harmed if a few 8-year-olds voted? If the response is that they will vote as parents instruct them to do this may be no bad thing. The parents of 8-year-olds are likely to belong to the age group that has the highest level of political competence: thus it would increase the number of competent voters.

Giving the vote to children will have important consequences. Children will be less easy to marginalize. Politicians will have to take the 'best interests' principle more seriously. Children's rights will be placed more firmly on the agenda. It would also have a positive impact on education. Article 29 of the UNCRC requires that children develop a respect for human rights and fundamental freedoms, as well as being prepared for a responsible life in a free society. If they had the vote, we would have to take the obligation more seriously. A population with a respect for human rights would be a healthier population, and one less tolerant of the abuses which we are regaled almost daily.

Whether children (or children of 16) are given the vote or not, there are, it should not be forgotten, other ways of ensuring we treat them

309 See O Stevens, *Children Talking Politics* (Oxford, 1982), 148. See also M Drakeford, J Scourfield, S Holland, and A Davies, 'Welsh Children's Views on Government and Participation' (2009) 16 *Childhood* 247-64 (8-year-olds thought their views should be considered on local issues).

as citizens. Children's Parliaments is one option: this would encourage children to express views on matters affecting them and put flesh on the bones of Article 12. It would also give more meaning to Article 13 (freedom of expression) and Article 15 (freedom of association and assembly). Some progress has now been made in relation to democracy in schools. The Education and Skills Act 2008 has, at long last, introduced a duty on all schools to 'invite and consider pupils' views' about prescribed matters, having regard to age and understanding.[310] Regulations are anticipated requiring governing bodies to seek and take account of pupils' views on such matters as uniform, school food, health and safety, and, as the Government Minister stressed, 'not simply on what colour to paint the walls'.[311] In Wales school council meetings must he held six times a year. We must wait and see what impact this reform has. It can all too easily become tokenistic.

## Some Concluding Thoughts

We have a long way to go, but we have come a long way in a relatively short time. Children's rights are now being discussed seriously, if critically. In the UNCRC we have a benchmark, and a foundation upon which we can build. No international treaty commands as much support. But paying lip-service to its ideals is insufficient, and too many countries fall down on their obligations under it. Our own record is especially poor, particularly in relation to poverty and to the criminal justice system. There is a need for more child-centred policies, for better structures to protect children and their rights, above all for a child-centred philosophy. This will proclaim the end of a discourse that children are not fully human, and will emphasize their dignity. A healthy democracy is one in which all its citizens can participate; it is one where authority and tradition can he challenged. The burden lies on those who would deny rights to children. It is often said, but it bears repeating, that you can judge a society by the way it treats its weakest members. The world will be a better place when this is recognized.

---

310 Section 157, inserting new s 29B into Education Act 2002. See further E Welton, 'Laying Down The Law: An Analysis of the Education and Skills Bill' (2008) 245 *Childright* 11.

311 *Per* Baroness Morgan of Drefelin, *Hansard*, HL 11 November 2005, col 573. On Wales see School Councils (Wales) Regulations 2005, SI 2005/3200, reg 3(2). Jane Fortin, *supra*, n 258, discusses this at 221-3.

CHAPTER 2

# A Time to be Born and a Time to Die

> To every thing there is a season, and a time to every purpose under the heaven: A time to be born, and a time to die...[1]

To the author of the book of *Ecclesiastes,* indeed until very recently, there was very little knowledge about the beginning and the end of life. If infertile you could, like Sarah and Hannah in the Bible, pray for a child:[2] if life had become an intolerable burden you could, similarly, pray that it be taken away from you.[3] Suicide,[4] like abortion,[5] attracted the severest penalties. But much has changed.

Not only can you be born after the death of your father, you can now be conceived after his death[6] and born after the death of your mother[7] (if we define death in terms of brain stem activity[8]). You can be born years after your twin.[9] It is likely soon, if this has not already happened, that you may be born without any sexual intercourse or fertilization having taken place.[10] You may have a genetic, gestational, and social mother, and they may be three different women.[11] Your mother may be post-meno-

1 *Ecclesiastes,* Chapter III, 2.

2 Sarah was 90 (*Genesis,* XVIII, 17). On Hannah see I *Samuel,* 1, 11.

3 Though this did not always work: *e.g.,* see *Jonah,* IV, 3-11, or *Job.*

4 See Thomas Szasz, *Fatal Freedom* (Syracuse, NY, 2002). For interesting linguistic insight, in particular into why 'suicide' was so called, see D. Daube, 'The Linguistics of Suicide' (1972) 1 *Philosophy and Public Affairs* 387-437.

5 See John M. Riddle, *Eve's Herbs* (Cambridge, Mass, 1997).

6 As in *R* v. *HFEA ex parte Blood* [1997] 2 All ER 287.

7 Which happened with the 'Erlanger baby'; see C. Anstötz (1993) 7 *Bioethics* 340-50.

8 See C. Pallis and D. H. Hartley, *ABC of Brain Stem Death* (London, 2nd edn, 1996). Legal authorities are *Re A* [1992] 3 Med LR 303 and, of course, the *Bland* decision (by implication), discussed below at pp. 642-45. For useful debate see (1990) 4(3) *Bioethics* 181-231.

9 Because of our ability to freeze embryos. On one of the more intriguing problems caused by cryopreservation see R. Atherton, 'En Ventre Sa Frigidaire: Posthumous Children in the Succession Context' (1999) 19 *Legal Studies* 139-64.

10 As a result of cloning (see below, pp. 614-24). Claims that this has happened have been doubted: see *The Independent,* 28 December 2002.

11 $M^1$ provides the egg, $M^2$ the womb, and $M^3$ the nurture.

 | DOI:10.1163/9789004219106_003

pausal.[12] Your parents may be two lesbians,[13] or two gay men.[14] You may have been chosen because when an embryo you did not have a genetic defect shared by your embryo siblings.[15] Or you may be deaf, for example, because your parents wanted a deaf child and were allowed to exercise 'reproductive autonomy'.[16] You may be a boy because your culture prefers boys and your parents exercised sex selection or used sperm sorting.[17] You might not have been born at all had your parents not needed you to help cure a child they already had.[18] Of course 'you' may not have been born at all: your mother's pregnancy may have been terminated, even in that third trimester,[19] or your mother may have used the 'morning-after pill'[20] or RU-486[21] to ensure you were not born at all. I raise merely a few possibilities.

And similarly with the end of life. The verities have gone. Once it was clear to us when someone was dead: they had stopped breathing. But now it hinges on brain-stem activity.[22] And this, of course, has important implications when it comes to the removal of organs for transplantation to others.[23] Science today can keep alive those who would have simply died.

12 On which see J. Harris, F. Fisher and A. Sommerville, G. de Wert and I. de Beaufort, in J. Harris and S. Holm, *The Future of Human Reproduction* (Oxford, 1998), at 19-21, 203, 221, and 238 respectively. But see C. Mihill, *The Guardian*, 20 July 1993.

13 See M. Spriggs (2002) 28 *Journal of Medical Ethics* 283.

14 See the account in D. Strah, *Gay Fathers* (New York, 2003).

15 See S. Holm, n. 12 above, 176. See also R.J. Boyle and J. Savulescu (2001) 323 BMJ 123.

16 Holm, n. 12 above, 186-7. See also L. Shepherd (1995) *Univ. of Illinois LR* 761 and below, pp. 631-32. On reproductive autonomy (or 'procreative liberty') see J. Robertson, *Children of Choice: Freedom and the New Reproductive Technologies* (Princeton, NJ, 1994). *Cf.* the rather more convincing case (in this context) for 'procreative beneficence' by J. Savulescu (2001) 15 *Bioethics* 413-26. See also n. 13 above.

17 See J. Harris, *Wonderwoman and Superman: The Ethics of Human Biotechnology* (Oxford, 1992), ch. 10.

18 The issue in the *Hashmi* litigation of 2002-2003, discussed below, pp. 627-29. See M. Spriggs and J. Savulescu (2001) 28 *Journal of Medical Ethics* 289.

19 English law allows abortion to term on three grounds: see Abortion Act 1967, s. 1(1) (b), (c), and (d), as amended by the Human Fertilisation and Embryology Act 1990, s. 37.

20 On which see *R Smeaton (on the application of) on behalf of SPUC* v. *Secretary of State for Health* [2002] 2 FLR 146, 153-4.

21 Mifepristone.

22 On which see Department of Health, *A Code of Practice for the Diagnosis of Brain Stem Death* (London, 1998).

23 On non-heart beating donors see D. P. T. Price (1996) 24 *Journal of Law Medicine and Ethics* 139 and (1997) 23 *Journal of Medicine and Ethics* 170. For criticisms of the brain stem death definition see R. D. Truog (1997) 27(1) *Hastings Center Report*

So moral questions arise as to whether to remove nutrition and hydration from someone in a persistent (or permanent) vegetative state:[24] the dilemma was not there for previous generations. Because we can keep alive, even if we cannot give a life to, PVS patients, those with 'locked-in' syndrome,[25] severely handicapped neonates,[26] we agonize about withholding and withdrawing treatment. We question futile treatment, though we are rarely clear about what 'futile' means.[27] We distinguish ordinary from extraordinary treatment,[28] as if the morality of an action should depend upon whether technology was involved. We forget that penicillin and antibiotics generally were once considered extraordinary interventions. We distinguish also killing from letting die, the active and the passive.[29] The law says the former is murder[30] and doctors have been prosecuted for giving lethal injections,[31] but would it have been more seriously wrong to have put Tony Bland[32] quietly to sleep rather than allowing him to die by denying him sustenance? At least those, like Bland, in a persistent vegetative state are allowed to die. The irony of responding to the incompetent more generously than to those able to make decisions for themselves would surely not have been lost on Dianne Pretty,[33] who

---

29. For an excellent discussion of the parallel historical evolution of brain death and organ procurement see M. S. Pernick in S. Youngner, R. Arnold, and R. Schapiro (eds.), *The Definition of Death: Contemporary Controversies* (Baltimore, MD, 1999), 3.

24 On PVS see B. Jennett, *The Vegetative State: Medical Facts, Ethical and Legal Dilemmas* (Cambridge, 2002).

25 The syndrome was in issue in *Auckland Area Health Board* v. *A-G* [1993] 1 NZLR 235.

26 See H. Kuhse and P. Singer, *Should the Baby Live? The Problem of Handicapped Infants* (Oxford, 1985).

27 See B. Brody and A. Halevy, 'Is Futility A Futile Concept?' (1995) 20 *Journal of Medical Philosophy* 123-44; B. Wilson, 'Futility and the Obligations of Physicians' (1996) 10 *Bioethics* 45-55; A. Lelie and N. Verweij, 'Futility without a Dichotomy: Towards an Ideal Physician-Patient Relationship' (2003) 17 *Bioethics* 21-31; D. Lamb, *Therapy Abatement, Autonomy and Fertility* (Aldershot, 1995).

28 See R. Gillon, 'Editorial' (1981) 7 *Journal of Medical Ethics* 56 ('The distinction has a dangerously deceptive appearance of simplicity').

29 A defence is M. Stauch, 'Causal Authorship and the Equality Principle: A Defence of the Acts/Omissions Distinction in Euthanasia' (2000) 26 *Journal of Medical Ethics* 237-41. See also R. W. Perrett, 'Killing, Letting Die and the Bare Difference Argument' (1996) 10 *Bioethics* 131-9.

30 *R* v. *Adams (Bodkin)* [1957] Crim LR 365.

31 Notably Dr Cox who injected potassium chloride: see *R* v. *Cox* (1992) 12 BMLR 38.

32 N. 24 above. See further below, pp. 643-45.

33 *R Pretty (on the application)* v. *DPP* [2002] 1 FLR 268; *Pretty* v. *United Kingdom* [2002] 2 FLR 45.

was denied assistance with her projected suicide, or Ms B,[34] forced into unseemly litigation before being allowed to refuse any further treatment.

We are knee-deep in a moral quagmire, and I suspect we will sink further. This paper will suggest an escape route out. It cannot possibly address all the issues concerning the beginning and end of life, even all those thus far raised. This may require a monograph. It will look for principles, rather as Ronald Dworkin did in *Life's Dominion.*[35] Both the range of subject-matter (Dworkin limited himself to abortion and euthanasia (broadly-defined)) and the principles adopted (Dworkin emphasizes the intrinsic sacred value of human life) are different. But we agree that 'questions about death require us also to think about life'.[36]

My paper is about two inter-linked principles, that of autonomy and that of dignity, as well as about their uses and abuses.[37] The principle of autonomy is clearly enunciated in Mill's *On Liberty:* 'Over himself the individual is sovereign'.[38] And it is a cornerstone of medical law. As Lord Goff noted in *Re F,* 'we have to bear well in mind the libertarian principle of self-determination'.[39] And, 'Even when his or her own life depends on receiving medical treatment, an adult of sound mind is entitled to refuse it. This reflects the autonomy of each individual and the right of self-determination'.[40] So much so that 'the principle of the sanctity of human life must yield to the principle of self-determination'.[41]

But the principle of human dignity is equally important.[42] As Brennan J explained in *Marion's* case, 'each person has a unique dignity which the

34 *Re B* [2002] 1 FLR 1090.

35 (London, 1993).

36 *Ibid.*, 26.

37 On the relationship see J. Raz, *The Authority of Law* (Oxford, 1979), 221: 'Respecting human dignity entails treating humans as persons capable of planning and plotting their future. Thus, respecting people's dignity includes respecting their autonomy, their right to control their future.'

38 (Cambridge, 1989, originally published in 1859.) See further the issue of *Social Philosophy and Policy* (2003) vol. 20(2) on 'Autonomy'.

39 *Re F* [1990] 2 AC 1, 73.

40 *Per* Judge LJ in *St George's Healthcare NHS Trust* v. *S* [1999] Fam 26, 43.

41 *Per* Lord Goff in *Airedale NHS Trust* v. *Bland* [1993] AC 789, 864.

42 According to Joseph Raz offences against a person's dignity can take one of three forms: 'if it consists of or implies a denial that he is an autonomous person or that he deserves to be treated as one. An action enslaves another if it practically denies him all options through the manipulation of the environment... One manipulates a person by intentionally changing his tastes, his beliefs or his ability to act or decide.'

law respects and which it will protect'.[43] 'The law,' he continued, 'will protect equally the dignity of the hale and hearty and the dignity of the weak and lame; of the frail baby and the frail aged; of the intellectually able and of the intellectually disabled'.[44]

Of course, there are other relevant principles: the sanctity of human life;[45] the integrity of the medical profession.[46] But too much attention may have been paid to these principles and they will play a subsidiary role in my discussion. Using the twin prongs of autonomy and dignity, I will offer a critical examination of the social practices which constitute the English law as it confronts what Dworkin has called the 'two edges'[47] of life.

## A Time to be Born

### *Not Being Born*

I start with abortion. The decision to choose a termination is central to reproductive autonomy.[48] But it is a right that women should exercise responsibly. Rosalind Hursthouse has so argued[49] and so has Robin West[50]

---

43 *Secretary, Department of Health* v. *JWB and SMB* (1992) 66 ALJR 300, 317.

44 *Ibid.*, 318.

45 See Helga Kuhse, *The Sanctity-of-life Doctrine in Medicine: A Critique* (Oxford, 1987). Despite Article 2 of the European Convention on Human Rights, the courts have frequently said the principle is not absolute (see n. 41 above *per* Lords Keith, Goff, and Mustill). A critique is J. Keown, 'Restoring Moral and Intellectual Shape in the Law After *Bland*' (1997) 113 LQR 481.

46 Identified most clearly in *Re Claire Conroy* 486 A 2d 1209 (1985). See also Thorpe J in *Secretary of State for the Home Department* v. *Robb* (1994) 22 BMLR 43. For the view that autonomy 'bears hard on relations of trust', and the implications that this has for medicine, see Onora O'Neill, *Autonomy and Trust in Bioethics* (Cambridge, 2002): note the excellent critique by Gerald Dworkin, 'Can You Trust Autonomy?' (2003) 33(2) *Hastings Center Report* 42-44.

47 N. 35 above, 27.

48 See Rosalind Petchesky, *Abortion and Women's Choice: The State, Sexuality and Reproductive Freedom* (Boston, 1985). Abortion, she says, 'represents the image of emancipated woman' (*ibid.*, 241).

49 *Beginning Lives* (Oxford, 1987).

50 'Taking Freedom Seriously' (1990) 104 *Harvard Law Review* 43-106, 84-85.

whom Dworkin quotes.[51] It is not like cutting one's hair[52] or fingernails. What Judge LJ said of a 36-week foetus, can be generalized to all foetuses: they are 'not nothing' and they are 'certainly human'.[53] As such some dignity must be accorded: there must be a recognition that the decision is important.

Abortion law should therefore be seen as part of a package that starts with sex education (our laws on this are found, and belatedly so[54] in Education Acts[55]), goes on to deal with the provision of contraceptive services (this duty is not found in the National Health Service Act 1977[56] but in the Medical Regulations[57]), before reaching the question of abortion. Nor would the package end with abortion: there would be provision too on maternity leave, maternity benefits, day care alternatives such as creches, etc.[58] But the English law of abortion could not be further from this model. Abortion was a capital offence until 1837.[59] The law even today is found in an antiquated criminal statute – the Offences Against The Person Act 1861[60] – and what most of us consider to be the abortion law (the Abortion Act of 1967, as amended in 1990) is grafted upon this criminal statute. The criminal statute astonishingly antedates the Papal interdict on early abortion by eight years (until 1869 abortions of male foetuses were allowed for 40 days and of female ones for 80, this being the time (or so it was believed) of ensoulment[61]).

---

51 N. 35 above, 57-58. Thus, according to Dworkin, West assumes that 'it is irresponsible to waste human life without a justification of appropriate importance' (*ibid.*, 58).

52 *Cf.* Jill Knight MP, who, during the debate on the Abortion Bill in 1966, said women who wanted abortions treat babies 'like bad teeth to be jerked out' (*Hansard,* HC vol. 732, col. 1100).

53 N. 40 above, 45.

54 See further D. Monk, 'Sex Education and HIV/AIDS: Political Conflict and Legal Resolution' (1998) 12 *Children and Society* 295-305.

55 Now the Education Act 1996, ss. 403-405.

56 This only provides for so-called 'personal medical services' (see s. 29).

57 National Health Service (General Medical Services) Regulations 1992, reg. 3(1)(c).

58 As there is, *e.g.* in Norway. See (1979) 30 *International Digest of Health Legislation* 126-8.

59 It was made a capital offence in 1803 (Lord Ellenborough's Act of 1803, s. 1). See further J. Keown, *Abortion, Doctors and The Law* (Cambridge, 1988).

60 Sections 58 and 59.

61 A belief that seems to go back to Aristotle. And see · R. Feen, 'Abortion and Exposure in Ancient Greece: Assessing the Status of the Fetus and "New Born" from Classical Sources' in W. Bonderson *et al.* (eds.), *Abortion and the Status of the Fetus* (Dordrecht, 1983).

The key word in the 1861 Act is 'miscarriage',[62] which today would be used only for spontaneous terminations. Nevertheless, the word is still used in the 1967 Act, as amended: s. 5(2) of that Act provides: 'For the purposes of the law relating to abortion, anything done with intent to procure a woman's miscarriage (or, in the case of a woman carrying more than one foetus, her miscarriage of any foetus) is unlawfully done unless authorised by section 1 of this Act….'[63] The abortion legislation does not define 'miscarriage': the Human Fertilisation and Embryology Act 1990 (in s. 2(3)) does – 'a woman is not to be treated as carrying a child until the embryo has become implanted' – but only for the purposes of the 1990 Act itself. This assumes there cannot be a miscarriage until there has been a 'carriage', that is an implantation.[64] This is crucial for understanding the status of various contraceptive techniques. It is easy to overlook the fact that our abortion legislation was passed before even the simplest of contraceptive devices, the condom, became at all common.[65] Bradlaugh and Besant were convicted of publishing an obscene libel in propagating the virtues of contraception in 1877[66] and, although the conviction was overturned on appeal, Mrs Besant was subsequently deprived of the custody of her seven-year-old daughter.[67] As James LJ put it: 'the future of a girl brought up in association with such a propaganda would be incalculably prejudiced'.[68]

As I have already indicated, abortion law should be constructed to be part of a code dealing with sex and reproduction. Although the challenge last year to the legality of the 'morning-after' pill was instructive and enlightening – and brought forth an outstanding judgment from

62 Which, as Munby J shows, 'is nota term of art introduced into the law in 1861' but 'the word which Parliament and the lawyers have been using in this context for some 200 years' (n. 20 above, 168). Munby J's decision had inevitably to turn not on what the word was understood to mean in 1861, but on what it means today (*ibid.*, 182).

63 Thus assuming that selective reduction involves miscarriage, rather than absorption, which is commonly the case (although, of course, selective reduction is very rare).

64 *Cf.* John Keown, 'Miscarriage: A Medico-Legal Analysis' (1984) *Criminal Law Review* 608, who relies on old Indian and Australian authorities.

65 Though in use in the eighteenth century and increasingly available in the nineteenth, it was expensive and had associations with disease and prostitution.

66 *R* v. *Bradlaugh and Besant* (1877) 2 QBD 569. The conviction was overturned on a technicality (see (1878) 3 QBD 607).

67 *Re Besant* (1878) 11 Ch D 508.

68 *Ibid.*, 521.

Munby J[69] – the case would never have been brought if abortion legislation had made it clear what being 'pregnant' meant. And modern legislation would do this.[70] Had the SPUC challenge succeeded, all forms of contraception capable of inhibiting the implantation of a fertilized egg – intra-uterine devices, progestogen-only pills (the mini-pill), and even the 'pill' itself – would have been called into question, and no woman could have taken the 'pill', for example, without two registered medical practitioners forming an opinion in good faith of one of four grounds and, presumably, her taking it in an approved place.[71] And it is this latter requirement which calls into question the drug RU-486 (or Mifepristone).[72] Since this can act to dislodge a fertilized egg which has implanted, it is an abortifacient. It must therefore be taken at an approved place, a hurdle which could be easily overcome were it not for the requirement that 'treatment', which is a process and not a single event, must be so situated and the woman could be anywhere by the time the 'treatment' has taken effect.[73] There is room for another challenge here, as perhaps also to menstrual extraction (or aspiration):[74] a modern Abortion Act could forestall such litigation.

But the law labours under a more distinct handicap than its lack of clarity. The whole ideology and structure of the law is wrong. The law is contaminated by its association with criminality and therefore by its need to find a route out of this, which it does by conferring powers on the medical profession.[75] That women, most of the time at least, have

69 N. 20 above.

70 It is easy to forget (or not to recognize) that the distinction between abortion and contraception only emerged in the 1920s. See B. Brookes, *Abortion In England, 1900-1967* (London, 1988).

71 Abortion Act 1967, s. 1(1), (3).

72 See I. Kennedy and A. Grubb, *Medical Law* (London, 2000), 1436-38. See also C. L. Meyer, *The Wandering Uterus: Politics and the Reproductive Rights of Women* (New York, 1997), 144-63.

73 And see Lord Keith in *Royal College of Nursing of the UK* v. *DHSS* [1981] AC 800, 834: 'termination of pregnancy… as… a process of treatment'.

74 Questioned by V. Tunkel, 'Abortion: How Early, How Late and How Legal?' (1979) *British Medical journal* 253-6. *Cf.* R. Chalker and C. Downey, *A Women's Book of Choices: Abortion, Menstrual Extinction, RU 486* (New York, 1982). Federal legislation in the US has recently outlawed dilation and extraction (see *The Guardian*, 6 June 2003).

75 See S. Sheldon, *Beyond Control: Medical Power and Abortion Law* (London, 1997); A. Grubb, 'Abortion Law in England: The Medicalisation of a Crime' (1990) 18 *Law, Medicine and Health Care* 146-61; T. Newburn, *Permission and Regulation: Law and Morals in Post-War Britain* (London, 1992), 136-57.

access to abortion on demand[76] should not delude us into thinking that they have a right to an abortion. Indeed, the grounds are vague – for example, they do not provide specifically for abortion when there has been rape or incest – and this may be to prevent women perceiving abortion as an entitlement. 'Entitlement' would also undermine the power of the medical profession. And this is clearly not Parliament's intention. And so the grounds do not even have to be satisfied: it is enough that doctors are of the 'opinion' in good faith that the woman's case comes within one of the grounds.[77] Ninety-eight per cent of abortions are on the so-called 'social' ground[78] since statistically the risk of carrying a baby to term is higher than that for an early abortion this ground is inevitably satisfied in most cases.[79] And, anyway, if a woman does not want to continue her pregnancy, it is difficult to see how her mental health (particularly when, as interpreted by the Royal College of Obstetricians and Gynaecologists, this means 'mental well being, not merely an absence of disease or infirmity'[80]) will not be affected by forcing her to continue.

The laws of abortion give too much power to the medical profession, and too little to women. This may have some, albeit unintended, valuable consequences: for example, in emphasizing that is the doctor's decision and not the woman's, the father's case to prevent an abortion is undermined.[81] But, in general, it deflects attention from the rationale for abortion, which is to sustain a woman's reproductive autonomy. Do we need doctors to form opinions – and they are opinions for the most part, not clinical judgements – or grounds to be established? Should not the law recognize, as it does elsewhere,[82] that termination is the woman's

---

76 Though, of course, women are refused terminations. Though dated, C. Francombe, *Abortion Practice* in *Britain and the United States* (London, 1986) is a valuable exploration of the issues.

77 Abortion Act 1967, s. 1(1). And see *R* v. *Smith* [1974] 1 All ER 376: 'the legality of an abortion depends on the opinion of the. doctor', *per* Scarman LJ at 381.

78 OCPS, *Abortion Statistics 1998* (London, 2000).

79 See Kennedy and Grubb, n. 72 above, 1420.

80 *The Care of Women Requesting Induced Abortion: Guidelines* (London, 2000), ch. 2.

81 The law anyway – and rightly – rejects it: see *Paton* v. *Trustees of British Pregnancy Advisory Service* [1979] QB 276. And, in relation to Scotland, *Kelly* v. *Kelly* 1997 SLT 896, See further D. Nolan, 'Abortion: Should Men Have a Say? ', in E. Lee (ed.), *Abortion Law and Politics Today* (London, 1998), 216-31 (who found that 84 per cent of men thought termination a 'joint resolution of the matter' (220)).

82 Not least in the United States where, since *Roe* v. *Wade* 410 US 113 (1973), abortion has been a constitutionally protected right during the first 12 weeks of pregnancy. On the battle to achieve this see D.J. Garrow, *Liberty and Sexuality* (New York, 1994).

decision, and that she does not need to give any reason? In many European countries where abortion is an entitlement, the time limit tends to be twelve weeks.[83] Our law by contrast allows abortion on the 'social' ground for twenty-four weeks[84] and on the other three grounds to birth.[85] In fact very few abortions take place after the twentieth week.[86] I believe we would wish to encourage early abortion, and de-medicalizing abortion and putting decision into the hands of women would be a step towards achieving this. Improving the provision of NHS-funded abortion would also help: currently abortion is the most common privately-funded health procedure.[87]

The case for reproductive autonomy is strong. It is women's bodies that carry and bear children. Women who do most of the nurturing. Most abortions are required because contraception has failed, not because it has not been used.[88] Some-however little, it is too much-pregnancy is the result of rape, sexual abuse, or domestic violence. Having to make a case for abortion also requires women to describe a scenario at its most extreme, to exaggerate and by implication to denigrate themselves. And abortion is not a deviant act: 35 to 40 per cent of women will experience one.[89]

I would give women full autonomy and open access to the NHS. And I would impose a maximum time limit of twelve weeks. Thereafter, abor-

---

More generally see M. Freeman, 'Abortion: What Do Other Countries Do?' (1988) 138 *New Law Journal* 233-5.

83 It is 12 weeks in Austria (see Penal Code, s. 96), Belgium (Law of 3 April 1990), Denmark (Law No. 350 of 13 June 1973), France (Law of 17 January 1975) (it was 10 weeks until recently), Germany (Penal Code, s. 218), Greece (Law 1609/1986), Italy (Law No. 194 of 22 May 1978) (12 weeks and 6 days), Portugal (Chapter II of Penal Code). See, further, S. D. Pattinson, *Influencing Traits Before Birth* (Aldershot, 2002), App. 1.

84 Abortion Act 1967, s. 1(1)(a). The Dutch law is similar (Law of 1 May 1981). In Sweden abortion is permitted up to 18 weeks.

85 Abortion Act 1967, s. 1(1)(b), (c), and (d). There are similar provisions in other European countries: see Pattinson, n. 83 above. See further R. Cook, 'Developments in Abortion Laws: Comparative and International Perspectives', in R. Cohen-Almagor (ed.), *Medical Ethics at the Dawn of the 21st Century* (New York, 2000), 74-87.

86 84 per cent during the first 12 weeks of pregnancy; about 1.5 per cent only after the 20th week (see n. 78 above).

87 As noted by E. Jackson, *Regulating Reproduction: Law, Technology and Autonomy* (Oxford, 2001), 85. There remain wide regional variations in NHS funding of terminations.

88 But K. Luker, *Abortion and the Politics of Motherhood* (Berkeley, Cal, 1984) found strong disapproval of using abortion as a method of contraception.

89 See A. Fureidi, 'Wrong But The Right Thing To Do: Public Opinion and Abortion' in E. Lee (ed.), n. 81 above, 159-71, 161.

tion would be available for 'emergencies' only, where the mother's life or health was in danger. That leaves the question of foetal abnormality. The law allows abortion where 'there is a substantial risk that if the child were born it would suffer from physical or mental abnormalities as to be seriously handicapped'.[90] And women are undoubtedly encouraged to undergo terminations where abnormality is detected. Indeed, it may be doubted whether they are allowed space to make their own decisions.[91] We do not permit children to be killed because they are seriously handicapped.[92] Smothering a premature seriously handicapped baby would be labelled murder, though the baby might well be younger than the foetus aborted on the foetal abnormality ground. It is difficult to see what the justification is for this ground. It is sometimes justified for eugenic reasons, but that would make it permissible where the child to be were merely a carrier, and no one suggests that the ground can embrace 'substantial risk' of a risk. So, it seems that the argument relates to the welfare of the parents and perhaps also of society at large. But this would apply equally in the case of severely handicapped babies and older children, indeed it might be stretched to embrace anyone with special needs. Has not the time come to reconsider the foetal abnormality ground? Is this not the point where the mother's autonomy should be trumped by the dignity to be accorded the disabled?[93] The foetal abnormality ground tells us more about us, our society and our values, than it does about those who will be born handicapped. I would suggest the time has come to reconsider this ground before, as it threatens, it expands and we get abortions for 'defects' not dreamt of by those who drafted the ground in 1967.[94]

---

90 Abortion Act 1967, s. 1(1)(d).

91 See, to like effect, M. Fox, in Harris *et al.*, n. 12 above, 77-100, 88.

92 And see G. Williams, *Textbook of Criminal Law* (London, 1983), 298.

93 *Cf.* Emily Jackson, 'Abortion, Autonomy and Prenatal Diagnosis' (2000) 9 *Social and Legal Studies* 467-94, 480-4. Policies differ strikingly as M. L. Gross has demonstrated. See his comparison of the UK, USA, Denmark, and Israel in 'Abortion and Neonaticide: Ethics, Practice and Policy in Four Nations' (2002) 16 *Bioethics* 202-30. On Dutch law see S. Gevers, 'Third Trimester Abortion for Fetal Abnormality' (1999) 13 *Bioethics* 306-13.

94 The Royal College of Obstetricians and Gynaecologists, *Termination of Pregnancy for Fetal Abnormality* (London, 1996), 3.3.1-3.3.3 makes some attempt to set out contours of serious handicap and urges caution 'as [it] has not been interpreted by the courts'. *Cf.* the Dutch Commission's report, discussed by Gevers, n. 93 above, 308-10. But could it extend, for example, to unintelligence (whatever this may mean)? And see M.J. Reiss, 'The Ethics of Genetic Research on Intelligence' (2000) 14 *Bioethics* 1-15.

*Being Born a Clone*

We would do well to be cautious about human reproductive cloning.[95] We do not yet know whether it can be achieved, and questions must be raised about how safe it is. Dolly was the sole survivor after the successful transplantation of nuclei to 277 enucleated ewe's eggs.[96] A high percentage of miscarriages, serious abnormalities, and other problems (Dolly's early arthritis is often alluded to) can be anticipated. But it is possible – I am inclined to say 'likely' – that cloning humans will become safe and, I suspect; quite soon. Should this happen, we will need to consider whether there are objections to cloning beyond alarmist concerns (mad scientists, lots of Adolf Hitlers, etc.) and what Devlin called, 'indignation, intolerance and disgust'.[97] I will examine possible objections after I have analysed the legislature's response to cloning. This has one thing in common with its response to abortion. In both cases it has had little understanding of the science involved. It first legislated against cloning in 1990. The Human Fertilisation and Embryology Act 1990, s. 3(3)(d), lays down that a licence cannot authorize

> replacing a nucleus of a cell of an embryo with a nucleus taken from a cell of any person, embryo or subsequent development of an embryo.

There is no doubt that Parliament intended to prohibit cloning[98] and, where the technique involves the replacing of the nucleus of a cell of an embryo with a nucleus taken from elsewhere (a person or another embryo), did so. But cell nucleus substitution and cell fusion do not involve the replacement of the nucleus of the cell of an embryo but rather the replacement of the nucleus of an unfertilized egg.[99] On a strict interpre-

---

95 I am distinguishing – and not discussing in this paper – therapeutic cloning, where single cells, not whole organisms, are replicated in the culture dish. In January 2001 the Human Fertilisation and Embryology Act 1990, Schedule 2(3)(2) was amended to permit HFEA to grant licences to carry out stem cell research.

96 See I. Wilmut *et al.*, 'Viable offspring Derived from fetal and Adult Mammalian Cells' (1997) 385 *Nature* 810-13.

97 *The Enforcement of Morals* (Oxford, 1965), 17.

98 See Lord Ennals in *Hansard*, HL vol. 513, col. 1013. See also P. Walsh and A. Grubb, 'I Want To Be Alone' (1997) 7 *Dispatches* 1.

99 See *Stem Cell Research: Medical Progress with Responsibility* (London, 2000), which contains helpful diagrams.

tation of the prohibition these techniques – and also embryo splitting[100] – would be allowed.[101]

In my view, the 'Dolly' technique, applied to human cloning, would not be caught by the 1990 Act for another reason. This Act defines an embryo as a 'live human embryo where fertilisation is complete', including, puzzlingly, 'an egg in the process of fertilisation'.[102] Fertilization does not take place when a cell is cloned. However, both the Human Genetics Advisory Commission (HGAC) and Human Fertilisation and Embryology Authority (HFEA) in their 1998 Report[103] and the Chief Medical Officer's Report *Stem Cell Research* in 2000[104] rejected these arguments, and concluded that cloning was either prohibited or subject to licensing (depending on the method used), and the HGAC and HFEA indicated that no licences for research into reproductive cloning would be issued.[105] The (HGAC) and (HFEA) concluded in their joint report that since it involved 'the use or creation of embryos outside the body' nuclear substitution fell within the Act and thus the 'jurisdiction of HFEA'.[106] Academic opinion[107] with varying degrees of confidence, agreed. Lee and Morgan, for example, were not concerned that it would require an 'extended interpretation of s. 1' (and presumably an even more liberal or purposive interpretation of s. 3(3)(d)). It was their view that whether a literal or purposive interpretation were adopted should depend on context.[108]

A challenge was inevitable and its instigator, the Pro-Life Alliance, unsurprising. It has brought forth a first instance ruling that an 'embryo' created by cell nucleus replacement was not protected by the 1990 Act, so that no licence was required for the creation or use of embryos cre-

100 It is thought that this would anyway 'probably not be very effective in the human', even though monozygotic twins and higher multiples do occur naturally. See Opinion of the Group of Advisers on the Ethical Implications of Biotechnology of the European Commission, in A. J. Klotzko, *The Cloning Sourcebook* (New York, 2001), 284, 285-6.

101 See P. Walsh and A. Grubb, n. 98 above.

102 Section 1(1)(a), (b).

103 *Cloning Issues In Human Reproduction, Science and Medicine* (London, 1998), para. 3.4.

104 N. 99 above.

105 N. 103 above, para. 5.4.

106 *Ibid.*, para. 3.4.

107 For example, M. Brazier, 'Regulating The Reproduction Business' (1999) 7 *Medical Law Review* 166, and D. Beyleveld and S. Partinson, *The Ethics of Genetics in Human Procreation* (Aldershot, 2000). *Cf.* Walsh and Grubb, n. 98 above.

108 R. G. Lee and D. Morgan, *Human Fertilisation and Embryology: Regulating The Reproduction Revolution* (London, 2001), 95.

ated by this process.[109] This literal interpretation so concerned Parliament that within nineteen days it had enacted the Human Reproductive Cloning Act 2001. As we will see, this Act has all the hallmarks of a rushed knee-jerk response to a moral panic. It was not an exercise in rational law-making. But soon after the Act came into operation – which it did on Royal Assent – the Court of Appeal allowed the Secretary of State for Health's appeal.[110] It held that an organism created by cell nucleus replacement came within the definition of 'embryo' in s. 1(1) of the 1990 Act. It achieved this result by a deliberate invocation of purposive construction.[111] Said Lord Phillips of Worth Matravers MR, 'the court has to ask, not what would Parliament have enacted if it had foreseen the creation of embryos by CNR, but, do such embryos plainly fall within the genus covered by the legislation and will the clear purpose of the legislation be defeated if the extension is not made'.[112] In his view 'the fact that the organism was created by fertilisation was not a factor of particular relevance to the desirability of regulation. The embryo created by cell nuclear replacement and the embryo created by fertilisation are essentially identical as far as structure is concerned. It is the capacity to develop into a human being that is the significant factor and that is the one that is shared by both types of embryo'.[113]

This decision has now been upheld by the House of Lords.[114] The Lords accept that s. 3(3)(d) of the 1990 Act did 'not prohibit cloning in general but only cloning when the host is an existing embryo',[115] that it was directed at nucleus substitution and not nucleus replacement. Like the Court of Appeal, the Lords adopted a purposive construction of the legislation.[116] Lord Bingham conceded that there were provisions in the 1990 Act which could not apply to embryos created by CNR,[117] but thought the 'discrepancies were not significant'.[118] As for the words 'where ferti-

109 *R (on application of Quintavalle)* v. *Secretary of State for Health* [2001] 4 All ER 1013.
110 [2002] 2 FCR 140.
111 [2002] 2 FCR 148.
112 *Ibid.*, 150.
113 *Ibid.*, 150-51.
114 R (on *the application of Quintavalle*) v. *Secretary of State for Health* (2003] 2 All ER 113.
115 *Per* Lord Hoffmann, *ibid.*, 127.
116 Lord Steyn observed that the 'pendulum has swung to purposive construction': *ibid.*, 123.
117 As the appellants argued forcefully. These provisions are s. 1(1), s. 3(4), s. 12(c), and Schedule 3.
118 [2003] 2 All ER 113, 121.

lisation is complete', these were not, so he ruled, 'intended to form an integral part of the definition of embryo but were directed to the time at which it should be treated as such'.[119] Lord Millett [120] observed that Parliament had not banned the placing of a human embryo in an animal where this was created by CNR. But, as he rightly commented, this would be no 'less abhorrent' [121] than doing so where an embryo was created by fertilization. Clearly, this is another case where a purposive construction would be called for. It was the Lords' view that the 1990 Act should be construed in the light of contemporary scientific knowledge,[122] a position I completely endorse. Seen thus, it was easy to conclude that Parliament did not intend to distinguish live human embryos produced by fertilization from those produced without such fertilization. [123]

This ruling must now run in tandem with the 2001 Act. [124] This makes it an offence to place a human embryo 'in a woman' if this has been created otherwise than by fertilization. So, it does not criminalize the incubation (by ectogenesis,[125] for example) and use of a cloned human embryo outside the body of a woman. Nor, it seems, would the time limits in the 1990 Act apply in such a case. The Act also will not prevent human clones being exported – and European legislation may assist this[126] – for implantation into a woman in a country where this is not prohibited[127] (in Italy, for example). In addition, the Act uses, but does not define, the concepts 'embryo' and 'fertilisation'. I suppose Parliament assumed these concepts would bear the meanings they had in the 1990 Act, but why? The question has thus been asked: '... would "fertilisation" encompass

---

119 Ins. 1(1)(a) of the 1990 Act. In 1990 it was assumed the *only* way to produce an embryo was by fertilisation, so that the four words were 'otiose'. See M. Warnock, *Making Babies* (Oxford, 2002), 100.

120 Lord Phillips of Worth Matravers similarly argued in the Court of Appeal, n. 110 above.

121 N. 114 above, 129.

122 See *e.g.* Lord Steyn, *ibid.*, 124.

123 See *e.g. per* Lord Bingham, *ibid.*

124 This has been described by Andrew Grubb as 'very clever': see 'Reproductive Cloning in the UK' (2002) 10 *Medical Law Review* 327-9, 328. As I indicate in the text, I am less convinced. But, of course, in the light of the Lords' ruling, we must expect it to be interpreted purposively.

125 If this were to become a practical possibility, which is not currently the case.

126 See n. 6 above for an illustration.

127 There is no legislation in Belgium on cloning. Nor is there any in The Netherlands or in Luxembourg. The law in Italy (which is often cited for its permissiveness in this area) is less clear. There was a ministerial decree aimed at cloning in 1997, and it has since been renewed, but there is no legislation as such.

kick-starting an organism created by CNR into growing by using sperm extracts of "artificial sperm"?'[128] Such sperm could in the future be engineered to be devoid of genetic material (and therefore falling outside the scientific definition of a 'gamete') but retain the ability to trigger growth of an organism created by CNR. The result would be a cloned human, genetically identical to the nucleus donor, but arguably 'created by fertilisation' and therefore not caught by the new Act. Purposive construction might target it, and the 1990 Act might also be construed as extending to this. But we cannot be sure.

It may be doubted whether Parliament has yet completely under stood cloning. It has certainly failed to define it in an Act which purportedly bans human reproductive cloning. If an embryo is created from one individual, and there is thus no mixing of genetic material, it is difficult to see how, short of further purposive interpretation, the 2001 Act impacts upon it.

But should human reproductive cloning be banned? Parliament clearly thinks so – breach of the 2001 Act is punishable by a ten year prison sentence – even if it has not thought so clearly. What is wrong with cloning?[129] I think the question must be put that way because, since the ban interferes with reproductive autonomy, the burden must rest with those who support outlawing the practice. So long as we cannot be sure of safety, they have the clinching argument. But when, as will happen, this objection is overcome, the case against cloning will require more convincing argument.

Many of the objections to cloning are rooted in the religious, the mystical, the metaphysical.[130] Thus, Leon Kass writes:

> There is wisdom in the mystery of nature that has joined the pleasure of sex, the inarticulate longing for union, the communication of

128 *Per* P. Wood and J. Good, 'Human Reproductive Cloning-Nipped in the Bud?' (2001) 151 *New Law Journal* 1760-62, 1762.

129 I am not discussing therapeutic cloning (and see n. 95 above). Although contentious (see, *e.g.*, the Special Issue of the *American Journal of Bioethics*, 2002, volume 2(1) on 'Stem Cells'), the pendulum seems to have swung in its favour. By banning reproductive cloning Parliament has forestalled the slippery slope argument against therapeutic cloning, viz. if you allow it 'it will lead to human reproductive cloning'.

130 There is no single religious view on cloning humans. An authoritative account of the Jewish view is J. David Bleich, 'Cloning: Homologous Reproduction and Jewish Law' (1998) 32(3) *Tradition* 47-86. But see Gregory E. Pence, *Who's Afraid of Human Cloning?* (Lanham, Maryland, 1998), ch. 9.

> the loving embrace, and the deep-seated and only partly articulate desire for children in the very activity by which we continue the chain of human existence and participate in the renewal of human possibility.[131]

Cloning, by contrast, is said by Kass to be 'rootless and narcissistic self-recreation'.[132]

It is easy to get the impression from critics of cloning that those who would allow it see it almost as the preferred option. But no one is suggesting that it becomes the main procreative route, any more than anyone has ever seen assisted reproductive techniques like IVF, GIFT, or DI as replacements for coitus. The argument that reproduction through cloning is not 'natural' is weak: so few things are.[133] Wearing clothes is not natural, but I doubt if any of those who attack cloning advocate nudity. The old joke, 'If God had intended us to fly, he wouldn't have given us the railway', is very apposite. Nor is the argument of those who attack cloning strengthened when they talk of clones being 'manufactured' or refer to them as 'artefacts'.

I accept that if cloning were to result in depersonalization, dehumanization, commodification – and these fears are raised – the opponents of it would have a strong case. The principle of human dignity dictates that we protect the integrity of the child, that we treat him/her as a person in his/her own right, and not as a means to someone else's end.[134] Those, like myself, who have fought for children's rights to be recognized would not wish to see them swept away by the imperative of scientific progress. But is there any real concern that a cloned child would be less wanted or loved, or that our expectation of such a child would pose an unreasonable burden upon him or her?

---

131 'The Wisdom of Repugnance', in G. McGee (ed.), *The Human Cloning Debate* (Berkeley, Cal, 1998), 149-80, 165.

132 *Ibid.*, 152.

133 Writing articles is certainly not!

134 Human cloning is often said to undermine human dignity (*e.g.*, by the Bioethics unit of UNESCO) but it is not made clear why. *As* Ruth Macklin notes, 'A child who came into the world through cloning would be no more the "property" or the "possession" of its creator than are children who are "begotten" or who result from *in vitro* fertilization ' ('Cloning and Public Policy', in J. Burley and J. Harris (eds.), *A Companion to Genethics* (Oxford, 2002), 206-15, 211). See further J. Harris, 'Cloning and Human Dignity' (1997) 7 *Cambridge Quarterly of Healthcare Ethics* 163-67.

Another of the objections posed is that cloning would violate the right to have one's own unique identity.[135] But, of course, human cloning already happens 'by accident'. No one suggests that identical twins lack individuality. Even genetically identical twins have different neural connections. Cloning is only gene deep. Different environments and different experiences ensure that twins develop into different people. How much more so when, as with clones, the environment they are born into is a generation apart. Much is said of a child's right to an open future[136] – and this is probably one of the most important rights we should give children – but why should a clone's future necessarily be foreclosed in any way, and at any rate to any greater extent than any other child's?

But would cloning distort family relationships? Cloned children would have a genetic relationship with only one of their parents. Although the HGAC and HFEA thought this would constitute a 'novel situation of which there is no previous experience'[137] – had they forgotten egg donation and donor insemination and some surrogacies? – should this really be a matter of overwhelming concern? Could it not be that the real concern, as was the case when the access provision[138] in the Human Fertilisation and Embryology Act 1990 was being formulated, is that cloning could enable single women and lesbians to have children without a man's gametes being used? We are offered the prospect, as Eskridge and Stein put it, of a 'community of women, unencumbered by men'.[139] The reproductive choices of gay men, bisexuals, transsexuals, and people with AIDS would also be enhanced. We would need much more evidence than we have that this increase in reproductive autonomy would be harmful,

135 The view of George Annas, 'Cloning: Crossing Nature's Boundaries', *Boston Sunday Globe,* 2 March 1997, D. I. and Daniel Callahan, 'A Step Too Far', *New York Times,* February 26, 1997, A23. But it is not clear whose 'right' would be violated since the 'initiator' would act voluntarily and the cloned individual would not exist were it not for the process objected to. On killing clones see J. McMahan, 'Cloning, Killing, and Identity' (1999) 25 *Journal of Medical Ethics* 77-86.

136 First articulated by Joel Feinberg: see 'The Child's Right To An Open Future' in W. Aiken and H. LaFollette (eds.), *Whose Child?* (Totowa, NJ, 1980), 124-53. And see Dena S. Davis, 'A Child's Right to An Open Future' (1997) 27(2) *Hastings Center Report* 7-15. For the argument that cloning undermines this see H. Jonas, *Philosophical Essays: From Ancient Creed To Technological Man* (Englewood Cliffs, NJ, 1974).

137 HGAC and HFEA, *Cloning Issues In Reproduction, Medicine and Science* (London, 1998), para. 4.7.

138 Section 13(5).

139 'Queer Clones', in M. Nussbaum and C. Sunstein (eds.), *Clones And Clones* (New York, 1998), 95-113, 99.

either to the institution of the family or, more especially, to children born in this way or children generally.[140]

If human cloning would increase the variety of people enabled to reproduce, and thus add to diversity of family form, it would also, say its critics, impair genetic diversity. Diversity may well be an intrinsic value which, I suppose, gets greater as the world's population increases. But, since the percentage of those who will opt for cloning is miniscule, it cannot really be pretended that it will have any impact on genetic diversity.[141] And, anyway, those who adduce this argument seem not to understand that the clone's genotype will be the product of two sets of genes (the DNA source's mother and father) and will inherit the mitochondrial DNA from the denucleated egg, with the result that its genetic inheritance is not identical to that of the nuclear DNA provider.

As with any new technology, concern is also expressed about where it will lead. Slippery slope arguments are, I find, rarely convincing whether they are used by common lawyers (if we allow liability for this, where will it stop?) or ethicists (who rarely distinguish logical and empirical slippery slopes).[142] But, to quote Kass again, 'the principle of reproductive freedom as currently enunciated by the proponents of cloning logically embraces the ethical acceptability of sliding down the entire rest of the slope to producing children ectogenetically from sperm to term (should it become feasible) and to producing children whose entire genetic makeup will be the product of parental eugenic planning and choice'.[143] We have become used to arguments like this: at the time of the birth of Louise Brown, the first IVF baby in 1978, we were given similar warnings and there was similar panic about what 'mad' scientists would do. Most of these concerns have evaporated, only to be focused now on cloning. And so the spectre is raised of crazed millionaires and evil dictators filling the world with clones of themselves. This will not happen. Even if it did, these clones would not be like xeroxed reproductions. And, most importantly, if we are concerned about the abuse of cloning,[144] we will

140 And, in this sense, it would enhance human dignity.

141 If this is a concern, we would restrict cloning by allowing a limited number in any case. Dorothy Wertz, in her evidence to the US National Bioethics Advisory Commission in 1997, suggested imposing a limit of 5.

142 On which see B. Williams, 'Which Slopes Are Slippery?', in M. Lockwood (ed.), *Moral Dilemmas In Modern Medicine* (Oxford, 1985), 126-37.

143 N. 131 above, 172-3.

144 It is interesting that with the focus on abuse there has been negligible attention given to its benefits. There is an excellent summary of these in A. Buchanan, D. W.

regulate it, not drive it underground to the nether world of the unscrupulous scientist.

It could be regulated through the Human Fertilisation and Embryology Authority.[145] But it would need primary legislation in addition to the Authority's Code of Practice. The 1990 Act offers some clues. Thus, there would need to be status provisions:[146] assigning parental responsibility might be easier than stipulating who are a cloned child's parents. Equally important would be consent provisions:[147] it would have to be made clear to what extent the DNA source was consenting, and how voluntary and informed the consent needed to be.[148] The liabilities, if any, flowing from cloning would need to be spelt out. And to counter one of the abuse concerns, a limit should be placed on the number of clones with the same DNA source.[149] The legislation should also have a 'welfare of the child' provision.[150] The one in the 1990 Act has been criticized, and rightly so, though it has its valuable uses, as will be seen later in this paper.[151] Its reference to the 'need of the child for a father', roundly condemned as a 'nonsense', may now be considered prescient. A cloning statute would need a more clearly targeted welfare provision, but it would need one at the least for reassurance or symbolic purposes, and perhaps more significantly as a barrier to abuse. Reproductive autonomy is the justification

---

Brock, N. Daniels, and D. Wikler, *From Chance to Choice: Genetics and Justice* (Cambridge, 2000), 200-201. See also J. Harris, '"Goodbye Dolly?" The Ethics of Human Cloning' (1997) 23 *Journal of Medical Ethics* 353-60.

145 As Lord Bingham explains inn. 114 above, 117, the 1990 Act 'imposes three levels of control ' (the Act itself, the powers of the Secretary of State, and the Authority, whose Code of Practice is now in its sixth edition).

146 It is possible to think of situations where a child might have one biological parent, and others where he/she would have three.

147 This is to confront some feminists who doubt if this is possible – they write in the context of IVF mainly – in a pronatalist society. An example is R. D. Klein, *Infertility: Women Speak Out About Their Experiences of Reproductive Medicine* (London, 1989), 246.

148 It is important to establish that the DNA source has given consent and that this is thoroughly informed.

149 See n. 141 above.

150 But *cf.* T. Hope, G. Lockwood, and M. Lockwood, 'The Interests of the Potential Child' (1995) 310 *British Medical journal* 1455-57: it is easy for the interests of society to 'masquerade' for the interests of the potential child.

151 See below, pp. 627-28.

for human reproductive cloning,[152] but it cannot be allowed to trump the dignity or the welfare of the child.

### *Being Chosen to be Born*

The advent of medically assisted reproduction has had many results barely anticipated at the time of the Warnock Report, and not provided for in our legislation of 1990. Cell nucleus substitution was one such example: pre-implantation genetic diagnosis (PGD) is another.[153]

PGD was first successfully used in 1989 by teasing a single cell from each of eight-cell embryos and testing the sex of the cells, so that a female embryo could be implanted and a sex-linked disorder that occurred only in males avoided.[154] Two years later, the same doctors tested for a genetic mutation that causes cystic fibrosis and enabled a high-risk couple to implant an embryo free of the disease. Today, PGD is used to screen for a handful of genetic diseases including haemophilia, Tay-Sachs, and fragile X syndrome. The procedure is expensive, is not available everywhere, and can be used to target only a small number of conditions.[155] But it is foreseeable that none of these limitations will last long. How are we to respond to it? It has already proved controversial in two areas: sex selection, where this is not for therapeutic purposes, and where it is used to produce a child to save the life of an existing child. To these controversies I will return.

As already indicated, PGD is not specifically tackled in the 1990 Act. But, since it involves the creation and use of embryos, it must be licensed by HFEA to be lawful.[156] It has indeed licensed PGD for certain severe or

---

152 Defined by Ronald Dworkin, n. 35 above, 148, as 'a right to control their own role in procreation unless the state has a compelling reason for denying them that control'. It is, he says, 'embedded in any genuinely democratic culture' (166-67). It is not without significance that countries which flout democratic principles – Romania is a recent example – tend to be remembered for the ways they flout procreative autonomy.

153 See J. R. Botkin, 'Ethical Issues and Practical Problems in Preimplantation Genetic Diagnosis' (1998) 26 *Journal of Law, Medicine and Ethics* 17-28.

154 See HFEA/ACGT Consultation Document, *Pre-Implantation Genetic Diagnosis* (London, 1999), para. 10.

155 And see D. Wells and]. K. Sherlock, 'Strategies for Preimplantation Genetic Diagnosis of Single Gene Disorders by DNA Amplification' (1998) 18 *Prenatal Diagnosis* 1389-1401.

156 See s. 3(1) and J. McMillan, 'Sex Selection In the United Kingdom' (2002) 32(1) *Hastings Center Report* 28-31.

life-threatening disorders at a limited number of clinics.[157] It has firmly rejected the use of PGD for sex selection for social reasons.[158] Some jurisdictions, for example Victoria, have specifically banned sex selection, in Victoria's case unless 'it is necessary for the child to be of a particular sex so as to avoid the risk of transmission of a genetic abnormality or a disease to the child'.[159] There is legislation in some US states too, and also in the Indian state of Maharashta.[160] English legislation does not ban sex selection where this is carried out for social purposes, and it is also known to take place using the technique for sperm sorting.[161] Abortions are also performed for sex selection reasons, using the s. 1(1)(a) ground. I doubt whether this fits, but anyway it would not be possible if the time limit for abortions were brought down, as I have advocated.

Sex selection may be thought to be a legitimate reproductive choice and its defenders, conscious of discrimination against women generally, may ask why this practice should be singled out for proscription when so many other discriminatory practices remain.[162] It has even been argued that it will make women 'more valuable'[163] and that the next generation will put a 'premium'[164] on women. These are not convincing argu-

157 This is said to be 'implicit' in the 1990 Act.

158 For an example see the Louise and Alan Masterson case, *The Guardian,* 16 October 2000. For the view that it should be legal see D. McCarthy, 'Why Sex Selection Should be Legal' (2001) 27 *Journal of Medical Ethics* 302-307.

159 Infertility Treatment Act 1995, s. 50. If, and when, the European Convention on Human Rights and Biomedicine comes to be signed and ratified Article 14 will have to be observed. This states: 'the use of techniques of medically assisted procreation shall not be allowed for the purpose of choosing the future child's sex, except where serious hereditary sex-related disease is to be avoided'.

160 See the Regulation of Pre-Natal Diagnostic Techniques Act 1988, discussed by F. Agnes, *State, Gender and the Rhetoric of Law Reform* (Bombay, 1995). See also the Pre-Natal Diagnostic Techniques (Regulation and Prevention of Misuse) Act 1994, where imprisonment for up to 5 years is prescribed for advertising or performing sex determination tests.

161 HFEA prohibits sperm sorting, but it is difficult to see on what legal basis. No licensed activity is performed where there is sperm sorting before artificial insemination in a woman receiving treatment together with the man whose sperm underwent this process. HFEA has now recommended a ban on sex selection. See *The Guardian,* 12 November, 2003, 13.

162 And see D. Bubeck, 'Sex Selection: the Feminist Response', in J. Burley and J. Harris (eds.), *A Companion to Genethics* (Oxford, 2002), 216-28.

163 So argued by J. Robertson, 'Genetic Selection of Offspring Characteristics' (1996) 76 *Boston University Law Review* 421-82, 459.

164 Or so John Harris thinks: see his *Clones, Genes and Immortality: Ethics and the Genetic Revolution* (Oxford, 1998), 192.

ments.[165] Once again, I would argue that the principle of human dignity dictates the banning of sex selection when it is used other than for therapeutic purposes. The practice undermines equality, denies respect, and degrades.[166]

HFEA allows for PGD in situations where abortion legislation would permit the termination of a pregnancy,[167] that is where there is 'a substantial risk that if the child were born it would suffer from physical and mental abnormalities as to be seriously handicapped'.[168] This must be right.[169] And, although he does not discuss PGD, it would have the support of Dworkin, for whom the wasting of 'natural investment'[170] would be so very much less at pre-implantation stage.

HFEA has also allowed PGD to be employed to produce a child who would be a good tissue match for a sibling who needed a bone marrow transplant.[171] PGD had already been used for this purpose in the USA (in the Nash case)[172] and a British couple had taken advantage of the facility there to do the same thing[173] before HFEA gave the go-ahead to the Hashmis in 2001. In doing so did HFEA exceed its remit?[174] When PGD was developed it was envisaged that embryos would be selected for their own intrinsic merit and not for their utility to another person. The legislation offers little guidance. A licence can be granted only if the activity is 'necessary or desirable'.[175] This hardly assists because it leaves open the ethi-

165 On gynicide see G. Corea, *The Mother Machine* (London, 1985), 206. *Cf.* L. Birke *et al., Tomorrow's Child* (London, 1990), 22-32.

166 On the argument that banning sex selection undermines reproductive choice see J. Raymond, *Women and Wombs* (New York, 1993). She maintains that this 'banalizes' choice (at 85).

167 And therefore not to test for 'any social and psychological characteristics, normal physical variations, or any other conditions which are not associated with disability or a serious medical condition'.

168 See n. 154 above, para. 22. And see Abortion Act 1967, s. 1(1)(d).

169 There is a useful discussion of this in B. Steinbock, 'Preimplantation Genetic Diagnosis and Embryo Selection', n. 162 above, 175-90, 175-81.

170 N. 35 above, 87.

171 Ethics Committee of HFEA, 'Ethics Issues In The Location and Selection of Pre-Implantation Embryos To Produce Tissue Donors', 22 November 2001.

172 See R. Dobson, '"Designer Baby" Cures Sister' (2000) 321 *British Medical Journal* 1040.

173 See S. Gottlieb, 'US Doctors Say Selection Acceptable for Non-Medical Reasons' (2001) 323 *British Medical Journal* 828.

174 Not so say J. A. Robertson, J. P. Kahn, and J. E. Wagner, 'Conception to Obtain Hematopoietic Stem Cells' (2002) 32(3) *Hastings Center Report* 34-40.

175 Schedule 2, para. 1(3).

cal evaluation. In addition there is the 'welfare provision' in s. 13(5), which requires account to be 'taken of the welfare of any child who may be born as a result of treatment ... and of any other child who may be affected by the birth'. Once again, although this is a much-criticized provision, it may be a useful resource in helping the determination of a case like that of the Hashmis. Indeed, it is difficult to think of a better example of where a treatment service will impact on the welfare of an existing child and do so positively (ironically the legislature's concern was that existing children might be harmed by the addition of a new child). But what of the welfare of the child created to save the life of an existing sibling? Is failure to take account of the Kantian categorical imperative [176] that no person should be a means to another's end, an admission that the child's welfare has not been suitably considered?

I find this ethical dilemma most troubling. A first instance court ruled that HFEA was wrong to allow PGD to be used in the Hashmi case to select an embryo which can be tissue-typed to find the best match for the existing child who has beta thalassaemia major.[177] The Court of Appeal, rightly, disagreed, and has given the go ahead.[178] Significantly, one of the judges, Mance LJ, was influenced by the welfare imperative in s. 13(5). This, he said, 'points towards a wider concern for the future child and siblings, which is better served if the legislation is read as permitting [the] screening'[179] envisaged in the Hashmi case. He had no doubt that 'the language [of s. 13(5)] does not exclude positive effects'.[180] Lord Phillips of Worth Matravers MR was persuaded that if the Act permitted the licensing of embryo research activities for the purpose of 'developing methods for detecting the presence of gene or chromosome abnormalities in embryos before implantation'[181] the clear inference was that Parliament approved of PGD to avoid implantation of embryos carrying genetic defects. 'Parliament chose to permit the licensing of research. It makes little sense for Parliament, at the same time, to prohibit reaping the benefit of that

---

176 *Grounding For The Metaphysics of Morals* (1785), transl. J. W. Ellington (Indianapolis, Indiana, 1981), para. 429.

177 *R (on application of Quintavalle)* v. *Human Fertilisation and Embryology Authority* [2003] 2 All ER 105.

178 *R (on application of Quintavalle)* v. *Human Fertilisation and Embryology Authority* [2003] 3 All ER 257.

179 *R* (on *application of Quintavalle*) v. *Human Fertilisation and Embryology Authority* [20031 3 All ER 283.

180 *Ibid.*, 286.

181 See Schedule 2, para. 3(2)(e).

research, even under licence.'[182] The Court of Appeal also had no doubt that genetic analysis for the purpose of tissue typing was 'necessary or desirable for the purpose of providing treatment services'.[183] Lord Phillips of Worth Matravers conceded that his 'initial reaction'[184] was the same as the first instance judge,[185] that is that the phrase suggests 'treatment designed to assist the physical processes from fertilisation to the birth of a child'.[186] But he now saw that 'if the impediment to bearing a child is concern that it may be born with a hereditary defect, treatment which enables women to become pregnant and to bear children in the confidence that they will not be suffering from such defects can properly be described as "for the purpose of assisting women to carry children"'.[187] He concluded that 'whether the PGD has the purpose of producing a child free from genetic defects, or of producing a child with stem cells matching a sick or dying sibling, the IVF treatment that includes the PGD constitutes "treatment for the purpose of assisting women to bear children"'.[188] Of the three Appeal Court judges only Mance LJ grasped the nettle of the so-called 'designer baby'.[189] Lord Phillips of Worth Matravers appeared to leave this entirely to the discretion of HFEA.[190] Mance LJ saw a clear distinction between 'screening out abnormalities' and 'screening in preferences' (for example, as to sex on social grounds only). 'Preferences', he noted, 'suggests personal indulgence or predilection and the luxury of a real choice' and, of course, the Hashmis 'are not seeking to indulge themselves'.[191] Mance LJ, however, noted that Parliament did not include 'any absolute prohibition in the area of sex selection for "social purposes"'.[192] The Hashmi request was 'much less obviously problematic'.[193]

In this case the intention is for blood to be taken from the baby's umbilical cord, which is rich in stem cells, and infused into the sick child. A more emotionally-fraught scenario, or ethical dilemma, it would be difficult to imagine. For that reason I return to the principles which inform

182 N. 178 above, 269.
183 *Ibid.*, 276.
184 *Ibid.*, 270.
185 N. 177 above, 111.
186 N. 178 above, 270.
187 *Ibid.*
188 *Ibid.*, 271.
189 *Ibid.*, 287.
190 *Ibid.*, 271.
191 *Ibid.*, 287.
192 *Ibid.*, 289.
193 *Ibid.*

this paper. Unless it harms, or misuses, or abuses the new child, the parents should be able to exercise their reproductive autonomy. It should be stressed – for autonomy can all too easily be seen in individualistic terms – that what the Hashmis want is 'relational autonomy'[194] that is to say the exercise of reproductive decision-making made with reference to others. It is not that they want their views to prevail so much as wanting to improve the welfare of one of their children and thus the whole family.[195]

We do not normally investigate the reasons why people decide to have children. If we did, we would find all sorts of less-than-worthy motives. But we must not ignore the dignity of the child-to-be. Will his/her interests be compromised in any way to promote those of the existing sick child? If the stem cells are from umbilical cord blood, there are no physical intrusions upon the baby (although there is with a bone marrow donation, these have been relatively uncontroversial for many years).[196] Provided, as is likely to be the case, the new child is wanted and will be loved and nurtured in his/ her own right, it is difficult why his/her dignity should be under mined. If there were no intention to bring the child up, the case would look different, though there would remain the argument that it is better to be an adopted child than a non-existent one. Even so, it is difficult to see how producing a child in such circumstances could be ethically acceptable. What would such a child be told about his/her origins? That he/she was indeed a means to someone else's end.

There is another question which is less commonly raised.[197] Do parents like the Hashrnis or the Nashs have an obligation to have another child in order to save an existing child? The legal answer must be that it is their choice. They cannot be compelled by a court to do so, any more than they can be compelled to donate blood, tissue, or organs to save a child of theirs.[198] It is clear that there is no legal obligation. However, I

---

194 See Nedelsky, 'Reconceiving Autonomy: Sources, Thoughts and Possibilities' (1989) 1 *Yale Journal of Law and Feminism* 7-36 and, of course, C. Gilligan, *In A Different Voice* (Cambridge, Mass, 1982).

195 Belinda Bennett's 'Choosing a Child's Future? Reproductive Decision-Making and Preimplantation Genetic Diagnosis', in J. Gunning and H. Szoke (eds.), *The Regulation of Assisted Reproductive Technology* (Aldershot, 2003), 167-76, was published after this paper was written. On this point we are in agreement (see 173).

196 And see C. H. Baron *et al.*, 'Live Organ and Tissue Transplants from Minor Donors in Massachusetts' (1975) 55 *Boston University Law Review* 159-93, 159.

197 But see J. Savulescu, n. 16 above, 415. J. A. Robertson *et al.*, n. 174 above, 36, say the question 'can be put swiftly to rest' and provide a negative conclusion.

198 The analogy is the medically-indicated caesarean section, on which see N. K. Rhoden, 'The Judge in the Delivery Room: The Emergence of Court-Ordered Cesareans'

would not find it difficult to justify imposing a moral obligation in these circumstances.[199] There are many situations in which we have rights but should allow our responsibilities to trump them.[200]

PGD raises a number of other issues and I will briefly address three of these.

First, after PGD whose decision should it be as to whether the embryo is implanted in the woman's uterus? Suppose doctors decide it is 'handicap-free' and want it transferred to the woman. Can she refuse? On principle, and on application of the principles I have used in this paper, the ultimate decision must belong to the woman.[201] This would promote her autonomy and recognize her dignity. The 'father' would have no rights.[202] Nor can it be argued that doctors have a legal duty to implant the embryo.[203] One consequence of this is that a woman may refuse to have an embryo implanted for any reason, which must include a preference for the other sex. But this enables sex selection for social or psychological reasons to creep in through the back door.[204]

Secondly – and conversely – if the doctors do not wish to implant the embryo because they perceive there to be a risk (which may fall below the abortion handicap threshold), but the woman wants the embryo transferred to her uterus, can she insist? Draper and Chadwick have argued that once women have parted with their gametes and the resulting embryos have been tested, 'it is possible for them to lose control over what happens next' and 'she cannot compel him to implant embryos against his wishes'.[205] But though this may not impugn her bodily integrity, it certainly undermines her reproductive autonomy, and arguably also her

---

(1986) 74 *California Law Review* 1951-2030. See also *McFall* v. *Shimp* (1978) 10 Pa D & C (3d) 90 (Ct Comm PI, Pa).

199 And note the ways courts try to find legal obligation, as in *Re Y* [1997] Fam 110. *Cf. Curran* v. *Bosze* (1990) 566 NE 2d 1319 (Illinois Supreme Court).

200 The 'lifestyle choices' of pregnant women, which exercised the Canadian Supreme Court in *Winnipeg Child and Family Services (Northwest Area)* v. *G (DF)* (1997) 152 DLR (4th) 193, offer a good example and discussion question.

201 Also the view of J. Harris: see in J. Harris and S. Holm, n. 12 above, 5-37, 33.

202 The abortion analogy may not always work – in this I agree with Harris, *ibid.* – but I think must hold here. See *e.g. Paton* v. *Trustees of British Pregnancy Advisory Service* [1978] 2 All ER 987.

203 But see the arguments of D. King, 'Preimplantation Genetic Diagnosis and the "New" Genetics' (1999) 25 *Journal of Medical Ethics* 176-82, 180.

204 Which is presumably why it is HFEA policy not to disclose this information.

205 'Beware! Preimplantation Genetic Diagnosis May Solve Some Old Problems. But It Also Raises New Ones' (1999) 25 *journal of Medical Ethics* 114-20, 119.

dignity. But one would not expect any court to compel a doctor to implant an embryo against his clinical judgement, nor, I suggest, would it have the authority to do so.

The third issue is the most difficult. Could a couple – interestingly, it is always a couple rather than a woman who are discussed here – choose to have a child with a particular disability? The most commonly cited example is the deaf couple wishing to have a deaf child. There has been considerable discussion of the ethics of this decision;[206] rather less about the law. Deliberately to produce a child with any disability,[207] whatever the justification – and in the case of deaf parents it is the value of 'deaf culture'[208] – is to deny the child the right to an open future, and cannot be countenanced. There is 'an asymmetry between the limitations on opportunity that deafness brings and the goods of membership in the deaf community'.[209] Any such exercise of reproductive autonomy is abusive and it pays scant attention to the dignity of the child. It follows that English law should not allow a deaf couple to use PGD to ensure that only a deaf embryo was implanted.

It could, I believe, prevent them by recourse to s. 13(5) of the 1990 Act. For Emily Jackson it is uncertain whether this can be done, because she says s. 13(5) *is* assumed to be 'concerned with *access* to infertility treatment, rather than choices made once treatment has begun'.[210] But this is to see access as a turnstile, rather than as a continuing process. Surely the better view is that implantation into a woman's uterus after IVF and PGD is a 'treatment service' and so is governed by the welfare principle. I can think of no way in which s. 13(5) could be better used than to justify a clinician's refusal to countenance PGD where the intention is to produce a deaf child, or, once there has been PGD, to refuse the express wishes of a couple to transfer an embryo known to be afflicted by congenital deafness. This argument is grounded on the premise that it is not in the best interests of a child to be born deaf, even to deaf parents. I am aware of

206 A stimulating recent contribution is R. Bennett and J. Harris, 'Are There Lives Not Worth Living? When Is It Morally Wrong to Reproduce?', in D. L. Dickenson (ed.), *Ethical Issues in Maternal-Fetal Medicine* (Cambridge, 2002), 321-34.

207 I accept that 'disability' is difficult to define, and confine. For the purpose of my argument here I am prepared to limit my case to those 'handicaps' which harm in the utilitarian sense of reducing capabilities normally taken for granted: the ability to hear (or see) is a paradigmatic example. See also N. Daniels, *Just Health Care* (New York, 1986), 28 (actions that detract from species-typical functioning).

208 But see J. Ree, *I See A Voice* (London, 1999).

209 *Per* A. Buchanan *et al.*, n. 144 above, 282.

210 N. 87 above, 245.

arguments to the contrary but neither that which extols 'deaf culture', nor that which says that being born deaf is better than not being born at all is particularly convincing.

At present, if PGD discovers genetic abnormality, the embryo is discarded. Pro-life objections to this are unlikely to be upheld. Pre-implantation gene therapy (PGT) is not yet possible, though it cannot be far away. Unsurprisingly, the issues that this will raise have not yet been addressed by legislation or HFEA. The issues are similar to those raised by PGD.[211] They can be reserved for a later discussion.

## A Time to Die

### *Choosing to Die*

Two of 2002's most controversial decisions were those concerning Dianne Pretty[212] and Ms B.[213] Both women wanted to die: Dianne Pretty by assisted suicide; Ms B by refusing any further treatment (an issue also raised in *Re AK*[214] the previous year). All three applicants were competent and conscious and capable of communicating their decision that they no longer wanted to live. Ms B and AK were allowed to refuse further treatment: Mrs Pretty was denied an assisted suicide. The law allowed her to commit suicide – it has done so since 1961[215] – but her husband risked a fourteen-year prison sentence if he assisted her to end her own life.[216] Nor would it have made any difference if she had requested doctor-assisted suicide.

The distinction between Ms B's and AK's cases, on the one hand, and Dianne Pretty's, on the other, may not be easy to grasp. All three persons wanted to die: Mrs Pretty wanted her husband's assistance (though it was not clear how); Ms B and AK wanted doctors to cease treating them. But did not all three acts amount to suicide? This may be of little consequence fors. 1 of the 1961 Act (which removes the criminal sanction from suicide and attempted suicide), but it is important in the context of the offences created by s. 2. If refusal of treatment amounts to suicide, a doc-

211 Jackson, *ibid.*, 246-7 throws some light on these issues.
212 N. 33 above.
213 N. 34 above.
214 [2001) 1 FLR 129.
215 Suicide Act 1961, s. 1.
216 Suicide Act 1961, s. 2.

tor who accedes to such a request might be said to aiding suicide. To Lord Goff in *Airedale NHS Trust* v. *Bland:*

> ... there is no question of the patient having committed suicide, nor therefore of the doctor having aided or abetted him in so doing. It is simply that the patient has, as he is entitled to do, declined to consent to treatment which might or could have the effect of prolonging his life, and the doctor has, in accordance with his duty, complied with his patient's wishes.[217]

The underlying premise seems to be that suicide requires an act, and cannot be perpetrated by an omission. What then of the person who refuses to leave a sinking ship?[218] Is the distinction that there is no intention to die? And what do we say of hunger-strikers? In *Robb's* case, Thorpe J said that 'refusal of nutrition and medical treatment in the exercise of the right of self determination does not constitute an act of suicide'.[219] Perhaps there are different forms of refusals of treatment, and they should not all be characterized alike. The hunger-striking prisoner does not intend to kill himself: he hopes the authorities will give in to his demands. Others may refuse treatment because it is no longer worthwhile, because it is futile or burdensome. The doctor who withholds or withdraws treatment in response is merely respecting the patient's decision not to have treatment disproportionate to what it can achieve. On this analysis we cannot describe the refusals by AK and Ms B to continue treatment as suicide. But what if the patient's intent is suicidal? Would the doctor who took him off a ventilator be assisting suicide and thus be exposed to the sanctions of s. 2 of the 1961 Act? Ian Brady's intention undoubtedly was, and, conveniently, he was found to be not competent to refuse nutrition.[220] But had he had the intention, would Thorpe J be right that it does not – that is can never – constitute suicide?

English law thus distinguishes the refusal of treatment from suicide, so that no question can arise about whether taking a patient off a ventilator at his/her request can amount to assisting a suicide. Thus, to treat them in the face of their refusal to continue treatment was tortious, and,

---

217 N. 41 above, at 864.

218 *Cf.* M. Otlowski, *Voluntary Euthanasia and the Common Law* (Oxford, 1997), 63.

219 *Secretary of State for the Home Department* v. *Robb* [1995] 1 All ER 677.

220 *R* v. *Collins and Ashworth Hospital Authority, ex parte Brady* [2002] 8 Lloyd's Rep. Med. 355.

indeed, Ms B sought and was awarded nominal damages in recognition of this.[221]

But is English law right to allow a doctor to turn off a ventilator at a competent patient's request, whilst denying the patient the assistance of a doctor to take his or her life? If there is an inconsistency, it could, of course, be solved both ways. There would, however, be little support for denying a patient a right to refuse treatment: few principles of medical law are more firmly established than self-determination.

And so can the ban on doctor-assisted suicide be justified? It was upheld both by the House of Lords[222] and the European Court of Human Rights[223] in the *Pretty* case. Mrs Pretty based her challenge on the European Convention.[224] The European Court thought that Article 8 (respect for private life) was engaged. Using principles I articulated earlier in this paper, it emphasized the concept of 'personal autonomy' as 'an important principle underlying the interpretation of [the] guarantees'[225] of the Convention and continued:

> The very essence of the Convention is respect for human dignity and human freedom. Without in any way negating the principle of sanctity of life... the Court considers that it is under Article 8 that notions of quality of life take on significance. In an era of growing medical sophistication combined with longer life expectancies, many people are concerned that they should not be forced to linger on in old age or in states of enhanced physical or mental decrepitude which conflict with strongly held ideas of self and personal identity.[226]

The Court was 'not prepared to exclude'-note its caution-that preventing Mrs Pretty from exercising her choice to avoid what she considered an undignified and distressing end to her life was an interference with her right to respect for private life.[227]

This was not the House of Lords' view. Thus, for Lord Bingham, 'any attempt to base a right to die on Art 8 founders on exactly the same objec-

221 N. 34 above, 1114.
222 N. 33 above.
223 *Ibid.*
224 Incorporated into English law by the Human Rights Act 1998.
225 N. 33 above, 81.
226 *Ibid.*, 81-82.
227 *Ibid.*, 82.

tion as the attempt based on Art 2, namely that the alleged right would extinguish the very benefit on which it is supposedly based'.[228] This begs a number of questions: we cannot talk about benefit without specifying whose. There are competing theories of the good.[229] Dame Elizabeth Butler-Sloss P appreciated this in Ms B's case.[230] There was drawn to her attention[231] an article by Kim Atkins in the *Journal of Applied Philosophy*,[232] in which this, and hence the value of autonomy, was explained. I will quote a couple of sentences from this article which proved highly influential in Dame Elizabeth's judgment:

> If we accept that the subjective character of experience is irreducible and that it is grounded in the particularity of our points of view, then we are bound to realize that our respect for other's differences and autonomy embodies a respect for the particularity of each other's points of view.
>
> ... While we can imagine, we cannot know objectively 'what it is like to be' another person, no matter how many facts we are in possession of...[233]

I would suggest that in tackling these difficult cases our courts strive to be as objective as possible, whereas they ought to be 'subjective'. To quote Atkins again:

> Insisting that a decision be made from a fully objective perspective can only produce a decision that is further from the patient's own point of view, not closer to it.[234]

This offers insight into 'private life' of which the Lords in *Pretty's* case would have done well to have taken advantage. Because, to quote another article by a philosopher, for someone in Mrs Pretty's situation it is her 'last

228 *Ibid.*, 280.

229 And see J. P. Safranek, 'Autonomy and Assisted Suicide' (1998) 28(4) *Hastings Center Report* 32-36.

230 N. 34 above, 1110.

231 By Dr Sensky, a consultant psychiatrist and Reader in Psychological Medicine at Imperial College London. In other words, the source was not from counsel.

232 'Autonomy and the Subjective Character of Experience' (2000) 17 *journal of Applied Philosophy* 71-9.

233 'Autonomy and the Subjective Character of Experience' (2000) 17 *Journal of Applied Philosophy* 71-9.

234 *Ibid.*, 78.

opportunity to exercise agency, to make a decision that truly expresses her own distinctive manner of living and dying'.[235] And Article 8 is about respect for *private* life. Would it not be better to read this as including control over the dying process? Dying is an act of living. How one dies is a component of the life cycle. Lord Bingham concedes that Article 8 protects 'the physical, moral and psychological integrity of the individual, including rights over the individual's own body'.[236] But how is integrity to be respected if such a basic decision is removed from the individual? Lord Hope seems to accept this argument: 'the way she chooses to pass the closing moments of her life is part of the act of living'.[237] He accepts 'a right of self-determination'.[238] But he is not prepared to draw the conclusion that there is a positive obligation to give effect to her wish to end her own life by means of an assisted suicide. He says this would 'stretch' the meaning of 'respect for private life' too far:[239] he does not indicate why. Nor am I sure that he is right to argue that he would be prepared to do so if there were evidence of international support for assisted suicide. First, because I do not see this as a principled argument and, secondly, because there is rather more sympathy for a benign approach to assisted suicide in other countries than he admits.[240] (It is an interesting reflection that the Government recently was economical with the truth when it gave evidence to[241] the House of Lords on the position in other countries.)

Even if Article 8(1) were engaged, both the House of Lords and the European Court of Human Rights were of the opinion that the challenge would founder on Article 8(2). This allows interference by a public authority with the Article 8(1) right 'in accordance with the law' if this is necessary in a democratic society in the interests of national security, public safety, or the economic well-being of the country, for the prevention of disorder or crime, for the protection of health or morals, or for the protection of the rights and freedoms of others'. The Lords were concerned with the possibility of abuse and the need to protect the weak and

235 A. Donchin, 'Autonomy, Interdependence and Assisted Suicide: Respecting boundaries/ Crossing Lines' (2000) 14 *Bioethics* 187-204, 197.

236 N. 33 above, 280.

237 *Ibid.*, 310.

238 *Ibid.*

239 *Ibid.*

240 And not just in The Netherlands and Belgium. See 'Taking the Law Into Their Own Hands?' (March 2003) *Professional Social Work* 18-19.

241 On 14 and 15 November 2002.

the vulnerable.[242] So was the European Court.[243] For both courts this was enough to justify disengagement from Article 8(1).

But if the concern is with abuse, is a ban the most effective strategy of control? Does anyone believe that because assisted suicide is proscribed that it does not take place? If we decriminalized it and regulated it,[244] if, in other words, we brought it into the open rather than sweeping it under the carpet, we would have in · place mechanisms to guard against abuse and to protect the vulnerable and the weak. The evidence from those jurisdictions which allow doctor-assisted suicide – The Netherlands[245] and Oregon[246] – does not provide proof of abuse.[247] There will be cases of abuse, but then there are at the moment. We need to rise to the challenge and design a structure that enables decisions to be taken sensitively and within a caring environment and that provides safeguards. We need to proceed cautiously, and the system will require careful monitoring. But we cannot reject assisted suicide out of hand as we have done in the past.[248] Nor can we pretend, as the Government did recently in its de-

242 And see the European Commission in *R* v. *United Kingdom* (1983) 33 DR 270. Lord Bingham thought it was not 'hard to imagine that an elderly person might opt for a premature end to life if that were available, not from a desire to die or a willingness to stop living, but from a desire to stop being a burden to others'. N. 33 above, 287. See also Lord Hope, at 310.

243 See n. 33 above, 83.

244 And see D. Orentlicher and L. Snyder; 'Can Assisted Suicide Be Regulated?', in L. Snyder and A. L. Caplan (eds.), *Assisted Suicide: Finding Common Ground* (Bloomington, Indiana, 2002), 55-69. Also useful is F. G. Miller, H. Brody, and T. E. Quill, 'Can Physician-Assisted Suicide Be Regulated Effectively ?' (1996) 24 *Journal of Law, Medicine and Ethics* 225-32. For Daniel Callahan, *The Troubled Dream of Life* (Washington, DC, 2000), regulating euthanasia is 'the last illusion' (91-119). On illegal (and uncontrolled) euthanasia see R. Magnusson, *Angels of Death* (Melbourne, 2002).

245 The literature on the Dutch experience is now huge. And there is a striking absence of consensus. Particularly critical is J. Keown, *Euthanasia, Ethics and Public Policy* (Cambridge, 2002), 81-149. Battin's 'caveats' are worth examining: see M. P. Battin, *The Least Worth Death* (New York, 1994), 130-44. An exploration of underlying principles is J. De Haan, 'The Ethics of Euthanasia: Advocates' Perspectives' (2002) 16 *Bioethics* 154-72.

246 On which see P. Curran, 'Regulating Death: Oregon's Death with Dignity Act and the Legalization of Physician-Assisted Suicide' (1998) 86 *Georgetown Law journal* 725-49.

247 Also Kennedy and Grubb's conclusion, n. 72 above, 1939.

248 And see M. Battin and L. Snyder, 'Should Older Persons Have The Right To Commit Suicide?', in A. E. Scharlach and L. W. Kaye, (eds.) *Controversial Issues in Ageing* (Boston, 1996), 92-102 (where opposing views are presented); D. W. Brock, 'Physician-Assisted Suicide Is Sometimes Morally Justified', in R. F. Weir (ed.), *Physician-*

fence of its position on Mrs Pretty's application, that our laws on assisted suicide are broadly similar to those in the rest of Europe. Our laws are the most restrictive and inflexible of anywhere in Europe, save Ireland: at the very least we could downgrade the criminal offence and lower the maximum penalty (by way of comparison, it is 60 days in Denmark and Norway). And why pretend? We do not prosecute anyway.[249]

This would not be far enough.[250] We have surely got to accept that it is intolerable for the state to dictate to us the manner of our death. This was recognized in 1961. Allowing suicide but banning assisted suicide does little more than discriminate against those unable to carry out their wishes.[251] McLachlin J recognized this in the *Rodriguez* case: 'the denial to Sue Rodriguez of a choice available to others cannot be justified'.[252] McLachlin J was in the minority, and the majority of the Canadian Supreme Court did justify it. In fact Sue Rodriguez was assisted to die by a doctor shortly after the ruling against her, but we know very little about

---

*Assisted Suicide* (Bloomington, Indiana, 1997), 86-103; J. J. Thomson, 'Physician-Assisted Suicide: Two Moral Arguments' (1999) 109 *Ethics* 497-518.

249 It is estimated that up to 26,000 people a year are 'helped to die' by their doctors. A few get publicity, like Reginald Crew who went to Switzerland for doctor assisted suicide. His widow, who took him there, could have been prosecuted under s. 2 of the Suicide Act 1961, but was not. So, arguably, could the BBC camera crew who accompanied them.

250 As I write, there is before Parliament the Patient (Assisted Dying) Bill 2003 proposed by Lord Joffe. Although passed by the House of Lords (see *The Guardian*, 7 June 2003, 6), it has no chance of becoming law, at least not just yet. Much of the criticism of this Bill comes from concerned 'disability' interest groups. But see A. I. Batavia, 'Disability and Physician-Assisted Suicide' (1997) 336 *New England Journal of Medicine* 1671-73, and A. Silvers, 'Protecting the Innocents from Physician-Assisted Suicide: Disability Discrimination and the Duty to Protect Otherwise Vulnerable Groups', in M. P. Battin, R. Rhodes, and A. Silvers (eds.), *Physician Assisted Suicide: Expanding the Debate* (New York, 1998), 133-48.

251 But for the argument that a right to assisted suicide does not follow from there being a right to suicide see M. Gunderson, 'A Right To Suicide Does Not Entail a Right To Assisted Death' (1997) 23 *Journal of Medical Ethics* 51-54. It has been argued also that PAS may undermine patient autonomy: see T. Salem, 'Physician Assisted Suicide: Promoting Autonomy-or Medicalizing Suicide?' (1999) 29(3) *Hastings Center Report* 30-36. A poll in October 2002 found that 81 per cent of the public supported the legalization of assisted suicide: see S. Gillen, 'A Dignified Exit?' (2003) *Community Care*, no. 1463, 28-29.

252 *Rodriguez* v. *British Columbia (Attorney-General)* [1993] 107 DLR (4th Series), 342, 415. She added that Rodriguez was being asked to 'bear the burden of the chance that other people in other situations may act criminally to kill others or improperly sway them to suicide' (417-18).

this.[253] The individual has the right to make important decisions, even if this exercise of autonomy robs him or her of the ability to take any further decisions. A belief in autonomy does not require us, as it did John Stuart Mill, to fetishize it. [254] As Dworkin points out, the manner of our death has a 'special or symbolic importance'[255] to us.

I have not analysed here all of the House of Lords or European Court of Human Rights reasoning in the *Pretty* case – I have done so elsewhere.[256] It is difficult to see how a different conclusion could have been reached. Mr Pretty was, after all, asking for a 'proleptic grant of immunity from prosecution'.[257] The answer lies in legislation,[258] the building blocks for which will emphasize autonomy and respect for human dignity. It will regulate, and it will protect the weak and the vulnerable.

## Having the Decision to Die Taken by Others

What of those not able to take decisions for themselves? Some who come into this category will have, when competent, expressed a view on what should happen to them if the circumstances which have now occurred should arise. The principled basis for recognizing the validity of an advance directive to refuse medical treatment is respect for the patient's autonomy.[259] Of course, very few do engage in end-of-life planning. We have no legislation on this: the Enduring Powers of Attorney Act 1985 is restricted to the 'property and affairs'[260] of the person in question, and 'affairs' is not wide enough to embrace health care decisions. But the common law is reasonably clear. Thus, Lord Keith in the *Bland* case was in no doubt that the liberty to refuse consent to treatment extended to

---

253 So R. Cohen-Almagor, *The Right To Die With Dignity* (New Brunswick, NJ, 2001), 93, points out. J. Martel, 'Examining The Foreseeable: Assisted Suicide As a Herald of Changing Moralities' (2001) 10 *Social and Legal Studies* 147-70 says her suicide 'may be regarded as a 20th century version of Socrates' crime' (158).

254 N. 38 above. Mill discusses this in relation to selling oneself into slavery.

255 N. 35 above.

256 'Denying Death its Dominion: Thought on the Dianne Pretty Case' (2002) 10 *Medical Law Review* 245-70. See also Antje Pedain, 'The Human Rights Dimension of the Diane Pretty Case' (2003) 62 *Cambridge Law Journal* 191-206.

257 *Per* Lord Bingham, n. 33 above, 289, discussed at n. 256 above, 259-61.

258 The Patient (Assisted Dying) Bill 2003 (see n. 250 above) is not without problems, but space precludes an examination of these here.

259 See for recent affirmation *Re B*, n. 34 above, 1095-96.

260 See s. 3(1).

'the situation where the person, in anticipation of his, through one cause or another, entering into a condition such as PVS, gives clear instructions that in such event he is not to be given medical care, including artificial feeding, designed to keep him alive'.[261] Lord Keith gives the example of PVS.[262] Lord Goff, in the same case, refers to consent expressed 'before he became unconscious or other wise incapable of communicating' and concedes that 'especial care may be necessary to ensure that the prior refusal of consent is still properly to be regarded as applicable in the circumstances which have subsequently occurred'.[263]

And this is the crucial question. We may regard autonomy as pivotal, but what do we mean by autonomy in these circumstances? The PVS case may be relatively straightforward in comparison with the one which fill much of the literature, the patient with Alzheimer's. Dworkin addresses this issue. He considers the case of Margo and asks us to suppose that

> years ago when fully competent, [she] had executed a formal document directing that if she should develop Alzheimer's disease... she should not receive treatment for any other serious, life-threatening disease that she might contract. Or even that in that event she should be killed as soon and as painlessly as possible.[264]

He argues that we should give effect to these wishes, even though, when afflicted with dementia, 'she seems perfectly happy with her dog-eared mysteries, the single painting she repaints, and her peanut-butter-and-jelly sandwiches.'[265] But is Margo the same person who gave the advance directive? Or has the 'very process that renders [Margo] incompetent and brings the advance directive into play... destroy[ed] the conditions necessary for her personal identity and thereby undercut entirely the moral authority of the direcrive?'[266] This is a serious objection, and if upheld will apply equally to those who succumb to persistent vegetative state as to those who become demented. But is this to place too much empha-

261 N. 41 above, 857.

262 *Ibid.*

263 *Ibid.*, 864.

264 N. 35 above, 226.

265 *Ibid.*

266 *Per* A. Buchanan, 'Advance Directives and the Personal Identity Problem' (1988) 17 *Philosophy and Public Affairs* 277-302, 280.

sis upon 'personal identity'?[267] Would we do better to look, as Buchanan does, to 'psychological continuity'[268] and to admit that this is a matter of degree? I am happier with Buchanan's reasoning than Dworkin's, but their conclusion is broadly similar and overemphasizes precedent autonomy.[269] However, the alternatives, proxy decision-making by the family and a professional judgement of what is in the patient's best interests, are both fraught with difficulties. The former is anyway rejected by English law,[270] and rightly so.[271] The latter is indeterminate and value-laden, and would ask us to give more weight to what doctors think than to what the patient when competent had indicated were his/her healthcare choices.[272]

We do not have 'living will' legislation in the United Kingdom. Nor is there any real impetus at present to introduce it.[273] It would be beyond my brief in this paper to set out the details of such legislation. There are many precedents in the United States and elsewhere.[274] In short, a lot of the spadework has already been done. Here I would do no more than urge the adoption of such legislation, and clear thought to the ethical principles underlying it. The crucial question is not so much about whether we should uphold the sanctity of life in these circumstances, but which decision (or decisions) best respects it. We would do well not

267 And see D. Morgan, 'Odysseus and The Binding Directive: Only A Cautionary Tale?' (1994) 14 *Legal Studies* 411-42. On the 'someone else' problem see D. Degrazia, 'Advance Directives, Dementia and "the Someone Else Problem"' (1999) 13 *Bioethics* 373-91.

268 N. 266 above, 280. Buchanan concedes the notion of 'psychological continuity' is 'inherently vague'.

269 And see R. Dresser, 'Dworkin on Dementia: Elegant Theory, Questionable Policy' (1995) 25(6) *Hastings Center Report* 32-38.

270 See *Re T* (1992) 9 BMLR 46, 50, *per* Lord Donaldson MR.

271 A. Grubb, 'Treatment Decisions: Keeping it in the Family' in A. Grubb (ed.), *Choices and Decisions in Health Care* (Chichester, 1993).

272 'Substituted judgment' is no better. See G. Dworkin, 'Law and Medical Experimentation' (1987) 13 *Monash University Law Review* 189-200. The test is justified by J. Robertson, 'Organ Donations by Incompetents and the Substituted Judgment Doctrine' (1976) 76 *Columbia Law Review* 48-78, 63-68. Use of the test is rejected by the House of Lords in *Bland's* case (n. 41 above): *e.g.*, Lord Goff says it does not form part of English law in relation to incompetent adults; and Lord Mustill described it as a 'fiction'.

273 Though recommended in the Law Commission Report, *Mental Incapacity* (Report No. 231) (London, 1995), this recommendation has now been dropped, perhaps because they are already recognized by the common law.

274 See D. Lanham and B. Fehlberg, 'Living Wills and The Right To Die With Dignity' (1991) 18 *University of Melbourne Law Review* 329-49.

to fetishize physical survival,[275] which offers no dignity, when the patient has indicated that this is not what he or she would want.

If we believe in autonomy we will encourage advance directives. But the majority will not make them, and decisions will have to be taken for those who have not said what should happen to them when, for example, they enter a persistent vegetative state. What decisions may be taken about the care and management of such patients, including withholding treatment and withdrawing nutrition and hydration, remains problematic and controversial ten years after the *Bland* decision. Not surprisingly there has been further litigation, some prompted by the Human Rights Act 1998, and professional guidance.

*Bland*[276] decided that doctors could withdraw artificial nutrition arid hydration from a young victim of the Hillsborough football disaster who had remained in a PVS condition ever since. There was no hope of any improvement or recovery. There was, unsurprisingly, no advance directive. The test adopted by the Lords was one of 'best interests'.[277] For the majority no benefit could accrue to Mr Bland by continuing the treatment. For Lord Goff, Mr Bland's condition was 'no more than a living death'[278] and treatment was 'futile'.[279] He referred to the 'invasiveness'[280] of the treatment and its indignity. For the minority, as Lord Mustill put it, although the termination of life was not in the best interests of Mr Bland, 'his best interests in being kept alive have also disappeared'. He had 'no further interest in being kept alive.'[281] In the Court of Appeal, Hoffmann LJ had said that Mr Bland was 'grotesquely alive':[282] he had no life in the sense that 'even the most pitifully handicapped but conscious human being has a life'[283] (presumably someone like Mrs Pretty).

The problem with conceptualizing decision-making in terms of interests and best interests is two-fold. First, it leads to a path where it is easy to say someone in a PVS condition has no interests. Certainly, he cannot express them. But he must have some interests. What would we

275 And see J. Gray, *Beyond The New Right: Markets, Government and the Common Environment* (London, 1993), 171.

276 N. 41 above.

277 *Ibid.*, 858, 866; but *cf.* 896-97 *per* Lord Mustill.

278 *Ibid.*, 869. But a Hillsborough victim did emerge from a coma: see *Daily Telegraph,* 27 March 1997. And there are other examples.

279 *Ibid.*

280 *Ibid.*, 869.

281 *Ibid.*, 897, 898.

282 *Ibid.*, 830.

283 *Ibid.*, 825.

say if it were decided that he could be used for medical research or experimentation? Or placed in a cubicle in the South Cloisters facing Jeremy Bentham? Or displayed in a circus? Secondly, it requires someone to determine what best interests and some criteria. The House of Lords decided the decision was for the medical profession,[284] with the courts exercising a supervisory role. It is not clear what this role is. Since the majority of the Lords tied the decision to what was in accordance with a practice acceptable to a responsible body of medical opinion (the *'Bolam'* test), is it to confirm that the doctor's decision to withdraw nutrition and hydration is supported by such opinion? Or does 'ultimate power and duty' to 'review' the doctor's decision rest with the court, as Sir Thomas Bingham MR said in the *Frenchay* case?[285] But should *Bolam* have a part to play at all? Granted that it governs diagnosis and treatment and, after *Sidaway*,[286] risk assessment, is it right that it should also be used to test the legality of a doctor's conduct as well as its reasonableness? Hoffmann LJ and Lord Mustill did not think so: according to the latter, the 'decision is ethical, not medical'. There was 'no reason in logic why on such a decision the opinions of doctors should be decisive'.[287] I venture to think they are right, and am delighted that a clear trend against *Bolam* can be detected in recent sterilization decisions.[288]

The question that continues to puzzle is why, if it is lawful to discontinue hydration and nutrition (indeed, according to Lord Browne-Wilkinson, unlawful to continue it when it is not in the best interests of the patient),[289] it is murder to end the life of someone like Anthony Bland by a lethal injection[290] (and would be so also where he requested 'mercy killing'). The House of Lords had no difficulty in distinguishing withdrawal of treatment – they held hydration and nutrition not uncontroversially to be treatment[291] – from a lethal injection. Lord Browne-Wilkinson was in no doubt that 'the whole purpose of stopping artificial feeding is to

---

284 Following *Bolam* v. *Friern Hospital Management Committee* [1957] 1 WLR 582.

285 *Frenchay NHS Healthcare Trust* v. *S* [1994] 2 All ER 403, 411.

286 *Sidaway* v. *Board of Governors of the Bethlem Royal Hospital* [1985] AC 871.

287 N. 41 above, 898. *He* thought the proposed withdrawal of nutrition and hydration was 'ethically acceptable' (899).

288 *Re A* [2000] 1 FLR 549 and *Re S* [2000] 2 FLR 389.

289 N. 41 above, 883.

290 Clearly so stated by Lord Goff, *ibid.*, 865, 866.

291 *Ibid.*, 873.

bring about the death of Anthony Bland'.[292] The discontinuance of life support is categorized as an omission. Lord Goff admitted that

> it may be difficult to describe what the doctor actually does as an omission... But discontinuation of life support is... no different from not initiating life support in the first place. In each case, the doctor is simply allowing his patient to die in the sense that he is desisting from taking a step which might... prevent his patient from dying as a result of his pre-existing condition.[293]

And he distinguishes the 'malicious interloper' from the doctor.[294] The interloper's conduct in turning off the machine 'cannot possibly be categorised as an omission.'[295] That may be so, but I share with Lord Mustill 'acute unease' about basing the *Bland* decision on the act/omission distinction because, as he puts it, 'however much the terminologies may differ the ethical status of the two courses of action is for all relevant purposes indistinguishable'.[296]

If so, we must ask what is wrong with the lethal injection. For Lord Goff, 'reasons of policy,'[297] not further explained, militate against the law allowing a lethal injection. And they do so, as is evident from the *Cox* case,[298] even where this is requested by the competent patient. But is it more seriously wrong? Is the difference morally significant? Many will be familiar with James Rachels' famous Smith/Jones scenario:[299] both were greedy and both stood to inherit from a young nephew. One drowned the nephew, the other stood gleefully by and watched him drown in a few inches of water. Rather than posing the dilemma in terms of a conceptual difference (acts and omissions), would it not better to ask about the risks and benefits of the different courses of action? Are the risks (abuse, etc.) any greater if we were to allow lethal injections? I doubt it, provided it was properly regulated. The benefits in terms of the dignity of the patient involved do, however, look better. As for autonomy, we cannot ask what this patient wants, but I would expect that most of us in Tony Bland's

292 *Ibid.*, 881.
293 *Ibid.*, 866.
294 *Ibid.*
295 Clearly so stated by Lord Goff, 866.
296 *Ibid.*, 887.
297 *Ibid.*, 866.
298 N. 31 above.
299 J. Rachels, *The End of Life* (Oxford, 1986).

position would prefer a lethal injection to a week's dying (however painless). And if we can impute altruism to such persons, we might assume also that they would realize their families would suffer less from their speedy death rather than any further prolongation of their now meaningless life.

If *Bland* provokes disquiet, case law post *Bland* does nothing to reassure. Thus, the Irish Supreme Court, following *Bland,* allowed the withdrawal of artificial nutrition from a patient who was not in a PVS and retained some cognitive function.[300] The Court of Appeal in the *Frenchay*[301] case declared that it was lawful not to reinsert a feeding-tube which had become disconnected. There was no independent neurological opinion: the case was an 'emergency' and there was no time to commission one. There was even some doubt as to whether the patient was PVS. The patient was a failed suicide. Was the court influenced by this? It didn't say it was, nor did it remark on the irony of allowing in effect an assisted suicide!

A challenge to the *Bland* reasoning was expected under the Human Rights Act. It came in *NHS Trust A* v. *M; NHS Trust B* v. *H*[302] within days of the Act coming into operation. It failed. The court held that a person in a PVS state was alive and therefore entitled to the protection of Article 2 of the Convention. But a responsible decision by a medical team not to provide treatment could not amount to intentional deprivation of life and therefore did not fall within the negative obligation imposed by Article 2 to refrain from taking life intentionally. As Dame Elizabeth Butler-Sloss P explained: 'Although the intention in withdrawing artificial nutrition and hydration in PVS cases is to hasten death, in my judgment the phrase "deprivation of life" must import a deliberate act, as opposed to an omission.[303] The act/omission distinction is thus once again upheld. Of course, the giving of palliative drugs – a morphine drip for example – is an act. Alerted to the problem the judge responded: 'This judgment is dealing only with the situation where treatment is to be discontinued and is not concerned with nor relevant to acts by doctors or other members of the health service, such as the giving of palliative drugs to a ter-

300 *In the Matter of a Ward of Court* [1995] 2 ILRM 410. For concern over misdiagnosis see K. Andrews *et al.,*'Misdiagnosis of the Vegetative State: Retrospective Study In The Rehabilitation Unit' (1996) 313 *British Medical Journal* 13-16.

301 N. 285 above. See also *ReD* [1998)1 FLR 411 and *Re H* [1998]2 FLR 36.

302 [2001]2 FLR 367.

303 *Ibid.*, 376.

minally ill patient, which might have the effect of shortening his life'[304] The intention in such a case is not deprivation of life, so that Article 2 would not anyway bite. I say this though a possible implication of *R* v. *Woollin*,[305] a non-medical case where medical questions were accordingly not addressed, is that doctors who foresee that their palliative care will shorten life are committing murder. This is an unacceptable conclusion, as was the conclusion that separating the Maltese conjoined twins[306] would constitute murder of the weaker one who, it was known, would die. Good medical practice should be encouraged and not sanctioned, and the courts should not, as they had to in the 'conjoined twins' case, have to scramble about for defences like necessity. Rather better would be the creation of an exception that what was done accords with good medical practice.

This is an area of law resistant to change but urgently in need of radical rethinking. The court was right to hold that the withdrawal of nutrition and hydration was not incompatible with Article 2, but was it right to remain ensnared within the act/omission distinction? It is not a true distinction, as the most cursory of examinations reveals. Is there any moral difference between not starting treatment when life could be saved, perhaps on a futility argument, and turning off a respirator or stopping nutrition and hydration? The law says there is no distinction, but it does so merely by categorizing both actions as omissions. Is it then also an omission if fifteen minutes after a patient has been placed on a respirator, the spouse of the patient arrives and presents the doctors with the patient's advance directive which indicates that in these circumstances he would not wish to be kept alive, and the doctors respond by turning off the respirator? It is consistent with the autonomy thesis presented in this paper that they should, but this is surely an act and not an omission. But if we allow acts, should we allow all ads, such as the lethal injection? We will need to reconsider the dichotomy, and much else in this area: the meaning of futility, for example. We cannot allow the law to continue to operate with simplistic notions which are often out of line with medical ethics and good medical practice.

304 *Ibid.*
305 [1999] 1 AC 82.
306 [2001] 1 FLR 1.

## Conclusions

My conclusions can be brief.

I have emphasized the importance of ethical thinking to the resolution of a number of practical problems that the law confronts in the area of medicine (and briefly also in science). I have shown the value of principled argument and the ways in which an emphasis on autonomy and human dignity can assist us to find good answers (I desist from calling them the 'right' answers) across a range of issues relating to birth decisions and decisions at the end of life. It is, I believe, significant that similar arguments are valuable at both edges of life. It is puzzling and troubling that these principles should have penetrated so little into the decision-making process at the end of life, when their impact upon beginning-of-life decisions is so profound.

Ethical thinking can help to inject some coherence into the law. This is important for many reasons, but not least, because the law is a response to problems and its answers do not always fit as well as they should. Ask yourselves why chain novels are never as good as novels![307] It can also introduce us to concepts and to ways of thinking of which we know little (or nothing), and it can reveal problems with our thinking. It can also offer insights into ways of reforming the law. Our courts work best when familiar with the ethical literature. This is clear when we read a judgment like that of Dame Elizabeth Butler-Sloss P in the *Ms B*[308] case, or Hoffmann LJ in the Court of Appeal in *Bland*[309] (it is obvious that he had read Dworkin's *Life's Dominion*).[310]

We need to see more ethical issues addressed, more ethical argument adduced, and more attention paid in judicial reasoning to the insights of ethical thinking. At present, our judges are more likely to hear about ethical issues from interest groups[311] than from ethicists. And this can distort the shape of the law, as well as undermining its rationality and integrity.

We have to begin this process by looking at the ways we educate our students. We've only just begun to realize that law students should study legal ethics. So it is hardly surprising that ethics as such and medical eth-

---

307 *Cf.* R. Dworkin, *Law's Empire* (London, 1986).

308 N.34 above.

309 N. 41 above.

310 This was apparently given to him in manuscript.

311 A clear example of this was the brief submitted by the Archbishop of Westminster in the 'conjoined twins' case: n. 306 above. And see C. Harlow, 'Public Law and Popular Justice' (2002) 65 MLR 1-18.

ics (within the context of medical law) should figure so little in the law curriculum. Students at UCL do rather better than many of their fellow students at other universities: we have a course in Medicine, Ethics and the Law, though this is unlikely to survive syllabus revisions in its present form. We need also to look at professional courses and at the ways we train the judiciary. How many, I wonder, can say with Lord Hoffmann that they have read *Life's Dominion?*[312] Or to have read articles in, or even to have heard of, the *Journal of Applied Philosophy*?[313]

The issues I have addressed will not go away. If anything they will become more difficult. And we must equip ourselves to find solutions. We must think more about the interface between law and ethics, and not just in the areas I have used. As the author of the book of *Ecclesiastes* reminds us, 'He who increaseth knowledge, increaseth sorrow'.[314] Or to put it into modern, but rather less elegant parlance, 'the more you discover, the less you realize you know'.

312 N. 41 above, 826. He had also had conversations with Bernard Williams.

313 I cite this journal here because of its influence in *Re B*, n. 34 above. But of greater value in the context of medical law and ethics is *Bioethics* or the *Journal of Medical Ethics*. Are these accessible to the profession or the judiciary?

314 N. 1 above, Chapter I, 18.

CHAPTER 3

# Upholding The Dignity and Best Interests of Children: International Law and the Corporal Punishment of Children

## I. Introduction – A Pre-History

Early legal statements are conspicuously silent on children's rights: the Ten Commandments, arguably the most influential of all legal codes, contains a clear normative pronouncement on parent-child relations – "Honor, thy father and thy mother."[1] But the commandment is in terms of respect for parents, and it is silent on the obligations of parents to love and nurture their children.[2] Is it then surprising that well into early modern times children were being prosecuted in England for abusing parents, but that prosecutions of parents for beating children appear not to have taken place?[3]

One of the earliest recognitions of children's rights is found in the Massachusetts *Body of Liberties* of 1641. Parents are told not to choose their children's mates and not to use unnatural severity against their children.[4] Children, furthermore, are given "free liberty to complain to the Authorities for redress."[5] But this is also the law that prescribes the death penalty for children over sixteen who disobey their parents.[6] There is no evidence that children did in fact successfully litigate against their parents, nor is there any evidence that any disobedient children were executed.[7] This recognition of children's rights nevertheless remains interesting in showing, as it does, that 370 years ago, protection of children went hand-in-hand with adding the power of the state to parental authority.

---

1 *Exodus* 20:12; *Deuteronomy* 5:16.

2 On religion and corporal punishment of children, see generally Philip Greven, *Spare the Child* (1991).

3 Richard Helmholz, 'And Were There Children's Rights in Early Modern England?', 1 *Int'l J. Child. Rts.* 23, 27 (1993).

4 Elizabeth Pleck, *Domestic Tyranny* 22 (1987).

5 *Id.*

6 *Id.* at 25.

7 *See id.* at 26-27.

 | DOI:10.1163/9789004219106_004

The two centuries that followed are hardly notable for their propagation of the rights of children. The Victorian novel is replete with floggings of children: *David Copperfield, Nicholas Nickleby, Oliver Twist, Jane Eyre, The Way of All Flesh* – the litany is almost endless. Indeed, graphic descriptions of floggings permeate novels well into the twentieth century: D.H Lawrence's *The Rainbow,* Richard Llewellyn's *How Green Was My Valley,* Lucy Maud Montgomery's *Anne of Avonlea,* and the popular *Billy Bunter* stories.[8] The nineteenth century, not surprisingly, also saw the birth of the child-saving movement, spawning institutions like the juvenile court.[9] Child-protection legislation also came about, commonly in the English-speaking world, after a campaign for its passage in England and after a similar campaign to protect domestic animals.[10] Yet cruelty remained a social construct, and founders of societies to protect children from abuse still vigorously defended corporal chastisement. Thus, one of the founders of the New York Society for the Prevention of Cruelty to Children (SPCC), Henry Bergh, was prepared to uphold "a good wholesome flogging" as appropriate for "disobedient children."[11] Others began to advocate children's rights and to voice some discomfort with corporal chastisement, as well.[12] Thus in 1892 the American children's novelist Kate Douglas Wiggin thought it likely that the "rod of reason" would have to replace "the rod of birch."[13] In Sweden, Ellen Key in *The Century of the Child* looked forward to "increasing limitations on the rights of parents over children," and to the end of corporal punishment.[14]

---

8 Charlotte Brontë, *Jane Eyre* (1847); Samuel Butler, *The Way of the Flesh* (1903); Charles Dickens, *David Copperfield* (1850); Charles Dickens, *Nicholas Nickleby* (1839); Charles Dickens, *Oliver Twist* (1839); D.h. Lawrence, *The Rainbow* (1915); Richard Llewellyn, *How Green was my Valley* (1939); Lucy Maud Montgomery, *Anne of Avonlea* (1909); Frank Richards, *Billy Hunter of Greyfriars School* (1947); *see generally* Edward Anthony, *Thy Rod and Staff* (1995); Hugh Cunningham, *Children of the Poor* (1991); John Waller, *The Real Oliver Twist* 109-15 (2006); James Walvin, *A Child's World* 45-60 (Penguin Books 1982), especially ch. 3.

9 *See* Anthony Plait, *The Child Savers: The Invention of Delinquency* 3 (1969).

10 *See* George K. Behlmer, *Child Abuse and Moral Reform in England 1870-1908* (1982).

11 *See* Joseph M. Hawes, *The Children's Rights Movement: A History of Advocacy and Protection* 21 (1991).

12 The etymology of chastisement is interesting. It originates in the same source as "chaste," and thus denotes "making pure." Nicholas Orme, *Medieval Children* 84 (2001).

13 Kate Douglas Wiggin, *Children's Rights* 19 (1892).

14 Ellen Key, *The Century of the Child* 317 (1909) (originally published in Swedish in 1900).

She described such punishment as "humiliating for him who gives it as for him who receives it."[15] She looked forward to the time when children would be treated as equals and be given "the same consideration, the same kind confidence" which is shown to adults.[16]

But the most significant of these early thinkers was Janusz Korczak, best known today as the man who voluntarily accompanied 200 children on their journey to Treblinka, where he and they were duly slaughtered.[17] His *How to Love a Child* and *The Right of the Child to Respect* contain a "Convention" on the Rights of the Child so far ahead of its time – formulated as it was in the 1910s – that it is not surprising the world barely noticed.[18] Even today Korczak's writings have not been fully translated into English.[19] Of the many rights Korczak accorded children was the right to a government that protects them from neglect, cruelty, and any exploitation of any kind.[20] This is as close as he got to emphasizing that corporal punishment was wrong, but this is what he believed: the institution he ran did not use corporal punishment. And a brief lecture he gave on child psychology makes it clear what his view was. Entitled *The Heart of The Child,* it was given in the X-ray room of the children's hospital.[21] Korczak entered with a small boy clutching his hand. Without a word he took the boy's shirt off, placed him behind a fluoroscope and turned off the overhead light. Everyone could now see the boy's heart beating rapidly on the screen. "Don't ever forget this sight," Korczak told his audience.[22] "Before you raise a hand to a child, before you administer any kind of punishment, remember what his frightened heart looks like."[23] That was the sum total of the lecture. Korczak also observed that there are many terrible things in this world, but "the worst is he who is afraid of his father, mother or teacher. He fears them instead of loving and trusting them."[24]

15 *Id.* at 327.

16 *Id.* at 109.

17 *See* Betty J. Lifton, *The King of Children* 338-45 (1988).

18 Janusz Korczak, *Loving Every Child – Wisdom For Parents* xi (Sandra Joseph ed., 2007).

19 *But see id.* (good selection of Korczak's writings in English). *See generally* Janusz Korczak, *Ghetto Diary* (2003) (recording Korczak's thoughts in the Warsaw Ghetto in 1942).

20 Janusz Korczak, *Prawo Dziecka Do Szacunku* [*The Child's Right to Respect*] (1929).

21 Lifton, *supra* note 17, at 144.

22 *Id.*

23 *Id.*

24 *Id.*

## II. International Declarations on Children's Rights: Guiding Principles

The first international declaration on children's rights was emerging as Korczak wrote, but it was limited in its aspirations. The 1924 Declaration of Geneva was premised on "mankind['s]" owing the child "the best it has to give."[25] It is stated in five terse principles, and these emphasize welfare.[26] The issue of corporal chastisement is not raised.[27] Interestingly, Korczak commented upon the Geneva Declaration, saying that its authors "ha[d] mistaken duties for rights. Instead of making demands they try to persuade. The Declaration is only an appeal for good-will, a request for more understanding."[28] Nothing came of the Geneva Declaration.

The next Declaration, the UN Declaration on the Rights of the Child, came thirty-five years later.[29] It repeated the exhortation that mankind owed the child "the best it has to give."[30] It mentioned the need for children to have "a happy childhood."[31] Principle 2 stressed that children should be given "opportunities and facilities... to enable [them] to develop physically, mentally, morally, spiritually and socially in a healthy and normal manner and in conditions of freedom and dignity."[32] This may have been the first time the "dignity" of the child was recognized in an international document. The same principle also stressed that "in the enactment of laws for this purpose the best interests of the child shall be the paramount consideration."[33] Two observations implicating corporal punishment may be made: First, although the corporal-punishment issue is not specifically addressed, one can read Principle 2 as discouraging its use. Second, by stating that children's best interests be paramount, the standard goes beyond "a primary consideration," the language of the Con-

25 Dominique Marshall, The Construction of Children as an Object of International Relations: The Declaration of Children's Rights and the Child Welfare Committee of the League of Nations, 1900-1924, 7 *Int'l J. Child. Rts.* 103, 103 (1999).

26 *Id.* at 129.

27 *Id.*

28 Philip E. Veerman, *The Rights of the Child and the Changing Image of Childhood* 96 (1992).

29 Declaration on the Rights of the Child, G.A. Res. 1386, U.N. Doc. A/4354 (Nov. 20, 1959).

30 *Id.* pmbl.

31 *Id.* pmbl.

32 *Id.* princ. 2.

33 *Id.*

vention adopted thirty years later.[34] Principle 7 is also significant: it states that the "best interests of the child shall be the guiding principle of those responsible for [the child's] education and guidance."[35] Since corporal punishment is not in a child's best interests, this principle is a further endorsement of the beginnings of an international understanding that hitting children is wrong.

## A. *Dignity*

The claim was emerging during the early part of the twentieth century that corporal punishment was inconsistent with "dignity," and that it was not in a child's best interests. What these concepts involve would require books: only the surface is scratched here.

"Dignity" comes from the Latin *dignitas*. The Latin term denotes both the status of an individual and the bearing that is associated with that status.[36] Immanuel Kant sought to derive man's dignity from autonomy and rationality; earlier thinkers had found it in revealed religion.[37] Radical Enlightenment thinkers like Tom Paine democratized human dignity: it no longer depended on whether one was an aristocrat or a labourer.[38] Dignity was to become a key normative principle in post-World War II Holocaust thinking. It is a foundational norm of the UN.[39] International legality was premised on a shared commitment to the value of the individual over and above the interests of the state. And these commitments are in turn supported by an appeal to human dignity. Yet "dignity" remains a contested and problematic concept.[40] Part of the reason why appeals to dignity are debated and contested is that they have an appearance of

---

34 *See* UN Convention on the Rights of the Child art. 3, para. 1, *opened for signature* Nov. 20, 1989, 1577 U.N.T.S. 3.

35 Declaration on the Rights of the Child, *supra* note 29, princ. 7.

36 Giorgio Agamben, *Remnants of Auschwitz: The Witness and the Archive* 66 (1999).

37 *See generally* Immanuel Kant, *Groundwork of the Metaphysic of Morals* 97 (H. Paton trans., 1948).

38 *See generally* Tom Paine, *Rights of Man* (Henry Collins ed., Penguin Books 1969). Paine did not go so far as to talk of the dignity of a child.

39 *See* Mary Ann Glendon, *A World Made New: Eleanor Roosevelt and the Universal Declaration of Human Rights* 144 (2001).

40 This article shall not address questions whether dignity can exist in a stratified society, even one like Nazi Germany, where, of course, dignity was denied to non-Aryans (as well as to Communists, homosexuals, et cetera). For these debates, see generally Christian Joerges & Navraj Singh Ghaleigh, *Darker Legacies of Law in Europe: The Shadow of National Socialism and Fascism over Europe and its Legal Traditions* 264-66 (2003).

finality about them. Once dignity is invoked, the inquiry collapses-one can go no further. Dignity asserts the worth of the person who is imbued with it. We cannot define what a human being is without recourse to an essential characteristic such as dignity. Animals do not have dignity; children, I would argue, do.

The UN Convention on the Rights of the Child emphasizes dignity in a number of places.[41] Article 37(a) lays down the right of the child not to be subjected to cruel, inhuman, or degrading treatment or punishment. This provision is designed to protect both the dignity and the physical and mental integrity of the child. Article 16 gives the child the right not to be subjected to "unlawful attacks on his or her honour and reputation" and the right to protection against such attacks.[42] Article 28(2) specifically invokes "dignity."[43] It requires that the signatory parties (States Parties) "take all appropriate measures to ensure that school discipline is administered in a manner consistent with the child's human dignity and in conformity with the... Convention." Punishment should rehabilitate, not mark a child's body.[44] Article 40(1) also invokes "dignity": States Parties are required to ensure that a child accused of violating penal law be "treated in a manner consistent with the promotion of the child's sense of dignity and worth...."[45] This "reinforces the child's respect for the human rights and fundamental freedoms of others."[46] The same emphasis is placed on the treatment of children who have been convicted. A child so deprived of liberty must be treated "with humanity and respect for the inherent dignity of the human person."[47] Some of these provisions refer to "dignity," others to "human dignity" and to "inherent dignity."[48]

Article 28(2) of the Convention, which evokes the child's "human dignity" in the administration of school discipline, does not mention disciplining specifically by parents or other caretakers. By contrast, Article 19 makes no mention of dignity, but it deals with the need "to protect the child from all forms of physical or mental violence, injury, or abuse...

---

41 *See* UN Convention on the Rights of the Child, *supra* note 34.

42 *Id.* art. 16.

43 *Id.* art. 28, para. 2.

44 *See generally* Anne McGillivray, '"He'll Learn It On His Body": Disciplining Childhood in Canadian Law, 5 *Int'l J. Child. Rts.* 193 (1997).

45 UN Convention on the Rights of the Child, *supra* note 34, art. 40, para. 1.

46 *Id.*

47 *Id.* art. 37, para. c.

48 The Preamble (in its first paragraph) recognizes "the inherent dignity" and "the equal and inalienable rights of all members of the human family" as the "foundation of freedom, justice and peace in the world." *Id.* pmbl.

*while in the care of* parent(s), legal guardian(s)," and other caretakers.[49] Though some would contest this, it is clear (and the UN Committee on the Rights of the Child regularly affirms) that, in this provision and others, corporal punishment by parents and others is outlawed by the Convention.

## B. *The Best Interests of the Child*

The international framework for a prohibition on corporal punishment of children also embraces a "best interests" principle.[50] This is set out in Article 3 of the UN Convention on the Rights of the Child, which states, "In all actions concerning children, whether undertaken by public or private social welfare institutions, courts of law, administrative authorities or legislative bodies, the best interests of the child shall be a primary consideration." The "best interests" is a new and controversial principle of interpretation in international law, for "[d]eciding what is best for a child poses a question no less ultimate than the purposes and values of life itself."[51] Of course, what is in a child's best interests is value-laden, and to some extent indeterminate. But it may be argued that there are some givens and that violence against a child may be considered one matter upon which there should be consensus. The best-interests principle can, of course, cloak prejudices: it can act as a smokescreen for a phobia about a particular religion, for example, or for anti-gay prejudices.[52] Attacks on male circumcision in the name of the child's best interests may reflect anti-Semitism or hostility towards Muslims.[53] The principle can also be a reflection of "dominant meanings."[54] The French sociologist Irene Théry sees it as an "alibi for dominant ideology, an alibi for individual arbitrariness, an alibi for family and more general social policies for which the law

---

49 *Id.* art. 19 (emphasis added).

50 *See generally* Michael Freeman, *A Commentary on the United Nations Convention on the Rights of the Child: Article 3 - The Best Interests of the Child* (2007).

51 Robert H. Mnookin, 'Child Custody Adjudication: Judicial Functions in the Face of Indeterminacy', 39 *Law & Contemp. Probs.* 226, 260 (Summer 1975).

52 *See* Helen Reece, 'The Paramountcy Principle: Consensus or Construct?' 49 *Current Legal Probs.* 267, 286-303 (1996) (criticizing the application of the "best interests" principle to deny homosexual parents custody of their children).

53 James G. Dwyer, 'Parental Entitlement and Corporal Punishment', 73 *Law & Contemp. Probls.* 189 (Spring 2010).

54 Irene Thery, '"The Interest of the Child" and the Regulation of the Post-Divorce Family', in *Child Custody and the Politics of Gender* 78, 81 (Carol Smart & Selma Sevenhuijsen eds., 1989).

serves as an instrument."[55] There is also a distinction between current best interests and future-orientated interests,[56] and the two can come into conflict. What makes a child happy at age seven (corporal punishment does not) may have adverse consequences at twenty-one (when the absence of discipline leads to conduct that may not be in his best interests).[57]

Article 3, which first mentions the child's best interests, does not refer to parents. The 1979 Polish draft to the Working Group would have applied the best-interests principle to all actions concerning children "whether undertaken by their parents, guardians, social or state institutions…."[58] It was at the behest of the United States[59] (ironically one of only two countries not to have ratified the Convention)[60] that the principle was limited to "official" actions (though this word is not used in the final formulation). The final text reflects a dominant view that obligations should not be imposed on parents and guardians.[61]

The best-interests principle is extended, if rather weakly, to parents in Article 18(1), which states that "[p]arents or… guardians have the primary responsibility for the upbringing and development of the child. The best interests of the child will be their basic concern."[62] The principle's weakness is in the use of the word "will," in contrast to the mandatory "shall" in Article 3(1), which addresses actions taken by institutional, legal, administrative, or legislative authorities, for all of which "the best interests of the child shall be a primary consideration."[63]

55 *Id.* at 82.

56 *See* Allen Buchanan & Dan Brock, *Deciding for Others: The Ethics of Surrogate Decision Making* 247 (1989) (discussing the two types of interests in the context of infants).

57 Mnookin, *supra* note 51, at 260.

58 Comm'n on Human Rights, 'Question on a Convention on the Rights of the Child', at 2-3, U.N. Doc. E/CN.4/1349 (Jan. 17, 1980).

59 Sharon Detrick, *A Commentary on the United Nations Convention on the Rights of the Child* 90 (1999) (citing U.N. Doc. E/CN.4/L.1575, para. 20 (1981)).

60 Somalia is the other, and it does not have a Government. It is said you should be known by the company you keep!

61 *See* Comm'n on Human Rights, 45th Sess., Item 13, paras. 117, 126, E/CN.4/1989/48 (Mar. 2, 1989).

62 UN Convention on the Rights of the Child, *supra* note 34, art. 18.

63 There is a clear preference for the nuclear family structure implicit in Article 18. *See* Prances Olsen, 'Children's Rights: Some Feminist Approaches to the United Nations Convention on the Rights of the Child', in *Children, Rights and the Law* 192, 199 (Philip Alston, Stephen Parker and John Seymour eds., 1992) (noting that the provision makes both parents responsible for children).

What is meant by "best interests," or at least what the UN Committee on the Rights of the Child (the Committee) believes it means, can be understood by examining its reports on the practices of States Parties. The Committee condemns corporal punishment, whether within the family, at schools, or in institutions, as not being in the child's best interests as addressed in both Article 19 and Article 3. Thus, in relation to Australia, the Committee expressed its concern about the lack of prohibition of corporal punishment "however light" in schools, at home, and in institutions.[64] This, it said, contravened many provisions in the Convention, including Article 3. In relation to Canada, the Committee recommended that physical punishment of children in families be prohibited: it cited both Articles 3 and 19.[65] In relation to the Czech Republic, the Committee was "concerned that corporal punishment [was] still used by parents and that internal school regulations do not contain provisions explicitly prohibiting corporal punishment, in conformity with articles 3, 19 and 28 of the Convention."[66] And the Committee has consistently criticized the United Kingdom for its refusal to ban corporal punishment by parents. In 1995, it suggested that the United Kingdom undertake "additional educational campaigns"

> in connection with the child's right to physical integrity... and in the light of the best interests of the child.... Such measures would help to change societal attitudes towards the use of physical punishment in the family and foster acceptance of the legal prohibition of the physical punishment of children.[67]

Since then, laws have been passed in England and Wales effecting a compromise: reasonable chastisement remains a defence only to common assaults on children (in lay language, when a mark is not left), but not to occasioning actual bodily harm.[68] The Committee, unsurprisingly, has

---

64 Comm. on the Rights of the Child, *Concluding Observations: Australia,* para. 15, U.N. Doc. CRC/C/15/Add.79 (Oct. 10, 1997).

65 Comm. on the Rights of the Child, 'Concluding Observations: Canada', para. 25, U.N. Doc. CRC/C/15/Add.37 (June 20, 1995).

66 Comm. on the Rights of the Child, 'Concluding Observations: Czech Republic', para. 18, U.N. Doc. CRC/C/15/Add.81 (Oct. 27, 1997).

67 Comm. on the Rights of the Child, 'Concluding Observations: United Kingdom of Great Britain and Northern Ireland', para. 31, U.N. Doc. CRC/C/15/Add.34 (Feb. 15, 1995).

68 *See, e.g.,* Children Act, 2004, c. 31, para. 58 (Eng., Wales).

condemned this half-way solution. And rightly so: the message it gives to parents is that they may hit their children.[69]

There are many other examples of the Committee's recommendations regarding corporal punishment, including those made to Fiji,[70] Ghana,[71] Ireland,[72] Jamaica,[73] Korea,[74] Kyrgyzstan,[75] Lebanon,[76] Senegal,[77] and Togo.[78] In the case of Ghana, the Committee referred specifically to caning (recommending that it should be "withdrawn from the Teachers Handbook").[79]

69 This was the evidence in Canada (which has effected a similar compromised measure). *See* Joan Durrant, Nadine Sigvaldason and Lisa Bednar, 'What Did the Canadian Public Learn from the 2004 Supreme Court Decision on Physical Punishment?', 16 *Int'l J. Child. Rts.* 229, 242-43 (2008) (study results indicated that a majority of parents focused on right to use force, not the limitations on the use of force, after Canada's Supreme Court issue a ruling on the corporal punishment).

70 Comm. on the Rights of the Child, 'Concluding Observations: Fiji', para. 16, U.N. Doc. CRC/C/15/Add.89 (June 24, 1998).

71 71. Comm. on the Rights of the Child, 'Concluding Observations: Ghana', para. 36, U.N. Doc. CRC/C/15/Add.73 (June 18, 1997).

72 Comm. on the Rights of the Child, 'Concluding Observations: Ireland', para. 16, U.N. Doc. CROC/15/Add.85 (Feb. 4, 1998).

73 Comm. on the Rights of the Child, 'Concluding Observations: Jamaica', para. 7, U.N. Doc. CRC/C/15/Add.32 (Feb. 15, 1995); Comm. on the Rights of the Child, 'Concluding Observations: Jamaica', para. 33, U.N. Doc. CRC/C/15/Add.210 (July 4, 2003).

74 Comm. on the Rights of the Child, 'Concluding Observations: Democratic People's Republic of Korea', para. 13, U.N. Doc. CRC/C/15/Add.88 (June 5, 1998); Comm. on the Rights of the Child, 'Concluding Observations: Republic of Korea', para. 38, U.N. Doc. CRC/015/Add.197 (Mar. 18, 2003).

75 Comm. on the Rights of the Child, 'Concluding Observations: Kyrgyzstan', para. 40, U.N. Doc. CRC/C/15/Add.127 (Aug. 9, 2000).

76 Comm. on the Rights of the Child, 'Concluding Observations: Lebanon', paras. 38-39, U.N. Doc. CRC/C/15/Add.169 (Mar. 21, 2002).

77 Comm. on the Rights of the Child, 'Concluding Observations: Senegal', para. 24, U.N. Doc. CRC/C/15/Add.44 (Nov. 27, 1995).

78 Comm. on the Rights of the Child, 'Concluding Observations: Togo', para. 40, U.N. Doc. CRC/C/15/Add.83 (Oct. 10, 1997).

79 Comm. on the Rights of the Child, para. 36, *supra* note 71. It is surprising that caning is not specifically cited in the reports of other countries where it remains prevalent. The Committee has also issued General Comment No. 8 on the topic of corporal punishment. *See infra* VI.

## III. The UN Convention on the Rights of the Child: Provisions and Interpretation

### A. *Article 19*

The UN Convention on the Rights of the Child is the first treaty to address directly the protection of children from violence. It requires the 193 States Parties to take

> all appropriate legislative, administrative, social and educational measures to protect the child from all forms of physical or mental violence, injury or abuse, neglect or negligent treatment, maltreatment or exploitation including sexual abuse, while in the care of parent(s), legal guardian(s) or any other person who has the care of the child.[80]

Although the Article imposes an obligation on States Parties, understood together with the objects and purposes of the Convention, it gives children the right to be protected against abuse and neglect, as defined in the Article. When the Article was being drafted, the Informal NGO *Ad Hoc* Group on the Drafting of the Convention on the Rights of the Child wanted a fuller exposition of what the Article was targeting. It proposed,

> [A]ll acts or omissions that are, or are likely to be, detrimental to the child's present or future welfare and development, including cruelty, injury, exploitation, discrimination and humiliating or degrading treatment, whether physical, psychological, emotional or sexual in nature, perpetrated by the child's parent(s), guardian or any other individual or social welfare institution responsible for the child's well-being.[81]

Such *travaux preparatoires* make evident the emphasis of Article 19 on prevention.[82] That is why Article 19(1) refers to "social and educational measures," and why Article 19(2) requires "effective procedures for the establishment of social programmes to provide necessary support for the

---

80 U.N. Convention on the Rights of the Child, *supra* note 34, art. 19. There is a good analysis of Article 19 in Detrick, *supra* note 59, at 318-29.

81 Detrick, *supra* note 59, at 321.

82 *See generally* Comm'n on Human Rights, 'Report of the Working Group on a Draft Convention on the Rights of the Child', Annex 11, U.N. Doc. E/CN.4/1983/62 (Mar. 23, 1983) (and papers cited therein).

child and for those who have the care of the child, as well as for other forms of prevention."

Article 19 does not specifically refer to corporal punishment, but the general guidelines for periodic reports do. States Parties are requested to indicate in their reports to the Committee all appropriate legislative, administrative, social, and educational measures taken for the implementation of Article 19.[83] In particular, reports must note

> [w]hether legislation (criminal and/or family law) includes a prohibition of all forms of physical and mental violence, including corporal punishment, deliberate humiliation, injury, abuse, neglect or exploitation, *inter alia* within the family, in foster or other forms of care, and in public or private institutions, such as penal institutions and schools.[84]

Other matters requested include complaint procedures, "educational and other measures adopted to promote positive and non-violent forms of discipline," and "awareness-raising campaigns to prevent situations of violence, abuse or negligence and to strengthen the system for the child[']s protection."[85]

And Article 19(2) requests that States Parties provide information in their reports on "system[s] of mandatory reporting for professional groups working with and for children…; confidential help lines, advice or counselling for child victims of violence, abuse or neglect…; [and] special training provided for relevant professionals."[86]

### B. *General Comment No. 8*

The Committee on the Rights of the Child has adopted a number of General Comments that pertain to corporal punishment. Among them is General Comment No. 8, entitled *The Right to Protection from Corporal Punishment and Other Cruel or Degrading Forms of Punishment.*[87] It aims

---

83 Comm. on the Rights of the Child, 'General Guidelines for Periodic Reports', paras. 88, 92, U.N. Doc. CRC/C/58, 22-23 (Nov. 20, 1996).

84 *Id.* para. 88.

85 *Id.*

86 *Id.* para. 89.

87 The comment pertains specifically to Articles 19, 28(2), and 37, inter alia. It was adopted by the Committee at its forty-second session in Geneva in May and June of 2006. Comm. on the Rights of the Child, 'General Comment No. 8: The Right of the Child to Protection from Corporal Punishment and Other Cruel or Degrading

"to highlight the obligation of all States Parties to move quickly to prohibit and eliminate all corporal punishment and all other cruel or degrading forms of punishment of children and to outline the legislative and other awareness raising and educational measures that states must take."[88] It emphasizes eliminating corporal punishment of children as "a key strategy for reducing and preventing all forms of violence in societies."[89]

The General Comment defines corporal punishment as

> any punishment in which physical force is used and intended to cause some degree of pain or discomfort, however light. Most involves hitting ("smacking", "slapping", "spanking") children, with the hand or with an implement – whip, stick, belt, shoe, wooden spoon, etc. But it can also involve, for example, kicking, shaking or throwing children, scratching, pinching, burning, scalding or forced ingestion (for example, washing children's mouths out with soap or forcing them to swallow hot spices). ... [C]orporal punishment is invariably degrading. In addition, there are other nonphysical forms of punishment which are also cruel and degrading, and thus incompatible with the Convention. These include, for example, punishment which belittles, humiliates, denigrates, scapegoats, threatens, scares or ridicules the child.[90]

The Committee accepts that children need discipline in the form of "necessary guidance and direction."[91] This is essential for the healthy growth of children. But such guidance is different, it rightly maintains, from violence and from humiliation.[92] The Committee also accepts that it may be necessary to intervene physically to protect children from harm: pulling a child back when he or she is running into the road or towards a fire.[93] But then, as John Stuart Mill noted in a famous example about an unsafe bridge, such actions are justifiable in the case of adults, too.[94]

---

Forms of Punishment', U.N. Doc. CRC/C/GC/8 (Mar. 2, 2007), *available at* www2.ohchr.org/english/bodies/crc/comments.htm.

88 *Id.* para. 2.

89 *Id.* para. 3.

90 *Id.* para. 11.

91 *Id.* para. 13.

92 *See Id.*

93 *Id.* paras. 14-15.

94 John Stuart Mill, *On Liberty* 158 (David Bromwich & George Kateb eds., Yale Univ. Press 2003) (1859).

The Committee recognizes the right of every person to others' respect for his or her dignity and physical integrity, and equal protection under the law:[95] "The dignity of each and every individual is the fundamental guiding principle of international human rights law."[96] This right, found, the Committee notes, in the original International Bill of Human Rights, is expanded upon in the Convention:

> There is no ambiguity: "all forms of physical or mental violence" does not leave room for any level of legalized violence against children. Corporal punishment and other cruel or degrading forms of punishment are forms of violence and the state must take all appropriate legislative, administrative, social and educational measures to eliminate them.[97]

The Committee responds to those who say that neither Article 19 nor Article 28 on school discipline refers to corporal punishment. In its view, this omission does not detract from the state's obligation to prohibit and eliminate corporal punishment. The Committee argues that the Convention (like all human-rights instruments) is "a living instrument."[98] Its interpretation therefore develops over time:

> In the 17 years since the Convention was adopted, the prevalence of corporal punishment of children in their homes, schools and other institutions has become more visible, through the reporting process under the Convention and through research and advocacy by, among others, national human rights institutions and non-governmental organizations (NGOs).

Once visible, it is clear that the practice directly conflicts with the equal and inalienable rights of children to respect for their human dignity and physical integrity. The distinct nature of children, their initial dependent and developmental state, their unique human potential as well as their vulnerability, all demand the need for more, rather than less, legal and other protection from all forms of violence.[99]

---

95 Comm. on the Rights of the Child, *supra* note 87, para. 16.
96 *Id.*
97 *Id.* para. 18.
98 *Id.* para. 20.
99 *Id.* paras. 20-21.

Even if the process of eliminating corporal punishment is an evolutionary one, the Committee emphasizes that it is "an immediate and unqualified obligation of States Parties."[100]

The Committee briefly addresses some arguments of the pro-corporal punishment lobby – for example, that "reasonable" or "moderate" corporal punishment is in the best interests of the child.[101] The Committee replies,

> [I]nterpretation of a child's best interests must be consistent with the whole Convention, including the obligation to protect children from all forms of violence and the requirement to give due weight to the child's views; it cannot be used to justify practices... which conflict with the child's human dignity and right to physical integrity.[102]

Second, proponents argue that how children are raised is up to parents, not the state.[103] The Convention fully upholds the importance of the family unit[104] a view that nonetheless treats as unproblematic those decisions that have been taken from parents, such as whether to educate their children.[105] In time, the decision not to hit a child will fall into an equally unproblematic zone. Third, the Committee recognizes that some justify the practice of corporal punishment in terms of their interpretation of religious teaching.[106] The Committee responds, "[The] practice of a religion or belief must be consistent with respect for others' human

---

100 *Id.* para. 22.

101 Comm. on the Rights of the Child, *supra* note 87, para. 26.

102 *Id.*

103 This view is commonly espoused by writers who take a negative view of children's rights. *See, e.g.*, Joseph Goldstein, Anna Freud, Sonja Goldstein & Albert Solnit, *The Best Interests of the Child* (1996); Martin Guggenheim, *What's Wrong With Children's Rights* (2005). My critiques of these books can be found respectively at Michael Freeman, 'The Best Interests of the Child? Is the Best Interests of the Child in the Best Interests of Children?', 11 *J.L. Pol'y & Fam.* 360, 360-88 (1997), and Michael Freeman, 'What's Right with Rights for Children', 2 *Int'l J.L. in Context* 89, 89-98 (2006).

104 *See* U.N. Convention on the Rights of the Child, *supra* note 34, art. 5.

105 *But see Wisconsin* v. *Yoder*, 406 U.S. 205, 232 (1972) (The "primary role of the parents in the upbringing of their children is now established beyond debate as an enduring American tradition" per Chief Justice Burger). *See also* M.D.A. Freeman, *The Rights and Wrongs of Children* 244-77 (1983) (discussing the role of the state in child-rearing decisions).

106 *But see* Greven, *supra* note 2 (deconstructing the arguments of the religious lobby by a careful examination of the texts and history).

dignity and physical integrity."[107] Further, "[the] freedom to practise one's religion or belief may be legitimately limited in order to protect the fundamental rights and freedoms of others."[108]

The Committee argues the need for legal reform. Such reform has taken place in at least twenty-nine countries to date.[109] The Committee advocates that all provisions that allow a "reasonable" degree of corporal punishment (whether in legislation or case law) should be repealed. But it is necessary to go beyond this, according to the Committee. Countries should include an "explicit prohibition" to make it "absolutely clear that it is as unlawful to hit or 'smack' or 'spank' a child as to do so to an adult, and that the criminal law on assault does apply equally to such violence, regardless of whether it is termed 'discipline' or 'reasonable correction'."[110]

But legal reform is not enough:

> [I]t is essential that the applicable sectoral legislation – e.g. family law, education law, law relating to all forms of alternative care and justice systems, employment law – clearly prohibits its use in the relevant settings. In addition, it is valuable if professional codes of ethics and guidance for teachers, carers and others, and also the rules or charters of institutions emphasize the illegality of corporal punishment and other cruel or degrading forms of punishment.[111]

The Committee stresses that law reform must be accompanied by awareness-raising, guidance, and training. The goal of the elimination of corporal punishment of children is not to put parents in prison, but to prevent its happening: "to prevent violence against children by changing attitudes and practice, underlining children's right to equal protection and providing an unambiguous foundation for child protection and for the promotion of positive, non-violent and participatory forms of child-

---

107 Comm. on the Rights of the Child, *supra* note 87, para. 29.

108 *Id.*

109 Children Are Unbeatable! Newsletter (April 2010), http://www.childrenareunbeatable.org.uk/ pdfs/newsletters/CAU-Issue02.pdf. A further twenty-four have made public commitments to full prohibition or are actually considering draft legislation to achieve this. *See* Global Initiative to End All Corporal Punishment of Children, www.endcorporalpunishment.org (last visited Oct. 11, 2009) (collection of the latest data country-by-country). Since the above works were written Poland and Lichtenstein have passed anti-spanking legislation and Tunisia and Kenya have become the first African countries to make it unlawful to hit children.

110 Comm. on the Rights of the Child, *supra* note 87, para. 34.

111 *Id.* para. 35.

rearing."[112] The Committee stresses that prohibition does not mean "all cases of corporal punishment of children by parents should lead to prosecution...."[113] Such cases need appropriate investigation to ensure protection from "significant harm," but the aim is to ensure that parents do not use "violent or other cruel or degrading punishment through supportive and educational, not punitive, interventions."[114] Effective prohibition requires "comprehensive awareness-raising of children's right to protection and of the laws that reflect this right."[115]

### C. *General Comment No. 1*

General Comment No. 8 was not the first one relevant to the corporal punishment issue. Five years earlier, in 2001, the Committee adopted its first General Comment concerned with violence against children. "Aims of Education," developing the norm now found in Article 29(1) of the UN Convention on the Rights of the Child, stressed that "children do not lose their human rights by passing through the school gates."[116] Education must be provided in a way that respects "the inherent dignity of the child"[117] and that "respects the strict limits on discipline... in Article 28(2) and promotes non-violence in school."[118] The Committee emphasized its repeated belief that corporal punishment does not respect the "inherent dignity of the child."[119] It continued, "Compliance with the values recognized in Article 29(1) clearly requires that schools be child-friendly in the fullest sense of that term and that they be consistent in all respects with the dignity of the child."[120]

### D. *The Committee's Jurisprudence on Corporal Punishment*

The Committee has been evaluating reports of States Parties since 1993, and in this period of sixteen years it has built up a substantial jurisprudence. This includes a body of comments on the States Parties' implementation (or nonimplementation) of Article 19. The Committee has ex-

112 *Id.* para. 38.
113 *Id.* para. 40.
114 *Id.*
115 *Id.* para. 45.
116 Comm. on the Rights of the Child, 'General Comment No. 1: The Aims of Education', para. 8, U.N. Doc. CRC/GC/200111 (Apr. 17, 2001), *available at* http://www2.ohchr.org/english/bodies/crc/ comments.htm.
117 *Id.*
118 *Id.*
119 *Id.*
120 *Id.*

pressed continuing concern at the persisting legal and social acceptance of corporal punishment of children in their homes, schools, and other institutions. It has consistently recommended prohibiting all corporal punishment.

Before these reports emerged, a few countries had already outlawed corporal punishment of children. Sweden was the first, in 1979,[121] and a number of other countries have done the same since the Committee began its scrutiny.[122] But in most countries corporal punishment is firmly entrenched, despite the Convention, the General Comments, and the Committee's responses to States Parties' reports. For those latter countries the process of their reporting and the Committee's responses has been one of give and take. When the Committee examined the United Kingdom's report in 1995, it was concerned about the law on reasonable chastisement within the family. It referred to "the imprecise nature of the expression of reasonable chastisement," which could be "interpreted in a subjective and arbitrary manner."[123] The Committee recommended that

> physical punishment of children in families be prohibited in the light of the provisions set out in Articles 3 and 19.... In connection with the child's right to physical integrity, as recognized by the Convention, namely in its articles 19, 28, 29 and 37, and in the light of the best interests of the child, the Committee suggests that the [United Kingdom] consider the possibility of undertaking additional education campaigns. Such measures would help to change societal attitudes towards the use of physical punishment in the family and foster the acceptance of the legal prohibition of the physical punishment of children.[124]

---

121 In 1979 Sweden added a provision to its Parenthood and Guardianship Code which (now) reads: "Children are entitled to care, security and a good upbringing. Children are to be treated with respect for their person and individuality and may not be subjected to corporal punishment or any other humiliating treatment." Föräldrabalk [FB] [Parents Code] 6:1 (Swed.). There are many accounts (in English) of the Swedish law and experience. *See, e.g.*, Susan H. Bitensky, *Corporal Punishment of Children – A Human Rights Violation* 154-60 (2006); *see also* Joan E. Durrant, 'Legal Reform and Attitudes Towards Physical Punishment in Sweden', 11 *Int'l J. Child. Rts.* 147, 147-73 (2003).

122 By now twenty-nine countries have outlawed corporal punishment of children by parents. *See* Children Are Unbeatable! Newsletter, *supra* note 109.

123 Comm. on the Rights of the Child, *supra* note 67, para. 16.

124 *Id.* para. 32.

The Committee was also concerned that private schools (anomalously called "public schools" in the United Kingdom) were still permitted to cane pupils, in clear breach of Article 28(2).[125] Shortly after its recommendation concerning corporal punishment in the context of families, the Committee recommended prohibition of corporal punishment in all private schools. There is no corporal punishment permitted in U.K. schools today.[126]

The Committee looked at the United Kingdom again in 2002.[127] Though pleased about the progress in schools, it "deeply regret[ted] that [the United Kingdom] persists in retaining the defence of 'reasonable chastisement' and has taken no significant action towards prohibiting all corporal punishment of children in the family."[128] It opined that the proposals – later implemented[129] – "to limit rather than to remove the 'reasonable chastisement' defence [did] not comply with the principles and provisions of the Convention…, particularly since they constitute a serious violation of the dignity of the child."[130] And, of course, the Committee observed that the proposals "suggest some forms of corporal punishment are acceptable, thereby undermining educational measures to promote positive and non-violent discipline."[131] It recommended removing the defence of reasonable chastisement and prohibiting "all corporal punishment in the family and any other contexts not covered by existing legislation," and promoting "positive, participatory and non-violent forms of discipline and respect for children's equal right to human dignity and physical integrity…."[132]

The Committee's third examination of the United Kingdom was in 2008.[133] It noted amendments to legislation that restricted the application of the reasonable chastisement defence, but expressed continued

125 *Id.* para. 16.

126 *See* School Standards and Framework Act, 1998, c. 31, § 131 (Eng.) (barring the use of corporal punishment in any school). Anecdotal evidence suggests it is still practiced "unofficially."

127 Comm. on the Rights of the Child, 'Concluding Observations: United Kingdom of Great Britain and Northern Ireland', U.N. Doc. CRC/C/15/Add.188 (Oct. 9, 2002).

128 *Id.* para. 36.

129 *See* Children Act, *supra* note 68, § 58.

130 Comm. on the Rights of the Child, *supra* note 127, para. 37.

131 *Id.*

132 *Id.* para. 38.

133 Comm. on the Rights of the Child, 'Concluding Observations: United Kingdom of Great Britain and Northern Ireland,' U.N. Doc. CRC/C/GBR/Co/4 (Oct. 20, 2008).

concern that the defence had not been removed.[134] It welcomed the commitment of the National Assembly in Wales to prohibit corporal punishment in the home, but recognized that the Assembly lacks the power to do this.[135] It recommended that the United Kingdom prohibit "as a matter of priority" all corporal punishment in the family.[136] The other recommendations reiterated those made in 2002.[137]

It is worth comparing the United Kingdom and Spain. Both are members of the Council of Europe and, as of the writing of this article, both have governments that are left of centre.[138] Spain, however, is only thirty-five years out of Fascism. When Spain's first report was examined in 1994, the Committee was concerned "at the wording of Article 154 of the Spanish Civil Code[,] which provides that parents 'may administer punishment to their children reasonably and in moderation,' and which may be interpreted to allow for actions in contradiction with Article 19 of the Convention."[139] When it examined Spain's Second Report in 2002, the Committee said it "deeply regret[ted]" that this law had still not been revised."[140] It reiterated its previous recommendation to amend Article 154 in order to delete the reference to reasonable chastisement.[141]

It further recommended the prohibition of all forms of violence including corporal punishment and awareness campaigns to promote alternative forms of discipline in families.[142] Spain has now implemented these recommendations and is one of the latest countries to make corporal punishment in families unlawful.[143]

It is possible to find the Committee's criticisms of corporal punishment of children in families, at school, and in institutions in its responses

---

134 *Id.* para. 40.

135 *Id.*

136 *Id.* para. 42(a).

137 *Id.* para. 42. The Committee added: the United Kingdom "should use these recommendations as a tool for action in civil society and in particular with the involvement of children, to ensure that every child is protected from all forms of physical, sexual and mental violence...." *Id.* para. 43.

138 In the United Kingdom's case this may be justifiably contested, but this is bow the Brown Government would identify itself.

139 Comm. on the Rights of the Child, 'Concluding Observations: Spain', para. 10, U.N. Doc. CRC/C/15/Add.28(oct. 24, 1994).

140 Comm, on the Rights of the Child, 'Concluding Observations: Spain', para. 30, U.N. Doc. CRC/C/15/Add.185 (June 13, 2002).

141 *Id.* para. 31.

142 *Id.* paras. 31(a), 31(b).

143 It did so in 2007, as indicated in Article 154 of the Spanish Civil Code. C.C. art. 154.

to reports of at least fifty-seven other countries.[144] A few of the criticized countries have since outlawed corporal punishment by parents: Bulgaria,[145] Cyprus,[146] Moldova,[147] the Netherlands,[148] New Zealand[149] and Romania.[150] One of the first countries to make it unlawful for parents to hit children, Finland[151] is under scrutiny because "the Committee is concerned at the number of cases of violence against children, including sexual abuse in their homes."[152] Several other countries are said to

144 *See* 2 Cynthia Price Cohen, *Jurisprudence on the Rights of the Child* 1565-780 (2005) (summarizing the Committee's criticisms of each country's implementation of Articles 19 and 39).

145 Bulgaria was criticized in Comm. on the Rights of the Child, *Concluding Observations: Bulgaria,* para. 30, U.N. Doc. CRC/C/15/Add.66 (Jan 24, 1997). It passed legislation in 2000. *See* Bitensky, *supra* note 121, at 197; *see also* Velina Todorova, 'Children's Rights in Bulgaria After the End of Communism' 17 *Int'lJ. Child. Rts.* 623, 630 (2009).

146 Criticized in 2003, Comm. on the Rights of the Child, 'Concluding Observations: Cyprus', para. 46, U.N. Doc. CRC/C/15/Add.205 (July 2, 2003). This criticism was strange, though, for Cyprus had already passed its Prevention of Violence in the Family and Protection of Victims Law (in June 1994) (now Law 119 (I) of 2000), *see* Bitensky, *supra* note 121, at 174-80.

147 Comm. on the Rights of the Child, *Concluding Observations:* 'Republic of Moldova', para. 31, U.N. Doc. CRC/C/15/Add.192 (Oct. 31, 2002). It passed legislation in 2008. Global Initiative to End All Corporal Punishment of Children, States with Full Abolition, http://www.endcorporalpunishment.org/pages/progress/prohib_states.html (last visited Apr. 3, 2010).

148 Comm. on the Rights of the Child, 'Concluding Observations: Netherlands', para. 17, U.N. Doc. CRC/C/15/Add.114 (Oct. 26, 1999) (exhorting the Netherlands to come into line with developments in other European countries). The Netherlands passed legislation in 2007. Global Initiative to End All Corporal Punishment of Children, *supra* note 147.

149 Comm. on the Rights of the Child, 'Concluding Observations: New Zealand', para. 16, U.N. Doc. CRC/C/15/Add.71 (Jan. 24, 1997). It passed legislation in 2007. Global Initiative to End All Corporal Punishment of Children, States with Full Abolition, *supra* note 147. New Zealand was the first English-speaking country to effect such a reform, but a threatened referendum might undo it. The referendum is being conducted as this is being written (July 2009). Eighty-seven percent of those voting opposed the ban (children did not, of course, have the vote). Voting results are available at http://www.electionresults.govt.nz/2009_citizens_referendum/2009_referendum_results.html.

150 Comm. on the Rights of the Child, 'Concluding Observations: Romania', para. 42, U.N. Doc. CRC/C/15/Add.199 (Mar. 18, 2003). It passed legislation in 2004. Global Initiative to End All Corporal Punishment of Children, *supra* note 147.

151 Parental corporal punishment ceased to be lawful in 1983 (though there was an attempt to achieve this even earlier in 1969). Bitensky, *supra* note 121, at 161.

152 Comm. on the Rights of the Child, 'Concluding Observations: Finland', para. 39, U.N. Doc. CRC/C/15/Add.132 (Oct. 16, 2000).

have laws targeting corporal punishment, though there is real doubt as to whether this is true. Haiti's law is said to date from 2001,[153] and Zambia's is said to derive from a Constitutional Court case in 1998.[154] Many countries in which corporal punishment is known to be prevalent, for example in Anglophone Africa and in the Caribbean, are not cited in the Committee's jurisprudence. Trinidad and Tobago are the only Caribbean countries to be criticized,[155] though violence against children (not specifically corporal punishment) is condemned in a report on Jamaica.[156] The African countries criticized by the Committee are Algeria[157] Cameroon,[158] Egypt,[159] Guinea Bissau,[160] Libya,[161] Malawi,[162] Morocco,[163]

---

153 Comm. on the Rights of the Child, 'Concluding Observations: Haiti', para. 36, U.N. Doc. CRC/C/15/Add.202 (Mar. 18, 2003) (The August 2001 Act prohibiting corporal punishment is "welcome[d]" by the Committee.). I have been unable to verify the existence of this Act, but the Global Initiative, *see supra* note 109, makes no reference to it, nor does Bitensky, *supra* note 121).

154 *See* Comm. on the Rights of the Child, 'Concluding Observations: Zambia', para. 30, CRC/C/15/Add.206 (July 2, 2003) (citing the Constitutional Court case as *John Banda* v. *the People,* HPA/6/1998). The Committee comments that corporal punishment is still practiced and accepted in schools, families, and in care- and juvenile-detention facilities, and recommends legislation. *Id.* paras. 30-31.

155 Comm. on the Rights of the Child, 'Concluding Observations: Trinidad and Tobago', para. 31, U.N. Doc. CRC/C/15/Add.82 (Oct. 10, 1997).

156 Comm. on the Rights of the Child, 'Concluding Observations: Jamaica', paras. 32-33, U.N. Doc. CRC/C/15/Add.210 (July 4, 2003).

157 Comm. on the Rights of the Child, 'Concluding Observations: Algeria', paras. 21, 35, U.N. Doc. CRC/C/15/Add. 76 (June 18, 1997).

158 Comm. on the Rights of the Child, 'Concluding Observations: Cameroon', para. 41, U.N. Doc. CRC/C/15/Add.164 (Nov. 6, 2001).

159 Comm. on the Rights of the Child, 'Concluding Observations: Egypt', paras. 37-38, U.N. Doc. CRC/C/15/Add.145 (Feb. 21, 2001).

160 Comm. on the Rights of the Child, 'Concluding Observations: Guinea Bissau', para. 30 U.N. Doc. CRC/C/15/Add.177 (June 13, 2002).

161 Comm. on the Rights of the Child, 'Concluding Observations: Libyan Arab Jamahiriya', para. 29, U.N. Doc. CRC/C/15/Add. 84 (Feb. 4, 1998); Comm. on the Rights of the Child, 'Concluding Observations: Libyan Arab Jamahiriya', para. 34(b), U.N. Doc. CRC/C/15/Add.209 (July 4, 2003).

162 Comm. on the Rights of the Child, 'Concluding Observations: Malawi', para. 33, U.N. Doc. CRC/C/15/Add.174 (Apr. 2, 2002).

163 Comm. on the Rights of the Child, 'Concluding Observations: Morocco', para. 42, U.N. Doc. CRC/C/15/Add.211 (July 10, 2003).

Mozambique,[164] Niger,[165] Sudan,[166] (where apparently there has been a move against corporal punishment at least in the south of the country)[167] Togo,[168] and Zimbabwe.[169] Only two of these countries are Anglophone: reference has already been made to Ghana,[170] but, for example, nothing appears in the reports on Nigeria or any of the East African nations. There is no report on Somalia (because it has not ratified the Convention) nor on the United States for the same reason. As far as the developing world is concerned, it may be that the problems of children are greater than being beaten by their parents. But, if this is the view, it would be short-sighted. Once the nail is stuck in the coffin of corporal punishment, the burial of child abuse and much else besides will be signalled.

## IV. The UN Secretary General's Study on Violence against Children

In 2001, on the recommendation of the Committee on the Rights of the Child, the UN General Assembly requested the UN Secretary General to undertake an in-depth investigation into violence against children and to put forward recommendations for consideration by member states to take appropriate action.[171] This led to the first comprehensive global study on violence against children.

The report on the investigation, by independent expert Paulo Sergio Pinheiro, notes that violence against children exists in every country

164 Comm. on the Rights of the Child, 'Concluding Observations: Mozambique', para. 38, U.N. Doc. CRC/C/15/Add.172 (Apr. 3, 2002).

165 Comm. on the Rights of the Child, 'Concluding Observations: Niger', para. 45, U.N. Doc. CRC/C/15/Add.179 (June 13, 2002).

166 Comm. on the Rights of the Child, 'Concluding Observations: Sudan', para. 35, U.N. Doc. CRC/C/15/Add.190 (Oct. 9, 2002).

167 *See* Daksha Kassan, 'The Protection of Children from All Forms of Violence-African Experiences,' in *Children's Rights in Africa: A Legal Perspective* 165, 176 (Julia Sloth-Nielsen ed., 2008).

168 Comm. on the Rights of the Child, 'Concluding Observations: Toga', para. 40, U.N. Doc. CRC/C/15/Add.83 (Oct. 10, 1997).

169 Comm. on the Rights of the Child, 'Concluding Observations: Zimbabwe', para. 18, U.N. Doc. CRC/C/15/Add.55 (June 7, 1996).

170 *See supra* text accompanying note 71.

171 Office of the UN High Commissioner for Human Rights, 'The United Nations Study on Violence Against Children', *available at* http://www2.ohchr.org/englishlbodies/crc/study.htm.

of the world.[172] Violence does not respect culture, class, education, income, or ethnic origin.[173] The report starts with the assertion that the study should "mark a turning point – an end to adult justification of violence against children, whether accepted as 'tradition' or disguised as 'discipline.' There can be no compromise in challenging violence against children."[174] It draws attention to General Comment No. 8 and calls for prohibition of all violence against children to be completed by 2009.[175] (It hardly need be said, but this has not happened.) It recognizes that

> eliminating and responding to violence against children is perhaps most challenging in the context of the family, considered by most as the most 'private' of private spheres.
>
> However, children's rights to life, survival, development, dignity and physical integrity do not stop at the door of the family home, nor do States' obligations to ensure these rights for children.[176]

In his report, Pinheiro makes a number of recommendations. He wants prevention to be prioritized.[177] He advocates that states and "civil society" should aim to "transform attitudes that condone or normalize violence against children, including stereotypical gender roles and discrimination, acceptance of corporal punishment and harmful traditional practices."[178] He emphasizes that children's rights should be understood, "including by children." He suggests public-information campaigns to "sensitize" the public about the harmful effects of violence on children.[179] He stresses, as well, the Convention's relationship to Article 12: states should "actively engage with children and respect their views in all aspects of prevention, response and the monitoring of violence against them, taking into account Article 12…."[180] And he flags the importance of child-friendly reporting systems and services.[181]

---

172 The Secretary-General, 'Report of the Independent Expert for the United Nations Study on Violence Against Children', para. 1, U.N. Doc. A/61/299 (Aug. 29, 2006), *available at* http://www.unicef.org/violencestudy/reports/SG_violencestudy_en.pdf.

173 *Id.*

174 *Id.* para. 2.

175 *Id.* para. 116.

176 *Id.* para. 38.

177 *Id.* para. 99.

178 The Secretary-General, *supra* note 172, para. 100.

179 *Id.*

180 *Id.* para. 103.

181 *Id.* para. 104.

Pinheiro's report makes more specific recommendations, too. Those relating to the family include the development of programs to "support parents and other care[givers] in their child-rearing role";[182] targeted programs for families in especially difficult circumstances, for example those caring for children with disabilities;[183] and gender-sensitive education programs focusing on nonviolent forms of discipline.[184] As far as schools are concerned, "all children must be able to learn free from violence, ... curricula should be rights based, and... schools [should] provide an environment in which attitudes condon[ing] violence can be changed and non-violent values and behaviour learned."[185] Pinheiro makes recommendations as well for the care and justice systems, the workplace, and the community.[186]

## V. United Nations Committees

### A. *The Human Rights Committee*

The Human Rights Committee monitors the implementation of the UN International Covenant on Civil and Political Rights. Article 7 of the Covenant states, "No one shall be subjected to torture or to cruel, inhuman or degrading treatment or punishment."[187] In 1992, the Human Rights Committee adopted General Comment No. 20 relating to this language, saying,

> The prohibition in Article 7 relates not only to acts that cause physical pain but also to acts that cause mental suffering to the victim. In the committee's view, moreover, the prohibition must extend to corporal punishment, including excessive chastisement offered as a punishment for a crime or as an educative or disciplinary measure. It is appropriate to emphasize in this regard that Article 7 protects pupils and patients in teaching and medical institutions.[188]

182 *Id.* para. 110 (a).

183 *Id.* para. 110 (b).

184 The Secretary-General, *supra* note 172, para. 110 (c).

185 *Id.* para. 111.

186 *Id.* paras. 112, 113, 114.

187 UN International Covenant on Civil and Political Rights art. 7, *opened for signature* Dec. 16, 1966, 999 U.N.T.S. 171.

188 Human Rights Comm., 'General Comment No. 20: Replaces General Comment 7 Concerning Prohibition of Torture and Cruel Treatment or Punishment (Art. 7)',

In its examination of the states' reports, the Committee has expressed concern about the use of corporal punishment and has recommended its prohibition in the family, schools, and penal systems.[189]

B. *The Committee on Economic, Social, and Cultural Rights*

The UN Committee on Economic, Social, and Cultural Rights monitors the implementation of the UN International Covenant on Economic, Social, and Cultural Rights. In 1999 it issued General Comment No. 13 on "The Right To Education,"[190] opining that

> corporal punishment is inconsistent with the fundamental guiding principle of international human rights law enshrined in the Preambles to the Universal Declaration of Human Rights and both Covenants: the dignity of the individual. Other aspects of school discipline may also be inconsistent with human dignity, such as public humiliation. Nor should any form of discipline breach other rights under the Covenant such as the right to food.[191]

A footnote explains that note had been taken of the "practice evolving elsewhere in the international human rights system."[192]

The Committee has also commented on corporal punishment within the family. Its concluding observations on the United Kingdom's periodic report in 2002 state:

> Given the principle of the dignity of the individual that provides the foundation for international human rights law... and in the light of Article 10.11 and 10.3 of the Covenant, the Committee recommends that the physical punishment of children in families be prohibited, in line with the recommendation of the Committee on the Rights of the Child.[193]

---

para. 5, U.N. Doc. HRI/GEN/1/ Rev. 9 (Mar. 10, 1992), *available at* http://www.unhchr.ch/tbs/doc.nsf/(Symbol)/6924291970754969c12563ed004c8ae5?Opendocument.

189 One example is Poland. Human Rights Comm., 'Concluding Observations: Poland', para. 25, U.N. Doc. CCPR/C/79/Add. 110 (July 29, 1999).

190 Comm. on Econ., Soc. and Cultural Rights, 'General Comment 13: The Right to Education (Art. 13)', U.N. Doc. E/C.12/1999/10 (Dec. 8, 1999).

191 *Id.* para. 41.

192 *Id.* n.18.

193 Comm. on Econ., Soc. and Cultural 'Rights, Concluding Observations: United Kingdom of Great Britain and Northern Ireland', para. 36, U.N. Doc. E/C.12/1/Add.79

### C. *The Committee against Torture*

The UN Committee against Torture, which monitors the implementation of the United Nations Convention against Torture and Other Cruel, Inhuman, and Degrading Treatment or Punishment, has also condemned the corporal punishment of children.[194] It may be argued that what constitutes torture and cruel, inhuman, and degrading treatment or punishment must be understood in relation to the person against whom it is perpetrated, and that what constitutes torture is different for adults and for children. The threshold for experiencing pain and the sensitivity to degrading punishment may be lower for children than for adults.

The Special Rapporteur on Torture of the UN Commission on Human Rights wrote that "any form of corporal punishment is contrary to the prohibition of torture and other cruel, inhuman or degrading treatment or punishment."[195] He called upon states to take adequate measures (in particular legal and educational ones) to ensure that "the right to physical and mental integrity of children is well protected in the public as in the private spheres."[196]

He drew attention to the condemnation of all corporal punishment by the Committee on the Rights of the Child, as well as by other treaty bodies.[197] And he welcomes information on measures taken to eradicate the practice of corporal punishment.[198]

---

(June 5, 2002). They made a similar recommendation to Malta in 2004, recommending that Malta consider an explicit prohibition on corporal punishment within the family. Comm. on Econ., Soc. and Cultural Rights, 'Concluding Observations: Malta', paras. 22, 40, U.N. Doc. E/C. 12.1/Add.101 (Dec. 14, 2004).

194 *See, e.g.,* Comm. Against Torture, 'Concluding Observations of the Committee Against Torture: Jordan', para. 177, U.N. Doc. A/50/44 (July 26, 1995); Comm. Against Torture, *Report of the Committee Against Torture,* para. 65(i), U.N. Doc. A/51/44 (July 9, 1996).

195 Special Rapporteur Against Torture, 'Report of Special Rapporteur Against Torture on Cruel, Inhuman or Degrading Treatment or Punishment, para. 28, delivered to the General Assembly', U.N. Doc. A/60/316 (Aug. 30, 2005).

196 Special Rapporteur Against Torture, 'Report of Special Rapporteur Against Torture on Cruel, Inhuman or Degrading Treatment', para. 26, U.N. Doc. E/CNA/2003/68 (Dec. 17, 2002).

197 *Id.*

198 *Id.*

## VI. The European Convention on Human Rights

The Statute of the Council of Europe requires every member state to "accept the principles of the rule of law and of the enjoyment by all persons within its jurisdiction of human rights and fundamental freedoms."[199] The Council of Europe's Convention for the Protection of Human Rights and Fundamental Freedoms was opened for signature in 1950 and entered into force in 1953.[200] Optional protocols have since been added. The Convention was the first international instrument to protect civil and political rights through a treaty binding on all member states. Victims may challenge breaches of their rights before the European Court of Human Rights.[201] The Committee of Ministers of the Council of Europe supervises governments' execution of judgments of the court. These are final and binding on the respondent state.[202]

A number of judgments of the European Court of Human Rights have found corporal punishment of children to be breaches of the European Convention on Human Rights. Most of these cases were brought against the United Kingdom. The earliest (in 1978) challenged judicial birching (then used in the Isle of Man).[203] Schools were the second object of scrutiny,[204] and most recently the court has examined corporal punishment within the family home.[205] The first case was that of *Tyrer* v. *United Kingdom.*[206] Tyrer was a fifteen-year-old birched after a conviction for assault. The judgment states,

> After waiting in a police station for a considerable time for a doctor to arrive [to certify he was fit to receive the punishment], Mr. Tyrer

199 Statute of the Council of Europe art. 3, *opened for signature* May 5, 1949, Europ. T.S. No. 001, *available at* http://conventions.coe.int/Treaty/en/Treaties/Html/001.htm.

200 Convention for the Protection of Human Rights and Fundamental Freedoms, *opened for signature* Apr. 11, 1950, Europ. T.S. No. 005, *available at* http://conventions.coe.int/Treaty/en/Treaties/ Html/005.htm.

201 Until 1998 there was a two-stage process, with cases first being examined by the European Commission on Human Rights and, only if a breach was revealed and no settlement could be reached between the applicant and the state, by the court.

202 Council of Europe, Committee of Ministers, 'Supervision of Judgments of the European Court of Human Rights', http://www.coe.int/t/cmlhumanRights_en.asp.

203 *Tyrer* v. *United Kingdom*, 26 Eur. Ct. H.R. (ser. A) (1978).

204 *See, e.g., Campbell and Cosans* v. *United Kingdom*, 48 Eur. Ct. H.R. (ser. A) (1982) (the first of the school-related cases).

205 Notably in *A.* v. *United Kingdom,* No. 35373/97, 27 Eur. H.R. Rep. 611 (1998).

206 *Supra* note 203.

> was birched late in the afternoon of the same day. His father and a doctor were present. The applicant was made to take down his trousers and underpants and bend over a table; he was held down by two policemen whilst a third administered the punishment, pieces of the birch breaking at the first stroke.[207]

The court found that the birching amounted to degrading punishment in breach of Article 3 of the Convention:

> [A]lthough the applicant did not suffer any severe or long lasting physical effects, his punishment – whereby he was treated as an object in the power of the authorities – constituted an assault on precisely that which it is one of the main purposes of Article 3... to protect, namely[,] a person's dignity and physical integrity.[208]

The court did not rule out the possibility that the punishment may have also had adverse psychological effects on Tyrer. Those inflicting the punishment were "total strangers" and Tyrer was also subjected to the "mental anguish of anticipating the violence he was to have inflicted upon him."[209]

In the 1980s many applications were brought concerning school corporal punishment in the United Kingdom. Two cases were brought by Scottish mothers and resulted in a 1982 judgment, *Campbell and Cosans v. United Kingdom*.[210] The mothers alleged that the corporal punishment used in their sons' schools – the use of a thick leather strap (a tawse) on the palm of the hand – was contrary to Article 3. Neither boy had in fact received corporal punishment; this allegation was therefore rejected.[211] But the Commission did find that the United Kingdom had failed to respect the parents' philosophical convictions against the use of corporal punishment. Article 2 of Protocol 1 to the Convention states, "No person shall be denied the right to education. In the exercise of any functions which it assumes in relation to education and to teaching, the State shall respect the right of parents to ensure such education and teaching in

207 *Id.* para. 10.
208 *Id.* para. 33.
209 *Id.*
210 *Supra* note 204.
211 *Id.* para. 25.

conformity with their own religious and philosophical convictions."[212] Since Jeffrey Cosans had, at fourteen, been suspended from school for a year for refusing to accept the tawse, the court found he had been denied his right to education. The court defined "philosophical convictions" as views relating to "a weighty and substantial aspect of human life and behaviour, namely the integrity of the person, the propriety or otherwise of the infliction of corporal punishment and the exclusion of the distress which the risk of such punishment entails."[213] The court found that the parents' philosophical convictions were compatible with human dignity and worthy of respect in a democratic society. They were therefore distinguishable from opinions "that might be held on other methods of discipline or on discipline in general."[214]

*Campbell and Cosans* did not establish that corporal punishment in itself is a violation of Article 3. It established only that a child's right to education includes the right to attend a school where he will not be subjected to corporal punishment if that is what the parents want and they can justify this in terms of their "philosophical convictions." The case did not further children's rights but rather those of their parents.

At roughly the same time, in an unnamed case, the U.K. government issued a circular stating that in certain circumstances the use of corporal punishment might amount to treatment contrary to Article 3 of the Convention.[215] The case centred on a girl of fourteen caned by her headmistress. The caning left welts and caused discomfort for a considerable period of time.[216] The case was settled-so there was no decision-but the circular remains important.

Numerous other cases in the United Kingdom challenged corporal punishment as a violation of Article 3 of the Convention, and most led to friendly settlements with *ex gratia* payments being made to families. The sums of money paid were relatively small. But these decisions led to the abolition of corporal punishment in state schools in the United Kingdom

---

212 Protocol to the Convention for the Protection of Human Rights and Fundamental Freedoms art. 2, *opened for signature* Mar. 31, 1952, Europ. T.S. No. 009, *available at* http://conventions.coe.int/ Treaty/en/Treaties/Html/0009.htm.

213 *Campbell and Cosans, supra* note 204, para. 36.

214 *Id.*

215 World Corporal Punishment Research, The Archive, http://www.corpun.com/uksc8202.htm (last visited Apr. 3, 2010).

216 *Id.*

in 1987.[217] Corporal punishment lingered for pupils in private schools not receiving state support in England and Wales until September 1999.[218] In Scotland it remained lawful until 2000;[219] in Northern Ireland it was finally abolished in 2003.[220]

But what of corporal punishment by parents? The landmark decision here is *A* v. *United Kingdom.*[221] The European Court of Human Rights found that corporal punishment with a garden cane of a boy of nine by his stepfather was a breach of Article 3. The stepfather had been prosecuted in an English court but had been acquitted on the grounds that the punishment satisfied the common-law test of "reasonable chastisement."[222] The European Court of Human Rights found the United Kingdom to be responsible because its domestic law, in allowing "reasonable chastisement," failed to provide children with adequate protection. The court ordered the United Kingdom to pay £10,000 compensation to the boy. The court ruled, "Children and other vulnerable individuals, in particular, are entitled to state protection, in the form of effective deterrence, against serious breaches of personal integrity...."[223] It cited, inter alia, the UN Convention on the Rights of the Child, Articles 19 and 37.[224] The court quoted the judge's instructions to the jury:

> What is it the prosecution must prove? If a man deliberately and unjustifiably hits another and causes some bodily injury, bruising or swelling will do, he is guilty of actual bodily harm. What does unjustifiably mean in the context of this case? It is a perfectly good defence that the alleged assault was merely the correcting of a child by its parent, in this case the stepfather, provided the correction be moderate in the manner, the instrument and the quantity of it. Or,

---

217 *See id.* (example of settlement). *See* Education (No. 2) Act, 1986, c. 61, para. 47 (Eng., Wales) (abolishing corporal punishment in publicly supported schools).

218 *See* School Standards and Framework Act, 1998, c. 31, § 131 (Eng., Wales) (abolishing corporal punishment in all schools).

219 *See* Standards in Scotland's Schools Act, 2000, (A.S.P. 6) § 16, *available at* http://www.hmso.gov. uk/legislation/scotland/acts2000/20000006.htm.

220 *See* Education and Libraries (Northern Ireland) Order, 2003, SI 2003/424 (N. Ir. 12), para. 36 (abolishing corporal punishment in all schools).

221 *Supra* note 205.

222 *Id.* para. 23. The defence is usually assumed to derive from Chief Justice Cockburn's judgment in *R* v. *Hopley,* (1860) 175 Eng. Rep. 1024 (Q.B.).

223 *A* v. *United Kingdom, supra* note 205, para. 22.

224 *Id.*

> put another way, reasonable. It is not for the defendant to prove it was lawful correction. It is for the prosecution to prove it was not.[225]

The execution of judgments of the European Court of Human Rights by the state government is supervised by the Committee of Ministers of the Council of Europe. It is still supervising the execution of *A* v. *United Kingdom.*[226] This is not surprising because legislation in England and Wales still permits a parent to hit a child. As recently as 2007, the Crown Prosecution Service in England and Wales[227] advised that if a parental assault on a child leads to an injury that "amounts to no more than reddening of the skin, and the injury is transient and trifling, a charge of common assault may be laid against the defendant for whom the reasonable chastisement defence remains available to parents or adults acting *in loco parentis.*"[228]

The law in England and Wales,[229] as in Canada,[230] effects a bungling compromise that satisfies no one. Abolitionists find it offensive, those who support corporal punishment do not know where the line has been drawn, the police are puzzled as to what their powers are, and social workers have no clear advice as to when intervention is appropriate.[231] The new law, according to one of England's local Safeguarding Children Boards, can be seen as "a licence to hit rather than promoting more constructive and positive alternatives."[232]

Another Safeguarding Children Board commented that there is no evidence that the new law has "improved the protection of children in any way. [It]... has caused general confusion. ... [I]t is virtually impossible

225 *Id.* para. 10.

226 Council of Europe, Committee of Ministers Publishes Decisions on the Execution of Judgments of the European Court of Human Rights, https://wcd.coe.intNiew-Doc.jsp?id=1455657&Site=DC (last visited Apr. 3, 2010).

227 The Service is in charge of criminal prosecutions.

228 *The Crown Prosecution Service, Reasonable Chastisement Report* (2007), *available at* http://www.cps.gov.uk/publications/research/chastisement.html#_Ol.

229 Children Act, 2004, c. 31, para. 58 (Eng., Wales).

230 *See* Anne McGillivray and Joan Durrant, 'Child Corporal Punishment: Violence, Rights and Law', in *Cruel But Not Unusual: Violence in Canadian Families* 177, 194 (Ramona Alaggia and Cathy Vine eds., 2006) (summarizing law in Canada and recommending reforms).

231 *See* Michael Freeman, *Understanding Family Law* 197-98 (2007).

232 *Children Are Unbeatable! Alliance, Briefing* (2009) 1, *available at* http:// www.rcpch.ac.uk/doc.aspx?id_Resource=4296.

to persuade/convince parents not to use physical chastisement."[233] And the British Association of Social Workers asks, "Are we teaching perpetrators to become more skilled in physical abuse, perfecting the art of not leaving bruises?"[234] In New Zealand, by contrast, where smacking was banned in June 2007, the Deputy Commissioner of Police reported (in December 2008) "a decline in the total number of child assault events," as well as "a corresponding decrease in the number of child assault events involving smacking and minor acts of physical discipline."[235] Nevertheless, the law in New Zealand remains under scrutiny and the legislation may be reversed.[236]

It was inevitable that some parents would object to legislation curtailing their liberty to use physical chastisement on their children. A challenge was mounted by Swedish parents belonging to a Protestant free church congregation in Stockholm, who believed that corporal punishment was right, necessary, and supported by their interpretation of Biblical texts.[237] But the European Commission in 1982 declared their application inadmissible.[238] The Commission concluded,

> The fact that no distinction is made between the treatment of children by their parents and the same treatment applied to an adult stranger cannot, in the commission's opinion, constitute "an interference" with respect for the applicant's private and family lives since the consequences of an assault are equated in both cases.... The Commission finds that the scope of the Swedish law of assault and molestation is a normal measure for the control of violence and that its extension to apply to the ordinary physical chastisement of

233 *Id.* at 3.

234 *Id.*

235 Rob Pope, *Third Review of Police Activity Following the Enactment of the Crimes (Substituted Section 59) Amendment Act* 2007 at 1 (2008), http://www.police.govt.nz/resources/2008/section-59-activity-review/section59_crime_ammendment_act_2007.pdf.

236 A portion of the New Zealand population demanded the change be reversed, and a referendum was held on the subject (in 2009). *See* 3 News, 'Anti-Smacking Debate Goes to Referendum' (June 15, 2009), http://www.3news.co.nz/Anti-smacking-debate-goes-to-referendum/tabid/423/articleID/108706/Default.aspx.

237 *Seven Individuals* v. *Sweden*, Application No. 8811179 (1982), *available by searching at* http://cmiskp.echr.coe.int/tkp197/search.asp?skin=hudoc-en.

238 *Id.*

> children by their parents is intended to protect potentially weak and vulnerable members of society.[239]

Another case was brought in England by Christian fundamentalist parents and teachers who alleged that the legislation which prohibited corporal punishment in private schools infringed their rights.[240] The parents wanted the teachers to be able to use corporal punishment, and the teachers believed the practice of corporal punishment was right. The House of Lords (the highest court in the United Kingdom, now replaced by the Supreme Court) accepted that the legislation did interfere with the right to religious freedom in Article 9 of the European Convention on Human Rights, but held that the interference could be justified.[241] Lord Nicholls explained, "Corporal punishment involves deliberately inflicting physical violence. The legislation is intended to protect children against the distress, pain and other harmful effects this infliction of physical violence may cause."[242] However, the same judge indicated that corporal punishment does not necessarily infringe a child's rights under Article 3 or Article 8. In other words, he did not rule out corporal punishment.[243] But Baroness Hale, who showed her full commitment to children's rights in a wonderful passage on the subject of her judgment, was not so categorical. She stated, "If a child has a right to be brought up without institutional violence, as he does, that right should be respected whether or not his parents and teachers believe otherwise."[244] She also said, however, that in a free society parents should have a "large measure of autonomy" in deciding how to raise their children.[245] In England and Wales, as in most of the world, such autonomy extends to physical discipline.

---

239 *Id.*

240 *R* v. *Sec'y of State for Educ. and Employment ex parte* Williamson, (2005] 2 A.C. 246 (H.L.) para. 8 (appeal taken from Eng.).

241 *Id.* para. 21.

242 *Id.* para. 49.

243 *Id.* para. 26.

244 *Id.* para. 86.

245 *Id.* para. 72.

## VII. European Bodies Concerned with the Protection of Children

### A. *The European Committee of Social Rights*

The original version of the European Social Charter, initially in Article 17, required states to take "all appropriate and necessary measures" to ensure the "effective exercise of the rights of mothers and children to social and economic protection."[246] The revised Article 17, inspired by the UN Convention on the Rights of the Child requires states to take all appropriate and necessary measures "to protect children and young persons against negligence, violence or exploitation…."[247]

By January 2007, the European Committee of Social Rights (ECSR), which monitors compliance with the Social Charter and Revised Social Charter, found eighteen member states not to be in conformity with Article 17 because the corporal punishment of children was not fully prohibited in those states. The eighteen states not in conformity are Belgium,[248] the Czech Republic,[249] Estonia,[250] France,[251] Greece (the law was changed in 2006),[252] Hungary (the law was changed in 2004),[253] Ireland,[254] Lithuania,[255] Malta,[256] Netherlands (the law was changed in

246 European Social Charter art. 17, *opened for signature* Oct. 16, 1961, Europ. T.S. 035, *available at* http://conventions.coe.int/Treaty/en/Treaties/Html/035.htm.

247 European Social Charter (revised), art. 17, *opened for signature* May 3, 1996, Europ. T.S. 163, *available at* http://conventions.coe.int/Treaty/en/Treaties/Html/163.htm.

248 European Comm. of Soc. Rights, *European Social Charter (revised): Conclusions 2007 Volume I*, 226-27 (Dec. 2007), *available at* http://www.coe.int/t/dghllmonitoring/socialcharter/Conclusions/ Year/2007Voll_en.pdf.

249 European Comm. of Soc. Rights, 'European Social Charter: Conclusions XVII-2 Volume I', 149 (Sept. 2005), *available at* http://www.coe/int/t/dghl/monitoring/socialcharter/Conclusions/Year/ XVII2Voll_en.pdf.

250 European Comm. of Soc. Rights, 'European Social Charter (revised): Conclusions 2005 Volume I', 193 (Sept. 2005), *available at* http://www.coe.int/t/dghllmonitoring/socialcharter/Conclusions/ Year/2005Voll_en.pdf.

251 European Comm. of Soc. Rights, *supra* note 248, at 240-41.

252 European Comrn. of Soc. Rights, *supra* note 249, at 326.

253 *Id.* at 422.

254 European Comm. of Soc. Rights, 'Decision on the Merits; Collective Complaint No. 18/2003 from the World Organisation Against Torture (OMCT) Against Ireland', paras. 65-66 (2004).

255 European Comm. of Soc. Rights, *supra* note 250, at 368.

256 European Comm. of Soc. Rights, 'European Social Charter: Conclusions XVII-2 Volume II', 568-69 (Sept. 2005), *available at* http://www.coe/int/t/dghl/monitoring/socialcharter/Conclusions/Year/XVII2Vol2_en.pdf.

2007),[257] Poland (the law was changed in 2010),[258] Moldova,[259] Romania (the law was changed in 2004),[260] Slovak Republic,[261] Slovenia,[262] Turkey,[263] and the United Kingdom.[264]

In 2001 the ECSR made a General Observation which concluded "that Article 17 requires a prohibition in legislation against any form of violence against children, whether at school, in other institutions, in their home or elsewhere."[265] The ECSR added that any form of degrading punishment or treatment of children must be prohibited in legislation "and combined with adequate sanctions in penal or civil laws."[266]

In 2003 the ECSR issued a finding of nonconformity with Article 17 in the case of Poland.[267] This was the first time it had done so in relation to corporal punishment in the family. It examined Poland's report on its implementation of Article 17 and concluded,

> Ministerial regulations prohibit the corporal punishment of children in public schools. The committee requests information about the situation in private schools and in institutions; it notes that the corporal punishment of children in the home is not prohibited.... The Committee concludes that the situation in Poland is not in conformity with Article 17 of the Charter on the following grounds: corporal punishment of children in the home is not prohibited.[268]

257 *Id.* at 607.

258 *Id.* at 659.

259 European Comm. of Soc. Rights, 'European Social Charter (revised); Conclusions 2005 Volume 2', 474 (Sept. 2005), *available at* http://www.coe/int/t/dghllmonitoring/socialcharter/Conclusions/Year/2005Vol2_en.pdf.

260 *Id.* at 612.

261 European Comm. of Soc. Rights, 'European Social Charter: Conclusions XVI-2 Volume 2', 805 (2003), *available at* http://www.coe.int/t/dghllmonitoring/socialcharter/Conclusions/Year/XVI2Vol2_en.pdf.

262 European Comm. of Soc. Rights, *supra* note 259, at 650.

263 *Id.* at 792-93.

264 *Id.* at 835-36.

265 Council of Europe, Commissioner for Human Rights, 'Children and Corporal Punishment: "The Right Not to Be Hit, Also a Children's Right"' (Jan. 2008) *available at* https://wcd.coe.int/ViewDoc.jsp?id=1237635&Site=CommDH&BackColorInternet=FEC65B&BackColorIntranet=FEC65B&BackColorLogged=FFC679#P136_10286.

266 *Id.*

267 European Comm. of Soc. Rights, *supra* note 261, at 660.

268 *Id.* at 660-61.

The ECSR came to similar conclusions in reports on a number of other countries including France, Romania, the Slovak Republic, and Slovenia.[269] In relation to France, the ECSR commented,

> ... [T]he Committee noted that the Penal Code prohibits violence against the person and provides for increased penalties where the victim is under 15 years of age or where the perpetrator is related to the child or has authority over the child, but does not necessarily cover all forms of corporal punishment which it found not to be in conformity with the revised Charter.[270]

Two years later (in 2005) the ECSR noted that neither Poland nor France had made any progress towards the goal of eliminating corporal punishment.[271] And in its conclusions on Belgium and Greece,[272] it referred to decisions in the complaints brought against these states by the World Organisation Against Torture under the collective-complaints procedure.[273]

Under this mechanism, the ECSR decides whether a complaint is admissible, and if it is, takes a decision on the merits of the complaint. It then forwards this to the parties concerned and to the Committee of Ministers in a report made public within four months of being forwarded. The Committee of Ministers adopts a resolution, if appropriate, and may recommend that the state take specific measures to bring the situation into line with the Charter.[274] In December 2003, collective complaints were declared admissible against five countries (Belgium, Greece, Ireland, Italy, and Portugal). The complaints alleged that the countries were not in conformity with the Charter because all corporal punishment and other humiliating treatment of children were not prohibited. A decision on these cases was made by the Committee of Ministers in January 2005. It found a violation in the cases of Greece, Belgium, and Ireland.[275]

---

269 European Comm. of Soc. Rights, *supra* note 250, at 240-41 (France); European Comm. of Soc. Rights, *supra* note 259, at 612 (Romania), 650 (Slovenia); European Comm. of Soc. Rights, *supra* note 261, at 805 (Slovak Republic).

270 European Comm. of Soc. Rights, *supra* note 250, at 240.

271 *Id.* at 240-41 (France); European Comm. of Soc. Rights, *supra* note 256, at 659.

272 European Comm. of Soc. Rights, *supra* note 249, at 85, 326.

273 *Id.*

274 *See* Council of Europe, 'Building a Europe for and with Children' (Aug. 2006), *available at* http://www.coe.int/t/transversalprojects/children/pdf/booklet_en.pdf.

275 *See* Council of Europe, 'List of Complaints and State of Procedure', *available at* http://www.coe.int/t/dghl/monitoring/socialcharter/Complaints/Complaints_

In *World Organisation Against Torture (OMCT) v. Greece,* the ECSR found a breach of Article 17 on the ground that corporal punishment was not adequately prohibited in the home, in secondary schools, and in institutions caring for children.[276] It stressed that, even if violence against the person is punished under the criminal law and subject to increased penalties when the victim is a child, this is not enough to satisfy Article 17.[277] The ECSR found that the legal provisions relied upon by the Greek government did not constitute an adequate legal basis.[278] In 2006 Greece introduced legislation prohibiting corporal punishment in all settings.[279]

In *World Organisation Against Torture (OMCT) v. Belgium,* the Committee reached a similar decision. It found that Belgian law did not adequately prohibit all forms of violence, including corporal punishment by parents and "other persons." [280]

In *World Organisation Against Torture (OMCT) v. Ireland,* Ireland too was found to be in violation of Article 17.[281] The ECSR noted that Ireland, like other common-law jurisdictions, had the defence of "reasonable chastisement."[282] Thus, as far as parental discipline was concerned, Ireland was in breach. In relation to foster care, residential care, and certain child-minding settings, the ECSR noted there were guidelines, standards, and inspection requirements, but these did not have the force of law and that the reasonable chastisement defence probably applied too.[283]

---

en.asp (list of complaints with information about subsequent activity in each case).

276 European Comm. of Soc. Rights, 'Decision on the Merits; Collective Complaint No. 17l2003 from the World Organisation Against Torture (OMCT) Against Greece', paras. 34-46 (2004).

277 *Id.* para. 38.

278 *Id.*

279 *See* 'Greece Outlaws Corporal Punishment in the Home', http://www.endcorporalpunishment.org/pages/news/greece-2006.html (describing Greek statute 3500/2006 passed on October 19, 2006) (last visited Apr. 3, 2010).

280 European Comm. of Soc. Rights, 'Decision on the Merits; Collective Complaint No. 21l2003 from the World Organisation Against Torture (OMCT) Against Belgium', paras. 37-41 (2004).

281 European Comm. of Soc. Rights, 'Decision on the Merits; Collective Complaint No. 18l2003 from the World Organisation Against Torture (OMCT) Against Ireland', paras. 58-66 (2004).

282 *Id.* para. 65.

283 *Id.* para. 66.

The ECSR did not find a breach of Article 17 regarding Italy[284] or, initially, Portugal.[285] In both countries court decisions effectively ruled out corporal punishment. Italy's dated from 1996.[286] But in 2006 the Supreme Court in Portugal ruled that slaps and spankings are "legal" and "acceptable" in child-rearing, and that failure to employ these punishment methods could even be "educational neglect."[287] The case concerned cruelty and ill treatment of mentally disabled children in a children's institution. Not surprisingly, the OMCT submitted a second complaint against Portugal, alleging that it does not explicitly or effectively prohibit all corporal punishment of children. In 2007 the ECSR agreed with the complainant and concluded that Portugal was in violation of Article 17.[288] Portugal has now banned the corporal punishment of children, and so is no longer in breach of Article 17 (or so it is assumed).[289]

### B. *The Committee of Ministers of the Council of Europe*

The Committee of Ministers of the Council of Europe was one of the first institutions to turn its attention to corporal punishment, and one of the first to condemn the practice. Recommendation No. R (85) 4 proposed in 1985 that states review their legislation on the power to punish children, to limit or prohibit corporal punishment, even if violation of such a prohibition does not necessarily entail a criminal penalty.[290] This was a cau-

284 European Comm. of Soc. Rights, 'Decision on the Merits; Collective Complaint No. 1912003 from the World Organisation Against Torture (OMCT) Against Italy', paras. 40-52 (2004).

285 European Comm. of Soc. Rights, 'Decision on the Merits; Collective Complaint No. 2012003 from the World Organisation Against Torture (OMCT) Against Portugal', paras. 33-43 (2004).

286 *See* Bitensky, *supra* note 121, at 247-54 (discussing the Italian Supreme Court's decision in *Cambria*).

287 Peter Newell, *Briefing from Global Initiative to End All Corporal Punishment of Children* 2 (2007), *available at* http://www.endcorporalpunishment.org/pages/pdfs/briefings/CAT%20briefing%20Apr-May%202007.pdf.

288 European Comm. of Soc. Rights, 'Decision on the Merits; Collective Complaint No. 3412006 from the World Organisation Against Torture (OMCT) Against Portugal', paras. 17-22 (2006).

289 It outlawed corporal punishment by parents in 2007 in an amendment to the Penal Code, in Article 152 of law 59/2007. *See* Global Initiative to End All Corporal Punishment of Children, State Reports: Portugal, http://www.endcorporalpunishment.org/pages/progress/reports/portugal.html (last visited May 26, 2010).

290 Council of Europe Comm. of Ministers, 'Recommendation No. R (85) 4 of the Committee of Ministers to Member States on Violence in the Family', para. 12 (Mar. 26, 1985).

tious and somewhat limited response, but it was twenty-five years ago, when only Sweden and Finland had banned corporal punishment in the home. The Committee of Ministers' explanatory memorandum described corporal punishment as "an evil which must at least be discouraged as a first step towards outright prohibition."[291] In the memorandum the Committee asked the public to question the assumption that corporal punishment of children is "legitimate": this, the committee thought, opened the way to "all kinds of excesses" (and presumably to child abuse).[292]

In 1990, in "Social Measures Concerning Violence in the Family," the Committee of Ministers noted that "trends towards the democratisation of the family, implying respect for members of the family as individuals with equal rights and equal opportunities, can help to discourage violence."[293] In its "measures for children," the recommendation states, "The importance should be emphasised of the general condemnation of corporal punishment and other forms of degrading treatment as a means of education, and of the need for violence-free education."[294]

In 1993, in Recommendation R (93) 2 (Medico-Social Aspects of Child Abuse), the Committee, referencing the UN Convention on the Rights of the Child, urged member states "to emphasise the rights of all children and young people to freedom from abuse and the need to change patterns of upbringing and behaviour which threaten this," and "to minimise levels of violence within society and the resort to violence in child-rearing practices."[295]

In 2006 the Committee issued a recommendation again calling for nonviolent positive parenting in the context of respect for, and the implementation of, children's rights.[296] In the same year the Council of Europe published a document and began a campaign entitled *Building a*

291 Council of Europe Parliamentary Assembly, 'Report: Europe-wide Ban on Corporal Punishment of Children', para. 22 (June 4, 2004), *available at* http://assembly.coe.int/documents/WorkingDocs/doc04/EDOC10199.htm.

292 *Id.*

293 Council of Europe Comm. of Ministers, 'Recommendation No. R (90) 2 of the Committee of Ministers to Member States on Social Measures Concerning Violence Within the Family', para. 18 (Jan. 15, 1990).

294 *Id.* app. B, para. 14.

295 Council of Europe Comm. of Ministers, 'Recommendation No. R (93) 2 of the Committee of Ministers to M ember States on the Medico-Social Aspects of Child Abuse', app., para. 1.2 (Mar. 22, 1993).

296 Council of Europe Comm. of Ministers, 'Recommendation (2006) 19 of the Committee of Ministers to Member States on Policy to Support Positive Parenting', para. 2 (Dec. 13, 2006).

*Europe for and with Children.*[297] The Council described the abolition of all corporal punishment as "a human rights issue,"[298] one with "serious consequences for the health and development of children and for society as a whole."[299] The emphasis was on "changing attitudes, not prosecuting parents."[300] The Council described a role for the media ("the dissemination of an unequivocal message against corporal punishment").[301] and described children as "prime actors in this process."[302] In response, the Committee of Ministers commented positively on the program's breadth:

> Given that the member states of the Council of Europe have entered into numerous commitments under general human rights conventions and specific conventions on children's rights and that human rights treaties of the Council of Europe (as well as the UN Convention on the Rights of the Child) require states to prohibit and fight all forms of violence and ill-treatment of children, the programme will assist member states in fulfilling their obligations under such treaties. It will be done in particular by implementing prevention policies and alerting professional circles and the general public to the problem. The programme will address all forms of violence, wherever it takes place (family, school, resident institutions, the community, media and cyberspace) with a special attention to fighting sexual abuse and corporal punishment.[303]

### C. *The European Network of Ombudspersons for Children*

The European Network of Ombudspersons for Children (ENOC) was formed in 1997. There are now thirty-two institutions in twenty-three member states of the Council of Europe in the network. These institu-

---

297 Council of Europe, 'Building a Europe for and with Children' (Aug. 2006), *available at* http://www.coe.int/t/transversalprojects/children/pdf/Booklet_en.pdf.

298 Council of Europe, 'Highlights - Building a Europe for and with Children' 18 (Apr. 2006), *available at* http://www.coe.int/t/transversalprojects/children/pdf/Highlights_GB.pdf.

299 *Id.* at 19.

300 *Id.*

301 *Id.*

302 *Id.*

303 Council of Europe Comm. of Ministers, 'Written Question No. 492 to the Committee of Ministers by Mrs Bargholtz: "Collective complaint 1812003 under the Revised Social Charter against Ireland" – Reply of the Committee of Ministers', CM/AS(2006)Quest492 (Sept. 29, 2006), *available at* http://wcd.coe.intViewDoc.jsp?Ref=CM/AS(2006)Quest492&Language=lanEnglish&Ver=final.

tions are pledged to work collectively to advance children's rights, in particular by encouraging the fullest possible implementation of the UN Convention on the Rights of the Child.

In 1999 the network adopted a position statement on corporal punishment of children. It urged "the governments of all European countries, the European Union, the Council of Europe and other European institutions and non-governmental organisations concerned with children to work collectively and individually towards ending all corporal punishment of children."[304] It argued that this would improve "children's status as people," and reduce "child abuse and all other forms of violence in European societies."[305] It stated, "Hitting children is disrespectful and dangerous. Children deserve at least the same protection from violence that we as adults take for granted for ourselves."[306] It noted that, although corporal punishment had been eliminated from schools and other institutions in almost all European countries, it remained "common and legally and socially accepted in the family home in most countries."[307] The ENOC position statement was critical of the "reasonable" or "moderate" chastisement defence and noted, "Where the law is silent, corporal punishment tends to be accepted in practice."[308] The network committed itself to working actively on what it called "this fundamental human rights issue."[309]

## VIII. The African Charter on the Rights and Welfare of the Child

The African Child Policy Forum[310] considers violence to involve a violation of rights that every human being (including children) must have: the

304 *Building a Europe for and With Children Programme, Council of Europe, Eliminating Corporal Punishment: A Human Rights Imperative for Europe's Children* 67 (2d ed. 2007).

305 *Id.*

306 *Id.*

307 *Id.* In the ten years since this statement there has of course been a lot of progress, with at least twelve European countries banning corporal punishment by parents.

308 *Id.*

309 *Id.* at 68.

310 This is an independent advocacy organization working for the realization of children's rights. It was founded in 2003, with headquarters in Addis Ababa, Ethiopia. Among the reports it has published that may be singled out are *Violence against Girls within the Home in Africa* (2006) and *Born to High Risk: Violence against Girls in Africa* (2006).

right to life, security, dignity, and physical and psychological well-being. Article 16 of the African Charter on the Rights and Welfare of the Child provides,

> States Parties to the present Charter shall take specific legislative, administrative, social and educational measures to protect the child from all forms of torture, inhuman or degrading treatment and especially physical or mental injury or abuse, neglect or maltreatment including sexual abuse, while in the care of a parent, legal guardian or school authority or any other person who has the care of the child.[311]

There is concern with corporal punishment in Africa, but other forms of violence against children, including rape, domestic violence, incest, domestic slavery, and female genital mutilation, assume a greater profile, and for obvious reasons. This is reflected in reports of the African Child Policy Forum, which held a conference in Addis Ababa, Ethiopia in May 2006.[312] The reports observed that it is primarily girls who are the victims of violence.[313] This is not to say that boys are not also affected: many are forcibly recruited into armed conflict (as, indeed, girls are, too).[314] All African countries, except Somalia, have ratified the UN Convention on the Rights of the Child and most have ratified the African Charter and therefore have aspirations to further children's human rights, but these countries' diversity of cultures and legal systems makes change less easy to achieve. Africa's pluralistic culture is undoubtedly a barrier to the enforcement of children's rights.[315]

---

311 African Charter on the Rights and Welfare of the Child art. 16, *entered into force* Nov. 29, 1999, OAU Doc. CAB/LEG/24.9/49 (1990); *see also id.* art. 11(5) (A child subjected to discipline "shall be treated with humanity and with respect for the inherent dignity of the child…."); *Id.* art. 17 (discussing protection of children against torture and inhuman or degrading treatment or punishment in the context of juvenile justice); *Id.* art. 21 (titled "Protection against Harmful Social and Cultural Practices"); *Id.* art. 27 (States Parties shall "protect the child from all forms of sexual exploitation and sexual abuse."); *Id.* art. 22 (armed conflict).

312 African Child Policy Forum, *Born to High Risk: Violence against Girls in Africa, supra* note 310.

313 *Id.* at 2.

314 Kathy Vandergrift, 'Challenges in Implementing and Enforcing Children's Rights', 37 *Cornell Int'l L.J.* 547, 550 (2004).

315 Chuma Himonga, 'Implementing the Rights of the Child in African Legal Systems: the Mthembu Journey in Search of Justice', 9 *Int'l J. Child. Rts.* 89, 90 (2001). *See gen-*

Nevertheless, many African countries are reviewing their child-protection legislation, recognizing that it is not in conformity with either the UN Convention or the African Charter. A number of African countries, including South Africa and Uganda, have included children's rights provisions in their constitutions.[316] Although the symbolic importance of these provisions cannot be underestimated, their impact is not as great as would be hoped.

The physical punishment of children is widespread in Africa and can be severe. Even where it has been abolished in schools, the practice continues. Sanctions against it are limited and seldom imposed. Teachers can get away with maiming children: in one widely reported case in Ghana, a girl was blinded.[317] Teachers will say they have few alternatives. In families, the use of physical violence to discipline children is culturally and legally tolerated. A characteristic shared by almost all of the countries in Africa is the belief that children are traditionally meant to be submissive, so that physical discipline is seen as a necessary element of child-rearing, and not in any way as problematic.[318]

The UN Study on Violence Against Children, Middle East and North Africa Region (the 2005 MENA Report) noted these factors contributing to violence against children: economic factors (poverty, unemployment); social factors (dysfunctional families, family conflicts, marital disputes, large families, polygamy); prevalent cultural beliefs; a lack of awareness regarding appropriate child-rearing practices; the role of the media and programs that encourage violence; the lack of provisions in legislation

*erally* N. Barney Pityana, 'The Challenge of Culture for Human Rights in Africa', in *The African Charter on Human and Peoples' Rights* 219 (Malcolm Evans and Rachel Murray eds., 2002).

316 S. Afr. Const. 1996, § 28(1) (South Africa); *see* Julia Sloth-Nielsen and Benyam D. Mezmur, '2+2=5? Exploring the Domestication of the CRC in South African Jurisprudence (2002-2006)', 16 *Int'l J. Child. Rts.* 1, 1-28 (2008) (South Africa); Julia Sloth-Nielsen, 'Domestication of Children's Rights in National Legal Systems in African Context: Progress and Prospects', in *Children's Rights In Africa – A Legal Perspective* 53, 62 (Julia Sloth-Nielsen ed., 2008) (Uganda).

317 Nicole O'Neal, 'Corporal Punishment in Public Schools: A Call for Legal Reform', 8 *Afr. Hum. Rts. L.J.* 60, 61 (2008).

318 Farhana Zuberi, *Assessment of Violence against Children in the Eastern and Southern African Region: Results of an Initial Desk Review for the UN Secretary General's Study on Violence against Children* 19 (2005), *available at* www.crin.org/docs/ESA_Regional_Assessment_Final.doc.

that target the protection of children; and, where such provisions exist, inadequate enforcement.[319]

The African Commission on Human and Peoples' Rights is a quasi-judicial institution that handles individual complaints of breach of the African Charter. Though it has been criticized for its ineffectiveness in ensuring compliance, it has ah increasingly important role in setting regional standards, and, in doing so, it has raised some awareness of the issue of corporal punishment. A good example is the case of *Doebbler* v. *Sudan.*[320] This action, brought by a human rights lawyer, was a challenge to the judicial corporal punishment of juveniles in Sudan. Several students had been convicted of violating "public order" contrary to Sudanese criminal law. The girls had been wearing trousers, kissing and dancing with men, crossing legs with men, sitting with boys, and sitting and talking with boys at a picnic. They were sentenced to fines and between twenty-five and forty lashes. These lashes were administered on bare backs with an unclean plastic whip and without a doctor present.[321] It was alleged that this amounted to cruel, inhuman, or degrading punishment. The Commission was influenced by the decision of *Tyrer* v. *United Kingdom* and noted that even when birching had been carried out in private in the presence of a doctor and in hygienic conditions, it was regarded as "degrading punishment."[322] The Commission decided that the Sudanese use of judicial corporal punishment was contrary to the African Charter and incompatible with international human-rights law. It recommended that the Sudanese Government amend the criminal law to ensure its conformity with the Charter and with relevant human-rights instruments. It also recommended that the judicial punishment of lashes be abolished and that its victims in the present case be paid compensation.[323]

Evidently, the Sudanese Government has failed to comply with the Commission's recommendations in this case.[324] But this does not mean its effect is nugatory. If nothing else, the case encourages pressure on gov-

---

319 U.N. Study on Violence Against Children, Middle East and North Africa Region.

320 *Curtis Francis Doebbler* v. *Sudan*, Comm. No. 236/2000, Africa n Comm'n on Human and Peoples' Rights (2003), *available at* http://wwwl.umn.edu/humanrts/africa/comcases/236-2000.html.

321 *Id.* para. 31.

322 *Id.* para. 38. *See also Tyrer, supra* note 203.

323 *Id.* para. 44.

324 *See* Frans Viljoen and Linette Louw, 'State Compliance with the Recommendations of the African Commission on Human and Peoples' Rights, 1994-2004', 101 *AM. J. INT'L L.* 1, 5 (2007).

ernments from lobbying groups and NGOs, and it does, of course, have some educational value.

There has now been some progress. The Interim Constitution of Southern Sudan (2005) includes a provision that prohibits the use of corporal punishment by parents. The draft has a section devoted to the rights of children, and this includes the following provision: "Every child has the right:... to be free from corporal punishment and cruel and inhuman treatment by any person including parents, school administrations and other institutions...."[325] The Children's Bill of South Sudan, however, now in the process of becoming law, does not include parents in the category of persons prohibited from using corporal punishment on children.[326] Daksha Kassan comments that this omission "could" be seen as a retrogressive step, though she attempts, rather unconvincingly, to defend the omission because the phrase "any other person in any other place" covers parents.[327] But, of course, it does not specifically say so. At any rate, consideration of corporal punishment by anyone in Sudan is progress in this poor, war-torn country.

Kassan also refers to a Kenyan decision, *Isaac Mwangi Wachira* v. *Republic High Court of Kenya (Nakuru)*,[328] in which the father appealed his conviction of subjecting a child to torture. The case against him alleged that in order to punish her – she was three years old – he pinched her with his fingernails in her face, ears, back, and thighs. He was sentenced to three years' imprisonment. This was, on appeal, reduced to one year. The length of the sentence is immaterial: the court's decision, supported by the appellate court, is an unequivocal disapproval of this kind of conduct. The appeal court (the High Court) observed that the father had "no justification in injuring... his own daughter." Further, the court reasoned that the action "could not be said to have been disciplining a child of three years," nor could "the child... be said to have been at fault to deserve the punishment that was meted out to her by [her father]."[329] The offence was subjecting a child to torture, and therefore the case cannot be considered to constitute rendering unlawful any corporal punishment by a parent of a child. Nevertheless, the decision is significant. As Kassan

325 Interim Const. of S. Sudan, 2005 para. 21(f). *See* Kassan, *supra* note 167, at 176 (describing the development of the Interim Constitution).

326 Kassan, *supra* note 167, at 176 n. 16.

327 *Id.*

328 *Id.* at 177. The case (Application 185 of 2004) is unreported. *See also* Godfrey Odongo, 'Kenyan Law on Corporal Punishment in the Home', 1 Article 19, 6, at 7 (2005).

329 Odongo, *supra* note 328, at 7.

notes, "[I]t confirms the power of the Kenyan court to judicially subject the status of corporal punishment by parents to scrutiny and... brings to the fore a need for an explicit legislative ban on corporal punishment by parents."[330] The decision is particularly significant, too, in demonstrating the legal procedure of challenging corporal punishment in Anglophone Africa.

## IX. The Inter-American Human Rights System: The Declaration of The Rights and Duties of Man

In 1948 the Organization of American States (OAS) adopted the American Declaration of the Rights and Duties of Man.[331] This is similar to, but not identical with, the Universal Declaration of Human Rights adopted by the UN shortly thereafter. The Inter-American Commission on Human Rights is expected to implement this Declaration. The Declaration applies to all member states of the OAS, even those that are not parties to the American Convention on Human Rights. Article 7 lays down that "all children have the right to special protection, care and aid."[332] The OAS has also adopted the American Convention on Human Rights.[333] The powers of this go beyond its European counterpart: the Inter-American Commission has an advisory jurisdiction and the power to order provisional measures in cases of extreme urgency and gravity.

Again unlike its European counterpart, the Inter-American Commission has a specific article on "The Rights of the Child,"[334] which provides, "Every minor child has the right to the measures of protection required by his condition as a minor on the part of his family, society and the state." Article 5 more broadly prohibits any torture or cruel, inhuman, or degrading punishment or treatment. Though cases decided under Article 5 apply specifically to adults, they offer some guidance on the attitude

330 Kassan, *supra* note 167, at 177.

331 Declaration of the Rights and Duties of Man, adopted by the Ninth International Conference of American States (1948), *reprinted* in Organization of American States, Inter-American Commission on Human Rights, *Basic Documents Pertaining to Human Rights in the Inter-American System,* OAS/Ser.LN/1.4 rev.12 (Jan. 31, 2007).

332 *Id.* art. VII.

333 American Convention on Human Rights, *entered into force* July 18, 1978, O.A.S.T.S. No. 36.

334 *See id.* art. 19.

of the Inter-American institutions to corporal punishment. The first is *Winston Caesar* v. *Trinidad and Tobago*, in 2005.[335]

Caesar was sentenced to twenty years' imprisonment with hard labour plus fifteen strokes of the cat-o'-nine tails for the offence of attempted rape. The Corporal Punishment Act of Trinidad and Tobago allowed for the imposition of corporal punishment to male offenders above the age of sixteen.[336] The evidence was that Caesar was in poor physical condition when the punishment was administered, and he suffered adverse physical and psychological effects of the lashes he received.[337] The Inter-American Court of Human Rights emphasized that the prohibition of torture and of inhuman and degrading punishment or treatment had reached the status of a "peremptory norm [] of international law."[338] It based this on a reading of international human-rights instruments as well as on regional case law. It took into account the institutionalized nature of the violence against Caesar, his extreme humiliation, and his severe physical and psychological suffering, and concluded that there had been a violation of Article 5 of the American Convention on Human Rights. In addition, the court ruled that Trinidad and Tobago's Corporal Punishment Act contravened Article 5. That legislation should therefore have been abrogated when Trinidad and Tobago ratified the Convention; failure to do so was a breach of the state's obligation.[339]

The second case was *Prince Pinder* v. *Bahamas* in 2007.[340] Pinder was convicted of armed robbery and sentenced to a lengthy term of imprisonment and to be flogged (six strokes in two instalments).[341] The flogging had not yet been carried out, but, according to the Inter-American Commission, "the mere anticipation of flogging is within the parameters of the cruel, inhuman and degrading elements of judicial corporal punishment. Corporal punishment is not simply about the actual pain or humiliation of a flogging, but also about the mental suffering that is generated by anticipating the flogging."[342] Pinder had waited nearly a decade by the time these words were pronounced. The delay had aggravated his

---

335 2005 Inter-Am. Ct. H.R. (ser. C) No. 123 (Mar. 11, 2005).

336 *Id.* at 2.

337 *Id.* at 14.

338 *Id.* at 24.

339 *Id.* at 29.

340 Case 12.513, Inter-Am. C.H.R., Report No. 79/07, OEA/Ser.L.N/II.130, doc. 22, rev. 1 (2007).

341 *Id.* para. 1.

342 *Id.* para. 35.

suffering and was "compounded even more by the fact that he has been sentenced to receive the flogging in two installments."[343] The Commission concluded that Pinder's rights under Article I, XXV, and XXVI of the American Declaration had been violated.[344] Article I lays down the right to "security of his person." Article XXV generates the right to "humane treatment" in custody, and Article XXVI creates the right "not to receive cruel, infamous or unusual punishment."[345] The Commission accordingly recommended commutation of the sentence of corporal punishment and abrogation of the punishment of flogging by the state of Bahamas.[346]

## X. Corporal Punishment in Asia

A number of Asian states have abolished corporal punishment in schools.[347] None, apart from Israel, as yet, has banned it in the home.[348] Asia lacks a regional human-rights mechanism analogous to those that exist in Europe, Africa, and the Americas. There are, however, subregional cooperations.

The South Asian Association for Regional Cooperation (SAARC) has adopted the SAARC Social Charter. This Charter recognizes the principles of human dignity and nonviolence, and provides for the legal protection and respect for the dignity of the child.[349] The Association of Southeast Asian Nations (ASEAN) has also set up a working group for an ASEAN human rights mechanism. As yet, though, neither of these institutions has moved to tackle corporal punishment. But individual countries are

---

343 *Id.*

344 *Id.* para. 36.

345 *Id.* para. 24.

346 *Id.* para. 42.

347 The group includes China, Japan, Philippines, and Thailand. *See* Global Initiative to End All Corporal Punishment of Children, Global Progress Towards Prohibiting All Corporal Punishment, http://www.endcorporalpunishment.org/pages/pdfs/charts/Chart-Global.pdf (last visited May 26, 2010).

348 Abolition is under discussion in several countries: for example, Bangladesh, Sri Lanka, and Pakistan (these countries made a commitment to abolition at the July 2006 meeting of the South Asia Forum). Taiwan stated its commitment to prohibition in August 2005. In the Philippines various bills have been filed but not heard. There is draft legislation in Mongolia also (this was due for consideration in 2008). See links to tables with individual states' progress reports available at http://www.endcorporalpunishment.org/pages/progress/global.htm.

349 South Asian Association for Regional Cooperation Social Charter, *available at* http://www.saarc-sec.org/SAARC-Charter/5/.

beginning to express a concern about corporal punishment. It is therefore possible that the subregional cooperations may also take the initiative. The example of other regional human-rights systems may also eventually have an impact.

## XI. Conclusion

There are grounds for optimism. Twenty-nine countries, mostly in Europe, have now outlawed corporal punishment by parents. More will do so. Sadly, others, predominantly in the English-speaking world, will resist change. There can be few more-dismal documents than a so-called consultation paper issued by the British government in 2000.[350] This paper stated outright that the government did "*not* consider that the right way forward is to make unlawful all smacking and other forms of physical rebuke and this paper explicitly rules out the possibility."[351] The paper makes no reference to children's rights, their dignity, or their best interests. It conceded that "we all have an interest in making sure that children thrive [] and are helped to grow up into healthy and socially responsible adults."[352] It took no note of the overwhelming evidence that such an objective was likely to be frustrated by the practice of corporal punishment. The consultation then sought opinions on the perimeters of reasonable chastisement. Should the law state that physical punishment that causes or is likely to cause injuries to the head including the brain, eyes, and ears never be accepted as "reasonable"?[353] It is difficult to believe such a question can even have been asked. But this was from a government that believed in "loving smacks," a classic oxymoron.[354]

350 U.K. Dep't Of Health, *Protecting Children, Supporting Parents: A Consultation Document on the Physical Punishment of Children* (2000), *available at* http:// www.dh.gov.uk/en/Consultations/Ciosedconsultations/DH_4083513.

351 *Id.* para. 1.5.

352 *Id.* para. 1.8.

353 *Id.* para. 5.7.

354 Tony Blair, the former Prime Minister, referred to "loving smacks." *See, e.g.*, 'Children in Anti Smacking Protest', BBC NEWS, Apr. 15, 2000, http://news.bbc.co.uk/1/hi/uk/713992.stm.

CHAPTER 4

# Whose Life is it Anyway?

The 'conjoined twins' case raises many issues. This paper addresses principally only one. Was it right to take the decision to separate the twins away from their parents? It is the view of many, including leading ethicists, that 'when neither the law nor ethics can provide anything other than a very tortuous path out of such a dilemma, we ought to be willing to respect the parents' decision and let them shoulder the responsibility for their decision'.[1] In this paper I ask why. I offer a critical examination of the premises and implications of prioritising parental autonomy. I conclude we should not do so, and that on this at least the Court of Appeal was right.

The context is the legal doctrine of parental responsibility. The contours of this must therefore first be sketched.

## I. Parental Responsibility and Medical Treatment

English law formerly emphasised parental rights (indeed, not so long ago the rights of fathers). Only with the Children Act 1989 did the concept of parental responsibility find its way into English law.[2] Parental responsibility is defined (sort of) in section 3 of the Act. Ward L.J. in *Re A* was rightly critical of the definition,[3] which cynics may think was concocted during a 'Yes, Minister' episode. 'Parental responsibility,' we are told

1 I quote here from Dr Richard Nicholson's Editorial in *Bulletin of Medical Ethics and EACME News* 160 (July/August 2000) 1. He has expressed this view also in 'Don 't Take One Child's Life To Save Another', *Observer*, 27 August 2000. It is also the opinion of Professor Raanan Gillon expressed at a seminar at University College London Medical School on 30 October 2000, of Barbara Hewson 'A (Children) – Cruel and Unnatural' (2000) 150 *New Law Journal* 1562, of Deborah Orr, 'Loving Parents Have A Right To Choose', *Independent*, 5 September 2000. See also L.P. Knowles, 'Hubris in the Court' (2001) 31 (1) *Hastings Center Report* at 50.

2 Children Act 1989 section 3. West Germany was the first country to accept this change: it did so in 1970. Norway followed in 1981.

3 *Re A* [2001] 1 F.L.R. 1, 32 (it is, he says, rather unsatisfactory). In a debate on the Children Bill Lord Meston described it as a 'non-definition' (*Hansard*, H.L. Debs. 502, col. 1172).

 | DOI:10.1163/9789004219106_005

means 'all the rights, duties, ... responsibility and authority which by law a parent of a child has in relation to the child and his property.'

This gives 'outmoded pre-eminence to the "rights" which are conferred',[4] which is most unfortunate. It also assumes a knowledge of the common law, of which it purports to be declaratory. On very few parental responsibilities is it easy to state the law with certainty, and in relation to medical treatment it is especially difficult. The importance of the shift to parental responsibility lies in the ideas it represents: first, that parents must behave dutifully towards their children; secondly, that responsibility for bringing up a child belongs to parents, not the State.[5] And thirdly and most importantly, it emphasises that children should be beneficiaries of parenting rather than possessions of parents.[6] Whether it also deflects attention away from children's rights – and it would be most unfortunate if it did – can be, and has been, debated. It is not an issue with which I will engage here.[7]

It is the second of these points that courts have frequently emphasised. In *Re K.D.,* for example, Lord Templeman stated:

> The best person to bring up a child is the natural parent. It matters not whether the parent is wise or foolish, rich or poor, educated or illiterate, provided the child's moral and physical health are not endangered.[8]

And in the same case Lord Oliver explained:

> Parenthood, in most civilised societies, is generally conceived of as conferring on parents the exclusive privilege of ordering, within the family, the upbringing of children of tender age, with all that that entails. That is a privilege which... would be protected by the courts.[9]

---

4 *Per* Ward L.J. in *Re S* [1995]2 F.L.R. 648 at 657.

5 See to this effect John Eekelaar's authoritative article 'Parental Responsibility: State of Nature or Nature of the State?' (1991) *J. Social Welfare Law* 37.

6 Lord Mackay L.C., when introducing the Bill, said as much (*Hansard,* H.L. Debs. 502, col. 490). See also Department of Health, *Introduction to the Children Act 1989* (HMSO 1989) para. 1.4.

7 I addressed this briefly in M.D.A. Freeman, *Children, their Families and the Law: Working with the Children Act* (Macmillan 1992) at 19.

8 [1988] A.C. 806 a t 812.

9 *Ibid.* a t 825. This statement is approved by Ward L.J. in *Re A* at 49.

Not long ago this principle under the cover of pseudo-science was erected into a firm rule that the 'blood tie' dictated with whom a child should live.[10] And for long we contended with the 'unimpeachable parent' doctrine: no one seemed to notice that unimpeachable parents were always fathers. It was strategy, successful to the late 1970s, to displace the maternal custody presumption.[11]

One incident of parental responsibility is the power[12] to give a valid consent to their child's medical treatment. The legislation makes it clear that a parent with parental responsibility has greater powers than others who may have acquired parental responsibility: this is particularly the case where parental responsibility has vested by virtue of an emergency protection order.[13]

This power may be said to derive from the parent's duty to the child. This was Blackstone's view,[14] and it has the support of Lord Scarman in *Gillick*[15] and the clear endorsement of Ward L.J. in *Re A*.[16] Ward L.J. adds that 'failure to perform the duty may be a culpable omission'.[17] Of course, if willful, it is also, he may have added, a criminal offence.[18] The case for giving parents this power is put eloquently by McHugh J. in *Secretary, Department of Health and Community Services* v. *J.W.B. and S.W.B.* (Marion's case):

> These grounds include respect for the family as the decision making unit, the appropriateness of giving the power to those who possess

10 Notoriously in *Re Thain* [1926] Ch. 676 and in *Re* C (*MA*) [1966] 1 All E.R. 838 (the so-called 'blood tie adoption' case).

11 It was 'finally quashed' (*per* N. Lowe and G. Douglas, *Bromley's Family Law,* (9th edn.) (Butterworths 1998) at 309) in S (*B. D.*) v. *S* (*D.J.*) [1977] Fam. 109.

12 I use the concept 'power' in Hohfeldian terminology, while admitting that correct conceptualisation is not straightforward.

13 Children Act 1989 s. 44(5)(b). Such a person may only take such action 'as is reasonably required to safeguard or promote the welfare of the child'. There is a 'clear' difference between day-to-day decisions and major elective surgery.

14 *Commentaries,* 17th edn (1830) vol. 1 at 452.

15 *Gillick* v. *West Norfolk and Wisbech A.H.A.* [1986] A.C. 112 a t 184. McHugh J. in *Department of Health and Community Services* (*N.T.*) v. *J.W.B. and S.M.B.* (1992) 175 C.L.R. 218 at 313 rejected Lord Scarman's view, but does not convince me (or I. Kennedy and A. Grubb, *Medical Law,* (3rd edn.) (Butterworths 2000) at 775).

16 *Op. cit.,* n. 3 at 32.

17 *Ibid.*

18 Children and Young Persons Act 1933 s. 1 (see esp. s. 1(2)(a)). On recklessness see *R.* v. *Sheppard* [1981] A.C. 394 and *R.* v. *Senior* [1899] 1 Q.B. 283 (where there was a religious objection to calling in medical aid).

> a moral duty to protect the child and who are, therefore, likely to have the child's best interests in mind, and the cost and inconvenience of vesting the power in others such as government officials.[19]

There are limits on the exercise of parental power. As Lord Scarman put it in *Gillick* 'parental right must be exercised in accordance with the welfare principle and can be challenged, even overridden, if it be not'.[20]

'Best interests' means the best interests of the child and not another. Thus, parents cannot consent to a procedure which is in the interests of a sibling[21] or in their own interests.[22] This point was glossed over in *Re* A:[23] it is difficult to see how parents can lawfully consent to a separation of conjoined twins, unless it can be shown (as it was to Robert Walker L.J.[24]) that it is in the best interests of both. And I will argue, in agreement with Robert Walker L.J., that it was, though not for the reason given by the judge.

There is another limit on the exercise of parental responsibility as it relates to medical decisions. Parents are not empowered to consent to all forms of treatment. There can be no doubt that throughout history they have done so,[25] and it was only the chance intervention of an educational psychologist 25-years-ago in the 'Sotos Syndrome' case[26] that forced the courts to question whether there were decisions a parent could not take.

---

19 *Op. cit.*, n. 15 at 316.

20 *Op. cit.*, n. 16 at 184. See also Lord Hailsham in *Re B* [1987] 2 All E.R. 206 at 212 and Butler-Sloss L.J. in *Re* C (*HIV Test*) [1999] 2 F.L.R. 1004. See also Mason C.J., Dawson, Toohey and Gaudron J.J. in *Department of Health and Community Services, op. cit.*, n. 15 ('the overriding criterion of the child's best interests is itself a limit on parental power' at 240). That the paramountcy principle is said in the Children Act 1989 s. 1(1) to apply to 'courts' does not mean that parents do not have to act in their child's best interests.

21 *Re Y* [1996] 2 F.L.R. 787 (illegal unless shown to be in the best interests of the defendant and therefore 'lawful' at p. 791). In this case 'best interests' was expansively interpreted to cover 'emotional, psychological and social benefit' (p. 794). Best interests are not limited to 'best medical interests', *per* Butler-Sloss L.J. in *Re M.B.* (1997) 38 B.M.L.R. 175,188.

22 *Re Eve* (1986) 31 D.L.R. (4th) 1; *Department of Health and Community Services* (*N.T.*) v. *J.W.B. and S.M.B., op. cit.*, n. 15 at 316, *per* McHugh J.

23 *Re Y* is not referred to in any of the judgments: it is not clear whether it was cited to the court.

24 See *supra* at 118 and 119.

25 In relation to sterilisations see (if you can, because the book was 'suppressed') S. Trombley, *The Right to Reproduce* (Weidenfeld and Nicolson 1988).

26 *Re D* [1976] Fam. 185. Trombley (*op. cit.*, n. 25) discusses the background to the case at 207-13.

It is now clear that *inter alia* parents cannot take the decision to have a learning disabled child sterilised, at least where this is being done for non-therapeutic reasons.[27] Whether parents in the future will be able to consent to elective surgery to separate conjoined twins (certainly where one will die) is unlikely. Surprisingly, the court did not address this issue.

*Re* D[28] established that the High Court can override a decision by a parent to consent or refuse consent to their child's medical treatment. Conversely, in *Re B*[29] the court sanctioned, contrary to the parents' wishes, a life-saving operation for a newly born Down's syndrome baby and in *Re B*[30] overruled a mother's objections and gave permission for a 12-year-old to have an abortion. In *Re* C[31] the court approved a proposal by a hospital to withdraw ventilation and thereafter not reinstate it in the case of a 16-month-old child suffering from a fatal disease. Life-sustaining treatment would simply delay death without significantly alleviating suffering. The parents were Orthodox Jews and could not contemplate a course of action that would indirectly shorten life.

## II. The Importance of a Parent's Wishes

The Court of Appeal in *Re A* recognised the importance of the parents' views. They are Catholics (we now know) from *Gozo*,[32] a small island off Malta. In their eyes the twins were equal and God's will should be allowed to prevail. It is not entirely clear what they understood by God's will. The twins were delivered by caesarean section, which the mother could have refused.[33] The parents accepted the jurisdiction of the English court:[34] whether they also accepted the application of English law was discreetly

27 Only Lord Templeman in *Re B* [1988] A.C. 199, 205 expressly stated this but it has been accepted since, at least as a matter of good practice. On therapeutic sterilisations see *Re E* (1991) 7 B.M.L.R. 117 and *F.* v. *F.* (1991) 7 B.M.L.R. 135. See also Law Commission, *Mental Incapacity* (Law Corn. No. 231 (1995) para. 6.4). On chemotherapy for cancer see Lord Chancellor's Department, *Who Decides?* (London 1997) Cm. 3803.

28 *Op. cit.*, n. 26.

29 [1981] 1 W.L.R. 1421.

30 [1991] 2 F.L.R. 426.

31 [1998] 1 F.L.R. 384.

32 It is a sad reflection of our society that Ward L.J. had categorically to deny that they were Kosovan refugees.

33 *St. George's Healthcare N.H.S. Trust* v. *S* [1999] Fam. 26.

34 *Op. cit.*, n. 3 at 26.

passed over by the court.[35] No other law was pleaded. Perhaps it was felt the case raised enough issues without having to question whether the best interests principle was procedural or substantive and, if substantive, whether it applied to children domiciled in Malta.

Not surprisingly, they did not understand why they could not make the decision.[36] As already indicated, others shared their concern that the decision was being taken away from them. In Ward L.J.'s view their decision had to be 'respected'.[37] 'The hospital would be no more entitled to disregard their refusal than they are to disregard an adult patient's refusal.'[38] However, 'overriding control is vested in the court':[39] the court could not hide behind parents or doctors.

They were, said the court, devoted and responsible parents. And there were, as articulated by Robert Walker L.J., strong reasons for having regard to the parents' views:

> They have sincerely-held religious views (formed after discussion with a priest... and now backed by the Archbishop of Westminster). Their views might be described as controversial but (unlike the objections to blood transfusion held by Jehovah's Witnesses) they are not obviously contrary to any view generally accepted by our society. Still less are their views contrary to those generally accepted in the remote community from which they have come to this country... No one suggested that it was selfish or unreasonable that they should have concerns about their ability, either financially or personally, to care for [the surviving twin] at home.[40]

This was a case of sincerely-held religious views, not one where opposition was 'prompted by scruple or dogma'.[41] This line is not an easy one to hold. Sincerely-held religious views are often rooted in dogma. And why should religious views be afforded respect which other sincerely held and

35 Though they are quoted as saying – Ward L.J. even italicises it – that they understand that they have 'to be governed by the law of England' (p. 26). I think we can take it for granted that they do not understand the difference between questions of jurisdiction and those of choice of law.

36 *Op. cit.*, n. 3 at 26.

37 *Ibid.* at 32.

38 *Ibid.*

39 *Ibid.* at 33.

40 *Ibid.* at 104.

41 *Ibid.* at 52. According to Walker L.J. the views were entitled to great respect 'especially' so far as they were religious convictions (*ibid.* at 118).

(perhaps) controversial views are not?[42] For example, the views of the parents in *Re C* (*HIV Test*)[43] about the transmission from mother to child of HIV or the views of the Russian parents in *Re* M.M.[44] (who would eventually return to a country with health services little better than Gozo[45]) who disputed intravenous replacement immunoglobulin for their seven-year-old. Why the emphasis on parents' views at all? As Ward L.J. pointed out, whilst admitting this was unduly harsh on desperate parents, 'it is the *child's* best interests which are paramount, not the *parents*'.[46]

## III. Autonomy in Child-Rearing

How important, then, should the parents' decision be? Children need parents. All children have certain needs, physical and psychological. Sick children and children with special needs have greater needs. Parents, of course, do generally act in their children's best interests. And, even were it desirable, the state in whatever manifestation is no substitute for flesh and blood parents. Goldstein, Freud, Goldstein and Solnit in *The Best Interests of The Child* argue that:

> The law does not have the capacity to supervise the fragile, complex interpersonal bonds between child and parent.... The legal system has neither the resources nor the sensitivity to respond to a growing child's ever-changing needs and demands. It does not have the capacity to deal on an individual basis with the con sequences of its decisions, or to act with the speed that is required by a child's sense of time.[47]

The costs of intervention may also be great. It may undermine family stability and harmony. It may even polarise the family. By intervention the state may achieve nothing valuable and may destroy that which is. The minimal intervention principle in the Children Act 1989 is a recognition of this.[48] It is accepted that child-rearing is a risk-taking enterprise.

42 And see R.J. Ahdar, *Law And Religion* (Ashgate 2000).
43 *Op. cit.*, n. 20.
44 [2000] 1 F.L.R. 224.
45 Their home was in the Urals, 1600 km east of Moscow.
46 *Op. cit.*, n. 3 at 52.
47 *The Best Interests of the Child* (Free Press 1996) a t 91.
48 Section 1(5).

Because parental autonomy is considered important, the argument for confining state intrusion into the family is frequently put by legal, philosophical and social welfare commentators, as well as by judges. Most famously in the US Supreme Court Justice Rutledge said that 'it is cardinal with us that the custody, care and nurture of the child reside first in the parents, whose primary function and freedom include preparation for obligations the state can neither supply nor hinder'.[49]

There was, he argued, 'a private realm of family life which the state cannot enter'.[50] More recently, also in the US Supreme Court, Justice Burger spoke of '[t]he history and culture of western civilisation [which] reflect a strong tradition of parental concern for the nurture and up bringing of their children'.[51]

It is against this background that the fullest, modern statement of minimum state intervention in parent-child relations was articulated. In its definitive formulation,[52] Goldstein, Freud, Goldstein and Solnit argue:

> The child's need for security within the confines of the family must be met by law through its recognition of family privacy as the barrier to state intrusion upon parental autonomy. These rights – parental autonomy, a child's entitlement to autonomous parents, and privacy – are essential ingredients of family integrity.[53]

It will be noted that the child's psychological need for security is conflated into a right – it is not clear whether this is a legal or moral right – without so much of a hint of justification. But their justification of minimum state intervention is four-pronged.

First, there is biology. To be a child is 'to be at risk', whereas to be an adult is 'to be perceived to take risk'. Children are 'incomplete beings'.[54] Secondly, there is justification sought within psychology, or rather within Freudian psycho-analytic theory. These analyse 'complex and vital devel-

---

49 *Prince* v. *Massachusetts* (1944) 321 U.S. 158.

50 *Ibid.* at 166. See also *Pierce* v. *Society of Sisters* (1925) 268 U.S. 510; *Meyer* v. *Nebraska* (1923) 262 U.S. 390 and, most recently, *Troxel* v. *Granville* (2000) 120 S.Ct. 2054.

51 *Parham* v. *J.R.* (1979) 442 U.S. 382.

52 The earliest statement is in *Before the Best Interests of the Child* (Free Press 1979) (Sonja Goldstein was not one of the authors of this).

53 *Op. cit.*, n. 47 at 90.

54 *Ibid.* at 89.

opments' that 'thrive in the protective enclave of family life under guardianship by parents who are autonomous'.[55] It is argued:

> When family autonomy is broken or weakened by state intrusion [the child's] needs are thwarted, and her belief that her parents are omniscient and all-powerful is shaken prematurely. The effect on the child's developmental progress is likely to be detrimental.[56]

Two purposes, they say, underlie the parents' right within the family to be free of state intrusion:

> The first is to provide parents with an uninterrupted *opportunity* to meet the developing physical and emotional needs of their child in establishing the familial bonds critical to every child's healthy growth and development. The second purpose, and the one on which the parental right must ultimately rest, is to safeguard the continuing *maintenance* of these family ties – of psychological parent-child relationships – once they have been established.[57]

This is presented as if it were uncontentious. Those who disagree – reference is made in end-notes to a number of behavioural psychologists – are peremptorily dismissed. Arguments about the resilience of cognitive functions are cast aside, and those about social resilience are ignored.[58]

Thirdly, they offer a philosophical rationale. 'A policy of minimum intervention by the state… accords with our firm belief as citizens in individual freedom and human dignity,' they state.[59] This is, of course, to ignore the impact that the exercise of freedom can have on relation ships where there is, as there is with parent-child relationships, an imbalance of power. Failure to intervene can, therefore, mean that a parent's will prevails over a child's legitimate interests and, even if some of these interests may seem relatively trivial, others may have profound effects on children's lives.

The fourth strand in their argument points to the dangers of state intervention. Attention has already been drawn to this. Thus, they ar-

---

55 *Ibid.* at 90.

56 *Ibid.*

57 *Ibid.*

58 *Ibid.* at 259-60.

59 *Ibid.* at 91.

gue, 'by its intrusion' into the family 'the state may make a bad situation worse; indeed, it may turn a tolerable or even good institution into a bad one'.[60] There is some truth in this but it underestimates the dangers in non-interference, and in drawing the line for interference (as they do) too conservatively.[61]

It is accepted that intervention must not be excessive, and it must be based on standards which are formulated as precisely as possible. Vague standards invite arbitrary and unwarranted interventions. Where standards are insufficiently precise, decision-making can be left to the *ad hoc* responses of health and welfare professionals, and judges. And, of course, vague standards can be employed all too easily to impose the standards of one section of the population on another[62] – a problem accentuated where there is, as in *Re A,* a multi-cultural setting. And standards should be as value-neutral as possible: value-laden standards can impose unwarranted biases and intrude oppressively into parent child relationships.

The writings of Goldstein, Freud and Solnit have been very influential:[63] Lainie Friedman Ross's book, *Children, Families and Health Care Decision-Making,* as yet less so.[64] Her case for, what she calls, 'constrained parental autonomy',[65] offering as it does a reformulation of Goldstein, Freud and Solnit, must also be examined. First, she rejects two well-known models of the family: Jeffrey Blustein's, in which parental duties are given priority over parental rights;[66] and Laurence Houlgate's communal model of the family based on the characteristics of a *Gemeinschaft* in contrast to a *Gesellschaft.*[67] These approaches are respectively deontological and utilitarian. What is wrong with Blustein's model, according to Ross, is that it does not permit parents to consider their own needs and interests and those of other family members when making decisions for their children. The problem with Houlgate's model, as Ross sees it, is that its utilitarianism ignores the distinctive values of the family.

---

60 *Ibid.*

61 I criticised this in *The Rights and Wrongs of Children* (Frances Pinter 1983), and 'The Best Interests of the Child? Is *The Best Interests of the Child* in the Best Interests of Children?' (1997) 11 *Int. J. Law Pol. Fam.* 360.

62 *Re W* [1999] 1 F.L.R. 869 is a graphic (and frightening) illustration.

63 The English Children Act 1989 is heavily permeated with notions and concepts drawn from Goldstein *et al.*

64 Clarendon Press 1998.

65 *Ibid.* at 50-2.

66 *Parents and Children: The Ethics of the Family* (Oxford University Press 1982).

67 *Family and State: The Philosophy of Family Law* (Rowman and Littlefield 1988).

Ross posits instead the principle of 'constrained parental autonomy'. This differs from Blustein's thesis because it allows parents to balance the competing claims of other family members (including their own) against the child's interests, provided 'parents procure a threshold level of each primary good for their child'.[68] Beyond that, parents can consider not only the child's self-interests, but also the interests of the child as a member of a particular family and community. Arguably, this would include the weaker conjoined twin's interest in the healthy future of her stronger sister. This could be considered part of the weaker twin's 'well-being'.[69]

Ross's thesis is consistent with offering the child a very limited range of life options: certainly she rejects the child's right to an 'open future'.[70] Further, because she allows for balancing, she rejects submitting cases to a child's 'best interests' standard.[71] Whatever the defects of this standard – and they need not be rehearsed here – it does impress upon the decision-maker that the child is the focus of the decision. When balancing is allowed all sorts of extraneous considerations become legitimate factors. Ross's thesis differs from Houlgate's because the principle of 'constrained parental autonomy' acknowledges the family's uniquely valuable role in providing the goods of intimacy to its members.

The scope of the 'intimate family' is not clear. It could be drawn over-widely. Its meaning[72] is not clear. Within intimate families we are told:

> ... one member's well-being is an integral part of the other member's well-being. Intimates take on one another's goals... To the extent that each family member incorporates the other members' ends into his own ends, the difference between altruism and egoism collapses. Other-regarding activities become self-regarding activities.[73]

So, parents may adopt a goal which may not be congruent with the goals (or, of course, best interests) of any particular child. It is not entirely clear what these 'goals' are. It would seem that the intimate family is some kind of community with its own goals. But where do these goals come from? It

68 *Op. cit.*, n. 64 at 24.

69 And see J. Raz, *Ethics in the Public Domain* (Clarendon Press 1994).

70 *Cf.* J. Feinberg, 'The Child's Right to an Open Future' in W. Aiken and H. LaFollette (eds.), *Whose Child?* (Littlefield and Adams 1980).

71 *Op. cit.*, n. 64 at 41.

72 There are dangers of reification too.

73 *Op. cit.*, n. 64 at 31.

should not be forgotten that the parent-child relationship is a microcosm of asymmetry of power.

To be fair, Ross does emphasise restrictions. Her thesis is about 'constrained parental autonomy'. Why constrained? Because, she accepts, children are owed respect.[74] Not the equal respect that Kant[75] and Dworkin[76] speak of – though neither of course does in the context of children – but one which is commensurate with cognitive and emotional development. She rejects the liberationist thesis.[77] She also rejects the philosophy of Article 12 of the United Nations Convention on the Rights of the Child[78] (though she demonstrates no awareness of its existence) and of Gillick[79] (which is relegated to an endnote). And she rejects self-determination by children, even where they are competent. Her reasons are:

- respect for a threshold of competency in children places the emphasis on short-term autonomy rather than on a child's lifetime autonomy.[80]
- the child's decisions are based on limited experience, so that his decisions are not part of a well-conceived life plan.[81] Children need to be protected from their 'impetuosity'.[82]
- ... family autonomy promotes the interests and goals of both the children and their parents. It serves the needs and interests of the child to have autonomous parents who will help her become an autonomous individual.[83]

The first argument employs a narrow concept of competency. The evidence suggests that many more children are competent of taking health care decisions than we are prepared to accept.[84] What Ross does is to

74 See the discussion, *op. cit.*, n. 64 at 44-50.

75 *Groundwork of the Metaphysics of Morals* (trans. H.J. Paton) (Hutchinson 1964).

76 *Taking Rights Seriously* (Duckworth 1977).

77 In particular that of Richard Farson (though she does not cite his leading work *Birthrights* (Penguin 1978) and H. Cohen, *Equal Rights for Children* (Littlefield and Adams 1980).

78 This emphasises the child's right to express views freely in all matters affecting him/her, and the opportunity to be heard in judicial and administrative proceedings affecting him/her.

79 *Op. cit.*, n. 15.

80 *Op. cit.*, n. 64 at 61.

81 *Ibid.*

82 *Ibid.* at 62.

83 *Ibid.*

84 See P. Alderson, *Children's Consent to Surgery* (Open University Press 1993).

construct for children both a higher and a different threshold of competency than would be standard in legal and bioethical literature when adult competency is in issue. She does not – and I would suggest cannot – justify this. The second argument is also wrong. Limited experience does not equate with incompetence. A more sophisticated theory of competency is called for. This would relate competence to the decision being made: taking the contraceptive pill[85] and agreeing to a heart transplant[86] require different skills. This is rarely recognised by legislation-which tends to be age-related-but was one of the remarkable insights of the *Gillick* decision.[87] The third argument of Ross is then as redundant as it is dangerous. Why emphasise family autonomy (in reality parental autonomy) when children can take their own decisions? Of course, young children will rarely be able to take their own decisions. But this does not mean that we can leave all such decisions to parents.

Like Goldstein, Freud and Solnit, Ross has 'great reservation about scrutinising the intimate family'.[88] It is clear where Goldstein and Ross and others who present the case for protecting the family enclave derive this from, and where their error lies. Classic liberalism – its most obvious source is John Stuart Mill's *On Liberty*[89] – *believes* that the state should stay out of our lives. Its paradigmatic conflict is between the citizen and the state. The state should stay out of the lives of citizens, out of respect for their moral autonomy and human dignity. But the paradigmatic family conflict is not between the citizen and the state: it is between two persons. If the state removes itself from concern with this type of conflict – if, for example, it takes no interest in domestic violence or child abuse[90] – the weak can easily be sacrificed to the strong. There is no moral autonomy or human dignity then for those whose interests can so routinely be trampled upon. It is not so long ago that we expected the parent to speak for the child, to represent the child's interests, even where that child had been abused by that parent.[91] We have moved on since then – but just how far?

---

85 At issue, if obliquely, in *Gillick* v. *West Norfolk and Wisbech A.H.A., op. cit.*, n. 15.

86 See *Re* M [1999] 2 F.L.R. 1097 (15-year-old girl's refusal to consent to a heart transplant overruled by court).

87 Particularly the judgment of Lord Scarman.

88 *Op. cit.*, n. 64 at 44.

89 First published in 1859.

90 But see F.E. Olsen, 'The Myth of State Intervention in the Family' (1985) 18 *journal of Law Reform* 835.

91 It took the Maria Colwell case in 1973-74 to bring us to our senses.

## IV. Why do Parents have Rights?

It tends to have been taken for granted that parents have rights (now as part of a responsibility package). But why do they have them? This is a critical question and must be investigated.

For John Eekelaar behind the granting of parental responsibility lie both 'a factual recognition of a state of affairs, and also a normative granting of approval by the state to a given situation'.[92] He sees it as a status which consists in, and is co-extensive with, practical action. But English law (and it is not alone in this) assigns parental responsibility to all mothers[93] and, where they are married, to their husbands.[94] It does not assign it to all fathers, even those who act as social fathers.[95] It assigns it to gestational mothers, even those who are not genetic mothers and have no intention of being social mothers.[96] Parents who have never looked after their children or do not now do so and who may never do so have parental rights.[97]

Different views have been expressed about why parents have rights. Many rest the case on biology. They assert that individuals have a right to their genetic offspring. As already indicated, English law has never subscribed in a coherent way to this. But even if it had, even if all other legal systems agreed, the question would remain as to why biology should confer rights. Some point to the unique biological relationship shared by parent and child. But, if genetic similarity alone were sufficient for ascription of parental rights, an identical twin would possess a greater claim than the parent, which looks odd, even absurd. And perhaps a conjoined twin would possess an even greater claim!

There are different versions of the genetic argument. On one, rights to biological children are derived from the property interest parents have in their genes. The parent owns, in John Locke's language, that which s/he

92 'Parental Responsibility: State of Nature or Nature of the State?' (1991) J.S.W.L. 37.

93 Children Act 1989 ss. 2(1), 2(2)(a).

94 Children Act 1989 s. 2(1).

95 Children Act 1989 s. 2(2)(b): but see s. 4(1) for methods of acquisition of parental responsibility by unmarried fathers.

96 Human Fertilisation and Embryology Act 1990 s. 27(1). And the husband of a surrogate is deemed the father of the child (s. 28(2)), unless he proves he did not consent to the infertility treatment.

97 For example, the parents of children in local authority care (see Children Act 1989 s. 33(3)(b)).

'mixed his/her labour with'.[98] The products of the body, like the products of hands, are that person's to do with as they please. Of course, this ignores the crucial steps which occur between production of reproductive materials and gestation and childbirth. If these were taken into account, the property rights of the mother would far exceed those of the father. The property rights argument is untenable today. Where support for it remains it tends to concentrate on the case for giving mothers parental rights. Thus, Katherine Bartlett points out that 'mothers have a kind of automatic responsibility for their children'.[99] The mother demonstrates this through decisions she takes during pregnancy, including whether she terminates this. But we have moved away from an exchange view of parenthood, where parental rights were based on an investment made by parents, to a more child-centred approach, where the best interests of children are considered especially important. However, as we shall see, there is a tendency for the child's best interests to be over-identified with the parents' interests. The assumption that parents know best what is in their child's best interests matches the equally entrenched presumption that the best place for children is with parents. The latter may not be empirically sound. There is concern that the former may equally lack a firm basis.[100]

A third attempt to explain why parents have rights is the so-called 'intention theory', propounded by Hill and Shultz.[101] Thus, according to Hill, what is essential to parenthood is not the biological tie between parent and child, but the pre-conception intention to have a child accompanied by undertaking whatever action is necessary to bring the child into the world. But, if married, a parent acquires status irrespective of intention, and unmarried fathers who demonstrate an intention to be a social parent do not automatically have parental rights. Both Hill and Shultz argue for this model in the context only of artificial reproduction.

98 See *Two Treatises of Government*, P. Laslett (ed.) (Cambridge University Press 1960) at 2, 26-30. A modern presentation is K. Roosevelt III (1998) 39 *Santa Clara Law Review* 79.

99 'Re-Expressing Parenthood' (1988) 98 *Yale Law Journal* 293.

100 A useful source is E. Bartholet, *Family Bonds: Adoption and the Politics of Parenting* (Harvard University Press 1993) a t 174-81.

101 J.L. Hill, 'What Does it Mean to be a "Parent"? The Claims of Biology as the Basis for Parental Rights' (1991) 66 *New York University Law Review* 353; M.M. Shultz, 'Reproductive Technology and Intent-Based Parenthood: An Opportunity for Gender Neutrality' (1990) *Wisconsin Law Review* 297.

At one time another justification posited for parental rights was marriage. If this argument was ever convincing – which I doubt – it is unlikely to persuade in a society in which close to 40 per cent of children are born outside marriage.

There is no convincing explanation as to why parents have rights, any more than there is, for example, a convincing justification for conferring personhood on newborn babies,[102] or for the institution of private property.[103] But, in all three cases, we must have a starting-point for our thinking and make some assumptions if we are to proceed at all.

Let us grant, then, that parents have rights whilst remembering not only their limits but the shaky foundations upon which the ascription rests.

## V. Whose Rights?

Courts in recent cases have eschewed any reliance as such on parents' rights. Even in *Re T* (the liver transplant case), for example, which I regard as the nadir of judicial thinking in this area, Waite L.J. said that this was 'not an occasion – even in an age preoccupied with "rights" – to talk of the rights of a child, or the rights of a parent, or the rights of the court'.[104]

It is notable that in a judgment which gave scant attention to a child's most basic rights the judge put children's rights before parents' rights, though I doubt whether in the light of the decision – in effect to condemn a toddler to death – much significance should attach to this. Butler-Sloss L.J. characterised mother and child as 'one'[105] – as in 'They two shall be one flesh' it is rather obvious who that 'one' is. In *Re T*, the Court of Appeal deferred to the mother's views. Said Butler-Sloss L.J.: 'The welfare of this child depends upon his mother.'[106] Fortin comments that the 'underlying message [is] that a mother may always have the upper hand... where the proposed surgery is invasive, the child very young and there is a need for intensive post-operative aftercare'.[107] Had the As read *Re T* they might have expected their opinions to prevail.

---

102 Those who believe this – myself included – have to contend with Michael Tooley and John Harris.

103 *Cf.* L. Becker, *Property Rights* (Routledge Kegan Paul 1977).

104 *Re T* [1997] 1 F.L.R. 502 at 512.

105 *Ibid.* at 510.

106 *Ibid.*

107 *Children's Rights and the Developing Law* (Butterworths 1998) at 261.

Between *Re T* and *Re A* the Court of Appeal was confronted with parents who refused to allow their child to be tested for HIV and a mother who persisted in breast-feeding whilst HIV positive herself.[108] After describing *Re T* as 'at the other end of the spectrum',[109] Butler-Sloss L.J. expressed the view:

> We are not talking about the rights of parents. We are talking about the rights of the child... The parents' views, which are not the views of the majority, cannot stand against the right of the child to be properly cared for in every sense. This child has the right to have sensible and responsible people find out whether she is or is not HIV positive... This child has her own rights.[110]

It would be easy to conclude that the judges speak in the rhetoric of children's rights only when they believe the parents' decision is manifestly wrong. Perhaps also that children's rights are accorded greater prominence when parents' views are aberrant.

*Re A*, however, makes little reference to rights at all. Parental rights are said, following *Re* K.D.,[111] to be subordinate to children's welfare,[112] but there is no other reference to parents' rights at all. As far as Jodie is concerned, Robert Walker L.J. acknowledges her 'right to life' which includes 'the right to have [her] own body whole and intact and (on reaching an age of understanding) to take decisions about [her] own body'.[113] But the intriguing vista is raised of an adult or Gillick-competent conjoined twin consenting to separation from the other twin, also adult or Gillick-competent, who refuses to consent to the operation.[114] And, presumably, if this will kill the refuser, that twin applying for an injunction to stop the surgery.[115] Ward L.J., on the other hand, is happy to conclude that Johnson J was 'plainly right to conclude that the operation would be in Jodie's best

108 In *Re* C (*HIV Test*) [1999] 2 F.L.R. 1004.
109 *Ibid.* at 1020.
110 *Ibid.* at 1021.
111 [1988] A.C. 886.
112 *Op. cit.*, n. 3 at 49.
113 *Ibid.* at 119.
114 The refusal could be overridden: see *Re R* [1992] Fam. 11, *Re* W [1993] Fam. 64. But is this a decision a court would take?
115 Raised by John Harris in his 'Gilbert and George' scenario. See paper in this issue.

interest',[116] and makes no attempt to justify the separation as recognising any right she might have, for example to life or to bodily integrity.

In relation to Mary, who is said to be 'designated', even 'self-designated',[117] for death, there is more resort to 'rights talk'.[118] There is reference to the 'universality of rights'.[119] her life is said to have 'equal value'.[120] She is alive,[121] is a separate individual,[122] and is most definitely not a 'monster'.[123] On the question whether she would benefit from the operation, there is some ambivalence. At one point in his judgment, Ward L.J. expresses the view that the only thing she will gain from the operation is her bodily integrity and dignity[124] (which Brooke L.J. adds, nature denies her).[125] Elsewhere he states she will get no benefit from the operation.[126] She has, he also says, a 'right to life' but 'little right to be alive. She is alive because and only because... she sucks the lifeblood of Jodie and she sucks the lifeblood out of Jodie'.[127] Robert Walker L.J. sees her as acquiring on death a 'body whole and intact'.[128] The operation would give her in death 'bodily integrity'.[129] This is of course puzzling for it is difficult to see why Mary, any more than someone on a life-support or dialysis machine, lacked 'integrity'. It is difficult, indeed, to understand what the judges mean by 'integrity'.

Did the characters in this tragedy have any rights not articulated by the court? They – and I include the health professionals in this – were given the opportunity to establish the facts and air the arguments in as neutral a forum as possible. All parties were represented (at the state's

116 *Op. cit.*, n. 3 at 37.

117 *Ibid.* at 98 *per* Brooke L.J. For Ward L.J. she is 'doomed', 'designated' for death: see at 54.

118 Mary Ann Glendon's expression in *Rights Talk* (Free Press 1991). Of course, whilst she is critical of the contemporary emphasis on rights, I applaud it.

119 *Op. cit.*, n. 3 at 71 *per* Brooke L.J. referring to *Perka* v. *The Queen* (1985) 13 D.L.R. (4th) 1, 31 per Wilson J.

120 *Ibid.* at 44 *per* Ward L.J.

121 *Ibid.* at 35 *per* Ward L.J. at 70 *per* Brooke L.J. at 100 *per* Robert Walker L.J.

122 *Ibid.* at 35 *per* Ward L.J. She has an existence separate from her mother *per* Ward L.J. at 37.

123 All three judges reject this derogatory language *per* Ward L.J. at 37; Brooke L.J. at 70; and Robert Walker L.J. at 101, who says it is 'redolent of superstitious horror'.

124 *Ibid.* at 39.

125 *Ibid.* at 99.

126 *Ibid.* at 46.

127 *Ibid.* at 54.

128 *Ibid.* at 119.

129 *Ibid.*

expense) and the decision was reasoned and transparent. A comparison with the events in Philadelphia in 1977 could not be starker.[130] It is inconceivable that any subsequent case in the United Kingdom would not also be taken to court, but the Court of Appeal should have made clearer the circumstances in which this is required. *Re A* would not have gone to court had the parents consented to elective surgery.[131] But in the light of the discussion of the lawfulness of the operation, could surgeons now risk a separation (certainly one likely to lead to the death of one twin) without the sanction of a court? And, despite what the Court of Appeal says, could a hospital allow conjoined twins to die if that is what parents wanted? Before *Re A* the map was relatively uncharted: after it the seas look uncomfortably choppy.

The religion-culture question is also troubling. Did too much hinge upon the religion and culture of the parents? Had they not been Catholics or had they been less committed Catholics or had they been Catholics from a less Catholic society than Gozo, the decision to separate the twins would have been less obstacle-ridden. If facilities on Gozo had been better the parents' reluctance might have been easier to overcome. The twins, of course, were oblivious to all of this. Should a child's right to life depend on her parents' religion or lack of it? Or on the facilities in her native land? And suppose there had been a conflict of religious views[132] or another difference of opinion between the parents. We can safely assume that despite section 2(7) of the Children Act,[133] this is not a decision which one parent can take.[134] But would it have been any easier to overrule one parent than two?

130 A three-judge panel of a local family court retired for only three minutes before deciding a separation might go ahead.

131 But could they do so unless the separation was in the best interests of both twins? How far can the reasoning in *Re Y* (1996) 35 B.M.L.R. 111 (an operation not in best medical interests but for emotional, psychological and social benefit approved by the court) extend? Could Raz's 'well-being' argument (see text at n. 69) be advanced here?

132 As in *Re J* [1999] 2 F.L.R. 678 (Wall J.); [2000] 1 F.L.R. 571 (Court of Appeal).

133 Which does not distinguish major decisions from everyday ones.

134 Following *Re J*, *op. cit.*, n. 132.

## VI. Best Interests?

The Court of Appeal concluded (by a majority)[135] that the operation could not be justified as in the best interests of Mary (the weaker twin) since it was not in her best interests to die.[136] It was, however, in the best interests of Jodie (the stronger twin).[137] Of course, the welfare of both twins was paramount.[138] It has been clear for thirty years that 'paramount' means 'only', even if this was not what Parliament originally intended.[139] It was inevitable that courts would be confronted with cases where the interests of children would be in conflict, and it would be impossible to apply the paramountcy principle to both.[140] The problem was anticipated, but not provided for. No one, it can safely be assumed, could have anticipated that the interests of children in conflict would be conjoined twins. The House of Lords in *Birmingham C.C.* v. *H*,[141] confronted with a conflict of interests between a mother who was a child and her baby, neatly avoided a solution.[142] Perhaps for this we should be grateful. Supposing it had decided that the younger child's welfare should prevail. Or had been attracted by Solomon's solution[143] or Jon Elster's.[144] The majority in *Re A* accordingly fell back on the Court of Appeal's resolution of the dilemma in the *Birmingham* case: as Evans L.J. put it, the paramountcy requirement 'must be regarded as qualified, in the cases where the welfare of more than one child is involved, by the need to have regard to potential detriment for one in the light of potential benefit for the other'.[145] So for Ward L.J. in *Re A* it was necessary to choose the 'lesser of the two evils'[146] and find 'the least detrimental alternative'[147] (a conscious or an unconscious

---

135 Brooke L.J. agreed with Ward L.J.'s judgment on the family law issues: see *op. cit.*, n. 3 at 62.

136 *Ibid.* a t 39.

137 *Ibid.* a t 37.

138 Children Act 1989 s. 1(1).

139 *J.* v. *C.* (1970] A.C. 668.

140 Examples are *Re T and E* [1995] 1 F.L.R. 581 and *F.* v. *Leeds C.C.* [1994] 2 F.L.R. 60.

141 [1994] 2 A.C. 212.

142 They saw as an issue of statutory construction: paramountcy was interpreted to apply only to the child in respect of whom the application was made.

143 Though in a sense the court in *Re A* came (literally) to Solomon's conclusion.

144 For Elster tossing a coin was as appropriate (more appropriate) as any other solution. See 'Solomonic Judgments: Against the Best Interest of the Child' (1987) 54 *University Chicago Law Review* 1.

145 [1993] 1 F.L.R. 883 a t 899.

146 *Op. cit.*, n. 3 at 49.

147 *Ibid.*

adoption of Goldstein, Freud and Solnit's hallowed phrase,[148] one wonders). It was not then difficult to conclude – I leave aside the lawfulness of the operation[149] – that since the weaker twin had only a few months to live and the stronger one had the prospect of a relatively normal life if the operation took place, that the operation should be performed.

For Robert Walker L.J., as for Johnson J., the proposed operation was in the best interests of both twins.[150] As far as Mary was concerned, to prolong her life for a few months 'would confer no benefit on her but would be to her disadvantage'.[151] Robert Walker L.J. argued:

> If Mary had been born separated from Jodie but with the defective brain and heart and lungs which she has, and if her life were being supported, not by Jodie but by mechanical means, it would be right to withdraw that artificial life-support system and allow Mary to die.[152]

Robert Walker L.J.'s analysis is more realistic and more convincing. Ward L.J. conceded that if Mary had been a singleton she would not have been viable and resuscitation would have been abandoned.[153] He also admitted that it was hard to see any benefit flowing from her continued life and that she existed 'pathetically on borrowed time'.[154] It is also said that she was doomed, self -designated for very early death and beyond help.[155] Of course, she had the right to life but she was unable to exercise it. A very premature baby, such as the one in *Royal Wolverhampton Hospitals N.H.S. Trust* v. *B*,[156] has the right to life. The child in *A N.H.S. Trust* v. *D*,[157] also premature but now 19-months-old with irreversible brain abnormality, severe chronic disabilities, heart failure, renal and hepatic dysfunction and severe developmental delay, has the right to life. But both of these children, and Mary, also have the right to die with dignity. We must ac-

148 *Op. cit.*, n. 47 a t 50.

149 I consider that on any positivistic interpretation of 'lawful' the operation to separate the twins was of dubious propriety. And see below, at 279.

150 *Op. cit.*, n. 3, at 104-5, 119.

151 *Ibid.* at 105.

152 *Ibid.*

153 *Ibid.* at 37.

154 *Op. cit.*, n. 3 at 38.

155 *Ibid.* at 54.

156 [2000] 1 F.L.R. 953.

157 [2000] 2 F.L.R. 677.

cept – as we did in *Bland*[158] – that sometimes this right trumps the more obvious and fundamental right to life.

Mary was 'alive'.[159] Unhappily, she was not 'living'[160] and could never do so. Had she been a singleton it would not have been worthwhile to treat her.[161] Cruel though it is to say so, her life was not worthwhile. Some (John Keown for example) draw a distinction between the worthwhile-ness of treatment and the worthwhile-ness of life.[162] I agree with John Harris[163] that the concepts cannot be distinguished, so that treatment is only worthwhile if life is worthwhile. Further, it is not an argument about resources or priorities. This argument is unacceptable. Nor is it because she was a parasite: I deprecate Ward L.J.'s use of this term.[164] Or because she was 'not innocent'[165] (comparing her to a six-year-old with a gun, as Ward L.J. does,[166] is obtuse and morally blind). It is because treatment would have achieved nothing for her beyond prolonging her 'aliveness' for a short period of time. Her body could not sustain life. She was, as Ward L.J. acknowledges, 'lost to [her parents] anyway'.[167] But to say she was 'designated' for death merely obfuscates. It is meaningless – all medical intervention is directed to persons who will die – and/or a nod in the direction of religion (the closest would be Calvinism – an odd ideology to inflict on parents whose own Catholicism was not allowed to dictate the decision). In fact the source relied upon, and misunderstood, is rabbinic:[168] it is even stranger to think that the responsum of an American talmudical scholar should have exerted so much influence on a secular court adjudicating on the moral dilemma of a Catholic family.

158 *Airedale N.H.S. Trust* v. *Bland* [1993] A.C. 789.

159 *Op. cit.*, n. 3 at 35 (Ward L.J.); 70 (Brooke L.J.); 110 (Walker L.J.).

160 Nor was she dying. *Cf. Re C* [1989] 2 All E.R. 782 (though a close examination of the facts reveals this was not so).

161 As in *Re J* [1991] Fam. 33.

162 'Restoring Moral and Intellectual Shape to the Law after Bland ' (1997) 113 L.Q.R. 481. Ward L.J. quotes the distinction with approval (at 43).

163 Paper earlier in this issue.

164 *Op. cit.*, n. 3 at 54.

165 *Ibid.* at 61.

166 *Ibid.*

167 *Ibid.* at 53.

168 For the source see J.D. Bleich, *Bioethical Dilemmas: A Jewish Perspective* (KTAV Publishing 1998) a t 283-328.

## VII. Conclusion

I have not addressed the lawfulness of the operation. This was not (fortunately) within my remit. For reasons given by other commentators it is difficult to see how the Court of Appeal could have concluded that separation was lawful. What has not been pursued – and must be reserved for a later discussion – is whether determination as unlawful terminates the argument. There are two possible approaches. One might have been adopted by the House of Lords had it heard a further appeal. This would have involved a reformulation of *Woollin*[169] to rule out *mens rea* in a case such as the conjoined twins. The second would require us to acknowledge that there are higher values beyond the law, that the decision was right though legally wrong, and that even judges have a discretion (to be exercised most sparingly) to disobey the law.[170]

As to the desirability of separation, as I have indicated, I believe the court came to the right decision, though I think the reasoning of the minority is the more convincing. But even with Robert Walker L.J. I cannot go the whole way. I cannot conceptualise Mary's right to life as including her right to a whole and intact body. This is a totally specious argument. It would suggest, for example, that those who have had a heart transplant are in some way less persons or less whole. The court was right to refuse to defer to the parents. It was better for all concerned that this was a decision taken out of their hands and subjected to a principled reasoning.

The majority was wrong to prioritise Jodie's interests (both were persons and Mary as important as Jodie): but it was, as Robert Walker L.J. argued, in the best interests of both twins that they be separated. The decision is one which upholds dignity: the right of Jodie to live with dignity, the right of Mary to die with dignity. Perhaps even the right of Mary to confer life upon her sister. These children had the right to expect a thorough investigation of their plight by a neutral decision-maker and they got it.

That there are dangers in putting the intimate family beyond scrutiny has been seen often, most recently in the 'liver transplant' case.[171] There are more important rights to confer upon children than the right to au-

169 *R.* v. *Woollin* [1999] 1 A.C. 82.

170 *Cf.* M.R. Kadish and S.H. Kadish, *Discretion to Disobey* (Stanford University Press 1973) a t 86 *et seq.*

171 *Re T, op. cit.*, n. 104.

tonomous parents. What Ross calls 'family autonomy'[172] (more accurately parental autonomy) does not necessarily promote, and in this case would certainly not have promoted, 'the interests and goals' of the children.

The case reveals the dangers of relativism (cultural or not), the over-emphasis on religion: accepting the Archbishop of Westminster's brief may constitute an unfortunate precedent, and the underplaying of rights, particularly children's rights. It is to be hoped that the parents will come to live with this decision and that Jodie will recover both from her early life experiences and from the loss of her sister. This is one case the facts of which cry out for continuing review. It is more likely to have a happy ending than many litigated disputes about children.

172 *Op. cit.*, n. 64.

CHAPTER 5

# The Morality of Cultural Pluralism

## Prologue – Pluralism and Children's Rights

In 1968 a man went to a doctor in South London for medical treatment of a venereal disease. He introduced his young wife to the doctor and let it be known that he had already taken her to a clinic to be fitted with a contraceptive appliance. The doctor was concerned and reported the matter to the police who brought a complaint to the juvenile court that she was in need of care because she was being exposed to moral danger.[1] The couple were Nigerian Muslims:[2] he was in his mid-twenties and she was at most 13, but may have been as young as 11. They had married in northern Nigeria shortly before coming to England. The court made a "fit person order"[3] under the Children and Young Persons Act 1963 and the girl was admitted to the care of a local authority. The reasons which prompted the court to conclude that she was in moral danger are encapsulated in the following statement:

> Here is a girl, aged 13, or possibly less, unable to speak English, living in London with a man twice her age to whom she has been married by Muslim law. He admits having had sexual intercourse with her at a time when according to the medical evidence the development of puberty had a almost certainly not begun... He further admits that since the marriage... he has had sexual relations with a prostitute in Nigeria from whom he has contracted venereal disease. In our opinion a continuance of such an association, notwithstanding the marriage, would be repugnant to any decent-minded English man or woman. Our decision reflects that repugnance.[4]

This decision was reversed on appeal by the Divisional Court. The Lord Chief Justice, Lord Parker, conceded that it was possible to hold that a

1 *Alhaji Mohamed* v. *Knott* [1969] 1 Q.B. 1.
2 They were domiciled in Nigeria.
3 Fit person orders were replaced by care orders in 1969.
4 *Op. cit.*, note 1, p. 15.

 | DOI:10.1163/9789004219106_006

validly married wife was in moral danger, but he refused to accept that the girl in this case was. He said:

> I would never dream of suggesting that a decision by this bench of justices, with this very experienced chairman, could ever be termed perverse: but having read that, I am convinced that they have misdirected themselves. When they say that 'a continuance of such an association notwithstanding the marriage would be repugnant to any decent-minded English man or woman', they are I think, and can only be, considering the view of an English man or woman in relation to an English girl and our Western way of life. I cannot myself think that decent-minded Englishmen or women, realising the way of life in which this girl was brought up, and this man for that matter, would inevitably say that this is repugnant. It is certainly natural for a girl to marry at that age. They develop sooner, and there is nothing abhorrent in their way of life for a girl of 13 to marry a man of 25... Granted that this man may be said to be a bad lot, that he has done things in the past which perhaps nobody would approve of, it does not follow from that this girl, happily married to this man, is under any moral danger by associating and living with him. For my part, as it seems to me, it could only be said that she was in moral danger if one was considering somebody brought up and living in our way of life and to hold that she is in moral danger in the circumstances of this case can only be arrived at, as it seems to me, by ignoring the way of life in which she was brought up, and her husband was brought up.[5]

The Divisional Court held that the marriage was entitled to recognition by the English courts. It followed from this that the husband was not committing the offence of unlawful sexual intercourse[6] – unlawful meant outside marriage.[7]

The case, understandably, provoked considerable controversy. The *Daily Express* was outraged. So was Baroness Summerskill who initiated a debate in the House of Lords.[8] The decision was branded as racist, a failure by white institutions to protect a vulnerable black child. Olive

5 *Ibid.*, pp. 15-16.

6 Sexual Offences Act 1956 s. 6(1) (intercourse with a girl under 16).

7 *Cf. R* v. *Chapman* [1959] 1 Q.B. 100 (on the interpretation of s. 19(1) of the 1956 Act).

8 *Hansard* H. L. vol. 290, cols. 1321-1323.

Stone thought the case "disturbing"[9] and Ruth Deech believed its "practical consequences would be disastrous".[10] It led Ian Karsten to call for a minimum age to be prescribed for recognition purposes.[11] But other commentators welcomed the decision. It showed a willingness to embrace the customs and culture of another society.[12] What was "moral danger" was being tested by the morality of the culture to which the couple belonged. The decision was seen to be consonant with an acceptance of moral pluralism.[13]

Whichever stance one adopted, the case had troubling features. An analysis of Lord Parker's judgment reveals prejudices and misconceptions galore, not least a concern that this understanding of Islamic culture in Northern Nigeria may not have been very deep, assumptions and biases filling in gaps in his knowledge base. It is not clear what evidence, if any, was given to either court about the life realities of Muslim Nigeria.

About the same time as *Mohamed* v. *Knott* was going through the courts, the question arose in a different context in *R* v. *Derrivierre*.[14] A West Indian father was charged with an assault upon his 12-year-old son occasioning him actual bodily harm. The boy had been disobedient and the father punished him by punching him a number of times in the face. English law provides a defense to the crime of willfully assaulting a child[15] if the purpose is chastisement and the punishment is moderate and reasonable.[16] The father was given a six months term of imprisonment for what the Deputy Chairman of the Inner London Quarter Sessions described as a "brutal attack". On an appeal against sentence the Criminal Division of the Court of Appeal upheld the decision and set out the broad principle involved:

> Standards of parental correction are different in the West Indies from those which are acceptable in this country; and the Court fully

---

9 *Family Law* (1977), p. 40.

10 "Immigrants and Family Law", (1973), 123 NLJ 110, 111.

11 "Child Marriages" (1969), 32 MLR 212, 215-216.

12 Brenda Hoggett (1977) *Parents and Children*, Sweet and Maxwell, p. 110.

13 M. D. A. Freeman (1974) *The Legal Structure*, Longmans, p. 48.

14 (1969) 53 Cr. App. Rep. 637.

15 See Children and Young Persons Act 1933 s. 1(7).

16 As to which see Cockbum, C. J. in *R.* v. *Hopley* (1860) 2 F & F 202. See further P. Newell (1989) *Children Are People Too*, Bedford Square Press. On the religious roots see P. Greven (1992) *Spare the Child*, Vintage Books. Echoes of this can be detected in M. Straus (1994) *Beating The Devil Out of Them: Corporal Punishment in the American Family*, Lexington Books.

> accepts that immigrants coming to this country may find initially that our ideas are different from those upon which they have been brought up in regard to the methods and manner in which children are to be disciplined. There can be no doubt that once in this country, this country's laws must apply; and there can be no doubt that, according to the law of this country, the chastisement given to this boy was excessive and the assault complained of was proved. Nevertheless had this been a first offence, and had there been some real reason for thinking that the appellant either did not understand what the standards in this country were or was having difficulty in adjusting himself, the Court would no doubt have taken that into account and given it such consideration as it could.[17]

In fact Derrivierre had a previous conviction for assaulting his daughter only a year before and thus had already received a fair warning of the unacceptable nature of this type of behaviour in England. But the case does show a willingness by English courts to take supposedly different standards of another culture into account in sentencing.[18] More recently, in a child care case,[19] the practices of a mother who was by origin Vietnamese were judged against the "reasonable objective standards of the culture in which the children have hitherto been brought up",[20] though the judge was careful to add, "so long as these do not conflict with our minimal acceptable standards of child care in England".[21] But, of course, the judge heard no evidence of what the "reasonable objective standards" of rural Vietnam were, though he was convinced that the mother's disciplinary measures were unacceptable in that culture too. Neither *Derrivierre* nor *Re H* (the Vietnamese case) provoked the interest or the controversy which *Mohamed* v. *Knott* fuelled. But that is hardly surprising, given our ambivalence to questions of the physical chastisement of children.[22]

17 *Op. cit.*, note 14, pp. 638-639.

18 On which matter see S. M. Poulter (1986) English Law and Ethnic Minority Customs, Butterworths, pp. 271-274.

19 *Re H* [1987] 2 FLR 12.

20 *Ibid.*, p. 17.

21 Idem.

22 This came to the fore yet again in Britain in 1994 over the question of the moral propriety and legality of a childminder smacking a child in her care. See *London Borough of Sutton* v. *Davis* [1994] 1 FLR 737. It has now been "resolved" by Government Guidance permitting a childminder to smack, but only where a parent gives consent (*The Times*, 3 December 1994).

These extended case studies are but two examples of the problem posed when legislation comes up against the practices of another culture.[23] It is a problem well known to drafters of international conventions and the two examples drawn from England could be added to by reference to confrontations in other countries. But the temptation to document such examples will be resisted and I will focus on two international conventions instead.

Seventy-five years ago the International Labour Organisation adopted a convention fixing the minimum age for admission of children to industrial employment.[24] Article 2 of this states:

> Children under the age of fourteen years shall not be employed or work in any public or private industrial undertaking, or in any branch thereof, other than an undertaking in which only members of the same family are employed.

For most Western States the age of fourteen was acceptable. But the Commission on Children's Employment, responsible for preparing the Labour Conference, met strong objection from countries in Asia where child labour under the age of fourteen was – indeed still is – widespread and where the financial resources for implementing rapid change did not exist. "Should modifications of the Convention be allowed in the case of those countries with special climatic and industrial conditions?", asked Sir Malcolm Delevinge of the United Kingdom.[25] A trades unionist from Britain, Margaret Bondfield, was in no doubt that such exceptions were unacceptable but a compromise at her initiative was effected. Speaking of what became Article 6 of the Convention, she said:

> With regard to one of the main objections, namely the nature of the Indian industries, we have carefully drafted this amendment to exclude all those industries that could be considered purely native

23 On scarification see *R* v. *Adesanya, The Times*, 16 and 17 July 1974 (and S. Poulter, (1975) Foreign Customs and the English Criminal Law, 24 ICLQ 136); on West African fostering practices see *Re O* (1973) 3 Fam Law 40, *Re E O* (1973) 3 Fam Law 48 and *Re A* (1978) 8 Fam Law 247. Also interesting is *Re H* [1978] Fam. 65 (returning a battered Pakistani child of 4 to her parents who were returning to Pakistan).

24 See Philip Veerman (1992) *The Rights of the Child and the Changing Image of Childhood*, Martinus Nijhoff, ch. XIII.

25 League of Nations, *International Labour Conference*, First Annual Meeting, *International Labour Conference*, First Annual Meeting, p. 96.

> industries or that are small industries. It is especially drafted to refer only to those industries which are being modelled on Western ideas, which are to some extent under control of factory legislation and which are mainly supervised by Western people.[26]

And so Article 6 declares boldly that Article 2 "shall not apply to India" and then sets a lower age (twelve) below which children are not to be employed in factories "working with power and employing more than ten persons" or in mines, transport or the docks. India continued to raise reservations, in particular relating to the "difficulties which local customs would place in the way of organising adequate primary education".[27] In the event India did not ratify this Convention though it did ratify (in 1921) another ILO Convention adopted in 1919 on the prohibition of night work.[28] The 1919 Convention on minimum age has been replaced by one adopted in 1973.[29] This states that every State Party is to undertake progressively to raise the minimum age for admission to employment or work "to a level consistent with the fullest physical and mental development of young persons".[30] Developing countries are, nevertheless, still allowed to specify a minimum age for employment at fourteen years.[31] The U.N. Convention on the Rights of the Child recognises the right of the child to be protected from economic exploitation and from performing hazardous work or work likely to interfere with education[32] but no minimum age is specified.

---

26 *Idem.*

27 International Labour Review vol. III, nos. 1-2, July-August 1921, p. 16.

28 Convention 6 (it is reproduced in Veerman, *op. cit.*, note 24, p. 420). India did originally ask for preferential treatment on this Convention too: so did Japan and Belgium (whose request to except the glass industry was rejected by the Conference).

29 ILO Convention No. 138 (reproduced in Veerman, *op. cit.*, note 24, p. 484).

30 Article I.

31 Article 2(4). They must state a reason or alternatively agree to renounce "the right to avail itself of the provisions in question as from a stated date" (Article 2(5)). India by the Child Labour (Prohibition and Regulation) Act 1986 has prohibited those under 14 working in certain hazardous employments and regulated their working conditions in certain other employments.

32 Article 32. States Parties must provide a minimum age for employment and provide for penalties or other sanctions to ensure effective enforcement. (Articles 32(2)(a) and (c)). On India see Myron Weiner (1991) *The Child and the State in India,* Oxford University Press.

But it is another Article of the U.N. Convention to which attention must now turn. Article 24, dealing with health and health services, confronts the issue of cultural difference in paragraph 3. This states:

> State parties shall take all effective and appropriate measures with a view to abolishing traditional practices prejudicial to the health of children.

There are many traditional practices which may harm children but no one is in any doubt that one practice in particular is targeted by this provision *viz.* female circumcision.[33] This is prevalent in wide areas of the world:[34] takes a number of forms[35] and infibulation – genital mutilation of the grossest kind – is particularly common in the Sudan, Somalia, Ethiopia and Mali. At least three Western countries have legislated against it,[36] including the United Kingdom in 1986,[37] and France has prosecuted and imprisoned parents involved in it. Nevertheless, in formulating Article 24, paragraph 3 caution had to be taken. Senegal, for example, warned that a more direct condemnation would force the practice underground.[38]

Four examples have now been used: child marriages, child labour, female circumcision and corporal chastisement practices. Of female child circumcision more will be said. But at this stage attention must turn to the concept of cultural pluralism and its justification. And pluralism

33 Delegates of Canada, the United Kingdom and the U.S.A. were in favour of formulations of the Article that would have referred specifically to female circumcision. See D. Johnson, "Cultural and Regional Pluralism in the Drafting of the U.N. Convention on the Rights of The Child", in M. Freeman and P. Veerman (1992) *The Ideologies of Children's Rights,* Martinus Nijhoff, pp. 95, 109-110.

34 See Alison Slack (1988) *Human Rights Quarterly* 10: 437. See also Stephen James (1994) *Bioethics* 8: 1.

35 See Efua Dorkenoo and Scilla Elworthy (1992) *Female Genital Mutilation: Proposals for Change,* Minority Rights.

36 The United Kingdom has the Prohibition of Female Circumcision Act 1986. There is also legislation in the United States (The Female Genital Mutilation Act of 1993, H.R. 3247). This is discussed in *Berkeley Women's Law Journal* 9: 206 (1994).

In France there is no specific law but the violence involved in circumcision brings the activity within a more general proscription: The recent *Greon* case in France, which led to a one year suspended sentence, promoted an outcry (see *The Guardian,* 17 September 1994).

37 For the view of social workers towards it see Lynn Eaton, "A Fine Line", *Community Care,* 21-27 July 1994, p. 16. See also Bryan Hartley (1994) *Archives of Diseases in Childhood.*

38 And pointed to son preference as another harmful traditional practice.

must be distinguished from two other political ethical theories, relativism and monism (or universalism).

## Cultural Pluralism

The fact of cultural pluralism was known as early as the Greek historian, Herodotus,[39] and it is traced through Montaigne,[40] Vico,[41] Hume[42] and Montesquieu[43] who perhaps was the first to try to explain cultural difference). But it is to twentieth-century anthropology that we must look for articulation of the concept.[44]

Pluralism is a theory about the sources of value (as are relativism and monism).[45] Pluralists believe that there are many reasonable conceptions of a good life and many reasonable values upon which the realisation of good lives depend. There are conflicts among reasonable conceptions of a good life as well as among reasonable values. Political ethics needs to cope with these conflicts, to attempt to surmount difficulties caused by the incompatibility and incommensurability of values whose realisation is thought to be essential. Where values are incompatible – for example a belief in equality of the sexes and a belief that men are superior – the realisation of one value must exclude the other. Values are incommensurable where there is no measuring rod by which they can be compared.

Incommensurable values need not necessarily be incompatible, and where they are not they can co-exist. If values were only incommensurable the problem would not be too great – a vision which allowed for and requited discrete but compatible conceptions of the good life is not

39 See his *Persian Wars* ("if one were to offer men to choose out of all the customs in the world such as seemed to them the best, they would examine the whole number, and end by preferring their own") (Book 3, Ch. 38).

40 See C. Geertz, "Anti Anti-Relativism", *American Anthropologist* 86: 263 at 264.

41 *The New Science* (1744).

42 See, in particular, his *A Dialogue* in *Enquiries concerning Human Understanding and concerning the Principles of Morals* L. A. Selby-Bigge (ed.), revised by P. H. Nidditch, Clarendon Press, 1975, p. 324.

43 *The Spirit of the Laws* (1748).

44 In particular to Franz Boas (see *e.g.* "The Mind of Primitive Man", *Journal of American Folklore* 14: I (1901)), Ruth Benedict (1934), Houghton Mifflin, and Melville Herskovits (1972) *Cultural Relativism: Perspectives in Cultural Pluralism,* Random House.

45 And see Charles Larmore (1994) "Pluralism and Reasonable Disagreement", *Social Philosophy and Policy* 11: 61, 64.

beyond the scope of imagination. It is the incompatibility of values that constitutes the stumbling-block.

Pluralists accept that conflicts among values can be resolved by appealing to some reasonable ranking of the values in question. They acknowledge that a plurality of reasonable rankings also exists.

### Monism

Monism or universalism,[46] by contrast, is committed to there being an over riding value or set of values and, if the latter, a ranking scheme on the basis of which values can be compared in a way that all reasonable people would find acceptable. Pluralists object to monism because they cannot accept the idea that there is an overriding value, that there is some consideration which always takes precedence over all other considerations. Monism also overlooks those cases of moral conflict where no standard can legitimately claim a monopoly of the truth (the issue of abortion[47] is the best example of this). Where pluralists and monists agree is in accepting the need for a reasonable method of resolving conflict.

### Relativism

Pluralists also reject relativism. Pluralism may have emerged out of relativism and the two are often confused.[48] Pluralists and relativists agree that there are no overriding values, that all values are conditional, that there is a plurality of incompatible and incommensurable values. They agree on the need for conflict resolution. But relativists go beyond pluralism and think that all values are conventional. Relativism emerged in reaction to cultural evolutionism, which was European and often racist.[49] As Hatch puts it: "It goes without saying that people who were thought

46 There are different models of monism, ranging from the Platonic "Idea of The Good" (see his *Republic*, 504-509) and to different versions of utilitarianism, using in its simplest model a felicific calculus (see Jeremy Bentham, *Introduction to the Principles of Morals and Legislation*).

47 And see Ronald Dworkin (1993) *Life's Dominion*, Harvard University Press.

48 Joseph Raz claims not to know what cultural pluralism is (see (1994) "Moral Change and Social Relativism", Social Philosophy and Policy 11: 139).

49 G. W. Stocking Jr. (1968) *Race, Culture and Evolution*, Free Press.

to be the least cultured were also thought to be the least intelligent and the darkest in pigmentation".[50] When cultural relativism emerged in the first third of this century it was seen as a challenge to racist, Eurocentric notions of progress.[51] Cultural relativism like pluralism is a theory about the way evaluations or judgments are made. But to the relativist, "evaluations are relative to the cultural background out of which they arise".[52] So to Ruth Benedict, one of the founders of relativism, tolerance is a key element of cultural relativism;[53] and to Herskovits it is necessary to recognise the "dignity inherent in every body of custom".[54] The philosopher Charles Taylor talks of the presumption of the equal worth of cultures.[55]

The attractions of relativism are difficult to ignore. It is rooted in egalitarianism, in liberalism, in modernism. It belongs perhaps to a disenchanted vision of the world.[56] It is anti-assimilationist, it is anti-imperialist, it is hostile to ethnocentrism.[57] It is sympathetic to, and would wish to protect, the traditions and rights of indigenous peoples.[58] It has the value also in a sort of Millian way,[59] of enhancing the prospects of achieving moral knowledge, though this presupposes the possibility of real communication across cultures and this is not always possible.[60]

Relativists regard all values as the products of the customs, practices and beliefs which have as a matter of fact developed within a particular tradition. They deny that any value has any authority, epistemological or moral, outside of this cultural context. They deny that conflict between values belonging to different traditions can be settled in any reasonable way, because, so they argue, what is reasonable is itself a product of par-

50 E. Hatch (1983) Culture and Morality: The Relativity of Values in Anthropology, Columbia University Press, p. 26.

51 Alison Dundes Renteln (1990) *International Human Rights: Universalism Versus Relativism,* Sage.

52 *Per* Melville Herskovits, *op. cit.*, note 44, p. 14.

53 *Op. cit.*, note 44, p. 37. See also Hatch, *op. cit.*, note 50, pp. 99-100.

54 *Man and His Works,* Alfred A. Knopf, 1947, p. 76.

55 *Multiculturalism and "The Politics of Recognition",* Prince ton University Press, 1992, p. 72.

56 Charles Larrnore so characterises it (*op. cit.*, note 45, p. 71).

57 See Abdullahi, A. An-Na'im (1987) "Religious Minorities under Islamic Law and the Limits of Cultural Relativism", 9 *Human Rights Quarterly* 1.

58 See Will Kymlicka (1989) *Liberalism, Community and Culture,* Oxford University Press. See also Alan Gewirth, "Is Cultural Pluralism Relevant To Moral Knowledge?", *Social Philosophy and Policy* 11: 22, 35.

59 See J. S. Mill (1859) *On Liberty.*

60 But see Chandran Kukarhas (1994) "Explaining Moral Variety", *Social Philosophy and Policy* 11: 1, 18.

ticular cultures. And so they demand of us that we ask not whether social practices like child marriage or female circumcision, or for that matter purdah, suttee or polygamy, are justified by the moral considerations that we find cogent, but rather whether they are sanctioned by the relevant social understandings of the cultures within which they are practised.

But, if that means that a culture can only be judged by endogenous value judgments, and that moral principles which derive from outside that culture have no validity, morality has become a slave to custom,[61] the "ought" has relinquished any transcendental power that it may have had to critique the "is". However, if, as Amy Gutmann has argued persuasively in a recent article, "cultural relativists agree that there can be standards for judging justice that are independent of social consensus, then they give up the distinctive premise of cultural relativism".[62] I would argue that they must. The argument for any practice must be more than that the practice exists. A culture which permits child marriage or female circumcision must be able to support these practices by a stronger argument, or series of arguments, than that there is – if, indeed, this is the case – social consensus. An examination of the social understandings within the culture may reveal that there is no social under standing at all or that there are conflicting understandings, misunderstandings or inconsistencies. Often, it will reveal that the so-called dominant understanding is in reality the understanding of the dominant.[63] Many cultural practices when critically examined turn on the interpretation of a male elite, with a consensus having been engineered to cloak the interests of a section of the society.[64]

Both monists and pluralists disagree. Monists because they believe that a practice can be judged by an overriding value: pluralists because they claim that there are values independent of the context of the culture in question to which we can reasonably appeal in settling conflicts. There is surely no dispute that there are certain needs which do not vary either temporally – they are historically constant – or culturally – they are the requirement of people everywhere. This does not mean that there are not differences in the ways in which these needs are met. There is a need

61 J. S. Mill wrote of the "despotism of custom".

62 "The Challenge of Multiculturalism in Political Ethics", *Philosophy and Public Affairs* 22: 171, 177 (1993).

63 *Ibid.*, p. 176.

64 Stephen A. James argues persuasively that this is the case with female circumcision in African societies. See "Reconciling International Human Rights and Cultural Relativism: The Case of Female Circumcision", *Bioethics* 8: I (1994).

for food: not a need for meat and two vegetables.[65] There is a need for shelter but it does not have to be a semi-detached house. Nor are these needs only physiological. There are psychological needs too: for comfort, affection, companionship. There are social needs: for order, security, dignity, respect, privacy. There are minimum requirements of human welfare. They must be met whatever the conception of what constitutes a good life and regardless of what other values are upheld in any particular culture.[66]

It is easy to distinguish this model of pluralism from one of relativism. Relativists do not acknowledge these primary values and therefore fail to see that there are standards independent of a particular culture by which it can be judged. It is less easy to distinguish it from monism, but it is a different claim for primary values may conflict with each other, in which case it may become necessary to put the conflict into its cultural context to determine which, if either, should prevail. The contribution that the achievement of the particular values makes to the life of the individual concerned may also be significant: which of two values, for example, enhances the goal of his or her "good life".

## Responding to the Case Studies – Relativism

We may return now to the examples used at the beginning of this essay: child marriages, corporal punishment practices, child labour and female circumcision. The relativist would situate each of the case studies into its cultural context and would, I would argue, be impotent to offer any real critique. It is surely one of the limitations of a belief in cultural relativism that it can lead us to conclude that "anything goes". A consequence of this is that we lack the ammunition to protect the individual against the group. The challenge of rights is easily snuffed out. We are forced to

65 And the need is for food as nutrition. Food may have secondary purposes such as the fulfilment of religious obligations. This is not addressed by Michael Walzer (1983) in *Spheres of Justice*, Basic Book s, p. 8 ("If the religious uses of bread were to conflict with its nutritional uses… it is by no means clear which should be primary"). Only a relativist could say this: it is crystal clear that the religious use of bread is of secondary importance to its use as nutrition. Nutrition is a basic, primary value: religion (*cf.* John Finnis (1980) *Natural Law and Natural Rights*, Clarendon Press, p. 89) is not.

66 And see John Kekes (1994) "Pluralism and the Value of Life", *Social Philosophy and Policy* 11 : 44, 49.

condone practices which we find repressive or intolerable because we are told that is only our opinion and had our enculturation been into the culture we are now criticising our opinion would be different. The relativist has little too offer the child either by way of protection or empowerment, any more I suggest than it could have offered Jews living in Nazi Germany or blacks in South Africa under apartheid.[67]

### The Monist Response

The monist response is more positive. It points to there being an evaluative consideration, an overriding value, which trumps all other considerations. It may take the form of a categorical imperative,[68] a harm principle[69] or a principle of generic consistency[70] or many other forms.

The epistemic relevance of these may be questioned. Certainly, a relativist might observe the use here of conceptions of reason and rationality firmly rooted within Western Enlightenment culture; there are other conceptions of "reason" to which other cultures appeal including myth, religious faith, intuition and tradition. Why, it may be asked, should alien reasoning processes be admitted when cultural practices external to the culture are ruled irrelevant? This is not unreminiscent of the debates about the relevance of human rights language to non-Western traditions.[71] And there are parallel debates about the meaning of childhood in different cultures and political economies.[72]

---

67 Renteln, *op. cit.*, note 51, believes that relativism is "out of favor" mainly because of this supposed impotence (p. 67). J. Cook described relativism as "nihilistic": see "Cultural Relativism as an Ethnocentric Notion" in R. Beehler and A. R. Drengson (1978) *The Philosophy of Society*, Methuen, p. 289.

68 As with Immanuel Kant.

69 As with John Stuart Mill (and see, *op. cit.*, note 59).

70 As with Alan Gewirth (1978) *Reason and Morality*, University of Chicago Press. See also (1984) "The Epistemology of Human Rights", *Social Philosophy and Policy 1: 1*, and, briefly, *op. cit.*, note 58. Deryck Beyleveld (1991) *The Dialectical Necessity of Morality: An Analysis and Defence of Alan Gewirth's Argument To The Principle of Generic Consistency*, University of Chicago Press, offers a sustained defence.

71 See *e.g.* Josiah A. M. Cobbah (1987) "African Values and the Human Rights Debate: An African Perspective," *Human Rights Quarterly* 9: 309; Donna E. Arzt (1990) "The Application of International Human Rights Law in Islamic States", *Human Rights Quarterly* 12: 202; Ann Mayer (1992) *Islam and Human Rights Tradition and Politics*, Westview Press.

72 See Philippe Aries (1962) *Centuries of Childhood: A Social History of the Family*, Jonathan Cape; Barbara A. Hanawalt (1993) *Growing Up In Medieval London: The*

The response of the monist to our four examples would depend upon the overriding value or values chosen. Abstracting values from international human rights norms[73] would lead to condemnation of female child circumcision[74] would result in castigation of countries which permitted child labour and would give no unequivocal answers on the other two matters. The U.N. Convention on the Rights of the Child has nothing to say on marriages of the very young and whether it allows corporal punishment at all depends upon how Article 19 is interpreted.[75]

### The Pluralist Approach

To the pluralist the practices found in the case studies at the beginning of this essay have to be looked at both in terms of primary values and the cultural context in which the individuals concerned lived. If one takes preservation of physical integrity to be a primary value, even situating this within relevant cultural contexts, leads to a condemnation of child female circumcision. Apart from ritualistic circumcision, where the clitoris is merely nicked and there is little mutilation or long-term damage, the term 'female circumcision' is a euphemism which has only the remotest similarity with male circumcision in terms of its physical effects. The practice has been described by Alison Slack as follows:

> The practice can be broken down into four basic forms that vary in degrees of severity. The first, and least severe form, is... ritualistic circumcision... The second form is simply called circumcision or "sunna" by the Muslims. This involves the removal of the clitoral prepuce – the outer layer of the skin over the clitoris, sometimes called the "hood"; the gland and body of the clitoris remain intact. Occasionally, the tip of the clitoris itself is removed. Sunna has been

---

*Experience of Childhood In History*, Oxford University Press; Rex and Wendy Stainton Rogers (1992) *Stories of Childhood: Shifting Agendas of Child Concern*, Harvester Wheatsheaf.

73 See John O'Manique (1990) "Universal and Inalienable Rights: A Search for Foundations", Human Rights Quarterly 12: 465.

74 Using the Universal Declaration of Human Rights, Article 25 (and 15). And see further James, *op. cit.*, note 64, pp. 12-22.

75 But a case can be put that it would proscribe it, as Sweden, amongst other countries including most recently Cyprus has done.

> equated with male circumcision, because the clitoris itself is generally not damaged.
>
> A third, and more harsh form of the practice, is called excision or clitoridectomy. This is the most common form and involves the removal of the gland of the clitoris – usually the entire clitoris – and often parts of the labia minora as well.
>
> Finally, the most severe form of the practice is infibulation..., where virtually all of the external female genitalia are removed – removing the entire clitoris and labia minora – and, in addition, much or most the labia majora is cut or scraped away. The remaining raw edges of the labia majora are then sewn together with acacia tree thorns, and held in place with catgut or sewing thread. The entire area is closed up by this process leaving only a tiny opening, roughly the size of a matchstick, to allow for the passing of urine and menstrual fluid. The girl's legs are then tied together – ankles, knees and thighs – and she is immobilized for an extended period varying from fifteen to forty days, while the wound heals.[76]

Often one of the harsher forms of the practice occurs, even though a milder type was intended because the girls struggle due to the blunt instruments used and the lack of anaesthesia. The instruments used range from kitchen knives, old razor blades, broken glass and sharp stones to scalpels: the wounds are frequently treated with animal dung and mud to stop the bleeding. The practice occurs most often on young girls between the ages of three and eight. It is primarily found in areas where there is considerable poverty, where hunger, insanitary conditions and illiteracy are rife, and where there is little in the way of health care facilities. It is also pertinent to note that the economic and social status of women characteristically is low where female child circumcision is prevalent.

The practices are supported by a number of arguments. The control of female sexuality is the central justification.[77] It prevents wantonness and

---

76 (1988) "Female Circumcision: A Critical Appraisal", *Human Rights Quarterly* 10: 437, 441-442. See also Efua Dorkenoo and Scilla Elworthy, *op. cit.*, note 35; K. Brennan (1989) "The Influence of Cultural Relativism on International Human Rights Law: Female Circumcision as a Case Study", *Law and Inequality* VIII: 367; K. Boulware-Miller (1985) "Female Circumcision: Challenges To The Practice as a Human Rights Violation", *Harvard Women's Law Journal* 8: 155. See also *International Journal of Children's Rights* 2: 1 (Special Issue (1993)).

77 Lawrence P. Cutner (1985) "Female Genital Mutilation", *Obstetrical and Gynecological Survey* 40: 438.

preserves the virginity of a future bride.[78] Where infibulation has taken place, the girl has to be "re-opened" surgically so that her husband may have sexual intercourse with her, reassured that he is the first to have done this. The preservation of virginity is essential for determining a woman's social position in these societies and in some areas the value of a prospective bride is based on the size of the infibulated opening.[79] There is a belief also that female circumcision is a religious imperative:[80] thus the belief is widely held among Muslims that the practice is scripturally mandated by the Koran.[81] Although the practice is often supported by Muslim leaders, there is no mention of either excision or infibulation in the Koran. Female circumcision is supported by these leaders as being a positive "sunna", or tradition, one that serves to attenuate sexual desire in women.[82] Muslim men in Africa hold uncircumcised women in contempt. One of the worst insults in Muslim Africa is to be called "Son of an uncircumcised mother".[83]

Justification of the practice also finds support in a number of myths including the belief that the clitoris represents the male sexual organ and, if not cut, will grow to the size of a penis,[84] that females are sterile until excised, the operation being thought to increase fertility, that the operation is a biologically cleansing process that improves the hygienic and/or aesthetic condition of female genitalia.[85] There is also the argument that the adherence to the tradition of female circumcision amounts to

---

78 See Slack, *op. cit.*, note 76, p. 445.

79 *Ibid.*, p. 446.

80 The practice does not exist in the teachings of any formal religion. Slack, *op. cit.*, note 76, p. 446 notes it is practised amongst Jews in Africa, but this is not correct. The Falashas in Ethiopia may have practised circumcision.

81 See Asma A. El Dareer (1982) *Woman, Why Do You Weep?*, Zed Press, p. 71.

82 Directing it, so it is said, to "the desirable moderation" *per* Marie Bassili Assaad (1980) "Female Circumcision in Egypt: Social Implications, Current Research, and Prospects for Change", *Studies In Family Planning* 11: 5. Hanny Lightfoot-Klein nevertheless found that sexual desire and pleasure were experienced by the majority of women subjected to the most extreme form of circumcision, in spite of their being culturally bound to hide these experiences. ("The Sexual Experience and Marital Adjustment or Genitally Circumcised and Infibulated Females In the Sudan", *Journal of Sex Research* 26: 375 (1989).) See also her *Prisoners of Ritual, An Odyssey into Female Genial Mutilation In Africa*, Haworth Press, 1989.

83 Raqiya Haji Dualeh Abodalla (1982) *Sisters In Affiliation: Circumcision and Infibulation of Women in Africa*, Lawrence Hill, p. 84.

84 Nayra Atiya (1982) *Khul-Khaal: Five Egyptian Women Tell Their Stories*, Syracuse University Press, p. 11.

85 Note, "Female Circumcision", *The Lancet*, 12 March 1983, p. 569.

a right to cultural self-determination and that the pursuit of this right brings psychological benefits to women. Research in Sudan, Egypt and Nigeria suggests that the importance of tradition[86] is the most significant of justificatory arguments for the practice, and that the support amongst women for the tradition is hardly less than that by men.[87]

These justifications can be examined utilising the cultural pluralist framework that I have offered. That there is a violation of physical integrity, at least in the case of clitoridectomy and infibulation, is incontestable. To the monist or universalist that is the end of the question. But the cultural pluralist must go on to ask how important a value physical integrity is to women in Sudan or Somalia, particularly when its preservation may lead to their being social outcasts. If an analogy may be given, it is clear that life is a primary value, but we can all think of circumstances, being in a persistent vegetative state for example, when we would not wish to continue to live. A PVS condition may constitute life but hardly a "good life".

What this overlooks is the age of those who undergo female circumcision. They are for the large part very young children in no position to give informed consent. And yet the operations carried out upon them may severely and irreversibly affect their future sexual experience. It may lead to their having difficulty with childbirth. There is an increased risk of sterility. Many are afraid of sex or can experience little enjoyment from sexual relationships. These are potential harms and years in the future. There are immediate harms too: severe pain, shock, infection, scarring, bleeding, even death.[88] According to a UNESCO report, emotional reactions "may present themselves as chronic irritability, anxiety, depressive episodes, conversion reactions or frank psychosis".[89] Circumcision is thus within the understanding of the cultures which legitimate the practice dysfunctional. Even so were it practised on adult women with their full and informed consents, we might be inhibited from attacking it (though whether the House of Lords, the final court of appeal in the United Kingdom, would find similar hesitation in the light of its condem-

---

86 Robert A. Myers *et al.* (1985) "Circumcision: Its Nature and practice Among Some Ethnic Groups in Southern Nigeria", *Social Science and Medicine* 21 : 584; El Dareer, *op. cit.*, note 81, p. 141 *et seq.;* Atiyo, *op. cit.*, note 84, p. 11.

87 El Dareer intervied over 4,500 adults in Sudan: 82.6 per cent of women approved of circumcision regardless of the type and 87.7 per cent of men approved the practice.

88 Slack. *op. cit.*, note 76, discusses these at pp. 450-455; Dorkenoo and Elworth, *op. cit.*, note 35, do so at pp. 8-10.

89 *Draft Report of the Working Group on Traditional Practice Affecting The Health of Women and Children.* U.N. Doc. E/CN.4/H.C.42/1985, 12 September 1985, p. 13.

nation in *Brown's* case[90] of sadomasochism may be doubted). We allow breast implants and even gender reassignments,[91] and both are carried out on the national health. Were girls purportedly to consent to circumcision we might still employ, what I have defended elsewhere, as "liberal paternalism", to protect them from the consequences of actions that will prevent them subsequently enjoying rationally autonomous adulthood.[92] But here we have a situation where many of the girls concerned cannot consent, but it seems that looking at their circumcision as adult women would have done so. There are real dilemmas here which cannot be avoided them by resorting to relativism, for then there would be no debate, or by seeking the refuge of monism, for this would impose a decontextualised overriding value. It would be comforting to rest in the moral certitudes of monism but this study has shown the fragility of the moral determinacy for which it stands.

How is then the cultural pluralist to respond? The answer lies in subjecting the practice to an internal critique, in deconstructing the arguments that are used to support it. The arguments in the case of female circumcision are, it will be recalled, four-fold. It is claimed as a control on female sexuality. Whilst there can be little doubt that it reduces sensitivity and responses to stimulation, it offers no guarantee that a woman has not had sexual experiences and, indeed, even infibulation is no guarantee: an unmarried woman can have sexual intercourse and then be re-infibulated immediately before her marriage to disguise this fact from her husband.

It is supposedly based on religion, but there is no evidence for this and at least a suspicion that it is an elitist religious fraud perpetrated by a clerical oligarchy on vulnerable women.

It rests also upon sexual myths and these – such as that the clitoris is a masculine feature and will grow to the size of a penis – need to be shown for what they are. If features of the other sex need to removed is there any move in any of these societies to excise male nipples?

And, as for the supposed benefits, it has already been shown that, to the contrary, there are physical and psychological harms which surely outweigh any social or cultural benefits.

---

90 [1993] 2 All E.R. 75.

91 Though we do not grant much in the way of rights to transsexuals: see *Corbett* v. *Corbett* [1971] p. 83, and *Rees* v. *U.K.* (1986) 9 EHRR 56.

92 *The Rights and Wrongs of Children*, Frances Pinter, 1983, pp. 54-60.

It would be easier to empathise with the arguments put if there were not in addition a suspicion that the cultural values upheld by the practices depicted here were not the values of a section of the society rather than the whole of it. Of what value are the norms of a community when they are directed at a group at best devalued but more likely excluded from it? It is concerns such as these which lead me to ask whether in a clash between the value of physical integrity and the value of cultural identity, the latter can possibly prevail.[93]

It also leads me to conclude – though it has not been necessary to discuss the question in this paper – that, using similar reasoning processes, it would not be difficult to show that in a similar clash over male circumcision it would be the latter value, namely cultural (or religious) identity that would prevail.

On the other case studies set out at the beginning of this paper, much briefer answers must be given. The cultural pluralist is likely to come to the same conclusion on child marriages as the Divisional Court did in *Mohamed* v. *Knott*. But s/he would need a deeper understanding of the cultural context than it would seem the English courts had.

The cultural pluralist's response to child labour in the developing world would require greater tolerance of the problems attendant on poverty, a greater understanding of the global economy and a more sophisticated approach to the relationship between child labour and education questions than is often found, but a conclusion not dissimilar from that in the U.N. Convention is likely to result from these deliberations.[94] On punishment practices s/he could be more categorical: there can be no reason for tolerating excessive punishment in the name of cultural difference; there is no cultural tradition or identity at stake. Of course, it would be so much easier if we knew what such punishment was different from.

93 Attacks on the practice of male circumcision have been launched by eminent thinkers like Alice Miller. There is also an organisation called NOHARMM in the United States (National Organization to Halt The Abuse and Routine Mutilation of Males). See also Denise Winn, "A Campaign to Save the Foreskin", *The Independent*, 20 April 1993.

94 *Cf.* Myron Weiner (1991) *The Child and the State in India: Child Labor and Education Policy in Comparative Perspective*. Oxford University Press, with Olga Nieuwenhuys (1994) *Children's Lifeworlds: Gender, Welfare and Labour in The Developing World*, Routledge. See also her review of his book in *Int. Journal of Children's Rights* 2: 205 (1994) and his article in *Int. Journal of Children's Rights* 2: 121 (1994).

### A Concluding Comment

I have set out in this paper three approaches that may be adopted towards cultural conflict and children's rights. I reject cultural relativism because it renounces normative judgment. The moral determinacy of monism offers blanket solutions but fails to address cultural difference. Cultural pluralism, a via media perhaps between two extremes, situates values within cultural context and offers dialogue and change. Nothing can provide solutions to the difficult cases thrown up by the ways different societies treat children, but cultural pluralism does, I believe, offer a challenge. It is one that those concerned with children, their welfare and their rights, must take up.

CHAPTER 6

# Cleveland, Butler-Sloss and Beyond – How are We to React to the Sexual Abuse of Children?

What should cause surprise is not that Cleveland happened, but that a Cleveland was so long in coming. The history books will record Middlesbrough as the place where the English conscience awakened to the sexual abuse of children. But they will also remember how the problem itself was clouded by revelations of ineptitude, of inter-professional rivalry, how Cleveland itself became the site for ideological conflict and the impetus for, and the battleground upon which, initiatives for reform were fought.

Despite the media attention, despite a lengthy inquiry leading to the Butler-Sloss report,[1] we do not know even today how many of the children removed from parents in Cleveland were sexually abused.[2] We are unlikely, accordingly, ever to know whether the paediatricians, Marietta Higgs and Geoffrey Wyatt, were Midases who turned everything they touched into sexual abuse or, like many pioneers, were more sinned against than sinning. That they were single-minded and zealous, at times even obsessed with what they considered to be the truth, that at times they, and those, notably Sue Richardson, who worked with them in social services, paid insufficient attention to rights or legal proprieties is clear from the report. Politicians they certainly were not. In the immediate aftermath of Cleveland it is their actions which are remembered and some of them leave a sour taste. But, in the perspective of history, Cleveland will be remembered as the place where we first faced up to the iniquity of the sexual abuse of children.

Why is it that sexual abuse of children has for so long been kept under wraps? How are we to explain our reluctance to accept its existence? A hundred years ago we grudgingly accepted that children were physically

1 Report of the Inquiry into Child Abuse in Cleveland 1987 (the Butler-Sloss report).

2 A point commented upon (after publication) both by M. Phillips in *The Guardian,* July 8, 1988, and S. Helm in *The Independent,* September 5, 1988. The issue erupted again in *The Guardian.* February 18, 1989 (a letter from 11 paediatricians claiming 90 per cent. were abused).

 | DOI:10.1163/9789004219106_007

abused.[3] A quarter of a century ago we awoke to the concept of the battered baby syndrome[4] and gradually became aware of non-accidental injury of children.[5] But revelations of sexual abuse continued to be greeted with disbelief. My book on *Violence In The Home,*[6] written in the mid-1970s, was to have contained a chapter on sexual abuse, but when the manuscript needed to be reduced, I readily acceded to the publisher's suggestion that the chapter to excise was the one on the sexual abuse of children. That chapter was separately published[7] but, I suspect, barely noticed. It was not that sexual abuse did not exist a decade ago: it was that we preferred to believe it did not exist. Why?

Professional interest in child sexual abuse can be traced to the publication of several incest histories in Krafft-Ebing's *Psychopathia Sexualis* in 1886.[8] But nothing seems to have come of this. The Kinsey reports in 1953[9] attracted a lot of interest but their revelations that many children had sexual experiences with adults seem to have caused little concern. Allegations of sexual abuse were dismissed as children's fantasies. In part we may attribute this response to the writings of Freud. He believed that an innate incest desire is evident in early childhood and that it continues throughout life in a repressed form.[10] Freud assumed that allegations of sexual abuse were primarily the result of a wish to have sex with a parent, usually the parent of the opposite sex.[11] Although more recent clinical writings have also stressed the presence of a strong incest desire,[12] there is no doubt that Oedipal fantasies are usually easily distinguished from

3 See C. K. Behlmer, *Child Abuse and Moral Reform In England 1870-1908* (1982); L. Gordon, *Heroes of Their Own Lives* (1989).

4 First revealed in C. H. Kempe *et al.'s* "The Battered-Child Syndrome," (1962) 181 Journal of the American Medical Association 17-24.

5 On the history of this see N. Parton, *The Politics of Child Abuse* (1985).

6 M. D. A. Freeman, *Violence In The Home – A Socio-Legal Study,* (1979).

7 M. D. A. Freeman, "sexual Abuse of Children," (1978) 8 Fam. Law 221-225.

8 R. Krafft-Ebing, *Psychopathia Sexualis: A Medico-Forensic Study* (1965) (originally published in 1886).

9 A. C. Kinsey, W. B. Pomeroy, C. E. Martin and P. H. Gebhard. *Sexual Behavior in the Human Female* (1953).

10 S. Freud, *The Complete Introductory Lectures on Psychoanalysis* (ed. and transl. by J. Strachey) (originally published in 1933).

11 See, further, R. Summit and J. Kryso, "Sexual Abuse of Children: A Clinical Spectrum" (1978) 48(2) Amer. J. of Orthopsychiatry 237; J. Herman, *Father-Daughter Incest* (1981); J. Masson. *The Assault on Truth* (1984); E. Ward, *Father-Daughter Rape* (1984), pp. 100-117.

12 *e.g.* K. C. Meiselman, *Incest: A Psychological Study of Causes and Effects with Treatment Recommendations* (1978).

allegations of sexual abuse. According to Kathleen Coulborn Faller, who gives good distinguishing examples, "they are likely to be expressions of a general desire for closeness to one parent and exclusion of the other, and do not have explicit sexual content."[13] In addition, she notes, "the child perceives them as desired events and experiences."[14] Freud's theories did not gel with anthropological evidence[15] or with that of historians of the family[16] or sociologists.[17] But it was, until recently, firmly entrenched as part of our cognition of sexuality.

Dating the breakthrough to a realisation of the existence of child sexual abuse is not easy. The "permissive" 1960s did not help advance the cause: too many professionals at the time were interested in liberalising sexual mores and this may have led them to downplay the importance of abuse. In the United States the label "child sexual abuse" first appeared in the federal Child Abuse Prevention and Treatment Act of 1974.[18] In the 1970s in the United States, and somewhat later in this country, advocates for children and feminist groups helped to acquaint both the public and professionals with the problem. They were the "moral entrepreneurs" who, in Howard Becker's memorable phrase, "blew the whistle."[19] It was the sexual abuse of adult women, in particular rape, which in the end stimulated research and inquiry. It came to be recognised that rape was the most under-reported of crimes and to be clear that, although the reasons for this were complex and manifold, legal processes,[20] both at the level of forensic investigation and proof in court,[21] which "blamed the victims,"[22] were to a large part responsible.

A television documentary in 1983, produced by Roger Graef, which revealed the bullying tactics of the Thames Valley police in investigating a rape allegation, shocked the nation. Judicial attitudes, in particular as regards sentencing, attracted a lot of adverse criticism at about the

---

13 *Child Sexual Abuse: An Interdisciplinary Manual for Diagnosis, Case Management and Treatment* (1988), p. 133.

14 *Ibid.*

15 B. Malinowski, *Sex and Repression in Savage Society* (1927).

16 E. Westermarck, *A Short History of Marriage* (1926).

17 J. R. Fox, "Sibling Incest," (1962) 13 British J. of Sociology 128-150.

18 D. K. Weisberg. "The 'Discovery' of Sexual Abuse: Experts' Role in Legal Policy Formation," (1984) 18 Univ. of California Davis Law Review 1-57.

19 H. Becker, *Outsiders* (1963).

20 On which see Jennifer Temkin's excellent *Rape and the Legal Process* (1987).

21 See Z. Adler, *Rape on Trial* (1987).

22 On which see W. Ryan, *Blaming The Victim* (1976).

same time.[23] On both levels there was a reconsideration. Women got the right to request examinations by female officers and doctors, and some attempt was also made to ensure that sentences for rape reflected the seriousness of the offence.[24] More rapes began to be reported. Rape crisis centres became deluged not just with adult rape survivors but also with those who had experienced, or were experiencing, sexual abuse. In retrospect the explosion had to come and, as so often, as in the United States also, it took a scandal to ignite the fuse.[25]

In the United States the issue of child sexual abuse was dramatically brought to the public's attention with the arrest in 1984 in Manhattan Beach, California, of Virginia McMartin and six of her employees for allegedly sexually abusing 125 children over a 10-year period at a day-care centre.[26] Shortly thereafter, indictments were brought against 24 adults and a juvenile (who included in their number a police officer and a deputy sheriff) for allegedly sexually abusing over 50 children in Jordan, Minnesota, a small town with a population of barely three thousand.[27] The McMartin case has not as yet been concluded. The Jordan affair has. The trial collapsed after a convicted child molester, who had confessed to molesting more than a dozen Jordan children and had agreed to testify for the State had his testimony struck from the record. This led to the acquittal of the Bentzes, whose six-year-old son had testified in court that they had sexually abused him, and to the dropping of all charges against the remaining defendants.[28] As in England, over Cleveland,[29] there were al-

23 *e.g.* Judge Bertram Richards' suggestion that hitch-hiking amounted to contributory negligence (*The Times*, January 7, 1982). This, and other examples, led to the Prime Minister announcing that only High Court or experienced Circuit Court judges would try rape cases.

24 See *R.* v. *Billam* [1986] I W.L.R. 349; see also *R.* v. *Roberts* [1982] 1 All E.R. 609 (see also *op. cit.*, note 20, pp. 16-25).

25 See D. Hechler, *The Battle and the Backlash* (1988).

26 L. Coleman, *The Reign of Error: Psychiatry, Authority and Law* (1984). See also D. Hechler, *op. cit.*, note 25. Chap. 8. Appendix 5 (an interview with a defence attorney in the case) is instructive.

27 *Hechler*, Chap. 6. See also M. A. Tester, "The Scott County Sexual Abuse Cases: A Closer Look at What Went Wrong," Dept. of Psychology, University of Virginia (1986).

28 E. R. Shipp, "Children Testify Against Parents Over Abuse," *The New York Times*. September 3, 1984. On the cases and the problem generally see also J. Crewdson, *By Silence Betrayed* (1989).

29 Notably by a local M.P., Stuart Bell, in his book *When Salem Came to the Boro* (1988).

legations of a witch-hunt.[30] Explicit parallels were drawn between Salem 1692 and Manhattan Beach 1985.[31]

In the United States, as here, the battle to expose child sexual abuse has led to a backlash.[32] In Cleveland, as we shall see, there undoubtedly were injustices perpetrated. Some decisions were taken that were "dictatorial, insensitive or prejudiced."[33] Far too much emphasis was placed on the anal dilatation test. But out of Cleveland, the Butler-Sloss report and its aftermath has come a recognition that child sexual abuse is a real problem with which all of us concerned with the interests of children must grapple.

Before the facts and issues can be considered, and the Butler-Sloss report evaluated, some basic questions about the sexual abuse of children must be addressed. What is it? (the question of definition.) How much abuse exists? (the issue of dimension.) And, why does it occur? (the problem of understanding its causes.) It is to a brief consideration of these matters that I now turn.

## What is Child Sexual Abuse?

In *Violence In The Home* I wrote of physical abuse of children that the difficulties of definition depended "on the purposes for which the definition is being sought."[34] A definition for a reporting law (such as exists in the United States) or management guidance has, I noted, very different functions from one constructed for operational or sociological research. Another problem, as I saw it then, concerned "the perspective from which the subject is approached."[35] How is one to emphasise the relative importance of the perpetrator's actions, the effects on the victim, the motivation behind the acts in question? Furthermore, solutions are often

30 In the United States, organisations like VOCAL and Men International have made such associations. (Hechler, *op. cit.*, note 25, discusses VOCAL at pp. 118-129).

31 An advertisement published in various Southern California newspapers in the summer of 1985, drawing the parallel between Salem and Manhattan Beach, is reproduced in Hechler, *op. cit.*, note 25, p. 4.

32 The most graphic and fullest description of which is in Hechler's book (*op. cit.*, note 25. Chaps. 6-9).

33 *Per* Lord Oliver in *Re K.D.* [1988] A.C. 806 a t 813.

34 Freeman, *op. cit.*, note 6, p. 11.

35 *Ibid.* See also J. Garbarino and G. Gilliam, *Understanding Abusive Families* (1980), esp. p. 5.

determined on the basis of problem definition.[36] Much, therefore, hinges on the definition accepted.

The definition of child sexual abuse is equally fraught with problems. The categories of sexual and physical abuse are, of course, not entirely separate categories. Some sexual abuse (certainly rape and arguably other forms) is gross physical abuse in addition to being sexual abuse. All sexual abuse is without question severe emotional abuse.[37] There has been a lot of discussion as to how much sexual abuse takes place. A figure commonly quoted in the Press suggests that 10 per cent. of adults were sexually abused when children.[38] This may have conveyed the impression that one in 10 adults experienced intercourse with an adult when they themselves were children. With all the discussion of the anal dilatation test, some may have come to believe that buggery of children too was commonplace. But the definition of sexual abuse employed by the researchers, whose data provided the media with the 10 per cent. figure, embraced a broad range of activities including exposure to pornographic material (including no doubt some of the very newspapers which reported the statistic) and talking about sexual things in an erotic way. There was similarly a lot of discussion at the height of the moral panic about the discoveries at Cleveland that fathers in particular would be reluctant to bath small daughters or show them physical affection for fear of such activities being interpreted as abuse. There may of course be borderline situations but it should not be difficult to distinguish sexual interference and affectionate physical contact. In many cases the distinguishing mark will be the feelings of the child: in others the presence or absence of genital involvement will serve as a sufficiently clear indicator. Too much has, I think, been made of this potential fear.

How, then, are we to define sexual abuse? There is no universally accepted definition of what constitutes child sexual abuse. There are differences in how far "sexual" extends: Finkelhor[39] defines "sexual victimisation" as "sexual encounters" of children under 13 with persons at least five years older than themselves and encounters of children between 13 and 16 with persons at least 10 years older. "Sexual encounters" are "inter-

36 N. Clapham and S. Nelson, "On Being Useful: The Nature and Consequences of Psychological Research on Social Problems," (1973) 28 American Psychologist 199-211.

37 See, for agreement, D. Glaser and S. Frosh, *Child Sexual Abuse* (1988), p. 9.

38 This statistic, discussed further below, is based on a study by A. Baker and S. Duncan, "Child Sexual Abuse: A Study of its Prevalence in Great Britain," (1985) 9 Child Abuse and Neglect 457-467.

39 D. Finkelhor, *Child Sexual Abuse* (1984), pp. 23-24.

course, anal-genital contact, fondling, or an encounter with an exhibitionist." Others include within sexual abuse any activity that brings gratification to the perpetrator. Should an act be regarded as sexual abuse if it is not so seen by the child? Not every child will identify the same acts as sexual. Very young children will not be capable of labelling in this way even the most overt sexual acts. For these reasons the intention of the abuser is crucial, and the inclusion within the definition of child sexual abuse of anything that gives him sexual gratification is meaningful. It is crucial to stress this element for two reasons: first, there are actions (for example, voyeurism) of which the child is unaware and, secondly, by emphasising what it does for the perpetrator, child sexual abuse can be seen as a wrong that reduces the child to a sexual object-her person is not the subject of "equal respect and concern."[40]

The age differential is also troubling. It is dearly postulated, by Finkelhor for example, to suggest coercion or undue influence. It is hardly satisfactory. It is not the age difference which is crucial but the ability to fend off advances and this is heavily dependent on development. Schechter and Roberge,[41] in a much-quoted definition, approved in the Butler-Sloss report,[42] take account of this. They define sexual abuse as:

> the involvement of dependent, developmentally immature children and adolescents in sexual activities that they do not fully comprehend and to which they are unable to give informed consent or that violate the social taboos of family roles.

The concept of "informed consent" is crucial. Victims of sexual abuse often do not object to participating in sexual activities but either lack knowledge of the social meanings and psychological impact of sexual encounters or, because of the powerless and dependent position they occupy, lack true free choice. It is impossible to say at what age children can give informed consent. A girl can consent to sexual intercourse at 16[43] and children of both sexes can consent to medical treatment at that age.[44] The American Psychological Association has argued that a 14-year-

40 See R. Dworkin, *Taking Rights Seriously* (1977), pp. 180-183. See also M. D. A. Freeman, "Taking Children's Rights Seriously," (1988) 1(4) Children and Society 299-319.

41 "Child Sexual Abuse" in R. Heifer and C. Kempe (eds.). *Child Abuse and Neglect: The Family and the Community* (1976), p. 60.

42 *Op. cit.*, note 1, p. 4, para. 4.

43 Sexual Offences Act 1956. s.6.

44 See Family Law Reform Act 1969, s.8(1).

old is competent to consent to an abortion.[45] On one reading of the *Gillick* decision[46] a girl with sufficient maturity, knowledge and understanding should be able to consent to going on the pill before she attains the age of 16. This will, of course, depend on the individual girl but psychologists tell us that, in both moral and cognitive development, many children reach adult levels between 12 and 14.[47] But, given the relationship of dependency, would it not be wiser to assume that children cannot give informed consent to sexual relations with adults?

*A fortiori* this should be the case where the relationship is close, whether within or without the incest test (for example, a step-parent). The reason for this is not brought out in the Schechter-Roberge definition, save in the reference to dependency. Abuse is about the exploitation of power: abusers are always more powerful than their victims.[48] The sexual abuser manipulates his victim for his own gratification. Because of the position children occupy within a family it is difficult to see a sexual relationship with an adult family member on whom they are dependent as anything other than sexual abuse. Most sex abusers are men and most victims are female (facts often glossed over in the Cleveland debates[49]): in this sense child sexual abuse is but a microcosm of the abuse, ranging from domestic violence,[50] through rape,[51] sexual harassment,[52] prostitution[53] and pornography[54] to which women are subjected.

Child sexual abuse takes many forms.[55] There is non-contact sexual abuse ("sexy talk," exposure and voyeurism). There is sexual contact, which includes any touching of the intimate body parts and frottage. There is oral-genital sex, involving the perpetrator's licking, kissing, suck-

45 See J. Bales "Brief Stresses Competence of Minors," APA Monitor, April 1987, p. 35.

46 *Gillick* v. *West Norfolk and Wisbech Area Health Authority* [1986] A.C. 112.

47 W. Damon, *The Social World of the Child* (1977); E. Douvan and J. Adelson, *The Adolescent Experience* (1966).

48 Recognised by the Standing Committee on Sexually Abused Children, *Definition of Child Sexual Abuse*. SCOSAC, 1984. See also B. Campbell, *Unofficial Secrets* (1988).

49 An attempt at a corrective is E. Welldon, *Mother, Madonna, Whore: The Idealization and Denigration of Motherhood* (1988).

50 R. Dobash and R. Dobash, *Violence Against Wives* (1979); E. Pizzey, *Scream Quietly Or The Neighbours Will Hear* (1974).

51 J. Rowland, *Rape: The Ultimate Violation* (1985); S. Estrich, *Real Rape* (1987) ; L. Clark and D. Lewis, *Rape: The Price of Coercive Sexuality* (1977).

52 C. MacKinnon, *Sexual Harassment of Working Women* (1979).

53 See E. Wilson, *What's To Be Done About Violence Against Women?* (1983), Chap. 5.

54 L. Lederer, *Take Back The Night* (1980).

55 *Op. cit.*, note 13, pp. 12-16. See also D. Finkelhor, *A Sourcebook on Child Sexual Abuse* (1986), pp. 22-27.

ing or biting the child's genitals or inducing the child orally to copulate with him. Fellatio is probably the most common example of this: the male perpetrator will insist on inserting his penis into a child victim's mouth. There is, fourthly, inter-femoral intercourse in which the perpetrator's penis is placed between the child victim's thighs. With younger children this technique is employed where the vaginal opening is too small: with older girls it may be used to avoid the risk of pregnancy. There is sexual penetration which may be digital (sometimes as a prelude to genital intercourse), use objects (electric vibrators, crayons, a carrot, a cucumber), involve the penis entering the vagina or the anus. There are also forms of sexual exploitation. This has to be distinguished from abuse. It is often done for financial gain, not sexual gratification. It includes child pornography[56] and child prostitution,[57] particularly loathsome forms of exploitation.

It may be useful to conclude this section with a working definition at least of child sexual abuse. The most comprehensive is that put forward by the Standing Committee on Sexually Abused Children in 1984. I quote it in full.[58]

> Any child below the age of consent may be deemed to have been sexually abused when a sexually mature person has, by design or by neglect of their usual societal or specific responsibilities in relation to the child, engaged or permitted the engagement of that child in any activity of a sexual nature which is intended to lead to the sexual gratification of the sexually mature person. This definition pertains whether or not this activity involves explicit coercion by any means, whether or not initiated by the child, or whether or not there is discernible harmful outcome in the short term.

## How Much Child Sexual Abuse is There?

The simple, and only honest, answer to this question is that we do not know. The assumption has always been that it is rare and this despite the Kinsey revelations that 24 per cent. of the women in their sample reported a sexual experience with an adult while they were children (though,

56 See F. Rush, "Child Pornography" in (ed.) L. Lederer, *op. cit.*, note 54, pp. 71-81.

57 See J. Ennew, *The Sexual Exploitation of Children* (1986).

58 See *op. cit.*, note 48.

when only sexual activity involving physical contact was considered, the rate fell to 9.2 per cent.).[59] More recently in this country, in the United States[60] and in Canada[61] attempts have been made to estimate the prevalence of sexual abuse. Many more cases are coming to light but this is a reflection of greater willingness to report and increased diagnoses, and not of greater occurrence. There was, almost certainly, more incest in Victorian Britain than there is today.

There are two types of information that assist us to estimate the frequency with which child sexual abuse occurs. There is data derived from studies of children referred to social services, doctors, police or therapeutic agencies. These suggest a low rate of abuse. For example, a survey by Mrazek, Lynch and Bentovim[62] of 1,599 family doctors, police surgeons, paediatricians and child psychiatrists uncovered a total of 1,072 cases seen in the year 1977-78. This would give an incidence figure of 1,500 per year, or one child in every six thousand. Over the entire childhood period (up to the age of 15), this study estimated that three children in every thousand are recognised as sexually abused. But (i) the overall response rate from the professionals was low (39 per cent.) and (ii) the figures are, as ever in this kind of survey, a gross under-estimate because they only take account of the cases which have been identified and processed through the relevant agencies.

The survey is interesting in that it reveals what incidence of abuse was coming to professional attention a decade ago. It does not, of course, uncover those cases which did not see the light of day because their victims were frightened, ashamed or confused, nor does it reveal anything about the cases that did not get beyond a disbelieving doctor.[63] With increased awareness of child sexual abuse, the numbers would be greater today. Thus, Wild[64] reports that referrals of child sexual abuse to paediatricians in Leeds increased from none in 1979 to 50 in 1984 and 161 in 1985. In 1984

---

59 *Op. cit.*, note 9. The sample (of volunteers) was 4.444 adult women.

60 See generally J. Haugaard and N. Reppucci, *The Sexual Abuse of Children* (1988), Chap. 3.

61 *Report of Committee on Sexual Offences Against Children* (1984). In New Zealand the one in 10 figure has been supported (see *The Independent*, April 15, 1988).

62 "Sexual Abuse of Children in the United Kingdom," (1983) 7 Child Abuse and Neglect 147-153.

63 As happened also with physical abuse. Doctors are now given guidance in DHSS, *Diagnosis of Child Sexual Abuse*, London, H.M.S.O. 1988.

64 "Sexual Abuse of Children in Leeds," (1986) 292 British Medical Journal 1113-1116.

in 60 per cent. of the referrals abuse was confirmed or considered probable: in 1985 the equivalent percentage was over 65 per cent.[65]

Another approach is to survey adults on their sexual experiences as children. There have been many American studies of this type. One of the best known is Diana Russell's, based on a probability sample of households in San Francisco. She reported that 38 per cent. of the women interviewed had experienced some form of sexual abuse involving physical contact before they were 18 (28 per cent. before they were 14).[66] The figures are 16 per cent. and 12 per cent. if only intra familial abuse is counted. The fullest British investigation was conducted by Baker and Duncan.[67] It involved a detailed interview of 2,019 women and men of 15 and over. It was a nationally representative sample. As indicated previously, it used a broad definition of sexual abuse. Respondents were asked if they had had experiences of sexual abuse (as defined) before the age of 16. Ten per cent. said that they had, 77 per cent. said that they had not: the remainder refused to answer the question. If these results can be generalised, it would mean that four-and-a-half million adults in Great Britain were sexually abused as children. Other British studies suggest the number is even larger. West[68] found that 46 per cent. of the 600 women he surveyed reported that they had been sexually abused as children and in Ruth Hall's sample of 1,236 women, 21 per cent. remembered that they had been sexually abused as children (for one-third of these the experience had occurred more than once).[69]

Obviously, these statistics must be treated with caution: the Butler-Sloss report admitted as much.[70] But, however exaggerated, they reveal the existence of a major problem.

65 The NSPCC h as also experienced large increases in reported cases (90 per cent. between 1984 and 1985).

66 "The Incidence and Prevalence of Intrafamilial and Extrafamilial Sexual Abuse of Female Children," (1933) 7 Child Abuse and Neglect 133-146.

67 *Op. cit.*, note 38.

68 West, *Sexual Victimisation* (1985).

69 *Ask Any Woman: A London Inquiry into Rape and Sexual Assault* (1985). For a very different view see D. Aitchison, *The Guardian*, August 11, 1988 (letter).

70 *Op. cit.*, note 1, p. 5, para. 7. Sue Richardson is quoted as suggesting that 30 per cent. of children may be abused (*The Independent*, July 1, 1987).

## How is Child Sexual Abuse to be Explained?

Do we know why it occurs? A lot of research effort has gone into trying to explain the aetiology of physical abuse and different models of explanation have emerged: one emphasising that abusers are "sick" (the medical or psycho-pathological model[71]), another that abuse is located in stress produced by socio-environmental factors such as the multi-faceted correlates of poverty,[72] and a third that abuse is to be explained in cultural terms, as an inevitable consequence of the fact that children are treated as property rather than persons, as social problems rather than as participants in the social process.[73] There is no agreement. It may be that a multi-dimensional explanation is what is needed.[74] But in many ways physical abuse is easier to understand than sexual abuse: most of us can empathise with the parent who lashes out in anger but few can comprehend sexual interference with a small child or intercourse with an adolescent daughter. How can it be explained? Are the models constructed to comprehend physical abuse of any assistance?

Although we will see striking parallels, one factor in child sexual abuse stands out and separates the two phenomena. Most perpetrators of child sexual abuse are men[75] and most victims are female.[76] The general source of the abuse must, therefore, be located in masculine sexuality.[77] It is surprising (or is it?) that the gender of the perpetrator is so rarely made

71 See M. D. A. Freeman, *op. cit.*, note 6, pp. 21-27 and N. Parton, *op. cit.*, note 5, Chap. 6 for critiques.

72 See L. Pelton "Child Abuse and Neglect: The Myth of Classlessness," (1978) 48 American Journal of Orthopsychiatry. 608-617 and see Freeman *op. cit.*, note 6. pp. 27-31 and Parton *op. cit.*, note 5, Chap. 7.

73 M. D. A. Freeman, "The Rights of Children in the International Year of the Child," (1980) 33 Current Legal Problems 1-32.

74 And see *op. cit.*, note 6, p. 32. And see D. Gil, *Violence Against Children* (1970). This was also recognised by the House of Commons Select Committee in its report on *Violence In The Family* (1977), H.C. 329, para. 32.

75 All surveys save one (G. V. Hamilton, *A Research In Marriage* (1929) – generally thought suspect on methodological grounds – demonstrate this. See D. Finkelhor, *op. cit.*, note 55, pp. 61-64; D. Glaser and S. Frosh, *op. cit.*, note 37, pp. 1 2-15. Russell, *op. cit.*, note 66, found a very small proportion of female abusers (4 per cent. where victims are girls.) Finkelhor, *op. cit.*, note 39, found 20 per cent. where the victims are boys.

76 A useful summary is Finkelhor, *op. cit.*, note 55, pp. 20-21. He estimates (p. 62) that there are 2.5 women victims for every man (*i.e.* 71 per cent. of victims are female).

77 See, for agreement, B. Campbell, *op. cit.*, note 48 ("Abuse is an expression of a patriarchal sexual culture"), p. 62; D. Glaser and S. Frosh, *op. cit.*, note 37, p. 13.

explicit. Discussion relating to Cleveland was invariably about "parents." The Baker-Duncan survey, referred to above, distinguishes "intra-familial," "extra-familial" and "stranger" abuse but never mentions the gender of the perpetrator.[78] Many of those who discuss sex abuse today would like to think that women were abusers too, but the evidence just does not support this. For example, in Russell's sample of 930 women, only 10 cases of incestuous abuse by women were reported, despite a wide definition of abuse.[79] Many of the early studies included women in the figures for perpetrators, not only when they had abused a child, but also when they had "simply 'allowed' sexual abuse to occur."[80] It is common to find mother blaming in the orthodox literature on child sexual abuse.[81] Nelson notes that "professionals cling to the collusive wife theory like drowning men grasping at flotsam." "Could it be," she asks most perceptively, "because it is such a powerful defence against admitting the male abuse of power? And because without it family therapists might be like emperors without clothes? These are harsh questions which they owe it to their own integrity to ask. "[82] They, that is orthodox theorists, in particular exponents of family systems theory,[83] do not ask them, but we must. If the male dimension in child sex abuse has been given such low profile, what is put in its place? How is sexually abusive behaviour explained in non-feminist literature?

As with the physical abuse of children, often it is individual factors in the abuser which are stressed. Some of the research findings can hardly be described as helpful.[84] Thus, abusers are described as being below av-

78 *Op. cit.*, note 38, p. 461.

79 *The Secret Trauma: Incest in the Lives of Girls and Women* (1986), p. 297.

80 D. E. H. Russell, *Sexual Exploitation: Rape, Child Sexual Abuse, Sexual Harassment* (1984), p. 219.

81 *e.g.* B. Justice and R. Justice, *The Broken Taboo – Sex in the Family* (1980); S. Forward and C. Buck. *Betrayal of Innocence: Incest and its Devastation* (1981); R. Kempe and C. H. Kempe, *Child Abuse* (1978).

82 S. Nelson, *Incest: Fact and Myth* (1987) (revised ed.), p. 108.

83 *e.g.* CIB A, *Child Sexual Abuse Within The Family* (1984); T. Furniss, "Conflict-Avoiding and Conflict-Regulating Patterns in Incest and Child Sexual Abuse," (1984) 50 Acta Paedopsychiat 299-313.

84 Good reviews of the literature are D. Finkelhor, *op. cit.*, note 55, Chap. 3; R. Langevin, *Sexual Strands: Understanding and Treating Sexual Anomalies in Men* (1983); K. Howells, "Adult Sexual Interest in Children: Considerations relevant to theories of Aetiology" in (eds.) M. Cook and K. Howells, *Adult Sexual Interest in Children* (1981).

erage intelligence,[85] of average intelligence,[86] and of above average intelligence.[87] They have been defined as aggressive,[88] and as passive.[89] The mothers similarly have been seen in contradictory terms: thus to some researchers they are inadequate and dependent,[90] to others dominant.[91] The explanation for this variation may be that different factors are important in different cases but it should trouble those who subscribe to a pathological model that the variations should be so great.

Weinberg[92] has tried to categorise abusers in a scheme which has proved influential. He distinguishes between "endogamic" abusers, who are oriented inwards towards their families, over whom they exercise a tightly possessive hold; "psychopathic" abusers, who treat all people within their power as sexual possessions, and "paedophic" abusers, whose psychological immaturity makes them fixate upon children as their sexual objects. Though not without interest, what the scheme implies is that children are abused only by sick or abnormal men. It is certainly convenient, even comforting, to think this: we would like to think of abusers as different, as a class apart.[93] But, when the characteristics of abusers are considered, they are found to be much like the rest of the male population, a diverse bunch whose range of sexual perceptions and responses are little different from "normal" men. Rarely does the literature which hypothesises individual pathology use control groups. It points to such factors as a harsh or deprived childhood,[94] to such matters

85 L. Bender and A. Blau, "The Reaction of Children to Sexual Relations with Adults," (1937) 7 Amer. J. of Orthopsychiatry 500-518. It was Bender and Blau, however, who, in the same article, suggested that the child was the seducer rather than seduced.

86 *Op. cit.*, note 12.

87 A. Mayer, *Sexual Abuse* (1985).

88 A. N. Groth and H. J. Birnbaum, *Men Who Rape* (1979).

89 B. Gottlieb, "Incest: Therapeutic Intervention In a Unique form of Sexual Abuse" in (ed.) C. C. Warner, *Rape and Sexual Assault: Management and Intervention* (1980).

90 V. De Francis, *Protecting the Child Victim of Sexual Assault* (1971); R. Sarles, "Incest," (1975) 22 Pediatric Clinics of North America 3.

91 M-J. Stern and L. Meyer, "Family and Couple Interaction Patterns In Cases of Father/Daughter Incest," in *Sexual Abuse of Children: Selected Readings* (1980).

92 S. K. Weinberg, *Incest Behavior* (1955).

93 E. Zigler. "Controlling Child Abuse in America: An Effort Doomed to Failure?"; in R. Bourne and E. Newberger (eds.), *Critical Perspectives on Child Abuse* (1979), pp. 171-213 (see particularly p. 176). See the example set out by K. C. Fuller. *op. cit.*, note 13, at pp. 101-103.

94 See Groth and Birnbaum (*op. cit.*, note 88) but *cf.* F.H. Knopp: *Remedial Intervention in Adolescent Sex Offences* (1982).

as parental marital discord,[95] multiple caretakers,[96] physical[97] or sexual abuse.[98] But why does this lead to these men becoming sexual abusers? If being sexually victimised predisposed to perpetrating sexual abuse, we would expect to find many more women committing sexual abuse. Those working within this paradigm do not explain why this does not happen: they content themselves with asserting that they marry abusing men and become pathological "colluding" mothers. There is no research on men who were abused as children and do not abuse their children. Such men do not come to the attention of clinicians. If there truly were a link between being victimised as a child and becoming an abuser, we would find many more boy victims than we do – a matter not satisfactorily explained by those who espouse an individualistic interpretation of child sexual abuse.

Not all of those who work within an individual personality framework present such a crude analysis. Finkelhor,[99] for example, links the individual psychological and the sociocultural in an attempt to construct a multi-dimensional explanation. He builds a theory of sexual abuse on a cluster of factors: emotional congruence ("sexual abusers choose children for sexual partners because children have some especially compelling emotional meaning for them");[100] sexual arousal to children, possibly produced by the effects of victimisation; blockage of alternative avenues of gratification (Finkelhor quotes Storr who claims that "a man... suffers from paedophilia... because he has been unable to find sexual satisfaction in an adult relationship. It is not from superfluity or lust, but rather because of a timid inability to make contact with contemporaries");[101] and disinhibitions of conventional social constraints (which includes explaining social and cultural elements that encourage or condone sexual behaviour directed toward children and thus weaken inhibitions – "anything that reinforces excuses for sexual abuse... acts to re-

95 K. Gruber and R. Jones, "Identifying Determinants of Risk of Sexual Victimization of Youth," (1983) 7 Child Abuse and Neglect 17-24. D. Finkelhor, *Child Sexual Abuse: New Theory and Research* (1984).

96 See, *e.g.* B. Justice and R. Justice, *The Broken Taboo* (1979).

97 M. De Young, *Sexual Victimization of Children* (1982); "Approaching the Incestuous and Sexually Abusive Family," (1983) 6 Journal of Adolescence 229-246.

98 H. Parker and S. Parker, "Father-Daughter Sexual Abuse: An Emerging Perspective," (1986) 56 Amer. J. of Orthopsychiatry 531-549.

99 See (with S. Araji) "Abusers: A review of the Research" (Chap. 3 of *op. cit.*, note 55).

100 *Ibid.* p. 94.

101 The quotation (at p. 107) is from A. Storr, *Sexual Deviation* (1965).

duce inhibitions."[102] Finkelhor, then, is not attributing abuse to personality traits alone but is combining these and experiences, such as being abused in childhood, with internal characteristics, such as lack of relationship skills, situating the whole within a socio-cultural context which makes some attempt to explain the effect of socialisation of men, the role of patriarchy in the denigration of women and children, the effect of pornography[103] and other disinhibiting factors. Of course, the feminist theories concentrate on the disinhibition factors. Finkelhor, by contrast, argues that these do not really offer full explanations of sexual abuse for they "take for granted some prior motive in the abuser to interact sexually with a child."[104] For Finkelhor they are, accordingly, a necessary but not a sufficient condition for abuse to occur. But, since the motive to indulge in a sexual relationship with a child hinges on man's sexuality or on social or cultural values, Finkelhor's thesis can be reconciled with a feminist interpretation of sexual abuse.

Again, as with physical abuse, the other dominant theory locates the source of sexual abuse in socio-environmental factors. The earliest writers[105] on sexual abuse hypothesised that it was an activity indulged in by the lowest social stratum. Thus Flugel in England (1926,[106] Sonden in Sweden (1936) and Guttmacher in the United States (1951)[107] reported that incest behaviour was inversely related to socio-economic status. These studies can be readily dismissed: the cases were limited to deviants already successfully prosecuted or to victims hospitalised in mental institutions. The evidence is, in other words, grossly distorted by sampling biases.[108] Similar criticisms can be made about any conclusions based on cases of sexual abuse which come to the attention of child protection agencies and the police.[109] These involve the poor disproportionately, but their behaviour is more likely to come under professional scrutiny.

---

102 *Op. cit.*, note 99, p. 113.

103 *Ibid.* pp. 105-106.

104 *Ibid.* p. 114.

105 As far as physical abuse is concerned, many still subscribe to a strong association between it and low social class. *e.g.* L. H. Pelton, *The Social Context of Child Abuse and Neglect* (1981).

106 J. C. Flugel, *The Psychoanalytic Study of the Family* (1926).

107 T. Sonder, "Incest Crimes in Sweden and Their Causes," (1936) 2 Acta Psychiatrica et Neurologica 379-401; M. S. Guttmacher, *Sex Offences* (1951).

108 I. B. Weiner, "On Incest: A Survey," (1964) 4 Excerpta Criminologica 37.

109 D. Walters, *Physical and Sexual Abuse of Children: Causes and Treatment* (1975). See also *op. cit.*, note 55, pp. 67-69.

With physical abuse the debate continues to rage over whether it is to be found predominantly amongst the poor.[110] Much, of course, depends on how physical abuse is defined (is corporal chastisement abuse?),[111] on how the "accident" in "non-accidental injury" is socially constructed.[112] As far as child sexual abuse is concerned, the evidence is so overwhelming that it crosses the social class barriers. The evidence here is American but there is no reason to believe it would not be replicated here. Thus Diana Russell's probability sample in San Francisco showed no association between sexual abuse and a father's education or occupation.[113] Peters' study of black and white women in Los Angeles could find no relationship between sexual abuse and either parental education or standard measures of social class.[114] And there are numerous other similar findings.[115] It could be that the middle-classes are more open about abuse experiences when questioned by middle class interviewers and so report more abuse, but there is no evidence or inferential support for this conclusion.[116] It is impossible to draw conclusions from the families of Cleveland where abuse was diagnosed, but certainly there the impression was created of a problem found both in poorer working and unemployed families and in the middle class, including professional families.

Even if poverty were linked with sexual abuse, it would still be necessary to demonstrate a causal relationship. What in poverty could be said to lead to abuse? Unemployment leading to greater access to the child (why then do not more women abuse children?), over-crowding and lack of privacy (but this may give the other parent greater opportunity to observe the abuse and to "collude" or report it to the authorities, so that it would show up in the statistics), social isolation?

Social isolation is a commonly-cited cause of sexual abuse. Thus, the Kempes in *The Common Secret* assert that "there are isolated communities or sub-cultures in which incest is accepted readily."[117] Is there any

110 D. E. H. Russell, *The Secret Trauma: Incest in the Lives of Girls and Women* (1986), (no association between sexual abuse and measures of father's education or occupation). For agreement, see Finkelhor, *op. cit.*, note 95.

111 *cf.* M. D. A. Freeman, *The Rights and Wrongs of Children* (1983), pp. 111-114.

112 See M. D. A. Freeman, "Child Welfare: Law and Control" in (eds.) J. Jowell and M. Partington, *Welfare Law and Policy* (1979), pp. 223-231.

113 *Op. cit.*, note 11 (2nd series).

114 S. D. Peters' Doctoral Dissertation, quoted in *op. cit.*, note 55, p. 67.

115 P. Miller's Doctoral Dissertation, also quoted *ibid.* pp. 67 and 69.

116 See *ibid.* p. 69.

117 R. S. Kempe and C. H. Kempe, *The Common Secret: Sexual Abuse of Children and Adolescents* (1984), p. 51.

evidence for this? Or does it just find its source in racist myths and class stereotypes? It is true that early researchers[118] did emphasise that incest rates were higher in rural than in urban environments and there is some anecdotal evidence[119] of concentrations of abusive families in rural areas. But the research studies, again American, do not associate abuse with isolated country communities:[120] indeed, the work of Miller[121] and Wyatt[122] suggests higher rates of abuse amongst women brought up in urban areas.

Studies do, however, confirm that sexual abuse victims appear to be isolated among their peers.[123] Those with fewer friends have been found to have more experiences of sexual abuse. But is this because they are looking for friendship and abusers take advantage of this, or is social isolation the "result of having been victimised rather than a risk factor?"[124]

Other socio-environmental factors do correlate with abuse. A number of studies have found higher vulnerability to sexual abuse among women who have lived without their biological fathers at some time during childhood,[125] though in several the finding is qualified.[126] There may also be a link between parental unavailability and abuse: girls who are victimised are more likely to have mothers who were employed outside the home, according to some studies;[127] they are more likely to have mothers who were disabled or ill[128] (but since the illnesses associated are alcoholism, depression and psychosis, one wonders which came first – the illness

118 *Op. cit.*, note 82, pp. 45-50 contains an insightful critique of the "subculture" interpretation.

119 See R. Summit and J. Kryso, *op. cit.*, note 11 (1st series).

120 Finkelhor, *op. cit.*, note 95, did find a significantly high rate (44 per cent.) among college student women who had grown up on farms.

121 Adoloscents from farm communities reported the lowest rates (*op. cit.*, note 15, 2nd series).

122 Higher rates in urban areas ("The Sexual Abuse of Afro-American and White American Women in Childhood," (1985) 9 Child Abuse and Neglect 507-519.)

123 *e.g.* Finkelhor (*op. cit.*, note 95) found that women with two or fewer friends at 12 had more experience of sexual abuse.

124 *Op. cit.*, note 55, p. 72.

125 See Finkelhor, *op. cit.*, note 95; also S. D. Peters, *op. cit.*, note 15 (2nd series) (but only for white women).

126 See *op. cit.*, note 55, p. 73.

127 See Russell, *op. cit.*, note 11 (2nd series); J. Landis, "Experiences of 500 Children with Adult Sexual Deviants," (1956) 30 Psychiatric Quarterly Supplement 91-109.

128 See J. Herman and L. Hirschman, "Families at Risk for Father-Daughter Incest." (1981) 138 Amer. J. of Psychiatry 967-970; also D. Finkelhor, *op. cit.*, note 95.

or the abuse?; more likely to witness conflict between their parents;[129] they are more likely to report a poor relationship with one of their parents.[130] Again, with these last two factors, there must be some doubt as to whether they are genuine risk factors rather than findings which result from abuse. A girl being abused by her father is likely to perceive there is conflict between her parents and/or perceive a poor relationship with her mother.

This leads us to the cultural interpretation of child sexual abuse. As with similar interpretations of other violence against women,[131] including domestic violence,[132] this is explicitly feminist. Such an interpretation is found in Florence Rush's *The Best Kept Secret*,[133] in Herman's study of father-daughter incest,[134] in the writing of Diana Russell,[135] of Mcintyre,[136] Taubman[137] and Wattenberg,[138] in Sarah Nelson's important study[139] as well as in the post-Cleveland analysis of Bea Campbell[140] and those who put together the special *Feminist Review* number[141] entitled "Family Secrets: Child Sexual Abuse." Feminism not only offers a different interpretation of child sexual abuse but also challenges the responses of orthodoxy, in particular those of "family systems" theory and family therapy.[142] It asks what is wrong with the functioning of the family and how can it be put back together again. It refuses to share responsibility or to blame victims. Its solutions are elsewhere, in cultural redefinitions to

129 See J. Landis, *op. cit.*, note 28 (2nd series); D. Finkhelor, *op. cit.*, note 95.

130 See J. Landis, *op. cit.*, note 28 (2nd series); D. Finkelhor, *op. cit.*, note 95; K. Gruber and R. Jones, *op. cit.*, note 95.

131 J. Chapman and M. Gates (eds.), *The Victimization of Women* (1978); J. Hanmer, *Women, Violence and Social Control* (1987).

132 K. Yllö and M. Bogard, *Feminist Perspectives on Wife Abuse* (1988).

133 Englewood Cliffs, New Jersey, Prentice Hall, 1980.

134 *Father-Daughter Incest* (1981).

135 *Op. cit.*, note 11 (2nd series); also *Sexual Exploitation* (1984).

136 K. Mclntyre, "Role of Mothers In Father-Daughter Incest: A Feminist Analysis," (1981) 81 Social Work 462-46.

137 S. Taubman, "Incest In Context," (1984) 29 Social Work 35-40.

138 E. Wattenberg, "In a Different Light: A Feminist Perspective in the Role of Mothers in Father-Daughter Incest," (1985) 64 Child Welfare 203-211.

139 *Op. cit.*, note 82.

140 *Unofficial Secrets: Child Sexual Abuse – The Cleveland Case* (1988).

141 No. 28 (Spring 1988). In particular, see M. MacLeod and E. Saraga, "Challenging the Orthodoxy: Towards a Feminist Theory," pp. 16-55. See also J. Hadley, "Mum is Not The Word," November 5, 1987 Community Care, pp. 24-26.

142 As in P. Mrazek and A. Bentovim "Incest and the Dysfunctional Family Systems" in P. Mrazek and C. H. Kempe, *Sexually Abused Children and Their Families* (1981) or R. Porter, *Child Sexual Abuse Within The Family* (1984).

tackle the problem at societal level, and in excluding and punishing the perpetrator to deal with the individual case.

For feminists child sexual abuse is an example of the inequality between the sexes produced by a patriarchal social system. Says Wattenberg: "The father rapes, abuses, brutalises and assaults the children and the mother, but somehow it is the mother's or child's fault."[143] Men have been taught that they have the right to have their sexual urges satisfied. Open access to wives is reinforced by the preservation even today of the marital rape immunity.[144] The extension to that other chattel, the daughter, seems quite logical, particularly if the wife for one reason or another is unavailable. And the structure of the family and society is such that both wife and children are trapped within dependency.[145]

An understanding of abuse requires an understanding of power. We have come to accept that rape is not so much a crime of sex, but a power trip.[146] In part sexual abuse has to be similarly understood. Herman, for example, documents the way in which the fathers of incest victims appear to those victims, when interviewed as adults, to have been dominating and authoritarian. These men exercise rigid and authoritarian control over wives and daughters, if necessary using force to impose their domination.[147] Jackson notes that "child molesters and child rapists are almost invariably men who have learnt to express their sexuality through aggression, to seek power over others and to be attracted to the vulnerable."[148] Is it possible to understand masculinity without seeing it in terms of aggression and violence?

There are those who respond by arguing that male sexuality is predetermined biologically, that it is produced by a biological drive, the function of which is the reproduction of the species. Men cannot help it: their sexuality is uncontrollable. To quote Ruth Porter's standard text: "these men may misunderstand the adolescent's behaviour and be sexually aroused by it; or physical chastisement may lead the perpetrator to

143 *Op. cit.*, note 39 (2nd series), p. 206.

144 An extraordinary defence of which is B. Amiel, "An Unwanted Act," *The Times*, March 24, 1989.

145 M. D. A. Freeman, "Legal Ideologies, Patriarchal Precedents and Domestic Violence," in M. D. A. Freeman, *State, Law and the Family: Critical Perspectives* (1984), pp. 51-78.

146 J. & H. Schwendinger, "Rape Myths," (1974) 1 Crime and Social Justice 18.

147 *Op. cit.*, note 11 (1st series), Chap. 5.

148 S. Jackson, *Childhood and Sexuality* (1982), p. 173.

the excitement that blends into sexual activity."[149] Clearly, these men are to be pitied! In one sense they are. They have not resisted or thrown off those definitions of masculine sexuality which most boys acquire during socialisation. After all, most do. Most sexual abuse may be perpetrated by males, but most males are not sex abusers.

It becomes important, therefore, to understand the processes by which masculine sexuality is constructed. Stephen Frosh's attempt to do so is most thoughtful.[150] I quote it at length:

> Some theorists... draw attention to differential patterns of conscious and unconscious socialisation for boys and girls which, together with wider social images of masculine sexuality, have the effect of constructing men as alienated from intimate relations and from our sexuality.... The characteristic patterns of masculinity, focussing on independence and 'hardness' and turning away from intimacy and nurture, follow from this. In particular it produces a severely narrowed rendering of sexuality, operating primarily in two convergent ways. First, sex is one of the few means by which men aspire to closeness with others, and as such it becomes the carrier of all the unexpressed desires that men's emotional illiteracy produces. However, this same process makes sex dangerous to men whose identity is built on the denial of emotion; sex then becomes split off, limited to the activity of the penis, an act rather than an encounter. At the same time, sex becomes tied up with competition, separation and power – something used to bolster a man's sense of masculinity rather than to create a bond with another. The link between such a form of masculinity and sexual abuse is apparent: it is not just present, but *inherent* in a mode of personality organisation that rejects intimacy. Sex as defence and as triumph slides naturally into sex as rejection and degradation of the other.

As he acknowledges, there are also important questions relating to the processes whereby most men learn not to abuse children. He sees these as connected with the "quality of their relationships in early life, internalisation of moral constraints, and the development of capacities to form positive sexual and emotional relationships with adults." But he adds: "if

149 *Op. cit.*, note 42, p. 9.

150 "Issues For Men Working With Sexually Abused Children" (1987) 3(4) British Journal of Psychotherapy 332-339. See also *op. cit.*, note 37 (1st series), p. 24.

there are systematic factors that make men more likely to sexually abuse children, then these factors will be present more or less strongly in all men." Sex, dominance and abuse do not have to be linked: there is no biological inevitability. But in our culture they are and they produce the conditions in which the sexual abuse of children occurs, and excuses are proffered.

Much more work needs to be done but, in the light of our existing knowledge and our understanding of closely-related phenomena like rape and domestic violence, it is the cultural explanation of child sexual abuse which most convinces. Armed with it, would we not look at orthodox solutions rather differently? With the kind of understanding it brings, would we not respond to Cleveland differently? How then are we to respond to the Cleveland crisis and its aftermath? What happened in Cleveland? What went wrong? Was sexual abuse properly managed? Were the resources of the legal system used efficiently, effectively and appropriately? What has emerged from Cleveland and the inquiry and litigation· that it spawned? Are there lessons for the future? It is to these questions that we must now turn.

### What Happened in Cleveland?

Cleveland hit the headlines in June 1987.[151] The chronology of events leading up to the crisis has been told, variously, elsewhere.[152] No more than a brief summary is required. The events identified reveal how the historian perceives the "crisis." One could dig in the nineteenth century for insights and parallels;[153] one could look back to the events surrounding the discovery of the battered child where there are parallels too.[154]

The more immediate background to Cleveland was the *Lancet* article of Hobbs and Wynne in 1986 with its assertion that anorectal abuse

151 Mainly in the *Daily Mail*. But see in particular F. Mount, "Children Need Justice Not Moral Panic," *Daily Telegraph*, July 3, 1987, E. Rantzen, "Listen To The Children's Cry," *Sunday Times*, July 5, 1987; M. Toner, "Should a Father Be Afraid To Kiss His Daughter Goodnight?," *Sunday Express*, July 28, 1987; S. Weir, "What If The State Kidnaps Your Child ?," *London Daily News*, July 23, 1987. On the role of the Press see M. Nava, "Cleveland and the Press," Feminist Review No. 28, pp. 103-121.

152 By Stuart Bell, *op. cit.*, note 29 (1st series), and Bea Campbell, *op. cit.*, note 48 (1st series).

153 See J. B. Twitchell, *Forbidden Partners* 1987.

154 See B. Nelson, *Making An Issue of Child Abuse: Political Agenda Setting For Social Problems*, (1984), and N. Parton, 1 *op. cit.*, note 5 (1st series).

was more common than the battered-child syndrome ("More children are buggered than battered"),[155] the NSPCC's focus on sexual abuse,[156] the BBC *Childline* project which commenced in October 1986[157] and the Blom-Cooper reports *A Child In Trust*[158] and, more particularly, the results of the inquiry into the death of Kimberley Carlile, *A Child in Mind.*[159] The reports were highly critical of the "rule of optimism"[160] that seemed to prevail in social services departments. They urged that greater emphasis be placed on the social control role of social workers and that, in particular, greater use should be made of the resource of law in tackling child abuse. Social workers in particular were castigated for not intervening swiftly enough or effectively.

The more immediate background to Cleveland itself was the declaration in 1986 by Cleveland County Council of child abuse as a priority and the appointment of a special child-abuse consultant, Sue Richardson. Dr. Marietta Higgs was appointed consultant paediatrician at Middlesbrough General Hospital in January 1987. Some months before she had seen for the first time the phenomenon of "reflex relaxation and anal dilatation." She had recently learnt from Dr. Wynne (the co-author of the *Lancet* article) that this is a sign found in children subject to anal abuse. The anal dilatation test is at the heart of the controversy surrounding Cleveland. Its novelty, so often stressed during the last couple of years, lies in its application to detect the buggery of children: the diagnosis is well-known in forensic pathology.[161]

Using this aid to diagnosis, though not it alone,[162] Dr. Higgs and a colleague, Dr. Geoffrey Wyatt, proceeded to diagnose a large number of cases in which, in their view, sexual abuse (in particular anal abuse) had occurred. In total 125 children in Cleveland were diagnosed as sexually abused between February and July 1987, 121 of them by Dr. Higgs and Dr.

155 C. Hobbs and J. Wynne, "Buggery In Childhood: A Common Syndrome of Child Abuse" (1986) 2 Lancet 792-796. Dr. Wynne now says the test was "given too much prominence" in the Cleveland affair (*The Independent*, July 13, 1988).

156 See T. Simmons, *Child Sexual Abuse – An Assessment Process*, London, NSPCC, 1986 (Occasional Paper No. 1).

157 Established by B.B.C. T.V. on October 31, 1986. On concern over how to handle cases brought to light by Childline see P. Hildrew, *The Guardian*, November 28, 1987.

158 The Jasmine Beckford report (published by L. B. of Brent, 1985).

159 Published by L. B. of Greenwich in 1987.

160 The phrase was coined by R. Dingwall *et al.* in *The Protection of Children* (1983).

161 In this sense it is not a "recent discovery" (and see *op. cit.*, note 1 (1st series), para. 11. 26).

162 *Op. cit.*, note 1 (1st series), para. 8.8.73.

Wyatt. In wardship cases brought by the local authority 27 of the children were dewarded and went home with the proceedings dismissed; 24 went home on conditions which included supervision orders and conditions as to medical examination, and two of them went home on interim care orders.

As at the time of writing of the Butler-Sloss report (the spring of 1988), nine other children who were wards of court remained in the care of the County Council and away from their families. Of those children not made wards of court, a further 27 were the subject of place of safety orders. In all, again using evidence available at the time the inquiry report was written, 21 children remain in care. Of the 121 children diagnosed by Drs. Higgs and Wyatt as sexually abused, 98 are now at home.[163] The sheer weight of cases, the number of them in which judges subsequently concluded that sexual abuse had not occurred, the over emphasis which Drs. Higgs and Wyatt gave to the anal dilatation test, the ways in which children were removed from families, the undermining of parental rights – all these matters naturally gave, and continue to give, cause for concern.

We may never know exactly what happened in Cleveland. There is no doubt that the events of the first half of 1987 created a moral panic and that the folk devils[164] were the two paediatricians, Drs. Higgs and Wyatt, and not those (in Cleveland and elsewhere) who were abusing young girls. There is a close parallel: in the aftermath of the Jasmine Beckford[165] and Kimberley Carlile[166] cases it was the social workers who, allegedly, had failed to prevent the deaths to whom opprobrium was attributed, not the men at whose hands the girls died. There is also a causal link: it was, in part, a response to the press social services departments had received when they failed to intervene in these well-publicised cases that Cleveland adopted, what appears in retrospect to have been, an over-interventionist policy.

Whilst not wishing to underestimate the importance of child sexual abuse, what Cleveland also reveals is abuse by the system. Cleveland was a battleground for personalities and social agencies. On one side were paediatricians and social workers who were too ready to diagnose sexual

---

163 This does not mean that some of these were not sexually abused. Further, we do not know how many of the fathers are also there.

164 See S. Cohen, *Folk Devils and Moral Panics* (1972); S. Hall, *Policing The Crisis* (1978); F. Fitzpatrick and D. Milligan, *The Truth About The Aids Panic* (1987).

165 As to which see *A Child In Trust* (1985).

166 See *A Child In Mind* (1987). This point is made in the Butler-Sloss report also (*op. cit.*, note 1 (1st series), p. 244, para. 15).

abuse. On the other were other doctors and the police who did not want to see signs of abuse.[167] In the process, parents' rights were ignored and many children were unnecessarily damaged. Dr. Higgs was right to believe that child sexual abuse had long gone undetected and right to believe that "paediatricians had a responsibility to right this wrong."[168] But she had unswerving confidence in her diagnosis and this was suspect too often for us to rely on the accuracy of her judgment. There is no evidence that Sue Richardson, the Cleveland child-abuse consultant, who saw sex abuse as a "unique constellation of trauma"[169] ever questioned a diagnosis. The techniques employed by the paediatricians (in particular the anal reflex dilatation test) and by the social workers and child psychiatrists (in particular the disclosure interview) are, I believe, both suspect and neither is criticised as rigorously in the Butler-Sloss report as it should be. In the other camp were the police who failed to consider or understand the complexities of child sexual abuse. With them was the police surgeon Dr. Alistair Irvine who adopted a position "where his examination was unlikely to support an allegation or complaint"[170] and who "rejected out of hand clinical symptoms and signs that other doctors considered significant."[171] The report notes that his personal and emotional involvement compromised his professional position.

In the middle of this battleground were the parents and the children. Parents like the Norths[172] whose two-year-old, brought to Dr. Higgs suffering from constipation, was diagnosed as having been anally abused. He had just had his first bowel movement in 17 days. This set in train a horrendous chain of events, with the other two children of the family being similarly diagnosed, and the Norths only winning their children back after seven months. The social services withdrew at the wardship stage and the Norths were awarded costs, but the true costs to them and their children are inestimable. Or like the Wests, another example of constipation in a two-year old being diagnosed as anal abuse. Mrs. West was 16

167 *Op. cit.*, note 1 (1st series), part 3, pp. 243-244. Also paras. 8.8.75; 7.37; 8.9.46; 9.3.22(1)(b).

168 *Op. cit.*, note 1 (1st series), para. 8.8.71.

169 *Ibid.* para. 4.187.

170 *Ibid.* para. 7.39.

171 *Ibid.* See also B. Campbell, "Heavy Hand of the Law Laid on Cleveland," *The Independent*, September 26, 1988.

172 Neither the "Norths" nor the "Wests" are the real names. They were the ones used in an I.T.V. programme transmitted on July 5, 1988 (the evening before the Butler-Sloss report was published).

weeks pregnant at the time and was left in no doubt that once delivered of her baby it would be taken into care forthwith. They could not believe this could "happen in England." They describe themselves as "members of the establishment" who believe in the system. At a case conference, to which they were not invited, it was decided that they could have one hour of access a week to their daughter. A second medical opinion diagnosed a mega-colon but not before the child had spent a month in care. And it was not just children taken to see a paediatrician with disorders which warranted anal examination who were given the anal dilatation test. According to some Cleveland parents, children with routine ailments like ear-ache and asthma were subjected to this test.[173] If, indeed, there were children unnecessarily tested in this way it is a sad reflection on the effect the crisis was having on the Cleveland paediatricians.

But they cannot be blamed alone. The Butler-Sloss report apportions responsibility. All the agencies involved, save one, are shown, in one way or other, to be at fault. No one person is singled out for blame. The criticism is spread wide, highlighting a lack of proper understanding between social agencies, and a lack of communication. Dr. Higgs and Dr. Wyatt are criticised for "the over-confidence with which they pursued the detection of sexual abuse in children referred to them."[174] But, they were not solely, nor indeed principally, responsible for the subsequent management of the children concerned.[175] Nevertheless, "the certainty of their findings in relation to children diagnosed by them without prior complaint, posed particular problems for the Police and Social Services."[176] The Director of Social Services is also criticised. He is said to have "reacted to events"[177] rather than controlled them, and to be at fault for not questioning the paediatric diagnoses and the need to take the children from their homes. The police are criticised for allowing a rift to develop between themselves and social services, and for "taking no effective steps to break the

173 There was no "routine screening for sexual abuse" according to the report (para. 9.3.22.1a). The report includes (*op. cit.*, note 1 (1st series), para. 8.8.75) that "she did not examine children for sexual abuse other than on occasions when in her professional judgment there were grounds to do so." "It was only rarely that she relied on R.A.D. as the 'only physical sign'" (para. 8.8.73).

174 *Op. cit.*, note 1 (1st series), p. 243, para. 7 (see also para. 8.8.81). See also Judge Cohen in *Cleveland C.C.* v. *D* [1988] F.C.R. 615 (their concern to find sexual abuse "paramount," so evidence not considered objectively).

175 *Ibid.*

176 *Ibid.*

177 *Ibid.* para. 4.186. His own account of events is found in Social Work Today, July 7, 1988, pp. 12-13.

deadlock."[178] The only agency not criticised are the magistrates. Since they appear to have granted every application for a place of safety order (without which authority none of the children could have been removed from home), the fact that they have got off virtually scot-free leaves one with a distinct feeling that those concerned with the administration of the law are immune from criticism. Could it be that Lord Justice Butler-Sloss would have felt embarrassment at subjecting legal personnel to criticism? The report describes the place of safety process as involving a "discretionary judicial act."[179] And so it should, but in what did the discretion consist in Cleveland, and what judicial qualities were being exercised? The part played by magistrates and the place of safety process is a matter for concern. It, together with other of the problematic features of Cleveland, will be considered in the next section of this article.

## Protecting Abused Children and Innocent Parents

The central dilemma of the child sexual abuse process is how to protect abused children whilst at the same time protecting innocent parents.[180] In Cleveland we did not get the balance right. As a result a number (we will never know exactly how many) of innocent parents and non-abused children suffered. We will never know either how many sick children were kept away from hospitals (and not just in Cleveland) because parents feared unfounded allegations of sexual abuse. We will never know the damage Cleveland has done to the credibility of a system, the aim of which was to protect abused children. What went wrong?

### (i) *The Reflex Anal Dilatation Test*

So much of the criticism of what happened in Cleveland has centred on the reflex anal dilatation test that it is appropriate to begin with it. It is not the technique that is new but its application to tackle a form of child sexual abuse is.[181] What appeared to cause both astonishment and horror in Cleveland was that it was being used to uncover so much anal abuse. Is anal abuse (as opposed to other forms of sexual abuse) so prevalent?

178 *Ibid.* p. 244, para. 9.

179 *Ibid.* para. 16.5.

180 *cf.*, D. J. Besharov, "Introduction" to H. Wakefield and R. Underwager, *Accusations of Child Sexual Abuse* (1988), pp. 3-15. See also A. Neustatter, "For the Sake of the Innocents," *The Guardian*, July 5, 1988.

181 *Op. cit.*, note 1 (1st series), para. 11.26.

The incidence studies all appear to suggest that, amongst girls at least, it is rare.[182] The Hospital for Sick Children in Great Ormond Street, London appears to think that anal abuse accounts for only 1 per cent. of that which it sees.[183] This could be explained by the fact that the test pioneered in Leeds was not being used. But it may also point to the unreliability of that test. The sign is as follows:

> When the buttocks are separated, the external sphincter and then the internal sphincter open so that the observer can see through the anal canal into the rectum. The anal sphincters are controlled in part automatically, in part by learned unconscious behaviour, and in part consciously; all in a very complex system not altogether understood by the experts. The controlling mechanism will change with age and will be influenced by levels of awareness and local sensations. ... In many children subject to anal abuse, Hobbs and Wynne found that the canal opened on buttock separation. Sometimes it opened and shut, (winking); sometimes it opened and stayed open so that the observer could look into the rectum.[184]

At times the impression is created of some kind of magic sign, a sort of infallible litmus test. But this is far from the truth. The signal emitted by the test requires interpretation and there is no consensus on its meaning. As the Butler-Sloss report conceded: "It is not known whether it occurs in normal individuals."[185] But it almost certainly does. John McCann's research at the Valley Clinic in Fresno, California (not picked up in the report) found signs of anal dilatation in 53 per cent. of a random sample of 268 non-abused children.[186] Dr. Graham Clayden,[187] a specialist in

182 *Op. cit.*, note 45 (1st series), p. 51. The Great Ormond Street book (ed. by A. Bentovim *et al. Child Sexual Abuse Within The Family* (1988), barely mentions it (see pp. 67, 79).

183 This figure was quoted in the I.T.V. documentary on child sexual abuse, transmitted the night before the Butler-Sloss report was published.

184 *Op. cit.*, note 1 (1st series), para. 11.26.

185 *Ibid.* para. 11.28.

186 This figure is somewhat higher than would be expected. But see now also A. Stanton and R. Sunderland, "Prevalence of Reflex Anal Dilatation in 200 children," (1989) 298 Brit. Med. Journal 802-803 who found such R.A.D. in 14 per cent. of the normal child population. They conclude that "it is a sign with poor discriminatory value in diagnosing anal abuse in children" (p. 803).

187 G. S. Clayden, "Reflex Anal Dilatation Associated with Severe Chronic Constipation in Children," (1988) 63 Archives of Disease in Childhood 832-836.

chronic bowel disorders at St. Thomas's Hospital in London, who gave evidence to the inquiry and who is quoted in the report, certainly believes that anal dilatation is a normal response of all of us. Anxiety or fear might cause the opening, and many of the children subjected to the test had plenty of opportunity to express this. The report states that it does not "usually occur in normal children,"[188] but this question-begs. Constipation, even chronic constipation, is not that abnormal in small children. The problem lies in drawing the conclusion that because anal dilatation is found in many children who have been anally abused that anal dilatation is a sign of sexual abuse when it may equally well be a symptom of other disorders or indeed a normal reaction. As the Butler-Sloss report notes: "Although most experts agreed that anal dilatation may follow anal abuse, there was considerable disagreement as to the other circumstances in which it might occur."[189]

The report concludes that the sign of anal dilatation is "abnormal and suspicious and requires further investigation."[190] But "it is not in itself evidence of anal abuse."[191] Did Dr. Higgs and Dr. Wyatt so interpret it, as a result of which interpretations children were removed from parents? Did the forensic examination, as Dr. Hobbs and Dr. Wynne indicate that it should, take place in the context of the whole child examination? Did Dr. Higgs and Dr. Wyatt often read too much into a complex sign and initiate a train of action which brought tragedy to a large number of families? The report is, I think, too kind to Dr. Higgs and Dr. Wyatt and, it should be added, far too severe on Dr. Raine Roberts,[192] whose experience of sexual abuse is wider than the Cleveland paediatricians and whose understanding of the issues and context far exceeds theirs.

### (ii) *The Use of Place of Safety*

It is surprising how little attention has been given to place of safety procedures in the past. Their implications, the inter relationship between

188 *Op. cit.*, note 1 (1st series), para. 11.26. In "only 18 cases of 121" was R.A.D. the sole physical sign (para. 9.3.22(b)).

189 *Op. cit.*, note 1 (1st series), para. 11.28. D.H.S.S., *Diagnosis of Child Sexual Abuse: Guidance for Doctors* (1988), p. 20 recommends that children with R.A.D. "be seen again at a later date for reassessment."

190 *Ibid.* para. 11.30.

191 *Ibid.*

192 She is said to have been unable to provide the inquiry with "cool, detached and considered testimony" (*op. cit.*, note 1 (1st series), para. 11.66). But *cf.* Judge Hall in *Cleveland C.C. v. C.* [1988] F. C. R. 607.

the procedures in the 1933 and 1969 Children and Young Persons Acts and the draconian effect of an order have been little understood. In Cleveland, in the first seven months of 1987, 276 place of safety orders were applied for by social workers under powers laid down in section 28 of the 1969 Act. Children having been medically diagnosed as abused, this was, it seemed, the next logical step. It was thought that, armed with such an order, the social services department could consent to the child being medically examined and further medical examination did usually follow the anal dilatation test. If the Cleveland social services department had read the Blom-Cooper report *A Child In Mind* it would have known that a place of safety order does not confer this power (he recommended accordingly a new order, a "child assessment order.") But this had clearly passed over its head.[193]

The social services department operated "a highly interventionist policy"[194] in the use of place of safety orders. A memorandum from the director directed social workers to apply for them on receiving a diagnosis of sexual abuse from a paediatrician. To enable "disclosure work" to be carried out, a decision was taken to reverse normal practice and request 28-day orders, the maximum period allowed by statute. Though most of the orders were granted during the day, most applications were also heard by a single magistrate at home and during the hours of court sittings. All but one application was *ex parte* and none was refused. Yet the Butler-Sloss report persists, rather formalistically, in describing the granting of an order as a "discretionary judicial act."[195] There is no doubt that that is what it *ought* to be, just as applications for search warrants by the police and for separate representation orders[196] ought to be judicial acts. However, it does seem that place of safety orders were so readily granted in Cleveland during the crisis of 1987 that it is difficult to accept that all decisions warranted the action taken by the magistrates.

The report is critical of much of the place of safety decision-making processes in Cleveland: the automatic assumption that the application should be *ex parte;* the lack of communication between magistrates granting orders and the clerk (is that why it appears that there were instances of more than one order on one child?); the use of the order to "ob-

193 *Op. cit.,* note 67 (2nd series), pp. 153-156. The pros and cons of this are debated in *Childright* no. 55 (April 1988) by A. Wilson (p. 12) and R. Osmond (p. 14).

194 *Op. cit.,* note 1 (1st series), para. 10.7.

195 *Ibid.* para. 16.5.

196 But *see R.* v. *Plymouth Juvenile Court ex p. F. and F.* [1987] 1 F.L.R. 169.

tain repeat examinations for forensic purposes or for information gathering rather than for continuing treatment";[197] the use of the order and the concomitant denial of access to facilitate "disclosure work," rightly condemned as an improper use of the legislation.[198] The report is "unhappy to see the acceptance of an automatic response by way of place of safety order to certain sets of facts"[199] and is especially critical of Sue Richardson's desire to use the place of safety mechanism "by way of control as the first stage of intervention and management of the family in situations where there was no immediate danger to the child."[200] This is seen, quite rightly as a "wholly unjustified use"[201] of the order, though, it has to be added, there is little unique in this reliance on the place of safety mechanism.[202] It should be added that the social services in Cleveland did also use "voluntary" care, a practice which has been officially approved.[203]

The Butler-Sloss report followed other recent critics in challenging the use made of the "place of safety" concept.[204] But it was already under sentence of death[205] and will disappear with the Children Act 1989 which will replace it with the better-designed and fairer emergency protection order.[206] This may account for the rather mild way in which the report considers the place of safety provisions and, in particular, the role of magistrates and their clerks in the process. It is a virtue of the report that it is even-handed and balanced, but the magistracy does get off rather lightly. It was carrying out a "discretionary judicial act." In what did its discretion consist? What judicial qualities were being exercised? If the magistrates exercised discretion, why were the orders invariably of 28 days' duration? This satisfied the administrative convenience of the social workers, but

197 *Op. cit.*, note 1 (1st series), para. 16.10.

198 *Ibid.* para. 16.12.

199 *Ibid.* para. 16.14.

200 *Ibid.*

201 See also p. 246. The views of Dr. James Appleyard (reported in *The Independent.* June 29, 1987) that sexually abused children are not in immediate danger of death or serious injury and so can be left until proper proceedings can be gone through is worth noting.

202 See J. Packman, *Who Needs Care? Social Work Decisions About Children* (1986).

203 Nevertheless, "child care practice traditionally relied heavily upon the use of statutory-based interventions and on place of safety orders" (para. 4. 27).

204 See Packman, *op. cit.*, note 3 (3rd series), pp. 52-54; T. Norris and N. Parton "The Administration of Place of Safety Orders" (1987) Journal of Social Welfare Law pp. 1-16; Dartington Research Unit, *Place of Safety Orders*, 1985 (unpubl.).

205 See the Government White Paper. *Law on Child Care and Family Services* Cm. 62. London, H.M.S.O.

206 See clauses 37 and 38.

it is generally accepted that 28 days was too long and that orders of this length were not in the interests of the children or their parents. Emergency protection orders will last for eight days only (with a possibility of extension by another seven days in strictly defined circumstances).[207] If the magistrates exercised a judicial function, how much evidence testing was there? The absence of the clerk from the processes is likely to have limited the possibility of this. We do not know how much evidence was questioned, how long the average application took, what magistrates were told or what they asked. How many of the magistrates who granted orders were on the juvenile panel? (At present there is no requirement that they must be).

It would have been appropriate for the inquiry to have probed rather more deeply into the work of the Cleveland magistrates. There is no reason why legal actors (even when lay persons) should remain immune from critical scrutiny.

### (iii) *Medical Procedures and Consents*

The Cleveland affair raises in acute form the question of who is capable of consenting to a medical examination. In many of the cases parents had taken the children to hospital for a paediatric examination. There can be little doubt that where this was, for example, for a bowel disorder that there was implied consent by the parents to an anal dilatation test. Parents complained, however, that this test was carried out when their child was brought to hospital with a complaint which could not possibly warrant an anal dilatation test. The Butler-Sloss inquiry found this did not happen.[208] Whether it happened or not, it is worth asking whether consent could be implied to such a test where a child suffering, for example, from ear-ache is taken to a doctor.

A letter from the Social Services Inspectorate,[209] dated February 1988 (*i.e.* long after the Cleveland storm), purports to rule that a doctor may conduct an examination to relieve distress, pain and suffering where this is "immediately essential" for the child's welfare. In many cases it is difficult to see how anal dilatation tests can have been "immediately essential." A parent could consent on behalf of his or her child: in certain

207 Clause 38(1), (5) and (6).

208 *Op. cit.*, note 1 (1st series), para. 8.8.75.

209 D.H.S.S. Circular (88) 2 (*Medical Examination of a Child Subject To A Place of Safety Order*).

circumstances the child herself can consent.[210] But, in default of such consents, the solution turned to by the local authority, *viz.* assuming that a place of safety order gave it the authority to consent to a medical examination for forensic purposes, though understandable, is clearly unacceptable. A place of safety order does not terminate parental rights.[211] Social workers who hold one have no more authority to consent to a medical examination on the child than they had prior to obtaining it.

This will change when the emergency protection order comes into operation. This will give the applicant (in most cases the social services department) "parental responsibility"[212] for the child, that is "all the rights, duties, powers, responsibilities and authority which by law a parent of a child has in relation to the child and his property."[213] Since the parent has the power to consent to medical treatment it will follow that a local authority vested with an emergency protection order will be in a similar position. But should any doubt remain the court, when making an emergency protection order, may give directions it considers appropriate regarding "medical or psychiatric examination of the child." It may, therefore, become the norm for a local authority to apply for such directions at the same time as seeking the emergency protection order.

### (iv) *Access to Children*

A major ground of complaint by parents was the fact that they were denied access or given it in restrictive conditions. This caused "great distress, much resentment and created great difficulties."[214] The reason why access was refused or restricted was to enable "disclosure work" with the child to take place to confirm the sexual abuse.

The Butler-Sloss report is rightly critical of this. It argues that the restriction or denial of access is:

> not... within the authorisation of a place of safety order, save where the safety of the child required it, for example a violent parent or the likelihood of removal of the child from the place of safety."[215]

---

210 Family Law Reform Act 1969 s.8(1) (if over 16): *Gillick* v. *West Norfolk and Wisbech A.H.A.* [1986] A.C. 112 (if she understands what is involved).

211 Part III of the Child Care Act 1980 does not apply (and see *op. cit.*, note 1 (1st series), para. 16.9).

212 Defined in clause 3 of the Children Bill.

213 A definition hardly more helpful than that in the Children Act 1975, s. 85(1).

214 *Op. cit.*, note 1 (1st series), para. 10. 19.

215 *Ibid.* para. 16.11.

The report also notes that:

> there was for the parents no recourse to the courts either under the place of safety order or under the interim care order" [save under section 12B of the Child Care Act 1980].[216]

The contradictions found in these two statements must be noted. On the one hand we are told that the local authority cannot by virtue of a place of safety order deny access (though this is qualified). On the other hand, the report draws attention to the absence of legal redress, where access is denied. The problem is accentuated because place of safety and interim care orders are drawn together. They are hardly juridical equivalents and the report rightly criticises social workers in Cleveland for treating place of safety orders as if they were interim care orders.[217]

Were Cleveland social services able to deny parents access? The matter was little discussed, and yet the answer is clear: a place of safety order does not terminate parental rights and this included (under section 85(1) of the Children Act 1975) a right of access. The Cleveland parents therefore had the right to unrestricted access to their children. Those who drafted the access provisions in 1983[218] realised that access could not be denied under a place of safety order: that is why they did not provide for parents denied access to apply to the juvenile court for an access order. Once an interim care order was made, such an application was allowed. Then why, one wonders, did Lord Justice Butler-Sloss suggest there was no recourse to the courts under an interim care order. This is clearly wrong. It follows from this analysis that a test case brought by a Cleveland parent for judicial review of the decision to refuse access where the local authority was retaining the child under a place of safety order should have succeeded. It may be added that the Code of Practice on Access to Children in Care was also ignored routinely in Cleveland.[219] The report could have been more forthright in its condemnation of the Cleveland policies on access. It could also have been clearer in its analysis of the concepts involved.

---

216 *Ibid.* para. 10.19.

217 *Ibid.* para. 4.114.

218 Health and Social Services and Social Security Adjudications Act 1983. Sched. 1.

219 Described in *M.* v. *Berkshire C. C.* [1985] F.L.R. 257, 263, "as an aid to construction" of the statute but in *R.* v. *Bolton M.B.C. ex p. B.* [1985] F.L.R. 343, 351 the Divisional Court refused to use the Code "as a guide to the proper meaning of the words of the statutes."

### (v) *Disclosure Interviews*

One of the most problematic features of the investigative process is the so-called "disclosure interview." Pioneered at the Great Ormond Street Hospital it is doubtless a valuable technique if used sensitively by trained professionals. But otherwise it can become coercive, intrusive and an affront to the dignity of the child. A fundamental problem of the "disclosure" approach is that it implies there is always something to disclose. At its worst, a point often reached in Cleveland interviews, the assumption is that the child who does not disclose is "in denial," that is to say cannot bring herself to accuse a parent. But, as Latey J. put it, "it would be helpful to the court if the questioners were alert to any indications of an innocent, as well as a sinister, interpretation and recorded them in their notes, reports and evidence."[220] There is, in other words, a third possibility – the child has no sexual abuse to disclose. The danger is that this is not considered a viable, meaningful option. The premise is that abuse has occurred and that the child must be helped to reveal her awful secret. The wheel has come full circle: not so long ago a child who claimed she had been sexually abused would rarely be believed and now one who insists she has not is also sometimes disbelieved. Allegations have been made in television programmes that some of the Cleveland interviews were quite ghastly with children hectored and bullied into saying they were abused when they had insisted throughout they had not been. Sometimes they were threatened they would not see their parents until they admitted they had been abused.[221] Many were made to feel "acutely uncomfortable"[222] as they were grilled by big, powerful adults and assured "You can trust me, darling."

Questions have been raised as to the value as evidence of diagnostic interviews.[223] A series of cases, conveniently reported in one issue of *Family Law Reports*,[224] goes some way toward answering these questions. Thus, the court is unlikely to give weight to anything the child has said in

---

220 *Re M.* [1987] 1 F.L.R. 293, 296.

221 Examples like this were shown in a number of T.V. programmes on the Cleveland affair, including that on I.T.V. on July 5, 1988.

222 *Per* Dr. Elizabeth Tylden, as quoted in I.T.V. programme on the Cleveland affair, July 5, 1988. According to Eastham J. in *Cleveland C.C.* v. *E.* [1988] F.C.R. 625 some children are left with "psychiatric scars" as a result of "relentless" questioning.

223 See G. Douglas and C. Willmore. "Diagnostic Interviews as Evidence in Cases of Child Sexual Abuse" (1987) 17 Family Law 151-154.

224 [1987] 1 F.L.R. 269-346.

response to leading questions.[225] The use of anatomically correct dolls as cues or prompts is said to be of limited value only and therefore must be treated cautiously.[226] The courts are unhappy to accept an interviewer's account and interpretation of the interview with the child unless a transcript and a videotaped recording are made available.[227] Further, the assistance that the recording can give is "limited to enabling the court to catch the flavour of the interview, noting the length of pauses, the attitude of the child, the tone of voice of the interviewer, and so on."[228] It could never be an acceptable substitute for the overall view which the court had to take of the evidence as a whole. There can be intervention (so that the child can be protected) even though the evidence does not indicate who has abused the child.[229] The court can conclude that a child has been abused on a balance of probabilities, that is on evidence short of what would be required to sustain a criminal conviction.[230] A higher degree of probability is needed to satisfy a court that an individual has sexually abused a child than that required to establish that the child has been sexually abused.[231]

But the diagnostic interview raises many more questions than have been addressed in the cases or in the Butler-Sloss report. A few of them will be raised here. Let us start with so-called "anatomically correct" dolls. These are in widespread use.[232]

Originally, they were used in therapy as toys and as aids to assist sexually abused children come to terms with their experience. Now they have come to be used as diagnostic tools in the investigation of suspected cases of sexual abuse. But, as Gabriel notes, many who work in the child protection field are untrained in play therapy. "The result has been that material produced by children in this manner can appear to confirm suspicions of sexual abuse when it may actually be no more than a normal reaction to

225 *Re E.* [1987] 1 F.L.R. 269.

226 *Re N.* [1987] 1 F.L.R. 280.

227 *Re M.* [1987] 1 F.L.R. 293; *Re G.* (*No.* 2) [1988] 1 F.L.R. 314.

228 *Re W.* [1987] 1 F.L.R. 297, 307.

229 *Re J. S.* [1981] 2 F.L.R. 146.

230 *Re W.* [1987] 1 F.L.R. 297. A higher degree of probability is required to satisfy the court that a parent is guilty of sexual abuse than to satisfy it that the child has been abused by an unknown person (*Cleveland C.C.* v. *A. & B.* [1988] F.C.R. 593).

231 *Re G.* (*No.* 2) [1988] 1 F.L.R. 314.

232 Discussed in the Cleveland report (*op. cit.,* note 1 (1st series)) at paras. 12.54-12.64. They are said to be "highly undesirable as a routine prop in initial interviews" (para. 12.64).

the dolls and the situation."[233] King and Yuille point out that "the dolls serve the function of a suggestive question with young children. The genitals and orifices of the dolls suggest a play pattern to children, and that play may be misinterpreted as evidence for abuse."[234] Gabriel describes a study of 19 non-abused children who were observed with the dolls. They demonstrated behaviour which could have been interpreted as indicating likely sexual abuse. Many showed overt interest in the genitals and/or unusual interaction with them. He concludes that "on the evidence of the dolls alone... the suspect will almost always be found "guilty," especially if the examiner is already biased in that direction."[235]

A leading study which claims to demonstrate the value of using anatomically correct dolls is by White, Strom, Santilli and Halpin.[236] They report that their sample of non-sexually abused children interacted differently with the dolls than did the abused sample. But the article gives us no information on other differences which may have existed between the two groups, without which it is impossible to draw conclusions.[237] Even the editors of *Child Abuse and Neglect,* in which the article appears, preface it by stating that:

> to date no data have been published which clearly delineate the responses to these interviews by children who have not been sexually abused. This study is necessary before the results of interviews of children who have been sexually exploited can be accurately interpreted.[238]

One of the most interesting studies was conducted by Jensen, Realmuto and Wescoe.[239] Twelve children, aged three to eight, were interviewed by a single therapist. Three of them were known to have been sexually

233 R. M. Gabriel, "Anatomically Correct Dolls in the Diagnosis of Sexual Abuse of Children," The Journal of the Melanie Klein Society (1982) 3(2), pp. 40-51 at p. 42.

234 M. A. King and J. C. Yuille, "Suggestibility and the Child Witness" in S. J. Ceci, M. P. Toglia and D. F. Ross (eds.), *Children's Eyewitness Memory* (1987) pp. 24-35, at p. 31.

235 *Op. cit.,* note 34 (3rd series), p. 49.

236 J. White, G. S. Strom, G. Santilli and B. M. Halpin, "Interviewing Young Sexual Abuse Victims with Anatomically Correct Dolls" (1986) 10 Child Abuse and Neglect, pp. 519-529.

237 See, for agreement, H. Wakefield and R. Underwager, *op. cit.,* note 80 (2nd series), p. 205.

238 Child Abuse and Neglect (1986) Vol. 10, p. 519.

239 J. B. Jensen, G. Realmuto and S. Wescoe, Paper To American Academy of Child Psychiatry, Washington, D. C., October 1986.

abused. Four had been referred for evaluation of other conditions (and were psychiatric controls). Five children were non-clinical controls. The interviews were videotaped and a panel, which included psychologists, then viewed the videotapes and rated the behaviours on a scale from "not at all suspicious" to "very suspicious." No differences between groups were found. Some of the nonabused children got the highest rating of "very suspicious" and some of the abused children got the lowest ratings of all. One of the psychologists identified none of the abused children, another rightly identified two but falsely identified a further three children.

The available data (none of which, incidentally, is picked up in the Butler-Sloss report) suggests that anatomically correct dolls cannot be used to distinguish abused from non-abused children.[240] No data supports the view that abused and nonabused children behave differently when dolls are used as diagnostic or assessment devices. Their use is likely to increase the rate of false positives, that is children said to have been abused when they have not.

Another questionable procedure is the use of children's drawings to diagnose sexual abuse. The assumption is that qualitative features of the drawings may be used as "signs" that suggest that the child has experienced sexual abuse.[241] But the variability from drawing to drawing is such that particular features of any one drawing are too unreliable to draw any conclusions from them. Non-psychologists, including clerks and typists, have been reported to do as well as psychologists and psychiatrists in interpreting children's drawings.[242] Nevertheless, they continue to be used. Existing evidence suggests that they can tell us very little and so should be used with the utmost caution, if at all.[243]

---

240 W. McIver, H. Wakefield and R. Underwager, "Behavior of Abused and Non-Abused Children in Interview with Anatomically-Correct Dolls" (1987), (unpublished manuscript, quoted *op. cit.*, note 80 (2nd series), pp. 206-208.)

241 D. B. Harris, *Children's Drawing as Measures of Intellectual Maturity: A Revision and Extension of the Goodenough Draw A Man Test* (1963); H. B. Roback, "Human Figure Drawings: Their Utility in the Clinical Psychologist Armamentarian for Personality Assessment" (1968) 70 Psychological Bulletin, pp. 1-19.

242 S. Fisher and R. Fisher, 'Test of Certain Assumptions Regarding Figure Drawing Analysis" (1950) 45 Journal of Abnormal and Social Psychology, pp. 727-732; E. Plaut and C. W. Crannell, "The Ability of Clinical Psychologists To Discriminate Between Drawings of Deteriorated Schizophrenics and Drawings by Normal Subjects" (1955) 1 Psychological Reports, pp. 153-158.

243 C. G. Watson, "Inter-judge Agreement of Draw-a-Person Diagnostic Impressions" (1967) 31 Journal of Projective Techniques and Personality Assessment. pp. 42-45.

The so-called "sexual abuse accommodation syndrome" also needs to be critically addressed. It is used by interviewers (and certainly was at Cleveland) to justify their questioning and interpretation of the responses of children during an interview. The concepts of the syndrome, described in an authoritative article by Ronald Summit,[244] are used to decide whether or not a child's statements about being sexually abused are valid or false. He proposes five categories of behaviour that constitute this syndrome:

(i) secrecy;
(ii) helplessness;
(iii) entrapment and accommodation;
(iv) delayed, conflicted and unconvincing disclosure;
(v) retraction.

Abused children, so Summit argues, will demonstrate these behaviours when interrogated. The syndrome has never been validated; yet it is widely adopted by professionals involved with sexual abuse allegations. Thus, the concept of secrecy is used to support the tactic of continuing to question when a child denies abuse. This syndrome has been enormously influential in practice in this country, in Cleveland and elsewhere. It is therefore worth quoting in full the authoritative observations of Wakefield and Underwager, two leading American experts:

> The application of the sexual abuse accommodation syndrome to children's statements means that nothing they say, nothing they do, can count against the belief that abuse happened. If they deny initially, that's because they have to keep it secret and if you keep at them long enough they will finally admit the secret. If they admit and then deny, that's because they are helpless, confused, and it means they are abused. If they deny, admit, and then retract, that's evidence that they were abused. Everything is evidence that the child has been abused. Once an allegation hits a professional who holds the sexual abuse accommodation syndrome concept and the dogma that children must be believed at all costs, nothing can falsify it.[245]

244 R. Summit, "The Child Sexual Abuse Accommodation Syndrome" (1983) 7 Child Abuse and Neglect, pp. 177-193.

245 *Op. cit.*, note 80 (2nd series), p. 215.

Finally, some comments on the interviewing techniques employed are in order. The C.I.B.A. textbook advocates that an interview should begin something like this: "You told your teacher/granny/foster-mother that Daddy put his hands in your pants/showed you his penis and that this was bothering you."[246] But all the research on memory and children as witnesses shows that the most reliable information from young children comes from a condition of free recall.[247] Closed or leading questions result in greater responses, but also greatly increase the risk that the children's answers will not be accurate.[248] The older the child, the more he or she will be able to produce in free recall. But it is generally agreed that even the few statements produced by young children in free recall are likely to be accurate.[249] Thus, to begin an interview with a question inviting spontaneous, free recall ("Tell me, what happened?") is likely to be much more productive and reliable than the sort of question advocated in the C.I.B.A. publication and commonly found in practice.

It is also not uncommon for interviewers subtly to suggest events to children. A recent American study (by Ceci, Ross and Toglia) showed that young children in particular appear more likely to incorporate "erroneous post-event information into their subsequent recollections than older children."[250] It seems that their high level of suggestibility is related to their conformity to what they believe to be the expectation of the adult. Young children are, in other words, not just vulnerable to sexual abuse: they are also vulnerable to adult social influence. They conclude that if erroneous information is introduced in a diagnostic interview it may "resurface in the form of the child's reconstruction of the events."[251] Legrand and Underwager comment: "In the light of their data and findings, it is difficult to locate the source of the optimistic belief that the majority of children's recollections are accurate."[252] Again, whilst this seems to have

246 (Ed.) R. Porter, *Child Sexual Abuse Within The Family*, (1984), p. 69.

247 E. F. Loftus and G. M. Davies, "Distortions In The Memory of Children" (1984) 40(2) Journal of Social Issues, pp. 51-67.

248 H. R. Dent and G. M. Stephenson, "An Experimental Study of the Effectiveness of Different Techniques of Questioning Child Witnesses" (1979) 18 British Journal of Social and Clinical Psychology, pp. 41-51; J. P. Lipton, "On The Psychology of Eyewitness Testimony" (1977) 62 Journal of Applied Psychology, pp. 90-95.

249 This was accepted by the Butler-Sloss inquiry (see *op. cit.*, note 1 (1st series), para. 12.34).

250 S. J. Ceci, D. F. Ross and M. P. Toglia, "Age Differences In Suggestibility: Narrowing The Uncertainties" in *op. cit.*, note 35 (3rd series), pp. 79-91, at p. 89.

251 *Ibid.*, p. 90.

252 *Op. cit.*, note 80 (2nd series), p. 79.

the ring of truth to it, it is not research that has been picked up in English child sexual abuse literature. It certainly was not brought to the attention of the Butler-Sloss inquiry. And yet, of course, like so much of this data it is only an application of well-known and well-respected psychological research into eye-witness testimony that amongst well-informed opinion is taken for granted in examinations of the criminal justice system.[253] Why is it not penetrating the consciousness of those who work in the child sexual abuse area in this country? Is it that in an effort to tackle the acknowledged evil of sexual abuse anything which appears as an obstacle is cast aside, or is it just plain ignorance? This question cannot be ignored for the civil liberties implications of misdiagnosis are profound and troubling.

### Where do We Go from Here?

Where do we go from here? How are we to get to grips with the evil of child sexual abuse whilst at the same time ensuring that intervention is properly targeted so that parents and children are not abused by the system. It is clear that the problem must be approached on two levels. Sexual abuse must be eradicated. This must be the primary goal, for prevention is always better than cure. But, whilst we must recognise this as an ultimate goal, an ideal to be striven for, we must also recognise that, short of a cultural revolution and even then, the problem will always be with us. And so effort must also go into improving our responses, managerial, social work and legal, to sexual abuse when it occurs. If the responses are seen as the problem, as has happened in Cleveland, our attention becomes diverted from the abuse itself. As I write this, a Children Bill is being published[254] and other reforms, such as those in the Criminal Justice Act 1988, are being implemented.

In this last section I focus on these two dimensions and ask how do we stop sexual abuse of children and how do we tackle it when it occurs. In discussing the latter question some comments are offered on the new and proposed legislation.

---

253 E. F. Loftus, *Eyewitness Testimony* (1979). See also M. S. Zaragoza, "Memory, Suggestibility and Eyewitness Testimony in Children and Adults" in *op. cit.*, note 35 (3rd series), pp. 53-78.

254 For the Second Reading debate in the House of Lords, see Hansard, H.L. Vol. 502, col. 487-540.

### (i) *Eliminating Abuse*

Child sexual abuse is essentially a problem of male sexuality. This is not predetermined biologically but is socially constructed. The socialisation processes which construct images of masculinity need to be re-examined. The role played by the legal system in these processes cannot be ignored. Can the law provide solutions to the problem of violence against women, of which the sexual abuse of girls is but a phenomenon, when it constitutes part of that problem?[255] Only a matter of two days ago, a judge in London said that a child sexual abuser had been driven to abuse his 12-year-old step-daughter, an epileptic with a mental age of seven, because his pregnant wife was not responding to his "healthy" desires.[256] There were three assaults. The first described by the judge as "not serious," the second involving manual contact with the girl's genitalia and the third the girl being induced to masturbate the man. On the third assault we are treated to the extraordinary comment: "there were no threats or bribes and more significantly, there was no change in the behaviour or temperament of the young lady." As so often, the mother is blamed and the inference drawn that the girl was at worst a "Lolita," at best a willing participant.[257]

It is not only male sexuality that needs to be rethought but also the position of children. Child sexual abuse cannot be explained only in terms of male-female power relationships, but needs to take account also of those between adults and children. For too long we have viewed them as property rather than persons.[258] Sometimes we have cloaked this in pseudo-scientific imagery by emphasising the "blood tie."[259] We deny

255 See M. D. A. Freeman, "Violence Against Women: Can the Legal System Offer a Solution When It Constitutes The Problem?" (1980) 7 British Journal of Law and Society, pp. 215-241.

256 The judge was Sir Harold Cassell (see *The Times*, November 29, 1988).

257 The judge concerned retired on grounds of ill-health the same week. His interpretation of events is far from unique; Judge Brian Gibbens was reported to have said that sex with a seven-year-old was "one of the kind of accidents that could almost happen to anyone." (*The Times*, December, 1983).

258 The Butler-Sloss report, in stressing that children are persons and not objects of concern (see *op. cit.*, note 1 (1st series), p. 245), strikes a significant blow for children. See also P. Newell, "Children's Rights After Cleveland" (1988) 2(3) Children and Society, pp. 199-206.

259 Attacked by J. Howells, *Remember Maria*, (1974); See also *Re* C. (*M.A.*) [1966] 1 W.L.R. 646.

children rights. In one authoritative recent book, children are said to have one right only – the right to autonomous parents.[260]

Intervention in the family ("the smack of statism" according to one of my critics)[261] is deprecated to uphold freedom and dignity.[262] But whose freedom and dignity are being upheld when children are allowed to suffer abuse and neglect? If we are to conquer the abuse of children, we must learn to "take children's rights seriously,"[263] we must accept their entitlement to "equal concern and respect."[264] But it is not just that children are reified. To understand sexual abuse we have to understand the ways in which the supposed sexuality of children is commodified. The commercialisation of child sexuality is as prevalent as the use of female images to sell products. We have begun to object (though not to much effect) to the misuse of a half-naked woman to sell cars, but when "the photograph of a prepubescent girl wrapped only in a towel, is used to advertise house insurance, there seems to be no objection."[265] The apparent precocity of a group of young girls has been deliberately exploited in the cinema also in the last decade.[266]

As the campaigns in the past few years have emphasised, children must be taught to say "no." But they must also be taught more about what they are saying no to. The child's right to education is universally accepted but her right to a sex education is still questioned.[267] Is it not somewhat ironic that a government committed to stamping out sexual abuse should also subscribe to the moral right's backlash against sex education? If we really care about sexual abuse we will commit ourselves to teaching children what sex is all about.

Improving the status of children requires many other things: an end to corporal punishment,[268] so clearly associated, not least in the minds of

260 J. Goldstein, A. Freud and A. Solnit, *Before The Best Interests of the Child* (1979), p. 9.

261 B. Amiel, "Smack of Statism," *The Times*, October 21, 1988.

262 *Op. cit.*, note 61 (3rd series). p. 12.

263 *Per* M. D. A. Freeman. "Taking Children's Rights Seriously" (1988) 1 (4) Children and Society, pp. 299-319.

264 *Per* R. Dworkin, *Taking Rights Seriously* (1977), pp. 272-278.

265 See J. Ennew, "Selling Children's Sexuality" (August 22, 1986) 77 New Society, No. 1 234, pp. 9-11, a t p. 10.

266 Tatum O'Neal, Jodie Foster, Nastassja Kinski and Brook Shields are the best-known examples.

267 *cf.* R. Ives, "Children's Sexual Rights," in B. Franklin, *The Rights of Children* (1986), pp. 143-162.

268 See Michael Freeman, "Time to Stop Hitting Children" (October 1988) 51 Childright. An attempt to undermine this failed in the House of Lords on January 24, 1989;

some sex abusers, with sexual gratification and therefore abuse; a greater say in the decision-making processes which affect them which makes the removal of automatic party status for children in care proceedings, as envisaged in the Children Bill, such a retrograde step;[269] better complaints procedures, an idea which is endorsed in the Bill;[270] a fuller recognition of the implications of the *Gillick* decision,[271] particularly as found in Lord Scarman's reasoning; an understanding that the removal of a child from its home environment into care is no panacea;[272] the adoption of more child-centred policies.[273]

### (ii) *Dealing with Abuse*

But sexual abuse will continue to occur. How are we to respond to it? First, we must examine existing approaches. As indicated, many of these are defective. By attributing the blame to the family system, they deflect it away from the perpetrator. We do not say burglars cannot help it or that people who go on holiday bear part of the responsibility for burglaries which take place in their absence. So, why do we respond to sexual abuse in this way? Sexual abuse is difficult to identify, but this does not excuse the development of techniques which lead to false positive identifications. Thus, the anal dilatation test must be used with the utmost caution and must never lead to a diagnosis of sexual abuse without more evidence. Those who carry out the interviewing of allegedly abused children must be better trained, must improve their techniques and must take on board the clear lessons of the psychological research to which reference has been made.

Interviewers[274] should:

(i) be aware of their biases;
(ii) minimise leading questions and ask open-ended ones;

---

Hansard Vol. 503, cols. 542-548.

269 See clause 36.

270 See clause 22.

271 [1986] A.C. 112.

272 See clause 1(4) and revelations about sexual abuse in care (*e.g.* Devon, *The Independent* November 2, 1987; Birmingham, *The Independent,* September 1, 1988. See also *The Guardian,* January 17, 1984: Liverpool).

273 See M. D. A. Freeman, *The Rights and Wrongs of Children* (1983).

274 A full account of the methods used in E. Vizard and M. Tranter, "Helping Young Children to Describe Experiences of Child Sexual Abuse" in *op. cit.,* note 82 (2nd series), pp. 84-129.

(iii) remain as objective and impartial as possible (this may require that the interviewer does not read background information prior to interviewing the child);
(iv) be alert to the cognitive and moral developmental level of the child (for example, young children confuse the concepts "know," "remember," "guess" and "forget");[275]
(v) minimise cues given to a child about what she is supposed to say;
(vi) avoid pressure or coercion to give a desired response (an affirmation obtained under pressure is worthless);
(vii) be calm and not show irritation when the child is not responding as desired;
(viii) conduct the interview in a way that does not contribute to the emotional trauma of the child.

There is reason to believe that many diagnostic interviews in England today fall well short of these optimal guidelines.[276] If it seems that a child has been abused, she must be protected. But this does not necessarily mean removal of that child from her home or cutting off or severely restricting contact with her family. Wherever possible, the least intrusive measure should be adopted.

The Children Bill is in part a response to Cleveland. Had it been in operation during the Cleveland crisis, would it have improved the processes and practices of the social agencies, would it have better protected the children involved, would it have safeguarded the rights of parents more fully? What differences would it have made?

The Bill is in many ways an improvement on the existing law. The emergency protection order[277] is a vast improvement on the place of safety order. It will last for a shorter period;[278] there will be a presumption of reasonable access[279] (or contact, as it is now to be called); the applicant (that is in most cases the local authority social services department) will have its powers and duties relatively clearly defined. But applications will still usually be *ex parte*. The granting of an E.P.O. will be a "discretionary

275 H. M. Wellman and C. N. Johnson, "Understanding of Mental Processes: A Developmental Study of 'Remember' and 'Forget'" (1979) 50 Child Development, pp. 79-88, (children up to six years of age).
276 See the cases reported in *Family Law Reports Special Issue* (note 25 (3rd series)).
277 Clause 37 *et seq.*
278 Eight days (cl. 38(1)).
279 See clause 29.

judicial act" (in theory): in practice its administration may not improve on that we associate with place of safety orders.

The whole process of care will be speeded up. A new provision requires a court hearing an application for a care order (or supervision order) to have regard to the general principle that "any delay" is likely to prejudice the welfare of the child.[280] The number of interim care orders is to be limited,[281] the intention being that the whole care process will be concluded in 12 weeks.[282] Whether this will be possible to achieve, we can only wait and see-and hope. To me it looks like a pious aspiration. One consequence is that care proceedings will, in the future, nearly always take place before criminal proceedings (if they are brought). This may prejudice some parents[283] but if the child's welfare is to be given priority this may be inevitable. It is anyway consonant with the recent decisions in the *Inner London*[284] *Exeter,* and *Waltham Forest Juvenile Court*[285] cases.

The grounds for a care order have been remodelled. They are wider in scope (they cover, for example, prognosis of harm where none has yet occurred,[286] and thus make it easier to remove new-born babies).[287] The ground is also subject to the general principle in the Bill that intrusion must be the least detrimental alternative[288] ("No court shall make any order under this Act... unless it considers that making the order would be better for the child than not making the order').[289] Given the standard of some substitute care,[290] the importance of this principle cannot be underestimated. One consequence of the widening of the care ground is that local authorities' power to use wardship will be severely restricted:

280 Clause 27(1).

281 Clause 33(1).

282 Clause 33(5)(a), (b) and (6).

283 Who will be tried for a criminal offence *after* the determination of care proceedings. The Government says speed is "vital" in prosecutions for child abuse (*The Times,* February 19, 1988).

284 [1988] 2 F.L.R. 58.

285 [1988] 2 F.L.R. 214.

286 Clause 26(2) ("is likely to suffer... harm.")

287 On the problems of which hitherto see M. D. Freeman, 10 Fam. Law 131-134 (1980).

288 The phrase (not in the Bill) was coined by Goldstein, Freud and Solnit, *Beyond the Best Interest of the Child* (1973) p. 53.

289 Clause 1(4).

290 On foster care breakdowns, see D. Berridge and H. Cleaver, *Foster Home Breakdown* (1987). See also references in note 73 (3rd series).

a local authority which cannot acquire parental responsibility using a statutory ground will not be able to use wardship as a safety valve.[291]

The law on access (what we must now call "contact") is also to be improved. There is to be presumption of reasonable contact[292] and, for the first time, a child[293] may apply to be allowed contact with a parent, a sibling or other persons. As the law stands at the moment, a parent may apply for an "access order" where access is terminated[294] by a local authority or it refuses to make arrangements for it.[295] Under the proposed legislation the decision will rest with the court which will be able to make an order authorising the authority to refuse to allow the child contact, if it is necessary to do so to safeguard the child's welfare.[296] Any authority's powers to refuse contact are most restricted: it will only be able to do so in matters of urgency, for a maximum period of seven days and then only if satisfied that it is necessary to do so to safeguard the child's welfare.[297]

There are other changes which may be viewed more cautiously. Neither parents nor children will get automatic party status, as the Bill stands. Whether they get it or not will depend on the court.[298] The 1986 Act giving parents party status where there is a separate representation order has only been in operation for a couple of months, so this seems a strange reversal of policy.[299] Denying children automatic party status could undermine their rights and is a measure which should be resisted. The Bill also seems to envisage children represented by guardians *ad litem* or solicitors, but not both.[300] Those who believe that solicitors perform a valuable role in care proceedings and in particular are better able to protect the rights of their child clients will be puzzled by this. Is it anything oth-

291 See clause 71. The authority will only be able to do so with leave (clause 71(3)) and where the result the authority wishes to achieve cannot be achieved otherwise and there is reasonable cause to believe that if the court's inherent jurisdiction is not exercised the child will suffer "significant harm" (clause 71(4)).

292 Clause 29(2).

293 Clause 29(3)(b).

294 And not where it is restricted. For a recent example see *Re Y.* [1988] 1 F.L.R. 299. See also *P.* v. *Staffs* C.C. [1989] F.L.R. 16.

295 And *see R.* v. *Bolron M.B.C. ex p. B.* [1985] F.L.R. 343.

296 Clause 29(4).

297 Clause 29(6).

298 Assurances have been given that regulations will provide for this. The provision, as it stands, is ominously close to that envisaged by the Green Paper issued by the Lord Chancellor's Department, *Improvements in the Arrangements for Care Proceedings* (1988).

299 Children and Young Persons (Amendment) Act 1986.

300 Clause 36.

er than an attempt to save money? The independent guardian *ad litem* panels, which were promised, have been forgotten: the existing, rather haphazard, system is therefore set to continue. There is, however, to be some streamlining of the court's jurisdiction, though, of course, no Family Court.[301] It seems to be envisaged that the county court[302] will bear the main burden of care proceedings. Such a transfer will sacrifice expertise acquired through experience for legal training, but will it necessarily improve the system? There will also be no Office of Child Protection,[303] but this is an ill-conceived concept, and few will regret its early demise.

It will be some considerable time before this new edifice is in working order. The provisions of the Criminal Justice Act 1988, which relate to children's evidence in sex abuse cases, already are in operation. Section 32 of this permits a child under 14 to give evidence through a live television link at a trial or an appeal.[304] The two-way video link may assist the child to give evidence, but the dangers inherent in this process remain. What will a jury think when it observes that the defendant is not permitted to confront the child face to face like other witnesses? Does not the fact that he is compelled to be physically separated from the child create inferences of his guilt and dangerousness?[305] In an effort to assist the child to give evidence, may we not have undermined the civil liberties of the alleged perpetrator of the sexual abuse? Section 34 removes the requirement (in section 38 of the Children and Young Persons Act 1933) that the unsworn evidence of a child must be corroborated by some other material evidence to convict. Judges will no longer have to warn juries against convicting defendants on the uncorroborated evidence of a child. The rule of practice that juries must be warned that it is not safe to convict on the uncorroborated evidence of a complainant does, however, remain, though of course they may do so if satisfied that the child is telling the truth. The repeal of section 38 makes it imperative that those who

---

301 What we get was described by Lord Justice Butler-Sloss in her Bentham Club lecture in 1989 as an "embryo" Family Court. It may be doubted if it will grow into a child.

302 This will only become clear when the rules are provided (see clause 69).

303 See C. M. Lyon, "Office of Child or Parent Protection?" [1988] Fam. Law 454 for a critique of this concept.

304 But not in trials or committals in magistrates' courts or in appeals therefrom.

305 G. B. Melton and R. A. Thompson, "Getting Out of a Rut: Detours To Less Travelled Paths in Child-Witness Research" in *op. cit.*, note 35 (3rd series), pp. 209-229. See also G. Fontaine and R. Kiger, "The Effects of Defendant Dress and Supervision in Judgments of Simulated Jurors" (1979) 2 Law and Human Behavior, pp. 63-72.

examine and cross-examine children in court also take on board what has been said about interviewing techniques and their pitfalls.

## Conclusion

Cleveland has come and gone but the shock waves it sent through the system continue to reverberate. It provoked passionate responses. There can be little doubt that in an attempt to rescue abused children, abuse was wrongly diagnosed. Diagnostic errors could have been avoided and must be eliminated in the future. But the errors that were made, and they were grievous, must not divert our attention from the evil of child sexual abuse. We must find ways of protecting abused children whilst at the same time protecting innocent parents. In the last analysis Cleveland was about sexual abuse, not Marietta Higgs or Geoffrey Wyatt. If the lessons of Cleveland enable us to conquer sexual abuse those whose lives were wrecked will not have suffered in vain.

CHAPTER 7

# Does Surrogacy Have a Future after Brazier?

## I. Introduction

Women have always carried babies for other women, or (perhaps more commonly) for men who are not their husbands or partners.[1] Examples (of sorts)[2] can be traced to the book of *Genesis*.[3] The first modern cases to attract public attention were *A* v. *C*[4] in 1978 (though this was not properly reported until the "Baby Cotton" case[5] in 1985 sensitised us to the problem), *Noyes* v. *Turane*[6] in 1981 and *Stiver* v. *Malahoff*[7] in 1983. All three cases had a sensationalist dimension and attracted media attention: in the first, the surrogate was a prostitute who was approached leaving the magistrates' court; in the second, the commissioning mother was a male-to-female transsexual; in the third case the child was rejected by the commissioning parents (he had microcephaly) but was revealed in a television show[8] to be the child of the surrogate's husband.

The cases coincide with early news (Louise Brown, the first IVF baby was born in 1978) and early concerns about the reproduction revolution. And, it was this, rather than surrogacy itself, which motivated the gov-

1 On male domination of reproduction see R. Rowland, *Living Laboratories* (Lime Tree 1992) at 6-14. See also C. Pateman, *The Sexual Contract* (Polity Press, 1988). For Debra Satz "markets in women's reproductive labor are especially troubling because they reinforce gender hierarchies in a way that other accepted labor markets do not" (see "Markets in Women's Reproductive Labor" (1992) 21 *Philosophy and Public Affairs* 107-31 at 110).

2 The oft-cited Biblical examples are not true surrogacies: the surrogates were slaves (or perhaps concubines: see Genesis XXV, 6).

3 See chapter XVI, 1-5 (Abram and Hagar) for the best known example.

4 (1978) 8 Fam. Law 170 and fully in [1985] F.L.R. 445.

5 [1985] F.L.R. 846. Kim Cotton's story is told in K Cotton and D Winn, *Baby Cotton For Love and Money* (Dorling Kindersley 1985).

6 No. CF7614 (LA. Cty. Super Ct. 1981) and see M.A. Field, *Surrogate Motherhood* (Harvard University Press 1988), 1.

7 See G. Corea, *The Mother Machine* (Harper and Row 1985) at 219-20, 230 and P. Singer and D. Wells, *The Reproduction Revolution* (Oxford University Press 1984) at 118-19.

8 The "Phil Donahue Show".

 DOI:10.1163/9789004219106_008

ernment in 1982 into setting up the Warnock inquiry.[9] But it was moral panic[10] over the "Baby Cotton" affair in January 1985 which led to legislation (the Surrogacy Arrangements Act 1985)[11] and this, as amplified in 1990,[12] remains the framework of surrogacy law today.

In 1997 a committee chaired by Margaret Brazier (hereafter "Brazier")[13] was established to review this law and current practice "to ensure that the law continued to meet public concerns". The review was prompted by examples of surrogacy reported in the press in 1996 and 1997.[14] In 1996 also the BMA declared surrogacy to be an "acceptable option of last resort", whilst stressing that "the interests of the potential child must be paramount and the risks to the surrogate mother must be kept to a minimum".[15] This was a long way from its position at the time of Warnock.

The time was ripe for a review. Surrogacy had divided the Warnock committee, the majority of which came down in favour of a conclusion ethically at odds with the pro-autonomy stand in the rest of the report.[16]

---

9 Mary Warnock, *A Question of Life* (Black well 1985), previously published as *Report of the Committee of Inquiry into Human Fertilisation and Embryology* (Cmnd. 9314) (London: HMSO, 1984).

10 See M.D.A. Freeman, "After Warnock-Whither The Law?" (1986) 39 *Current Legal Problems* 33-5. The Government insisted that "it was not as a result of the Baby Conon case that this Bill came forward" *per* the Earl of Caithness, *Hansard,* H.L. vol. 465, col. 925. See also C. Dyer, "Baby Cotton and the Birth of a Moral Panic", *The Guardian,* 15 January 1985 and A. Hutchinson and D. Morgan, "A Bill Born From Panic", *The Guardian,* 12 July 1985.

11 See M.D.A. Freeman, "The Surrogacy Arrangements Act 1985" in *Current Law Statutes Annotated* (Sweet and Maxwell 1986).

12 By the Human Fertilisation and Embryology Act 1990, on which see D. Morgan and R.G. Lee, *Blackstone's Guide To The Human Fertilisation and Embryology Act 1990* (Blackstone Press 1991).

13 The review team was Margaret Brazier, Professor of Law, University of Manchester; Alistair Campbell, Professor of Ethics in Medicine, University of Bristol and Susan Golombok, Professor of Psychology, City University, London.

14 In particular the Karen Roche case (see *The Independent,* 20 January 1997); also the arrival of the American, Bill Handel, who "advertised" his presence in the United Kingdom (without advertising in breach of the 1985 Act) and let it be known that payments of between £30,000 and £45,000 were available for willing surrogates.

15 *The Changing Conceptions of Motherhood – The Practice of Surrogacy in Britain* (BMA 1996) at 59.

16 See Freeman, *op. cit.,* note 10.

And the subject continues to divide: Van Dyck is able to detect no fewer than seven different feminist positions on surrogacy.[17]

There is, the Brazier Report acknowledges, "a policy vacuum",[18] an absence of a "coherent policy".[19] The 1985 legislation had not implemented the Warnock Report in full: had it done so, organisations like COTS and the Surrogacy Parenting Centre could not have operated, and full surrogacy would have been impossible.[20] Surprisingly, neither the Warnock Report nor the 1985 Act addressed the question of payment to surrogate mothers: both the committee and the legislature may have assumed that adoption law would act as a sufficient deterrent to money changing hands.[21] It did not do so: indeed, liberal construction by the courts facilitated the making of adoption orders where surrogates had been paid for their services.[22]

The Brazier Report, looking back to 1985, believes it was thought that surrogacy would "largely disappear",[23] that it would "wither on the vine".[24] Clearly, this has not happened, and, although accurate statistics are difficult to calculate, it has to be assumed that the number of surrogacy arrangements and births is on the increase.[25] And, contrary to early fears, it is only in a handful of cases (the Brazier Report estimates 4-5 per cent)[26] that the nightmare scenario occurs and a surrogate refuses to hand over the child.

---

17 J. Van Dyck, *Manufacturing Babies and Public Consent* (Macmillan 1995) at 172-3. See also Joan Mahoney, "An Essay On Surrogacy and Feminist Thought" in (ed.) Larry Gostin, *Surrogate Motherhood* (Indiana University Press 1990) at 183-97.

18 *Surrogacy: Review for Health Ministers of Current Arrangements For Payments and Regulation* (Cm. 4068) (Department of Health, 1998) at i (para 3).

19 *Ibid.*

20 *Ibid.*, para. 2.8.

21 This is the view of the Brazier report: see *ibid.*, para. 3.2.

22 See *Re An Adoption Application (Payment For Adoption)* [1987] Fam. 81 and *Re M.W. (Adoption: Surrogacy)* (1995] 2 F.L.R. 759.

23 *Op. cit.*, note 18, para. 3.5.

24 *Ibid.*, para. 3.44.

25 Statistics on the number of applications for parental orders are in a table on p. 6 of the *Report* (para. 1.27).

26 *Op. cit.*, note 18, para. 3.38.

## II. Brazier's Philosophy

The Brazier Report, in the words of the minister who set up the committee, looks to "provide a sensible and sensitive way forward within a framework that inspires public confidence".[27] It believes – and rightly so – that concerns have changed since the days of Warnock. Surrogacy for convenience, roundly condemned by Warnock as "totally ethically unacceptable",[28] is no longer thought to constitute a threat. Today rather, as the report sees it, it is the point at which surrogacy becomes an "acceptable alternative"[29] to other fertility treatment that is the matter in contention. But, again, we simply do not know the incidence of resort to surrogacy after failed IVF cycles. Nor today, though such concerns were voiced to the Brazier committee,[30] is opposition to surrogacy often couched in terms of the intrusion of a third party into the marriage relationship. It is perhaps surprising that this concern should have eased so much given the constant peddling of "back to basics" and the emphasis on "family values".[31]

The concerns today, as Brazier saw them,[32] are whether the law and practice adequately safeguard the welfare of the child; whether it protects the interests of the surrogate, her family and the commissioning couple – the report takes it as unproblematic that surrogacy is a service for couples – and whether it should do so; and whether payment of the surrogate is acceptable.

Although contemporary concerns differ from those current in Warnock's day, the ethical issues remain broadly the same. Warnock was concerned with the danger of exploitation: "that people should treat others as a means to their own ends, however desirable the consequences, must always be liable to moral objection. Such treatment of one person by another becomes positively exploitative when financial interests are involved".[33] Brazier acknowledges that it is not payment that makes peo-

27 *Ibid.*, para. 1.49, quoting Tessa Jowell M.P.

28 *Op. cit.*, note 9, para. 8.17.

29 *Op. cit.*, note 18, para. 4.7.

30 *Ibid.*, para. 4.5.

31 See Michael Freeman, "Family Values and Family Justice" (1997) 50 *Current Legal Problems* 315-59.

32 *Op. cit.*, note 18, para. 4.6.

33 *Op. cit.*, note 9, para. 8.17. On exploitation, see Michael Freeman, "Is Surrogacy Exploitative?" in (ed.) Sheila A.M. McLean, *Legal Issues In Human Reproduction* (Gower 1989) at 164-84. See also Alan Wertheimer, *Exploitation* (Princeton University Press 1996), ch. 4.

ple into a mere means, that, "on the contrary lack of payment (as in slavery or breadline wages) may be much more exploitative".[34] Despite this, the report advocates allowing surrogacy to continue – regulated, as we shall see – but strongly objects to surrogates being recompensed for their services.

But is it right to indict a service (or an occupation) because of its motivation? A fertility specialist who increases the happiness of many infertile couples may do so for personal aggrandisation or for wealth, but we focus on his/her results, not his/her motives for going into the occupation (or business). The objection may be to earning money by using your body, but no-one has suggested that fashion models, for example, should go financially unrewarded. Brazier's answer to this focuses on the supposed inability of surrogates to foresee the risks entailed. "Payment increases the risk of exploitation if it constitutes an inducement to participate in an activity whose degree of risk the surrogate cannot, in the nature of things, fully understand or predict".[35] The prospective surrogate's autonomy[36] must, it seems, be protected by a healthy injection of paternalism.[37] We do not purport to protect others who are economically vulnerable from entering into dangerous occupations and it is not a satisfactory answer to say that "people choosing to undertake such jobs do so with full knowledge and under standing of such risks"[38] because this is patently not so (since the examples of soldiers is given by Brazier, think of the Gulf War and its aftermath). Poor women have long worked in environmentally dangerous workplaces and where they have been excluded, for example from mines, it is not at all clear that this was to protect them.[39] More obviously, women have always taken risks with pregnancy, and much greater ones than they do now, and have done so for others (men or society at large) but, it seems, risk is only raised as a problem now that there is for the first time the prospect of financial remuneration. It is clear that Brazier would like surrogacy to come to an end. Even

34 *Op. cit.*, note 18, para. 4.23. And see Field, *op. cit.*, note 6 at 26 ("The most oppressive result of all is to allow surrogacy but prohibit the payment of any fee").

35 *Op. cit.*, note 18, para. 4.25.

36 On autonomy see S. Dodds and K. Jones "Surrogacy and Autonomy" (1989) 3 *Bioethics* 1-17, distinguishing occurrent and dispositional autonomy.

37 For agreement see L. Purdy, *Re producing Persons* (Cornell University Press 1996), ch. 11.

38 *Op. cit.*, note 18, para. 4.24.

39 And see J. Humphries, "Protective Legislation, the Capitalist State and Working Class Men: The Case of the 1842 Mines Regulation Act" (1981) 7 *Feminist Review* 1-33.

if its terms of reference had allowed it to consider the question, it would not have recommended the "full commercialisation of surrogacy".[40] In its view it is not an acceptable occupation: commercialisation would imply a "normalisation of... a difficult personal choice, with an unknown degree of psychological risk".[41] This may well be true – as yet we do not know – but it overlooks the fact that a surrogate's difficulties should be less than those of a mother relinquishing a child for adoption. On exploitation, Brazier concludes, that "there is not strong enough evidence to warrant attempts to ban surrogacy because of its effect on surrogate mothers", but "there is sufficient cause for concern to make regulation essential".[42] Whether regulation can overcome these perceived problems and risks is itself debatable: much will depend on how this is organised. Brazier's blueprint for this is discussed later in this paper.

Warnock was also concerned with the effect of a surrogacy arrangement on a child. It was "degrading to the child... since, for practical purposes, the child will have been bought for money".[43] In the Brazier Report this argument translates as "commodification".[44]

The Brazier Report does not use the concept of "commodification" in the usually accepted way. In Radin's seminal article it is the effects that surrogacy might have on children generally that is captured by the metaphor of commodification. She writes,

> If a capitalist baby industry were to come into being, with all of its accompanying paraphernalia, how could any of us, even those who did not produce infants for sale, avoid subconsciously measuring the dollar value of our children? How could our children avoid being preoccupied with measuring their own dollar value? This makes our discourse about ourselves (when we are children) and about our children (when we are parents) like our discourse about cars. In the worst case, market rhetoric could create a commodified self-conception in everyone, as the result of commodifying every attribute that differentiates us and that other people value in us, and could destroy personhood as we know it.[45]

40 *Op. cit.*, note 18, para. 4.25.
41 *Idem.*
42 *Ibid.*, para. 4.26.
43 *Op. cit.*, note 9, para. 8.11.
44 *Op. cit.*, note 18, para. 4.34.
45 M. Radin, "Market-Inalienability ", (1987) 100 *Harvard Law Review* 1849-937, at 1926.

This is an argument, though it has rather too much of the "slippery slope"[46] about it, which cannot be ignored. And the effect of surrogacy on the institution of childhood must be of concern. We have fought long enough for children to be recognised as persons (rather than perceived as property), and for their rights to be taken seriously not to compromise this success now.[47] For Brazier it is "legal considerations" (terms of a contract requiring the child to be handed over, in particular) that lead to the conclusion that "any financial arrangement that involves remuneration rather than simply expenses has to be regarded as a form of child purchase".[48] The core value, as Brazier sees it is, what Titmuss called,[49] "the gift relationship".[50] So "bearing a child for others should be seen within the context of a fully informed and free act of giving, and... neither the child nor the surrogate should be regarded as the subjects of a commercial transaction".[51] There is the assumption that gifts are unproblematic. Brazier – and the Report is not alone in this – has a model of the altruistic surrogacy with the surrogate as "virtue ethics"[52] personified. She has freely entered into the arrangement and there are no constraints. Nor will there be any problems. But how accurate a picture is this? Pressures and problems will exist, even if they are different ones.[53] Further, what has been overlooked is that the surrogate who has been paid may feel a greater obligation to hand over the child than one who has not. It could well be that in the surrogacy of the future as Brazier envisages it, there will be more "failures" than the 4-5 per cent, which is the current estimate.

46 On which see F. Schauer, "Slippery Slopes" (1985) 99 *Harvard Law Review* 361-83; W. Van Der Burg, "The Slippery Slope Argument", (1991) 102 *Ethics* 42-65 and D. Walton, *Slippery Slope Arguments* (Oxford University Press 1992).

47 And see Michael Freeman, *The Moral Status of Children* (Martinus Nijhoff 1997).

48 *Op. cit.*, note 18, para. 4.35.

49 R. Titmuss, *The Gift Relationship: From Human Blood To Social Policy* (Alien and Unwin 1970).

50 *Op. cit.*, note 18, para. 4.36.

51 *Ibid.*, para. 4.39.

52 See, for example, P. Foot, *Virtues and Vices* (University of California Press 1978); R. Hursthouse, *Beginning Lives* (Blackwell 1987); M. Slote, *From Morality To Virtue* (Oxford University Press 1992).

53 See J. Oakley, "Altruistic Surrogacy and Informed Consent", (1992) 6 *Bioethics* 269-87.

Like Warnock, Brazier rejects any suggestion that surrogacy should be prohibited by the criminal law. Warnock was anxious to avoid children being born to surrogates "subject to the taint of criminality".[54]

Brazier agrees and adds two other objections: it would constitute an unjustifiable violation of (an assumed but not proved) procreative liberty[55] (this could be justified if there were significant evidence that "any"[56] form of surrogacy resulted in significant harm); and a criminal prohibition could not be effectively policed. As far as this second consideration is concerned two points may be made. First, criminal legislation has functions other than criminal prosecution: in particular it sets moral standards.[57] It is no answer to the criminalisation of marital rape[58] that this would require the state to "police the bedrooms of the nation"[59] (the argument Brazier uses against criminalising surrogacy). The proposition – with which I agree – that surrogacy should not be criminalised is thus not supported by the argument presented. Secondly, what Brazier does not say is that by driving surrogacy "underground"[60] (the undoubted effect of a criminal prohibition), a crime tariff[61] would be created and the price of surrogacy would go up, in all probability as the quality of the service went down. The law would "protect" the market of the criminal entrepreneur. What Brazier does not appreciate is that under the scheme it designs this could anyway happen, as the supply of legitimate surrogates, starved of remuneration, dries up, and commissioning parents turn to shady agencies on the margins of the underworld who, for sums far in excess of those quoted in the Brazier report, will arrange surrogacies. Many of these surrogates will be drug addicts and doubtless some will be HIV-infected. We may live to rue the consequences of removing remuneration from surrogates.

54 *Op. cit.,* note 9, para. 8.19.

55 On which see J.A. Robertson, *Children of Choice* (Princeton University Press 1994).

56 *Op. cit.,* note 18, para. 4.38.

57 See the arguments of Karl Olivecrona in the first edition of *Law As Fact* (Einar Munksgaard 1939), at 150-61.

58 See *R* v. *R* [1992] 1 A.C. 599 and *Criminal Justice and Public Order Act 1994*, s.142.

59 *Op. cit.,* note 18, para. 4.38.

60 *Idem.*

61 See H. Parker, *The Limits of the Criminal Sanction* (Stanford University Press 1969), at 277-82.

## III. Brazier's Recommendations

Brazier recommendations relate to three matters: *payments to surrogates;* the *regulation of surrogacy;* and, *new legislation* to replace the 1985 Act and s.30 of the 1990 Act, tightening up the provisions of these Acts and providing for a new Code of Practice.

### A. *Payments to Surrogates*

It was concern about the "level"[62] of payments being made to surrogate mothers that was a major factor in the initiation of the review. Of course, information was (and is) sketchy but accounts from COTS and elsewhere suggest payments of "£15,000 or more"[63] are being made by commissioning couples to surrogates. Payments reported to Guardians Ad Litem "ranged from nothing to £12,000, averaging £3,800 where payments were made"[64] (and, therefore, though the report does not say so, less than this). In fact in cases known to Guardians Ad Litem (GALs)-those where applications for parental orders were made – in only 3 per cent of cases was payment more than £10,000.[65] The cynic might comment that if there was concern about the "level" of payments it ought to have been because the remuneration appears to be so low! That those who are not applying for parental orders are the "big spenders", as the report suggests,[66] can only be speculation. It is equally possible that they are ignorant of the law – a possibility which the report countenances in another context.[67] The review found a majority of respondents (56%) were against payments.[68] This excluded COTS members who generally favoured payments. A large majority (83 per cent) believed surrogates should not be "out of pocket as a result of their pregnancy".[69] There was less consensus in relation to loss of earnings: 75 per cent thought payments should reimburse loss of actual earnings[70] but only 31 per cent that potential earnings should be

62 *Op. cit.*, note 18, para. 3.1.
63 *Ibid.*, para. 3.4.
64 *Ibid.*, para. 1.31.
65 *Ibid.*, para. 5.6 and Annex C.
66 *Ibid.*, para. 5.7.
67 *Ibid.*, para. 6.33.
68 *Ibid.*, para. 5.8.
69 *Idem.*
70 *Ibid.*, para. 5.9.

compensated.[71] In fact, over one in six respondents wanted to prohibit payments of any kind.[72]

Brazier recommends that payments to surrogate mothers should cover only genuine expenses associated with the pregnancy[73] – a list of permissible expenses is provided[74] – and actual loss of earnings (the difference between the surrogate mother's usual earnings and state benefits).[75] A number of reasons are given to support this conclusion. First, children are not commodities to be bought and sold.[76] Of course, this is right, but Brazier is too readily dismissive of the distinction between payment for the purchase of a child and payment for a potentially risky, time-consuming and uncomfortable service. The Report also overlooks the point made by Laura Purdy[77] that paying a woman to bear a child forces us to recognise the process as socially useful and children as socially valuable creatures whose upbringing and welfare are critically important. Secondly, it is in line with emerging policy in relation to egg and sperm donors, as well as with the law on blood and live organ donation.[78] This inevitably treats the law and policy in these areas as unproblematic, which they clearly are not.[79] But it was outside the remit of the review to question beyond surrogacy, and it is equally outside the scope of this paper to do so.[80] Thirdly, women should not be influenced to become surrogate mothers by the lure of financial benefit. The review found (unsurprisingly) that many surrogates are "primarily motivated by payment".[81] The spectre of

71 *Idem.*
72 *Idem.*
73 *Ibid.*, para. 5.24.
74 *Ibid.*, para. 5.25.
75 *Ibid.*, para. 5.26.
76 *Ibid.*, para. 5.11.
77 *Op. cit.*, note 37, at 47.
78 *Op. cit.*, note 18, paras. 5.12-5.13. See also Nuffield Council on Bioethics, Human Tissue: Ethical and Legal Issues (London 1995) and European Convention for the Protection of Human Rights and Dignity of the Human Being With Regard To The Application of Biology and Medicine (1996), Article 21.
79 But see L.R. Cohen, "Increasing The Supply of Transplant Organs: The Virtues of a Future Market" (1989) 58 George Washington Law Review 1-51; C. Perry, "Human Organs and the Open Market" (1980) 91 Ethics 63-71; and G. Crespi, "Overcoming the Legal Obstacles To The Creation of a Futures Market in Bodily Organs", (1994) 55 Ohio State Law Journal 1-77.
80 In relation to organs, I questioned non-marketability in Michael Freeman, "Un Mercato Di Organi Umani?" in (ed) S Fagiuoli, *La Questione Dei Trapianti Tra Etica, Diritto, Economia* (Giuffre 1997), at 161-203.
81 *Op. cit*, note 18, para. 5.14.

surrogacy as a profession is also noted.[82] The fears here may well be exaggerated and regulation could police this. Fourthly, though conceded to be speculative, the report believes it is "not necessarily in children's best interests to learn that their surrogate mother benefitted financially from their birth or from giving them away to the commissioning couple".[83]

Clearly, children born of surrogacy arrangements have the right to be told this,[84] but done properly and at the right time, is there any reason to believe that they will be harmed by information that money passed hands? The Report implies that the right time to tell a child of his/her origins is when that child is a teenager.[85] This surely cannot be the right advice and makes one suspicious of the rest of the psychology embedded in the report.

The Report fails to appreciate that withdrawing remuneration from surrogates will only drive potential surrogates away from regulated surrogacy into an invisible and socially uncontrolled world where the regulators will be more like pimps than adoption agencies. There is every reason to control surrogacy and to guard against perceived problems, but most women will expect to be rewarded. Brazier agrees and believes that surrogacy will rarely be undertaken by strangers once its recommendations are implemented. This prognosis is misplaced: surrogacy will continue; it will probably grow as infertility increases; it will go underground and the fees will become larger. We cannot stop women exercising their autonomy, nor can we persuade them that being paid aggravates their exploitation, when common sense tells them the reverse.

### B. *Regulation*

Brazier proposes that surrogacy should be regulated. This was also the view of the minority in the Warnock Report[86] and it is supported by Singer and Wells[87] and others.[88] Brazier rests its case for regulation on protection.[89] Regulation, it says, "might reduce the more obvious hazards

82 *Ibid.*, para. 5.17.

83 *Ibid.*, para. 5.19.

84 And see Michael Freeman, "The New Birth Right? Identity and the Child of The Reproduction Revolution", (1996) 4 *International journal of Children's Rights* 273-97.

85 *Op. cit.*, note 18, para. 5.21.

86 Wendy Greengross and David Davies (see Expression of Dissent A). See also, D. Davies, "Hire-a-Womb, with Safeguards", *The Times*, 19 July 1984.

87 *Op. cit.*, note 7, at 126-8.

88 For example, the Ontario Law Reform Commission, *Human Artificial Reproduction and Related Matters* (1985) and Kim Cotton, *op. cit.*, note 5, at 69 and 186-7.

89 *Op. cit.*, note 18, paras. 6.5 and 6.6.

to the child and the others involved (including any children of the surrogate mother)".[90] The view that regulation is undesirable because its effect would be to aggravate the current situation – in effect the view of Warnock[91] – is dismissed: "the risks of not having a regulatory framework are greater than any entailed by introducing one".[92]

Like the minority in Warnock, Brazier would not outlaw surrogacy arrangements made outside the regulated service. Those not using this might find it more difficult to secure a parental order under the new section 30 of the Human Fertilisation and Embryology Act 1990, but that, it is envisaged, would be the only sanction.[93] It is my view that if surrogacy is to be regulated, as I agree it should, then all surrogacy arrangements should be thus controlled. The institution of adoption is a ready-made model: private placements, save within the context of the family, are banned and no adoption order can be made without first being vetted.[94]

Brazier investigates three options for regulatory bodies. It rejects conferring regulatory powers on infertility clinics or the Human Fertilisation and Embryology Authority: it is not right to perceive surrogacy arrangements as "merely another treatment for infertile people".[95]

Brazier is right to reject this option. Clinics and the HFEA have medical and scientific expertise and this is rarely required in the context of surrogacy. Other skills are, and these are more likely to be found in adoption-like agencies. It also rejected a new licensing authority on the ground that a "complex and expensive regulatory arrangement"[96] would be "an excessive reaction to current concerns about the practice of surrogacy".[97] It favours instead a "much simpler option":[98] "all agencies involved in surrogacy arrangements would be required to be registered by the UK Health Departments and to operate in accordance with a statutory Code of Practice".[99]

This modest proposal would not require the establishment of any new Authority. Brazier does not make out a strong case for this method of

90 *Ibid.*, para. 6.3.
91 *Ibid.*, para. 6.5.
92 *Ibid.*, para. 6.6.
93 Other sanctions are rejected: see para. 7.13.
94 See Adoption Act 1976, s.11(1), (3) and *Gatehouse* v. *Robinson* [1986] 1 W.L.R. 18.
95 *Op. cit.*, note 18, para. 6.13. See also para. 7.9.
96 *Ibid.*, para. 6.22.
97 *Idem.*
98 *Idem.*
99 *Ibid.*, para. 6.23.

regulation. Given how few surrogacy arrangements and surrogacy births there are, the logic of decentralisation is weak. Even within the control of a Code of Practice, there are bound to be differences of interpretation and whether surrogacy is approved may depend on geography. On a subject of such concern, should not authority speak with one voice? The case for a single licensing authority (Singer and Wells called it a "State Surrogacy Board")[100] is a strong one.

### C. *Reforming the Law*

Brazier recommends a new Surrogacy Act. This would address in one statute "the main legal principles" governing surrogacy arrangements and offer a surrogacy "code".[101] Rational, as opposed to panicked, legislation is to be welcomed. There are few better modern examples of morally panicked legislation than the 1985 Act (one MP said it "rightly outlaw[ed] the hell and wickedness that exists in America-where women are exploited and handled in an undignified manner for gain"),[102] and the parental order concept, introduced by the 1990 Act, was hastily conceived to respond to a problem of a constituent of its sponsor.[103]

The new Surrogacy Act would both consolidate and reform the law. Thus, Brazier recommends that surrogacy contracts should continue to be unenforceable.[104] The further question as to whether such contracts are valid or void or voidable is not addressed, but such an analytical investigation was outside the remit of the inquiry. The Report envisages the continuation of provisions in the 1985 Act prohibiting commercial agencies from assisting in the creation of surrogacy arrangements, and related provisions prohibiting advertisements.[105] Few will contest this, and Brazier desists from debating the issue. If surrogacy is to be totally regulated, this conclusion must be right. But if surrogacy is to be allowed to continue outside the framework of regulation, the proposal has less to commend it. Fertility clinics are allowed to profit from treating infertile couples. In my view the answer is clear: surrogacy should be totally regulated and the current bans on commercial activity continued.

The new Surrogacy Act would define and limit lawful payments to surrogate mothers allowing, as we have seen, only prescribed expenses and

---

100 *Op. cit.*, note 7, at 126-8.
101 *Op. cit.*, note 18, para. 7.2.
102 Harry Greenaway M.P., *Hansard*, H.C. vol. 77, col. 45.
103 Michael Jopling M.P. responding to *Re W. (Minors) (Surrogacy)* [1991] 1 F.L.R. 385.
104 *Op. cit.*, note 18, para. 7.3.
105 *Idem.*

actual loss of earnings.[106] It would also provide for the promulgation of a Code of Practice as a "model of good practice".[107] Although the details of this are to be left for the Department of Health to settle after a consultation process, the Report offers a detailed blueprint in chapter 8. This addresses a number of matters.

Commendably, the first concern is the welfare of the child.[108] The Report does not adopt a consistent line on this. In the discussion of the Code of Practice, as in the Executive Summary, the welfare of the child must be "the paramount concern of all parties to the arrangement, the courts and all other agencies involved".[109] Elsewhere in the Report, we are told that the welfare of the child "must be accorded the highest priority".[110] These are different standards. The paramountcy principle allows no space for other considerations. The child's welfare is more than just the "top item": it "rules upon or determines the course to be followed".[111] But according a child's welfare – in effect, of course, a child yet to be born – the highest priority, it becomes the "first consideration" but not the only one. It is weighted, though by how much is an unanswerable question.[112] A reading of the Report as a whole suggests that it must intend to accord the child's welfare only the "highest priority" (to use language found in other statutes[113] "the first consideration") because the interests of other parties, in particular the vulnerability of the surrogate, are constantly stressed.

The Report also gives its approval to section 13(5) of the Human Fertilisation and Embryology Act 1990[114] which, to say the least, is interesting since few others do.[115] This is the provision which, in relation to fertility services, stipulates that "A woman shall not be provided with treatment services unless account has been taken of the welfare of any child who may be born as a result of the treatment (including the need of that child for a father), and of any other child who may be affected by the birth". It is clear that surrogacy which uses fertility clinic facilities is already subject

106 *Ibid.*, paras. 5.24-5.26.
107 *Ibid.*, para. 8.1.
108 Nor all will agree: see, for example, Purdy's concern that recourse to a child's welfare is a "trump card" against a woman's autonomy. (see *op. cit.*, note 37, at 193).
109 *Op. cit.*, note 18, para. 8.3 (see also at ii).
110 *Ibid.*, paras. 4.46 and 4.50.
111 *Per* Lord MacDermott in *J* v. *C* [1970] A.C. 668, 710.
112 On which see Lord Simon of Glaisdale, *Hansard*, H.L. vol. 359, col. 544.
113 For example, the Adoption Act 1976, s.6.
114 *Op. cit.*, note 18, para. 4.33.
115 For criticisms see G. Douglas, "Assisted Reproduction and the Welfare of the Child" (1993) 46 *Current Legal Problems* 53.

to the imperative of this subsection.[116] And it is difficult to see how it can bite on those "non-tech" surrogacies which, for obvious reasons, do not. But, though the Report desists from discussing eligibility for surrogacy in these terms, its uncritical approval of section 13(5) must be seen as an endorsement not just of its content but also of its ideology. Section 13(5) was introduced and passed expressly to prevent the creation of one-parent families through assisted reproduction, and, implicitly, to prevent lesbian women from receiving treatment services. As Morgan and Lee commented: the provision "has all the hallmarks of a profamilist ideology. Assisted conception is to be, for the most part, for the married, mortgaged middle-classes".[117] Presumably, Brazier intends to rule out surrogacy for homosexuals – and this may well be right – but it ought to say so and to argue the case instead of covertly slipping in such a ban beneath the cloak of a contentious provision. Will a new section 13(5) include also the need of a child for a mother?

The Report does address eligibility, albeit briefly, and not in these terms. It argues that there should be a minimum and a maximum age for commissioning parents. It does not address criteria: the thorny question of surrogacy for post-menopausal women is thus not addressed. If the ethical arguments for not permitting post-menopausal women to receive egg donations are weak, and recent essays suggest they are,[118] *a fortiori* the case for limiting surrogacy to younger couples is unconvincing.[119] It is not clear what the Report has in mind. In 1994 the High Court upheld the decision of a Health Authority not to provide publicly-funded fertility treatment for a woman aged 37 on the grounds only of her age.[120] Is surrogacy to be similarly limited and, if so, on what grounds (the rationing of a scarce resource, surrogates?). Is it envisaged that the maximum age will apply to both men and women? Older women have a better claim to consider parenthood since in the natural order of things they will live longer than their male counter parts. On minimum age, the Report says

116 See *Principles of Medical Law* (eds.) I. Kennedy and A. Grubb (Oxford University Press 1998), at para. 10.61.

117 *Op. cit.*, note 12, at 146.

118 See F. Fisher and A. Sommerville, "To Everything There is a Season ?"; G. de Wert, "The Post-Menopause: Playground for Reproductive Technology? Some Ethical Reflections"; and I. de Beaufort, "Letter from a Post-menopausal Mother" in (eds.) J. Harris and S. Holm, *The Future of Human Reproduction* (Oxford University Press 1998) at 202-20, 221-37, 238-47.

119 Where there are no health problems.

120 *R* v. *Sheffield Health Authority, ex parte Seale* (1995) 25 B.M.L.R. 1 (the upper age limit set by the health authority for such procedures was 35).

little but implies that the age at which one can apply for a parental order, currently 18, should be raised.[121] It is anyway lower than the minimum age at which an adoption order can be applied for.[122] But whether the age specified is 18 or 21 (and it surely would be wrong to stipulate a higher age, say 25 or 30) is of no consequence: it is inconceivable that people not at least in their twenties would contemplate surrogacy. I have my doubts as to the necessity to specify an age at all.

On surrogates, the Report also indicates criteria: a minimum age (21);[123] a maximum age (no age is mentioned); having had a child and having one still living with her; a minimum period of two years between any pregnancies; a maximum number of surrogate births (one, "save where a commissioning couple seek a sibling for a previous child where the surrogate was the genetic mother").[124] The surrogate is to be provided with comprehensive information about the risks of surrogacy, and to have access to independent counselling and legal advice. The Report also recommends "a period of reflection between any initial approach to act as a surrogate and any attempt to establish a pregnancy".[125] The importance of "free, informed consent" in altruistic arrangements is also stressed.[126] The Report says nothing about the marital status of the surrogate but accordingly overlooks questions which relate to her husband's status, where she is married.

The Report sees the relationship between the surrogate and the commissioning parents as being based on a "memorandum of understanding"[127] (which, though non-contractual, would define and clarify the expectations of the parties).[128] This should record arrangements to secure the future welfare of the child, include agreements about contact between the surrogate and the child[129] (I note not between the child and the surrogate)[130] and/or what the child is to be told about his or her origins. Of course, this suggests that the Report sees contact and

121 *Op. cit.*, note 18, para. 8.4.

122 Applicants for an adoption order must be at least 21 years of age though a parent adopting his or her own child need only be 18 (Adoption Act 1976 ss.14 (1A)(1B), 15(1), as amended by the Children Act 1989, Sched. 10, para. 4).

123 *Op. cit.*, note 18, para. 8.8.

124 *Idem.*

125 *Ibid.*, para. 8.6.

126 *Idem.*

127 *Ibid.*, para. 8.12.

128 *Ibid.*, para. 8.14.

129 *Ibid.*, para. 8.13.

130 *Cf.*, the Children Act 1989, s.8.

identity questions as matters for negotiation between the commissioning parents and the surrogate, rather than as matters of public policy upon which the state has the right to dictate a clear line. On the conduct of pregnancy (matters such smoking and ante-natal care), the Report is ambivalent.[131] Are these matters of negotiation too? The Report says that they are matters to be addressed, but by whom, the regulatory body or the parties to a particular surrogacy arrangement? If regulation is to fulfill its role, then the screening out of unsuitable surrogates, which clearly includes smokers,[132] must be part of its remit.

### D. *The Revised Parental Order*

The Report makes a number of recommendations to reform the parental order scheme, currently in section 30 of the Human Fertilisation and Embryology Act 1990. First, it recommends that commissioning parents should only be eligible to apply for an order if they can establish that they have complied with the statutory limitations on payments:[133] otherwise impermissive payments should not be amenable to retrospective judicial authorisation, as is the case at present.[134] However, commissioning parents in breach would remain eligible to adopt the child. The adoption judge would thus retain the power, as now, to give retrospective authorisation to payments.[135] Adoption as a fall back position is far from satisfactory, but with Brazier I have to agree that some solution must be found so that children are not left in an unsatisfactory limbo position. The concept of a residence order only partially assists: the commissioning parents could acquire parental responsibility in this way but would share it with the surrogate[136] (and her husband if the child is produced by means of assisted procreation with his consent).[137] Since this is hardly satisfactory – it is potentially productive of disputes – adoption, however undesirable, would seem the only solution.

Brazier formulates one curious exception to the rule that surrogacy is to go through a registered agency if a parental order is to be sought

131 *Op. cit.*, note 18, para. 8.13.

132 On parental smoking as child abuse, see D. Ezra, "Sticks and Stones Can Break My Bones but Tobacco Smoke Can Kill Me: Can We Protect Children From Parents That Smoke?" (1993) 13 *St Louis University Public Law Review* 547-90.

133 *Op. cit.*, note 18, paras. 7.13.

134 See s.30(7).

135 *Op. cit.*, note 18, para. 7.13.

136 See Children Act 1989 s.l2.

137 See Human Fertilisation and Embryology Act 1990 s.28(2).

and made. Where neither the couple nor the surrogate were aware of the requirement that agencies be registered, "their lack of knowledge would not preclude the grant of a parental order"[138] where all other conditions were met. What looks like misplaced indulgence (why should ignorance of the law excuse in this context?) is compounded when, in the next sentence, it is suggested that a judge "might well be disinclined to exercise his or her discretion to grant a parental order" if it were established that the commissioning couple knew their surrogate "was only 16" and no attempt had been made to provide her with advice or counselling.[139] Those using unregistered agencies should therefore be careful to ensure 16-year-old surrogates are counselled or they use 17 or 18-year-olds or, perhaps, there is some other lesson that I have not grasped! To push the realm of fantasy further, what of a *Gillick*-competent 15-year-old surrogate?[140] If she is artificially inseminated, it is difficult to see what offence is committed.[141] If she receives counselling (after falsely representing her age), would Brazier countenance a parental order?

Secondly, Brazier recommends that parental orders should be obtained only in the High Court to ensure "the effective 'approval' of a surrogacy arrangement is given by judges of the highest experience".[142] I doubt whether this is really necessary or that, should surrogacy continue legitimately, this view will prevail in ten years time.

Thirdly, it is recommended that judges should be empowered to require DNA tests to establish the genetic relationship of the child to at least one of the commissioning couple.[143] As Brazier says, where this is not so, the parties have entered into a pre-natal adoption agreement and the general laws relating to adoption should apply.

Fourthly, Brazier recommends that guardians ad litem should have power to check criminal records to ascertain whether the commissioning couple has any criminal convictions likely to endanger the welfare of the child.[144]

Fifthly, it is recommended that the requirement in the present section 30 that at least one of the applicants be domiciled in a part of the

138 *Op. cit.*, note 18, para. 7.23.

139 *Idem.*

140 See *Gillick* v. *West Norfolk and Wisbech A.H.A.* [1986] A.C. 112.

141 Sexual intercourse with a girl under 16 is unlawful, but not the artificial insemination of such a girl.

142 See *op. cit.*, note 18, para. 7.24.

143 *Idem.*

144 *Idem.*

United Kingdom (or in the Channel Islands or the Isle of Man) be replaced by a provision that both should be habitually resident for a period of 12 months immediately preceding the application. As Brazier notes, domicile is a concept of "tortuous complexity" and "habitual residence", though far from simple, is more straightforward.[145]

The proposals for DNA tests (where necessary and it will only happen in the exceptional case), for criminal checks (presumably to establish whether either of the couple is a 'Schedule 1 offender') and for a change in personal connecting factor (though it will affect English domiciliaries who live abroad) should cause no problems.

However, if section 30 is to be revitalised (and it was, after all, a late and rushed amendment in 1990), other changes should be considered. First, if parental responsibility is to be extended to a wider category of unmarried fathers,[146] is it necessary (or desirable) to confine applications for a parental order to couples who are husbands and wives? The government proposals on parental responsibility were made late in Brazier's deliberations.[147] The Report is aware of the problems extensions may cause but throughout assumes that surrogacy arrangements are made with commissioning couples and, although it does not specifically say so, implies that they are persons who are married to each other. Would it be a step too far at this stage to allow those living together as husband and wife to apply for a parental order? If this continues not to be allowed, the unmarried couple is forced into the artificial position of one adopting and the other (or both) seeking a residence order.[148]

Secondly, the provision in s.30(2) which limits applications to the period of six months from the birth of the child seems unduly restrictive and could be relaxed or the limitation period dispensed with totally.

Thirdly, the provision in s.30(4) that at the time of the making of the order (note not the birth of the child) the husband and wife must have attained the age of 18 seems, as indicated above, unnecessary. But, if an age is to be specified, then, in accordance with Brazier's proposals, it will presumably need to be raised, though, it will be remembered, the Report does not indicate to what.

---

145 *Idem.*

146 As the Government announced in 1998.

147 They are briefly discussed at paras. 7.14 and 7.15. Too much depends on the details of the new law for its implications to be considered here. I agree with Brazier they are profound and may necessitate a rethink of the paternity provisions in the 1990 Act.

148 See *Re A.B.* (*Adoption: Joint Residence*) [1996] 1 F.L.R. 27.

Fourthly, the court must be satisfied that the surrogate and the legal father of the child "have freely, and with full understanding of what is involved, agreed unconditionally to the making of the order".[149] Where the surrogate is married, the legal father will usually be the husband (unless he can prove that he did not consent to the procedure).[150] But if he did, why should his agreement to a parental order be required? Where the surrogate is unmarried, the commissioning man will be the legal father if his sperm was used for donor insemination or in vitro fertilisation.[151] If there is medical intervention, whether he is the legal father will hinge on whether the surrogate and commissioning man are being treated "together".[152] If they are not being treated "together", and this must be the better view, neither he nor any other man is the child's legal father.[153] It may be too much to expect from surrogacy, reform that Parliament will look again at these legal parentage rules, but they are complex, confusing and ill-understood.

Fifthly, agreement cannot be dispensed with, though it is not required where the person concerned cannot be found or is incapable of giving agreement.[154] This "ground" is modelled on adoption law, but adoption law makes provision for dispensing with agreement if it is unreasonably withheld, and on a number of other grounds.[155] Consideration should be given to extending the model of adoption law to embrace these other grounds. If a surrogate freely hands over a child and subsequently refuses to agree to the making of a parental order, the opportunity to test her change of heart through the unreasonableness provision should be open. Why should she be treated any differently from any other mother who hands over her child and then changes her mind?

Sixthly, the statutory provision is currently filled out by the Parental Orders (Human Fertilisation and Embryology) Regulations 1994, which applies many of the provisions of the Adoption Act 1976 to section 30 applications and orders.[156] Thus, for example, applications are heard in private, a guardian *ad litem* is appointed for the child, and the court has a duty to safeguard and promote the welfare of the child. The child's welfare

---

149 See s.30(5).
150 Section 28(2).
151 This is the common law position and it is not affected by the 1990 Act.
152 See section 4(1)(b).
153 And see *Re Q (Parental Order)* [1996] 1 F.L.R. 369.
154 See section 30(6).
155 See Adoption Act 1976 s.16(2).
156 S.I. 1994/2767.

is the first consideration (as in adoption). However, the welfare checklist in section 1(3) of the Children Act, which explains the paramountcy test, is, we are advised, to be considered.[157] These a re matters which ought to be in primary legislation rather than in regulations or guidance, and, if there is to be a new Surrogacy Act, there is the opportunity for a rethink and a reformulation.

Seventhly, Brazier investigates the GAL's role only in relation to criminal searches. The Report overlooks the fact that children cannot be parties to section 30 proceedings. One result of this is that in this "extraordinarily complicated and sensitive area",[158] guardians are not able to instruct solicitors for the children whose interests they represent. The guardian is thus acting without the benefit of legal advice for the child. Section 30 was designed to satisfy the needs of adults, and here it clearly shows. As Cretney and Masson observe: "Despite the appointment of a guardian *ad litem* it appears that there is an expectation that all applicants who meet the basic qualifications for a parental order will obtain one".[159] Not surprisingly the Department of Health guidance envisages that it will be exceptional for a guardian to recommend that an order should not be made,[160] a view which was confirmed by evidence given to the Brazier inquiry by guardians.[161]

## IV. Conclusion

We need to make up our minds about surrogacy. Hitherto, policies pursued have been ambivalent: the 1985 Act sent a strong message of disapproval without attempting to outlaw the practice; the 1990 Act offered new resources to those who commissioned surrogates to bear children for them. The 1985 Act criminalised but did not do so totally, purporting to make a sharp separation between the public commercial world and the private world of the family. The 1990 Act offered new private family law remedies (the parental order), but in so far as other private yet commercial remedies remained (and the sting had already been removed

157 See para. 3.18.

158 See J.E. Timms, Children's Re presentation: A Practitioner's Guide (Sweet and Maxwell 1995), at 305.

159 *Principles of Family Law* (6th edn.) (Sweet and Maxwell 1997), at 947.

160 L.A.C. (94) 25.

161 *Op. cit.,* note 18, para. 3.19.

by the judiciary)[162] these were withdrawn (so contracts were declared unenforceable).[163] Neither pieces of legislation was rationally constructed or properly thought through: the first was a response to a moral panic with the surrogate the classic "folk devil";[164] the second was a hasty response to a constituent's problem.

The time is opportune for a new Surrogacy Act. Of the possible approaches to adopt, criminalisation will not work and contract has been rejected. Regulation is clearly the right answer: this was the view of the minority in Warnock and is now the way ahead as seen by Brazier. Regulation is not, however, an easy answer and regulated surrogacy will continue to throw up problems. Decentralised regulation, as favoured by Brazier, is likely to create more and greater problems. One of these will be the thorny question of recompense. If Parliament agrees with Brazier and denies women the opportunity to be financially rewarded for surrogacy services, an unregulated surrogacy with all the evils attendant upon such underground activities will emerge. Brazier would prefer surrogacy to have no future. But the Report points to a future in which it may thrive to the detriment of women, of children and of society.

162 See *Re P. (Minors)(Wardship: Surrogacy)* [1987] 2 F.L.R. 421.

163 Human Fertilisation and Embryology Act 1990 s.36.

164 See S. Cohen, *Folk Devils and Moral Panics* (McGibbon and Kee 1972).

CHAPTER 8

# Images of Child Welfare in Child Abduction Appeals

## I. Introduction

The abduction of a child – a phenomenon often involving members of ethnic minority groups – is the hangover from the concept of the child as "property".[1] Two international Conventions, one from the Council of Europe, the other the Hague Convention, have attempted to tackle the problem of international child abduction. The United Kingdom is a signatory to both Conventions, and both are incorporated in the Child Abduction and Custody Act 1985. The two Conventions have similar aims – to return abducted children promptly to home countries, so that any dispute as to their care can be determined there. The Conventions set their faces against the abductors gaining any tactical advantage from their wrongful behaviour. They can also be seen as intended to deter abductions. There is, accordingly, a presumption in favour of returning the child, and a reluctance to investigate residence and upbringing. In Children Act proceedings (at least in those which relate to a child's upbringing),[2] the child's welfare is paramount.[3] But in the context of the Conventions, the courts have interpreted welfare as congruent with the restoration of the child to her home environment.

A striking illustration of this is the case *N* v. *N*[4] where the mother had abducted the three children from Australia. In the words of the judge:

> The mother is seeking to obliterate the father from her life and the lives of the children, almost as though he were dead. If she succeeds in distancing him by ten thousand or more miles, directly or indirectly discouraging contact, what will be the long-term effect on the children of losing a devoted father in such way?[5]

1 See, *e.g.*, M.A. Mason, *From Father's Property to Children's Rights* (New York: Columbia University Press, 1994).

2 See *Re A* [1992] Faro 182.

3 Children Act 1989, s. 1(1).

4 [1995] 1 FLR 107.

5 *Ibid.*, at 112.

 | DOI:10.1163/9789004219106_009

There was some evidence, though the court thought that this should be evaluated in Australia, that this "devoted" father had sexually abused one of the children (the eight year-old-daughter). The court held that it had to weigh the psychological harm of returning the children against the psychological consequences of refusing such a return. Given that both risks were substantial, the court held that it had to speculate as to which was the more substantial and, further, in "exercising the discretion in such circumstances, due weight [had to] be given to the important primary purpose of the Convention to ensure the swift return of abducted children".[6] In the event, the welfare of the children was said to be important, but not a paramount consideration.[7]

The only reference in the Conventions-and thus in the Act-to children's welfare is in one of the Article 13 defences (which was an issue in *N* v. N).[8] To read welfare as important, rather than as paramount, is therefore a judicial construction rather than a literal reading of the legislative Act. Nonetheless it is necessary if the underlying objectives of the Conventions are to be carried through. What ought to be noted, however, is that not only is the emphasis on the child's welfare different in abduction cases, it is also located within a different objective. In Children Act cases, where paramountcy *is* the guiding principle, the courts are concerned with the best interests of the child whose upbringing is in question. But in international child abduction cases, the courts are concerned not just with the interests of the abducted child in the case in issue, but also with the interests of abducted children more generally. As Balcombe LJ explained in *Re N.*[9]

> The fact that the assistance of the court is invoked ... does not make this ordinary adversarial litigation between the father and the mother as the judge seems to have thought. Not merely is there a statutory duty to apply the Convention if the necessary facts are present, but in applying the Convention the court is concerned with the interests of the child in question and of abducted children generally.[10]

---

6 [1995] 1 FLR 107, at 113.

7 *Ibid.*, at 144. See also *Re K* [1995] 1 FLR 977.

8 An. 13(b) of the Hague Convention. This provision is discussed at some length, *infra*, in part II of this chapter.

9 [1993] 2 FLR 124.

10 *Ibid.*, at 131.

The most contentious part of the Convention – and the one which has caused most interpretational problems both in England and elsewhere – is the package of "defences" to international child abduction contained in Article 13. The "message" of the Convention is clear, and the English courts comply with it. So they "set their face against the removal of the child".[11] This should have led to Article 13 being construed strictly, but regrettably the courts have not been consistent.

## II. Assessing a Risk

Probably the most contentious provision empowers a court to refuse to return a child if there is "a grave risk that his or her return would expose the child to physical or psychological harm or otherwise place the child in an intolerable situation".[12] There are few English cases where this defence has succeeded.[13] This is the only provision in the Convention where the issue of the child's welfare can be legitimately raised, but the courts, aware as they are of the objectives of the Convention, have done their best to frustrate the endeavours of those who would invoke it. Thus, in *Re N*[14] Bracewell J said:

> it is plain that it is not a trivial risk and it is not a trivial psychological harm which is envisaged and which has to be justified and, furthermore, I am satisfied that the intolerable situation envisaged has to be something extreme and compelling.[15]

In *P* v. *P*,[16] the mother claimed that if the court ordered the return of the children to the USA she would become deeply unhappy, and this, in turn, would make the children unhappy as well. The argument was said to be "beside the point". But this was not because the courts were inhumane. "On the contrary" it was said, "there is a humane purpose underlying it in ensuring that children are not subjected to disruption through arbitrary movement by one parent".[17] On the other hand, the courts have accepted

11 *Re W* [1995] 1 FLR 878,889 *per* Wall J.
12 Arr. 13(b).
13 The first was *Re F* [1995] 2 FLR 31.
14 [1991] 1 FLR 413.
15 *Ibid.*, at 419. See also Re *C* [1989] 1 FLR 403.
16 [1992] 1 FLR 155.
17 *Ibid.*, at 161.

that psychological harm can include that suffered by the abducting parent. In *Re* G,[18] for instance, the court was convinced that to return a child to Texas would lead to the mother's mental condition worsening and a prognosis that the mother might become psychotic. Accepting the evidence provided by a consultant psychiatrist to the effect that the mother's psychotic state would import the likelihood that the mother "would be unable to look after the child",[19] Ewbank J concluded:

> I am satisfied that this is a case where Art 13 does apply and that I am not bound to send these children back to the USA, and taking into account all the circumstances of the case, I do not propose to make an order that these children should go back to the USA. In my view, the effect of an order returning the children to the USA would be that there would be a serious deterioration in the mother's condition and the children would be affected.[20]

It has also been judicially accepted that harm in this context can include financial detriments.[21] But the courts refuse to listen to the idea that a child would be in danger if she returned unaccompanied. In *Re* C,[22] the mother said she would refuse to accompany the child if he were to be returned to Australia. She asserted that the child would therefore suffer severe psychological harm. The Court of Appeal rejected this contention effectively on the basis that the mother ought to be estopped from relying on a psychological danger that she herself had created. Moreover, in *Re* L,[23] a baby of eighteen months was returned to Texas in the face of evidence that the mother might not get a visa to accompany him, and despite affidavits provided by two psychologists that stated that separation of a mother and a child of this age would be likely to cause grave psychological harm. Hollis J was of the view that, even if the mother failed to obtain a visa, the child would not be exposed to psychological harm of the necessary degree, reasoning that "[h]e knows, of course, his father although he has not seen him since last September" and "[h]e knows his paternal grandmother although less well than his father".[24] The evidence

18 [1995] 1 FLR 64.
19 *Ibid.*, at 68.
20 *Ibid.*, at 70.
21 Re M [1995] 1 FLR 1021.
22 [1989] 1 FLR 403.
23 [1993] 2 FLR 401.
24 *Ibid.*, at 405.

for these claims is not clear. On the face of it, this is an extraordinary decision, redolent of much-criticised cases in other contexts,[25] and one which it is thought, could never be reached today outside the context of an international abduction.

One of the few cases in which the defence has succeeded is *Re F*.[26] In that case, there was evidence both of domestic violence towards the mother and of physical abuse of the child.[27] The combined effect was of nightmares and bedwetting. Additionally, the child suffered from asthma. It was said that returning the child to the surroundings in which he had previously been not simply a witness to marital discord, but also a victim of it, would on the facts create a grave risk that his return would expose him to psychological harm and would place him in an intolerable situation. Even so, Butler-Sloss LJ admitted that she reached this conclusion with "considerable hesitation" noting in passing that, to her knowledge "there is no case which has been heard in an English appellate court in which that standard has been reached".[28]

The contrast with two very recent cases is striking. In *Re* S,[29] the return of a nine-year-old girl to Sweden was ordered, though there was genuine concern on the part of social services both in Camden and in Sweden that the cohabitant of the mother (the child had been brought to England on a vacation visit and not returned by the father) had sexually abused the girl. "Comity of nations"[30] seemed to weigh more with Sir Stephen Brown P than the girl's "understandable reluctance"[31] to go back to Sweden. Once in Sweden the uncomfortable process of disclosure would be repeated, this time, it seems, by the police.[32] So, together, the child and her mother would be placed in an "investigation home" where at least she would be relatively safe. It would then be up to the Swedish social authorities to find a way of protecting her.

Similarly, in *Re C*,[33] the Court of Appeal, overruling the first instance judge, ordered the return to California of children aged nine and eight

25 For example, *Re C* (MA) [1966] 1 All ER 838, the so-called "blood-tie adoption" case that caused considerable controversy.
26 [1995] 2 FLR 31.
27 See also, *Re M* [1996] 1 FLR 315.
28 *Supra*, n. 26, at 38.
29 [1999] 1 FLR 843.
30 *Ibid.*, at 848.
31 *Ibid.*, at 849.
32 *Ibid.*, at 845.
33 [1999] 1 FLR 1145.

despite the fact that this would mean, *inter alia*, contact with a father who beat them with a belt buckle. The judge was reassured that contact would be safe because it would be supervised. But he also quoted from the welfare report to the effect that "the children's thoughts and feelings about the father are dominated by their painful memories of what they consider to be his cruel and harsh mistreatment of them".[34] This, it will be observed, was readily discounted. So keen are we to uphold our international obligations to secure the return of abducted children that we forget that we also have an international obligation towards the children themselves (under the United Nations Convention on the Rights of the Child) to protect them from abuse.[35] The response – that this latter obligation ranks lower in the scale since it is not a directly enforceable right under English law – is further ammunition for those who would like to see the United Nations Convention "brought home" in a manner similar to that in which the European Convention on Human Rights and Fundamental Freedoms has been.[36]

## III. An Objecting Child

The Conventions also allow the courts to refuse to return a child in the face of that child's objections. But as a rider to this, the child has to have reached "an age and degree of maturity at which it is appropriate to take account of its views".[37] The Court of Appeal has ruled that the child's objection is an entirely separate matter from paragraph (b) of Article 13, and that there is no need to establish that the child will be at risk of physical or psychological harm before the discretion comes into play.[38]

34 *Ibid.*, at 1147.

35 Art. 19.

36 Contrary to what is often said, the Human Rights Act 1998 does not incorporate the European Convention on Human Rights and Fundamental Freedoms into English law. Rather, the Act provides, first, that wherever possible primary and subordinate legislation must be interpreted in a way which is compatible with Convention rights (s. 3), and secondly, that it is unlawful for any public authority to act in a way that is incompatible with a Convention right (ss. 6-8).

37 Art. 13.

38 In *S* v. *S* [1992] 2 FLR 492 Balcombe LJ was emphatic (at 499) that "the part of Art. 13 which relates to the child's objections to being returned is completely separate from para (b)". See also *Re M* (1990) 25 July (unreported) *per* Sir Stephen Brown P.

The Convention does not specify an age.[39] Nor does it embody a *Gillick-type* competency test.[40] In *Re R*,[41] Balcombe LJ was prepared to listen to the objections of a child of seven-and-a-half, though Millett LJ was not. Seven would appear to be the earliest age at which the English courts seem to have taken note of a child's objection.[42] What is required is not just "instinct", but "the discernment which a mature child brings to the question's implication for his or her best interests in the long and the short term".[43] Often the child's objection will be to a separation from the abducting parent, rather than to being returned to the home environment.[44] Frequently, too, the child's views will have been influenced by the abducting parent, and when the courts have deemed this to be so they have given little or no weight to those views. Balcombe LJ's remark in *S* v. *S*[45] is typical: "if the court should come to the conclusion that the child's views have been influenced by some other person, for example the abducting parent. then it is probable that little or no weight will be given to those views".[46]

Even if the child has reached the requisite level of maturity, her return may still be ordered, the child's views being merely one, not necessarily prevailing, consideration[47] (The seven-year-old girl in the case in which this was said appeared afraid to return to a home in which she recollected severe physical chastisement).[48] Where a child of sufficient maturity has expressed a wish to remain, the court must decide just how much weight to attribute to the child's views, bearing in mind the purposes of the Convention. Thus, in *S* v. *S*,[49] the court was alert to the danger that Article 13 could be interpreted in a manner which would undermine the notion that it is normally in the best interests of children that they should promptly be returned to the country from which they have

39 There is no chronological threshold in Balcombe LJ's judgment in *Re R*: see [1995] 1 FLR 716, 730.

40 See Lord Scarman's speech in *Gillick* v. *West Norfolk and Wisbech AHA* [1986] AC 112.

41 [1995] 1 FLR 716.

42 *B* v. *K* [1993] 1 FCR 382; *P* v. *S* [1992] 2 FLR 492.

43 *Re S* [1994] 1 FLR 819, 827 *per* Waite LJ.

44 See *S* v. *S* [1992] 2 FLR 492.

45 [1992] 2 FLR 492.

46 *Ibid.*, at 501. See also Thorpe J's approval of this approach in *N* v. *N* [1995] 1 FLR 107, 112.

47 See *Re K* [1995] 1 FLR 977. But this statement was made *obiter* because it was held that the child in this case had *not* reached the age and maturity required.

48 *Ibid.*, at 996.

49 [1992] 2 FLR 492.

wrongfully been removed. Balcombe LJ remarked that to give effect to a child's views where these have been influenced by some other person would be "to drive a coach and horses through the primary scheme of the Hague Convention".[50] In fact, in *S* v. *S*, the court took the view that the nine-year-old's reason for not wishing to be returned to France – she found being educated in English far easier-both independent and valid, and it upheld it.

## IV. Non-Convention Cases

When the Convention was drawn up and when the United Kingdom passed its legislation, there were comparatively few Convention countries. And in terms of understandings of child welfare the differences were not pronounced. In relation to child welfare, therefore, the Convention/non-Convention dichotomy may not always be as significant as interpretations of child welfare within Convention countries (Burkina Faso and many ex-Soviet Republics including Asiatic ones are Hague signatories). Where debates have arisen, however, is in relation to the application of Hague-type principles to non-Convention countries.

In non-Convention cases the welfare of children is the paramount consideration.[51] Accordingly, "the principles of the Convention are applicable only to the extent that they indicate what is normally in the interests of children".[52] But there is a concern that the courts are too willing to apply Hague principles to non-Convention cases. The courts have said that they will do so only where the non-Convention country applies principles not significantly different from those of the English courts.[53] But in *Re S*,[54] the case in which this statement was made, the children concerned were returned to Pakistan where, according to expert evidence, they could be deprived of the care of their mother if she re-married, formed a liaison with a man other than a close relation or was deemed unsuitable (for example, by living an un-Islamic way of life). The underlying assumption of the Convention is that:

50 *Ibid.*, at 491.
51 *D* v. *D* [1994] 1 FLR 137; *Re* Z [1999] 1 FLR 1270.
52 *D* v. *D* [1994] 1 FLR 137, 144 *per* Balcombe LJ.
53 *Re S* [1994] 1 FLR 297.
54 *Ibid.*

> the courts of all its signatories are equally concerned to ensure, and equally capable of ensuring, that both parties receive a fair hearing, and that all issues of child welfare receive a skilled, thorough and humane evaluation.[55]

But the children in *Re S* were returned to a system whose principles are not compatible with the welfare standard applied by the English courts. This does not always happen, however. In *Re JA*,[56] both Singer J and the Court of Appeal refused to return a two-year-old girl to her father in Sharjah. But the two courts gave different reasons for their decisions. Singer J relied on acquiesence and presumably therefore would have returned the child had the father not indicated an earlier willingness for her to remain. Ward LJ, however, situating his reasoning firmly within pre-Convention principles,[57] held that it would be an "abnegation of the duty of this court to the ward under its protection to surrender the determination of the ward's future to a foreign court whose regime may be inimical to the child's welfare".[58] He referred to the limited powers of the Emirates' courts and to the fact that there was no indication that welfare was the applicable test there. So, he said:

> if the mother returns to Sharjah with the child, there is no power in the court to permit her to return to this country if the father objects to that move, whatever the best interests of the child dictate. Once the mother and the child return to the Emirates, they are effectively locked in there.[59]

But there was also a welfare consideration (or transferred welfare consideration) in the opinion of Ward LJ. He was convinced by the argument that the mother's health – not merely her happiness – was at risk if she was forced to return to the Emirates. This was perceived as a risk of consequential harm to the child. If this swung the balance in favour of the mother and non-return to the child's habitual residence, one has to conclude that the mother (and the child) were fortunate to be able to point to psychiatric evidence (it can be found in the judgment)[60] which I

55 *P* v. *P* [1992] 1 FLR 155, 161 *per* Waite J.
56 [1998] 1 FLR 231.
57 *Re B's Settlement* [1940] Ch. 54; *McKee* v. *McKee* [1951] AC 352.
58 *Supra*, n. 57, at 243.
59 *Ibid.*, at 244.
60 *Ibid.*

suspect would fit any abducting mother ("adjustment disorder", "lowness of mood", "considerable anxiety accompanied by worry, disturbance in sleep and appetite and occasional bouts of crying").

The resurrection of pre-Convention sources is welcome, as is Ward LJ's reading of them. In particular, this is true of his emphasis on words in a judgment of Ormrod LJ in *Re R*[61] to the effect that "damage to a child's interest" from not making a summary order ought to be balanced against risks which include "the child being subjected to a regime of law under which the protection of their interests may be open to question".[62] Of course, there are dangers of chauvinism here in an arena in which comity is supposed to prevail.[63] Even worse, there is the suspicion that ethnocentrism (sometimes referred to as "anglo-centrism")[64] or just plain racism may intrude into decision making. These are dangers against which we must guard ourselves.

We are all further aware of the indeterminacy of the notion of welfare and best interests even within a purely domestic context.[65] Where the choice is between two jurisdictions, the problem is quite obviously accentuated. Even so, there are aspects of systems within rules, procedures and processes which militate against upholding a child's interests. There are inflexible rules related to age and gender.[66] There are systems which discriminate, often in effect penalising women and hence mothers. That we have done this ourselves in the past or come close to doing so (it is not so long ago that we abandoned custody presumptions, for example)[67] should not deflect us from trying to seek justice now, particularly when the future of vulnerable children is in issue. And we should remember that in all, or practically all, of the contested abduction cases the child is closely connected with this country, even if habitually resident elsewhere.

61 [1981] 2 FLR 416, 426.

62 *Supra*, n. 57, at 243.

63 And note Lord Diplock's language in a very different context-in The Abidin Daver [1984] AC 398, 411.

64 Identified again in a very different context: see N. MacCormick, "Children's Rights: A Test Case for Theories of Right" in N. MacCormick, *Legal* Right *and Social Democracy: Essays* in *Legal and* Political *Philosophy* (Oxford: Clarendon Press, 1982) pp. 154-7.

65 See R. Mnookin, "Child-Custody Adjudication: Judicial Functions in the Face of Indeterminacy" (1975) 39 *Law and Contemporary Problems* 226 and J. Montgomery, "Rhetoric and Welfare" (1989) 9 *Oxford journal of Legal Studies* 395.

66 An example is discussed by Ward LJ in *Re JA* [1998] 1 FLR 231 at 243.

67 And see *Re S* [1991] 2 FLR 388, 390 *per* Butler-Sloss LJ.

The courts have refused to be deflected by *forum conveniens* considerations,[68] but the truth of the matter is that often England is the most appropriate forum for the litigation of the dispute. In Convention cases, this is not a consideration that can properly be brought into the decision making process. On the other hand, it is not the least bit clear why this should not be a highly relevant factor.

## V. Looking at Other Systems – A Value Framework

The question remains as to how we should look at a child's best interests in international abduction cases. It is possible to take three distinct approaches. The first emphasises monism or universalism.[69] This directs us to believe that there is an overriding value (or set of values). International documents – the United Nations Convention on the Rights of the Child is the most obvious paradigm – are committed (or largely so) to just such an approach. On this account, what amounts to the best interests of the child should vary very little from one country to another.

The second approach, long popular, emphasises cultural relativism. Relativism emerged, early in the last century, in reaction to cultural evolutionism, which was European and often distinctly racist.[70] Cultural relativism is a theory about the way evaluations or judgements are made. To the relativist, "evaluations are relative to the cultural background out of which they arise".[71] And, according to Benedict, tolerance is a key element of cultural relativism,[72] while for Herskovits it is necessary to recognise "the dignity inherent in every body of custom".[73]

68 See *Re M* [1995] 2 FLR 224.

69 There are different models of monism: these range from the Platonic-the "Idea of the Good": see Plato, *The Republic* (Harmondsworth, Penguin, 2nd ed, 1974) (revised) pp. 504-9 – to different versions of utilitarianism, using its simplest model of a felicific calculus (as in Jeremy Bentham's *Introduction to the Principles of Morals and Legislation* (Oxford: Oxford University Press, 1996)).

70 See, *e.g.*, G.W. Stocking Jnr, *Race, Culture and Evolution* (New York: Free Press, 1968).

71 M. Herskovits, Cultural Relativism: Perspectives on Cultural Pluralism (New York: Random House, 1972) p. 14.

72 Patterns of Culture (New York: Houghton Mifflin, 1934) p. 37. See also E. Hatch, Culture and Morality: the Relativity of Values in Anthropology (New York: Columbia University Press, 1983) pp. 99-100.

73 *Man and his Works* (New York: Alfred A. Knopf, 1947) p. 76.

The contemporary philosopher, Charles Taylor, talks of the presumption of the equal worth of cultures.[74] The attraction of relativism is difficult to ignore. It is rooted in egalitarianism, liberalism and modernism. It belongs – at least, on Charles Larmore's account[75] – to a disenchanted vision of the world. It is anti-assimilationist, it is anti-imperialist, it is hostile to ethnocentrism.[76] It is sympathetic to, and would wish to protect, the traditions and rights of indigenous peoples.[77] It has the value also, in a sort of Millian way,[78] of enhancing the prospects of achieving moral knowledge, though this presupposes the possibility of real communication across cultures which, of course, is not always possible.

Relativists regard all values as the products of the customs, practices and beliefs which have, as a matter of fact, developed within a particular tradition. They deny that any value has any authority, epistemological or moral, outside of this cultural context. They deny, also, that conflict between values belonging to different traditions can be settled in any reasonable way because, so they argue, what is reasonable is itself a product of particular cultures. And so they demand of us that we ask not whether social practices like child marriage or female circumcision are justified by the moral considerations that we find convincing, but rather whether they are sanctioned by the relevant social understandings of the cultures within which they are practised.

The fundamental problem with this approach is that the culture can only be judged by endogenous value judgements, so that moral principles which derive from outside that culture have no validity. In effect, morality becomes a slave to custom.[79] But the argument in favour of any practice must be more than simply that the practice exists. A culture which permits child marriage, for example, must be able to justify legitimising this practice by a stronger argument (or series of arguments) than that there

74 *Multiculturalism and "The Politics of Recognition"* (Princeton, NJ: Princeton University Press, 1992) p. 72.

75 "Pluralism and Reasonable Disagreement" (1994) 11(1) *Social Philosophy and Policy* 61, at 71.

76 See A.A. An-Na'im, "Religious Minorities under Islamic Law and the Limits of Cultural Relativism" (1987) 9 *Human Rights Quarterly* 1.

77 See W. Kymlicka, *Liberalism, Community and Culture* (New York: Oxford University Press, 1989) and A. Gewirth, "Is Cultural Pluralism Relevant to Moral Knowledge" [1994] *Social Philosophy and Policy* 22, at 35.

78 See J.S. Mill, *On Liberty* (first published in 1859).

79 Mill referred to the "despotism of custom" in *On Liberty*. See also A. Gutmann, "The Challenge of Multiculruralism in Political Ethics" (1993) *Philosophy and Public Affairs* 171.

is – if, indeed this is the case – social consensus. An examination of the social understandings within a culture may reveal that there is no social understanding at all, or that there are conflicting understandings, misunderstandings or inconsistencies. Female circumcision, to take one example, is often justified *by* Muslims *by* reference to the Koran – but it is not there![80] Often, an examination will reveal that the so-called dominant understanding is in reality the understanding of the dominant.[81] Many cultural practices when critically examined turn upon the interpretation of a male elite (an oligarchy, clergy or judiciary): if there is now consensus, this was engineered, an ideology constructed to cloak the interests of only one section of society.[82]

Pluralism, which is the third and preferred approach, must be distinguished from relativism. For the cultural pluralist there are values independent of the context of the culture in question to which we can appeal in settling conflicts. Perhaps the biggest difference between relativism and pluralism is that the latter identifies primary values and therefore standards independent of a particular culture by which it can be judged. There are certain needs which do not vary either temporally – they are historically constant – or culturally – they are the requirement of people everywhere. There are physiological needs (food, clothing, shelter); psychological needs (comfort, affection, companionship, stimulation); social needs (dignity, respect, privacy). There are, in other words, certain minimum requirements of human welfare. They must be met whatever the conception of what constitutes a good life, and regardless of what other values are upheld in any particular culture.[83]

The monistic approach is unhelpful to any child abduction debate, though in a sense the presumption of return embodied in the Hague Convention is such a standard. Relativism is also not helpful. We cannot pretend that there is nothing to choose between the approach to child welfare in different systems. It is simply not true that "anything goes". Pluralism may offer an answer. Standards independent of culture can be identified. It is for this reason that we should not contemplate returning a child to a country where she would not be properly fed or where she

80 The practice does not exist in the teachings of any formal religion.

81 A point made forcefully by Gutmann: see A. Gutmann, *op cit.* n. 79, p. 176.

82 Also argued by Stephen A. James in relation to female circumcision in African societies: see S.A. James, "Reconciling International Human Rights and Cultural Relativism: The Case of Female Circumcision" (1994) 8 *Bioethics* 1.

83 And see J. Kekes, "Pluralism and the Value of Life" (1994) 11(1) Social Philosophy and Policy 44, at 49.

cannot be educated or where she would be violated by being forced into a marriage or compelled to undergo genital mutilation or where her needs would not be uppermost in any custody determination.

There is, I believe, in pluralism a framework which would assist the courts in making the difficult decisions that confront them when having to justify not returning a child to the country of her habitual residence. It may be argued in response that the framework offered by pluralism would plunge the judiciary into the non-justiciable. The argument would be that the judges are well qualified to evaluate systems of justice (procedures, processes, rules and principles of legal systems) but that their competence ends where issues of policy arise. But the boundary between principle and policy is unreal and unsustainable. A careful reading of reasoning processes of the judiciary in the difficult cases they have to decide in this area will demonstrate how difficult it is to maintain this boundary.

But if this is a process to commend in the context of non-Convention cases, should it stop there? The decision to admit countries to the Convention is currently taken on unduly narrow criteria – in fact little different from those employed by our judges. A framework could be created to assist the vetting process. And pluralism could offer this guidance as it could to judges even when the Convention applies. Nor should it be thought that explorations of this nature would take the judiciary beyond the remit of the Convention. Rather, it could be incorporated into the language of Article 13. Those who drew up this provision neither put flesh on a concept such as "intolerable situation" nor put that concept into any theoretical framework. The approach I have identified would fill both those lacunae.

## VI. Conclusion

We have been too ready to accept, and accept uncritically, that "welfare" bears a different meaning in the context of child abduction from that which it possesses elsewhere in legislation and litigation concerning children. Welfare is not necessarily congruent with a restoration of the *status quo ante*. Many, if not most, abductions are wrongful. Some, however, could more aptly be described as rescues. What is imperative is that we find better ways of protecting victims of abductions (and rescues) than those currently employed.

A final thought: what would the Convention have looked like had it been considered after the passing of the United Nations Convention on the Rights of the Child in 1989, rather than some years before it? The United Nations Convention, it is true, specifically repudiates abduction[84] and requires States to take all measures to combat it.[85] But it also states that "in all actions concerning children… the best interests of the child shall be a primary consideration".[86]

And it requires children to be given participatory rights in legal proceedings that go way beyond those accorded in Hague Convention litigation.[87] Hague Convention practice falls far short of these child-centred norms. It is time to rethink it.

---

84 Art. 35 states that "States Parties shall take all appropriate national, bilateral and multilateral measures to prevent the abduction, the sale of or the traffic of children for any purpose or in any form".

85 See Art. 11.

86 Art. 3.

87 See Art. 12.

CHAPTER 9

# The Limits of Children's Rights

There can be no doubt that children are amongst the most vulnerable and powerless members of our societies to-day. In the past thirty years, but not before, we have been reminded to this each time a dramatic incident of child abuse is brought to public attention. In Britain, if not elsewhere, the sad face or logo of Maria Colwell,[1] a victim at the hands of her step-father, still haunts the consciousness of society. It is perhaps fitting that the vulnerability of children should be associated with parental violence (and, now of course, sexual abuse) because for so long the argument prevailed that parents were the guardians of their children's welfare making the need for and development of children's rights otiose. It would not render children's rights advocacy redundant even were it true (as, of course, it is for most children most of the time) for the love, nurture, care and protection afforded children would still be that which particular parents deemed appropriate. Children are in this sense at their parents' 'mercy' and, as Joel Feinberg put it,[2] 'no amount of love and compassion' is an adequate substitute for the ability to demand what is ours by right.

## The Importance of Rights

Rights are important – few would now deny this. They have been called 'valuable commodities',[3] important moral coinage. In Bandman's[4] words, they 'enable us to stand with dignity, if necessary to demand what is our due without having to grovel, plead or beg'. If we have rights we are entitled to respect and dignity: no amount of benevolence or compassion can be an adequate substitute.

The children's rights movement, in some shape or form, has been with us for a century or more. An article with the title 'The Rights of Chil-

1 J. Howells, *Remember Maria,* Butterworths (1974).

2 'Duties, Rights and Claims', *American Philosophy Quarterly* 3, 137 (1966).

3 *Per* R. Wasserstrom, 'Rights, Human Rights and Racial Discrimination', *Journal of Philosophy* 61, 628 (1964). See also A. Buchanan, 'What's So Special About Rights?' *Social Philosophy and Policy* 2(1), 61 (1984).

4 'Do Children Have Any Natural Rights?, *Proceedings of the 29th Annual Meeting of Philosophy of Education Society* (1973), p. 234 at p. 236.

 | DOI:10.1163/9789004219106_010

dren' appeared as early as June 1852.[5] In France Jean Valles attempted to establish a league for the protection of the rights of children in the aftermath of the Paris Commune.[6] This was also the period of the child-saving movement and thus of the development of juvenile justice, as well as of the establishment of compulsory education. But, at this stage, it is the 'investment motive'[7] which is critical to the thinking behind children's rights: society's concern for the child is seen very much in terms of the child's usefulness to society. Children are objects of intervention rather than legal subjects. Talk of children's rights has been couched predominantly in child-saving language, in terms of salvation.[8] Its essential concern has been with protecting children, individual children, rather than with upholding the rights of children in general. And, although the distinction between two approaches to children's rights, between the 'nurturance' and 'self-determination'[9] orientation, has now been widely recognised, it is still the former that largely characterises public debate and social policy.

It is in part because of this that concern for children is still often firmly rooted in the individual child rather than children in general. With advocacy of children's rights it is not a question of protecting a particular child against an abusive or uncaring adult. The children's rights movement has now moved on to a plane where what is in issue is institutional discrimination, not a shortfall in parental or other adult behaviour.

## The Importance of Children's Rights

There are still those who argue that, however important rights are, it is not necessary to recognise as such children's rights. Where such arguments are put, they tend to employ one of two myths.

One, to which brief reference has already been made, idealises adult-child relations: it emphasises that adults (and parents in particular)

---

5 By, improbably, one Slogvolk (see *Knickerbocker*, No. 36 (1852), p. 489).

6 On which see T. Zeldin, *France 1848-1945* Oxford University Press (1973).

7 *Per* P. B. Mayer, 'The Exploitation of the American Growing Class', in D. Gottlieb (ed.), *Children's Liberation*, Prentice Hall (1973), p. 51.

8 See A. Platt The Child Savers, Chicago, University of Chicago Press (1977) and also C. R. Margolin, 'Salvation Versus Liberation: the Movement for Children's Rights In a Historical Context', *Social Problems* 22, 441 (1978).

9 See C. M. Rogers and L. S. Wrightsman, 'Attitudes Toward Children's Rights: Nurturance or Self-Determination', *Journal of Social Issues* 34(2), 59 (1978).

have the best interests of children at heart. Those who argue in this way tend, like Goldstein, Freud and Solnit[10] or indeed the British government which was recently responsible for major children's legislation,[11] to adopt a *laissez-faire* attitude towards the family.[12] Thus, the only right for children which Goldstein *et al.* would appear to accept is the child's right to autonomous parents.[13] A policy of minimum coercive intervention by the state accords, they maintain, with their 'firm belief as citizens in individual freedom and human dignity'.[14] But *whose* freedom and *what* dignity does this uphold? It certainly would not appear to be those of the child. The recent English Children Act of 1989 very much reflects this philosophy.[15] It is somewhat unfortunate that in an age when so much abuse is being uncovered that governments and writers should cling to the 'cereal packet' image of the family.

The second myth can be captured more succinctly. It sees childhood as a golden age, as the best years of our life. Childhood is synonymous with innocence. It is a time when we are spared the rigours of adult life; it is a time of freedom, of joy, of play. The argument runs that, just as we avoid the responsibilities and adversities of adult life in childhood, so there should be no necessity to think in terms of children's rights. Whether or not the premise underlying this is correct or not (and I think that the carefree nature of a child's life can be exaggerated), it represents an ideal state of affairs, and one which ill-reflects the lives of many of to-day's children and adolescents.

There are countries which to-day are systematically exterminating children as if they were vermin (Brazil and Guatemala are two well-documented examples).[16] Poverty, disease, exploitation are rife in every part

---

10 *Before The Best Interests of The Child*, Free Press, New York (1979).

11 Children Act 1989. Similar ideology is found in the recent New Zealand Children, Young Persons and their Families Act 1989.

12 To some associated with 'privatisation'. See, for example, A. Bainham, 'The Privatisation of the Public Interest in Children', *M.L.R.* 53, 206 (1990) and M. Freeman 'In the Child's Best Interests?' (1992) *C.L.P.* 173.

13 *Op. cit.*, note 10, p. 18. See also para. 10.7 on p. 189.

14 *Ibid.*, p. 12.

15 And see A. Bainham, *Children, Parents and The State*, London, Sweet & Maxwell (1988). See also L. Fox Harding, *Perspectives in Child Care Policy*, Harlow, Longman (1991).

16 See A. Vittachi, *Stolen Childhood*, Oxford, Polity Press (1989). According to a recent report a child a day is 'exterminated' in the streets of Rio de Janeiro (*The Times*, November, 30, 1991). Even in New Zealand children have been described as an 'en-

of the globe: the briefest of glances at the annual *State of the World's Children* publication soon reveals that.[17]

Even in the developed world the lives of children are fraught with deprivation. Thus, the latest data to 'emerge' from Britain reveals that, in a decade in which awareness of children's rights has heightened, child poverty numbers have nearly doubled. In a report just published[18] (written by Jonathan Bradshaw for the National Children's Bureau) the conclusion is drawn that during the 1980s 'children have borne the brunt of the changes that have occurred in the economic conditions, demographic structure and social policies of the United Kingdom'.[19] Three million children in Britain (that is 28 per cent of the total number) live on state benefits which force them to exist at or below (depending upon definition and interpretation) subsistence level. For contrast the percentage in 1979[20] was 17 per cent.

The case posited to attack those who espouse children's rights does not, therefore, command respect. Rights are important because possession of them is part of what is necessary to constitute personality. Those who lack rights are like slaves, means to others' ends, and never their own sovereigns.[21] It is surely significant that when we wish to deny rights to those who have attained chronological adulthood we label them (blacks in South Africa, the mentally retarded) children. To be a child, one does not have to be young. Foucault's aphorism[22] that 'madness is childhood' rings very true. Childhood is, of course, a social construct, a man-made phenomenon: those in authority determine who is a child.[23] That they have not done so with any consistency or, it would seem, coherent thought can not detain us here.

To say that rights are important, and important also for children, is not to gainsay the crucial part which other morally significant values, such as love, friendship and compassion, have and play in life's relationships.

---

dangered species'. See L. Max, *Children – Endangered Species*, Penguin, Auckland (1990).

17 Published by Oxford University Press on behalf of UNICEF.

18 *Child Poverty and Deprivation in the UK*, National Children's Bureau, London (1990).

19 *Ibid.* p. 51.

20 The year when the current Conservative Government came to power.

21 See I. Kant in translation by H. Paton, *The Moral Law*, Hutchinson, London (1948) (originally published in 1785).

22 *Madness and Civilisation*, Tavistock, London (1967), p. 252.

23 See A. James and A. Prout, *Constructing and Reconstructing Childhood*, Falmer Press, Basingstoke (1990).

John Kleinig[24] is surely correct to argue that 'a morality which has as its motivation merely the giving of what is due... is seriously defective'. But, short of a cultural revolution beyond our wildest dreams, rights will remain important.

And, it will remain important to recognise children's rights. As Howard Cohen put it,[25] when he explained the importance of associating the children's rights movement with other rights' movements (women, civil rights etc.), '"rights" is a militant concept to the extent that it is used as part of the ideology in a campaign for social change'. It is generally agreed that denial of rights is a bad thing, so that something should be done about it. 'Rights' enables one to talk in terms of 'entitlements'.

## Rights and Dignity

Ronald Dworkin[26] has not given any thought to children's rights but his thesis can be generalised. It is his thesis that if persons have moral rights to some thing, they are to be accorded these rights even if a utilitarian calculation shows that utility would be maximised by denying it to them. He invokes Rawls's *A Theory of Justice*[27] to illuminate the moral foundations of the rights thesis. Rawls proposes a methodology of reflective equilibrium whereby we try to fashion formulations of moral principles to the coat of moral judgment until we no longer feel inclined to change our judgments to fit the theory or our theory to fit the judgments. The ideal is a perfect fit. The mechanism for this reflective equilibrium is the social contract model: it conceives of persons in the 'original position' behind a 'veil of ignorance' (and thus ignorant of their identity, interests and entitlements) choosing the structure of the society in which they will live. Dworkin believes that these individuals 'have a responsibility to fit the particular judgments on which they act into a coherent program of action'.[28] He sees this as analogous to the way lawyers construct principles from precedent. Thus interpreted, he believes the contractual mechanism can be dropped: it is nothing more than a moral metaphor.

24 'Mill, Children and Rights', *Educational Philosophy and Theory* 8, 14 (1976).

25 *Equal Rights for Children*, Littlefield, Totowa, New Jersey (1980), p. 45.

26 See, in particular, *Taking Rights Seriously*, Duckworth, London (1978).

27 Published by Harvard University Press, Cambridge, Massachusetts in 1972. Rawls has refined his theory since. For a review of later developments see R. Arneson 'Symposium on Rawlsian Theory of Justice', *Ethics* 99, 695 (1989).

28 *Op. cit.*, note 26, p. 160.

Instead, he believes we can, and should focus on the idea that all other principles derive from the principle of equal concern and respect for each person.[29]

For Dworkin, anyone who proposes to 'take rights seriously' must accept the ideas of human dignity and political equality. He argues in favour of a fundamental right to equal concern and respect, and against any general right to liberty. The advantage of his so doing, as acknowledged by Mackie,[30] is that the right to equal concern and respect is a final and not merely 'a prima facie right' in the sense that one person's possession or enjoyment of it does not conflict with another's. Dworkin puts this forward as a 'postulate of political morality'.[31] a fundamental political right: governments must treat citizens with equal concern and respect.

## Rights – from Where?

It may be thought that, however persuasive, this argument does not take us far enough. The question still not answered is where rights come from?[32] Why do we 'have' the rights we do? In posing this question, I am asking why we have the 'moral' rights we have (and assuming that we have some), and not posing the same question about legal rights. It is obvious why we have legal rights: on *one* level the answer is that they are set out in laws (the right to consult a lawyer when in police custody[33] or the right, if adopted, to see one's original birth certificate);[34] on *another,* we have them because historical struggles to acquire them have been successful (for example the right to vote or to strike). But it is less clear why we have the moral rights we do. What 'is' there when there 'are' rights? There must be, Narveson argues, 'certain features or properties of those who 'have' them such that we have *good reason to acknowledge* the obligation to refrain from interfering with, or possibly to sometimes help

29 This is developed in *op. cit.* note 26, chs. 7, 9, 11-13. It is noteworthy that in Janusz Korczak's Declaration of Children's Rights the 'right to respect' was placed only after the 'right to love'. On the reverse (more common) see A. Miller, *The Drama of Being a Child,* London, Virago (1988), ch. 3.

30 'Can There Be a Rights-Based Moral Theory ?' in J. Waldron (ed.), *Theories of Rights,* Oxford, Oxford University Press (1964), p. 168.

31 *Op. cit.* note 26, p. 272.

32 See L. W. Sumner, *The Moral Foundation of Rights,* Oxford, Clarendon Press (1987).

33 In England, see Police and Criminal Evidence Act 1984, s. 58.

34 In England, see Adoption Act 1976, s. 51. But it is not an absolute right (see *R* v. *Registrar General ex parte Smith* (1991) 1 FLR 255).

other bearers to do the things they are said to have the right to do, or have those things they are said to have a right to have'.[35]

All then hinges on 'good reason', on moral argument. It is interesting, if surprising, that Robert Nozick,[36] an arch-apostle of rights, should do no more than assert peremptorily that 'individuals have rights'. A common justifying principle is sought in relating rights to interests.[37] Thus, Feinberg writes[38] that 'the sort of beings who can have rights are precisely those who have (or can have) interests.' Though superficially attractive this argument ultimately fails. More than the existence of an interest is required to establish a right. Conversely, so may less for if rights only exist when interests are expressed, we would have to deny rights to the comatose,[39] the mentally handicapped[40] and to babies (as well, of course, to trees,[41] rocks and animals[42] but then those who do this conflate our moral responsibilities to lesser beings and to the environment into rights-type language with unfortunate consequences).

Another argument often put forward is purely formal. It is that all persons ought to be treated alike unless there is good reason for treating them differently.[43] Dworkin accepts this: he sees the right to treatment as an equal as the morally fundamental idea. It is that which requires that each person be accorded the same degree of concern and respect as every other person. The problem with this argument lies in deciding what constitutes a 'good reason' for treating persons differently. Gender and colour are now almost universally accepted as indefensible distinctions, but age, of course, continues to ground (at both ends, be it noted) legitimate discrimination in the opinions of many. The principle looks

---

35 'Contractarian Rights in R. G. Frey (ed.), *Utility and Rights*, Oxford, Blackwell (1984), p. 161 at 164.

36 *Anarchy, State and Utopia*, Blackwell, Oxford (1974).

37 See for example, H. J. McCloskey, 'Rights', *Philosophical Quarterly* 15, 115 (1965).

38 'The Nature and Value of Rights', *Journal of Value Inquiry* 4, 243 (1970).

39 See H. Rolston, 'The Irreversibly Comatose: Respect for the Sub-Human in Human Life', *Journal of Medicine and Philosphy* 7, 337 (1982).

40 See M. D. A. Freeman, 'Sterilising The Mentally Handicapped' in M. D. A. Freeman (ed.), *Medicine, Ethics and The Law*, Stevens, London (1988).

41 See C. Stone, *Should Trees Have Standing?*, Los Altos, California, William Kaufmann (1974).

42 See T. Regan, *The Case for Animal Rights*, Berkeley, University of California Press (1983). And using Rawls, D. Van De Veer 'Of Beasts, Persons and the Original Position', *The Monist* 62, 368 (1979).

43 See P. Westen, *Speaking of Equality*, Princeton University Press, Princeton, New Jersey (1990).

egalitarian but it can backfire and become an argument used to undermine egalitarianism.

Dworkin himself, attempts to identify the existence of a moral right against the state when for 'some' reason the state would 'do wrong' to treat a person in a certain way, 'even though it would be in the general interest to do so'.[44] But, since what it is 'wrong' for the state to do is what the state has a duty not to do, Dworkin appears to be defining rights in terms of duties. It is 'wrong' for the state to act in a particular way when the individual has a 'right' on which state action of a particular sort would illegitimately trample. The circularity of the argument will be readily apparent.

The Dworkinian thesis then takes us so far – but not, it seems, far enough. Equality by itself cannot explain what Dworkin is trying to explain, namely that rights as such 'trump'[45] countervailing utilitarian considerations. Something more is needed: the concept of autonomy may supply this. A plausible theory of rights may take account not just of equality but of the normative value of autonomy, the idea that persons as such have a set of capacities that enables them to make independent decisions regarding appropriate life choices. The deep structure of the rights thesis is equality and autonomy. Kant expressed this by asserting that persons are equal and autonomous in the kingdom of ends. It is the normative value of equality and autonomy that lies at the root of the Rawlsian contractarian conception. To see people as both equal and autonomous is to repudiate the moral claim of those who would allow utilitarian calculations of the greatest happiness of the greatest number to prevail over the range of significant life choices which the rights thesis facilitates and enhances.

Utilitarianism, by contrast, insists that the pattern of individual life choices be overridden if others are those made better off. To treat persons as utilitarianism requires us to focus almost obsessively on aggregated pleasure as the only ethically significant goal. But this is to ignore the crucial fact that persons experience pleasure, and that pleasure has human and moral significance only in the context of the life that a person chooses to lead. It is the rights thesis that protects the integrity of that person in leading his or her life.

One of Dworkin's insights was to link Rawlsian contractarian theory to the language of rights. One of his failings was not to appreciate that

44 *Op. cit.*, note 26, p. 139.

45 *Ibid.*, p. 178.

both notions at the root of Kantian moral theory (equality and autonomy) were equally morally significant. When we take both equality and autonomy seriously we are back at the contractarian thinking to be found in Kant and centrally in Rawls's morality. The reason is that equality is best expressed as an original position of equal beings, and that autonomy cannot be expressed better than as the choice of those equal beings under a 'veil of ignorance'.

## Children and Double Standards

But what is the relevance of this to children? For, so the argument may be proferred, children are different. They (or at least some of them) have lesser abilities and capacities, are more vulnerable, need nurturance and protection. This, it may be thought, justifies the upholding of the double standard which is deeply embedded in our social practices and well-established in our laws, with one set of rights for adults (providing them with opportunities to exercise their powers) and another for children (providing them with protection and at the same time keeping them under adult control).

A double standard can be considered unjust where the distinction upon which it relies is not relevant: thus, for example, the colour of a person's skin is not a distinguishing mark to justify giving persons of one colour the right to vote and denying this right to persons of another (as institutionalised by the system of *apartheid* in South Africa or, indirectly, through the use of differential literacy tests in the United States before the 1964 Civil Rights Act). Is age then a relevant or a suspect point of distinction? Part of the problem lies in the fact that if we are going to give adults rights and deny them to children we must have a precise place at which to draw the line between the two (or at least that is received wisdom). Most developed countries currently draw the line at 18[46] (though it was common, previously, to set the line at 21 for no other sound reason than that 21 was the age at which medieval England deemed a man strong enough to bear full armour and fight as a knight). But no one can seriously believe there is a real distinction (in powers, competence etc.) between

46 Though this does not preclude conferring legal capacities to do specific things (make contracts, get married are examples) at earlier ages and 21 remains the age of majority for homosexual activity.

someone of 18 years and a day and someone of 17 years and 364 days.[47] The drawing of the line is arbitrary. The law abhors uncertainty and has a tendency accordingly to think in dichotomies[48] (guilty/not guilty, though the Scots with a greater penchant for indeterminancy retain a 'not proven' verdict; liable/not liable; male/female – most legal systems are ill at ease with transsexualism).[49] Similarly, the law categorises persons into adults with full capacity and minors with little or none.

But the arguments adduced to deny children and adolescents rights can equally well be produced to deny those of 'mature' years those very same rights. Take, for example, the right to vote. In England, and in most developed countries with sufficient political stability to allow political choice, the right to vote is exercisable at the age of eighteen. However, many 16 years olds, and doubtless many children of a younger age, are politically aware and are capable of making an informed political choice. We do not give them the vote because there is a widely-held belief that children in general are incompetent to exercise the responsibilities and discharge the obligations associated with full citizenship. But, if competence is the test, a by-no-means insignificant proportion of children must be granted full political status and a larger number of adults would have to be disenfranchised. Apart from incompetence, the other argument adduced is the child's lack of experience and understanding. It suggests, or at least implies, that these are gained during the traditional period of childhood. This argument typically adduces the fact (if fact it be) that children lack foresight, that given the capacity to make decisions they will make disastrous ones. But is this not the case with adults too? Look at the governments voted in by adults in Britain, the United States, Israel in recent years! If experience and/or understanding is the criterion, many children would have the vote and many adults would not.

A further argument would justify denying children the franchise in terms of a belief that the decisions of children are not based on rational considerations. Rationality can be judged from a number of perspectives, but it seems common that those who attack children's rights do so from utilitarian considerations. Thus, Scarre[50] (justifying paternalism and not specifically the withholding of democratic rights) argues for intervention in an individual's affairs 'when there is reason to believe his decisions are

47 *Cf.* H. Cohen, *op. cit.*, note 25, p. 49.

48 See V. Aubert, *In Search of The Law*, Oxford, Martin Robertson (1983), p. 93.

49 See I. Kennedy, *Treat Me Right*, Oxford University Press (1988), ch. 9.

50 See 'Children and Paternalism ', *Philosophy* 55 (1980), 117.

not based on rational considerations, and that they are likely to result in a diminution of his stock of existing good, or underachievement of his possible stock of good'. To Scarre 'rational actions are those which are directed to maximising the expected utility of the agent'. 'In addition', he says, 'actions backed by rational decisions typically manifest themselves as elements of a systematic approach adopted by the agent for maximizing his good'. Scarre's concept of rationality is unduly confined but leaving that aside, can it really be said that adults' actions are always motivated by rational considerations? Indeed, it would not be difficult to find examples of decisions motivated by rational considerations which did not maximise the agent's utility, nor were expected to do so.

It is relatively easy to demolish the arguments adduced to support the double standard employed in our treatment of adults and children. It is also not difficult to show that children to-day occupy a different status from that of the young in earlier centuries and in different cultures: the line between adulthood and minority was not drawn as clearly by earlier generations.[51] Thus children in past ages participated in what we designate as adult activities (work, sex, leisure) in ways that would shock today. What conclusions should we draw from this? If moral argument and history appear to be on the side of the enfranchisers and liberators, are we to admit that we are wrong? Should we abandon the distinction between children and adults, even if this means, as Hafen put it, 'abandoning children to their rights'?[52]

## Liberating Children

Few, it would seem, would go quite this far. Even the most extreme proponents of children's liberation would preserve some protective legislation, though wisely they would look at all claims to protect children with scepticism.[53] But the conclusion is nevertheless drawn by some that, if children worked in earlier societies then the sort of restrictions we find on child labour in developed societies should be removed. Thus Martin Hoy-

---

51 See P. Aries, *Centuries of Childhood*, J. Cape, London (1962). But *cf.* L. Pollock, *Forgotten Children*, Cambridge University Press, Cambridge (1983).

52 'Puberty, Privacy and Protection: the Risks of Children's Rights', *American Bar Association Journal* 63, 1383 (1977).

53 An excellent new history is H. Cunningham, *The Children of The Poor*, Oxford, Blackwell (1991).

les[54] in *Changing Childhood* can write of the 'crucial separation which modern children *suffer* (my emphasis) is the separation from work'. He can write this from the perspective of England (incidentally in 1979, IYC, in a book welcomed by the U.K. Association for the International Year of the Child). In England to-day, if anything, far too many children are *forced* to work,[55] allegedly part-time and often in conditions of exploitation - and they are lucky compared with children in much of the third world.[56] Certainly, when children had the 'right' to work (when 'Victorian values' so beloved of Thatcher and her cronies prevailed) they suffered.[57] Leading liberationalists, like Farson[58] and Holt,[59] would give children the right to work: in Parson's view it is part of the 'a right to economic power'.[60]

But they would give the child the right to do, in general, what any adult may legally do. Thus Holt writes:[61] 'In important matters, nobody can know better than the child himself'. So central is this to his thought that he italicises the sentence to emphasise its significance. But he recognises that young children are egocentric: they are 'animals and sensualists; to them what feels good *is* good. They are self-absorbed and selfish.... They are barbarians, primitives'.[62] Parson's manifesto is strikingly similar and so are his arguments. Thus, overriding all 'birthrights', he argues, is the right of selfdetermination. Children should have the right to decide 'the matters which affect them most directly'.[63] That these arguments are heard less volubly to-day attests to the experiences of the last decade when manifold forms of child exploitation, not least sex abuse, have captured the public imagination.

On the other hand, it must be asked how many of the structures, institutions and practices created, particularly during the twentieth-century and often under the influence of the child-saving or protectionist ideol-

---

54 Writers and Readers Publishing Co-operative, London (1979), p. 5.

55 See C. Pond and A. Searle, *The Hidden Army: Children at Work in the 1990s*, London, Low Pay Unit (1991).

56 The Anti Slavery Society publishes a continuing series on child labour.

57 The expression was first used by R. Boyson in *Down With The Poor* (1971). Mrs. Thatcher first used it in a speech reported in *The Daily Telegraph*, 16 April 1983, bottom of page.

58 *Birthrights*, Penguin, Harmondsworth (1978).

59 *Escape From Childhood*, Penguin, Harmondsworth (1975).

60 *Op. cit.*, note 58, p. 154.

61 *Op. cit.*, note 59, pp. 175-176.

62 *Ibid.*, p. 114.

63 *Op. cit.*, note 58, p. 12.

ogy, to 'protect' children actually achieve this goal.[64] Has this really been achieved, for example, by the juvenile court,[65] whatever its good intentions? Or by the institutions[66] to which children in need of protection are sent? Or by the whole panopoly of powers developed to protect children from abuse and neglect? Do systems of mandatory reporting, such as operate in the United States[67] and now elsewhere including parts of Europe,[68] or child 'protection registers' protect children or do they serve rather to ease adult conscience and offer insurance policies to social workers and others involved in the control of the problem?[69] The examples could be multiplied. But the essential failing of these systems as of others is our failure (that is the failure of all of us, and not just professionals) to recognise the moral integrity of children and treat them as persons entitled to equal concern and respect. Thus, for example, few countries only (the Nordic ones and Austria)[70] have now accepted that it is morally wrong to hit children – legislation which is likely to have a greater impact upon the conquest of child abuse than any system of reporting, registers or care legislation.[71]

## The Limits of Autonomy

In looking for a children's rights programme we must thus recognise the limits of protection: we must also note the dangers inherent in the liberationist prospectus. Too often writers on children's rights (like lawyers)

64 See L. Taylor, R. Lacey and D. Bracken, *In Whose Best Interests?*, London, Cobden Trust and Mind (1979).

65 See, for example, H. Parker *et al.*, *Receiving Juvenile Justice*, Oxford, Blackwell (1982). The juvenile court is to be renamed the 'youth court' in England in 1992.

66 See the account of 'pin-down': A. Levy and B. Kahan, *The Pindown Experience and the Protection of Children*, Stafford, Staffordshire CC (1991).

67 In the US it is reckoned that, despite the law, only a third of all instances of child abuse are reported (K. Burgdorf, *Recognition and Reporting of Child Maltreatment*, Rockville, Md, Westat (1980).

68 See J. Christopherson, 'European Child-Abuse Management Systems' in O. Stevenson (ed.), *Child Abuse*, Brighton, Wheatsheaf (1989), p. 74. Also see further K. Jones in J. Hutton *et al.* (eds.) *Dependency To Enterprise*, London RKP (1991) at p. 34.

69 See A. Solnit 'Child Abuse: The Problem' in J. Eekelaar and S. Katz (eds.), *Family Violence*, Toronto, Butterworths (1978), p. 143.

70 See the discussion in P. Newell, *Children Are People Too*, London, Bedford Square Press (1990).

71 See M. Freeman, *The Rights and Wrongs of Children*, London, Frances Pinter (1983), pp. 111-114.

have dichotomised: there is either salvation or liberation, either nurturance or selfdetermination – in Parson's pithy phrase[72] the one protects children, the other their rights. To take children's rights seriously requires us to take seriously both protection of children and recognition of their autonomy.

The view I put forward is premised on the need to respect individual autonomy and to treat persons as equals. It is not dependent on actual autonomy but on the capacity for it. For an understanding I turn again to Rawls's theory of justice.[73] It is, as I have indicated,[74] the normative value of equality and autonomy which form the substructure of the Rawlsian conception of the social contract. The principles of justice which Rawls believes we would choose in 'original position' are equal liberty and opportunity, and an arrangement of social and economic inequalities so that they are both to the greatest benefit of the least advantaged and attached to offices and positions open to all under conditions of fair equality and opportunity.[75]

The principles confine paternalism[76] (the philosophy at the root of salvation or protection) without totally eliminating it. Parties to a hypothetical social contract would know that some human beings are less capable than others; they would know about variations in intelligence and strength, and they would know of the very limited capacities of small children and the rather fuller, if incomplete, capacities of adolescents. They would take account of the in sights from cognitive psychology, which suggests that children even as young as 12 (and certainly children of 14) are as capable of making decisions about their lives as adults are for them.[77] They would also bear in mind how the actions of those with limited capacities might thwart their autonomy in a future time when their capacities were no longer as limited.

---

72 *Op. cit.*, note 58, p. 9.

73 This was set out in *A Theory of Justice*, Cambridge, Mass., Harvard University Press (1971). It has since gone through refinement and reformulation. This article starts from the 1971 statement, though draws in later developments.

74 *Ante*, p. 33.

75 In later Rawlsian writing parties in the hypothetical deliberations of the original position are now identified as giving priority to their Kantian interests in the development and exercise of their moral powers of rational autonomy and fair dealing.

76 See J. Feinberg, 'Legal Paternalism', *Canadian Journal of Philosophy* 1, 105 (1971).

77 See W. Damon, *The Social World of The Child*, San Francisco, Jossey Bass (1977); J. J. Conger, *Adolescence and Youth: Psychological Development in a Changing World*, New York, Harper and Row (1973).

These considerations would lead to an acceptance of interventions in people's lives to protect them against irrational actions. But what is to be regarded as 'irrational' must be strictly confined. Subjective values of the would-be protecter must not intrude. Irrationality must be defined in terms of a neutral theory capable of accommodating pluralistic visions of the 'good'. Further, we should be prepared to dismiss an action as irrational when it is manifestly so, 'severe and systematic', as David Richards puts it,[78] and when taking the action will lead to major, irreversible impairment of interests. We must tolerate mistakes, for, as Dworkin rightly observes[79] 'someone may have the right to do something that it is wrong for him to do'. We cannot treat persons as equals without also respecting their capacity to take risks and make mistakes. We would not be taking rights seriously if we only respected autonomy when we considered the agent was doing the right thing. But we also do not recognise a child's integrity if we allowed him to take an action (such as using hard drugs or refusing to attend school) which would seriously impair the attainment of full personality and development subsequently. The test of 'irrationality' must also be confined so that it justifies intervention only to the extent necessary to obviate the immediate harm, or to develop the capacities of rational choice by which the individual may have a reasonable chance of avoiding such harms.

The question we should ask ourselves is: what sort of action or conduct would we wish, as children, to be shielded against on the assumption that we would want to mature to a rationally autonomous adulthood and be capable of deciding on our own system of ends as free and rational beings? We would, I believe, choose principles that would enable children to mature to independent adulthood. One definition of irrationality would be such as to preclude action and conduct which would frustrate such a goal. Within the constraints of such a definition we would defend a version of paternalism. This version is not paternalism in its classical sense for within those perimeters there would be little room for children's rights at all. Furthermore, it has to be stressed that this version of paternalism is a two-edged sword in that, since the goal is rational independence, those who exercise constraints must do so in such a way as to enable children to develop their capacities.

---

78 'The Individual, The Family and The Constitution', *New York University Law Review* 55, 1 at p. 18 (1980). See also his 'Rights and Autonomy', *Ethics* 92, 13 (1981).

79 *Op. cit.*, note 26, pp. 188-189.

All paternalistic restrictions require moral justification. In many cases it is not difficult to adduce sufficient convincing reasoned argument. Thus, it is not difficult to present the case for protecting children against actions which may lead to their death or serious physical injury or mental disability. Nineteenth century legislation making it illegal for children to go down coal mines or be employed as chimney sweeps or undertake arduous work in factories (if paternalistic – for there were undoubtedly other sources also at play) can thus be defended without much trouble. So, I think, can laws designed to protect children from sexual exploitation and harassment. There are clear dangers that the suggestions of Holt, Farson and others that a child's right to self-determination includes the right to a sexual relationship with whomsoever he or she pleases could become a paedophile's charter.[80] On the other hand 'ages of consent', whether pitched at an age like 16 (as in England) or 12 (as new Dutch legislation proposes) are meaningless: the crucial factor is the presence or absence of exploitation, so that age *difference* may be of greater significance than the age of the child. A system of compulsory education (and, concomitantly, restrictions on employment) can also be defended, contrary to the arguments of some liberationists, though, it should be stressed, by 'education' is not necessarily meant education as conventionally defined. This has often been too narrow and now directed towards the development of capacities required for autonomous self-determination.

What should legitimise all these interferences with autonomy is, what has been called,[81] 'future-oriented consent'. The question is: can the restrictions be justified in terms that the child would eventually come to appreciate? Looking back, would the child appreciate and accept the reason for the restriction imposed upon him or her, given what he or she now knows as a rationally autonomous adult?

The dichotomy drawn is thus to some extent a false divide. Dichotomies and other classifications should not divert us away from the fact that true protection of children does protect their rights. It is not a question of whether child-savers or liberationists are right, for they are both correct in pointing out part of what needs recognising, and both wrong in failing to see the claims of the other side. To take children's rights seriously requires us to take seriously nurturance *and* self-determination,

80 See T. O'Carroll, *Paedophilia: The Radical Case,* Boston Alyson Publishers (1980). *Cf.* J. Ennew, *The Sexual Exploitation of Children,* Oxford, Polity Press (1986).

81 By G. Dworkin 'Paternalism' in R. Wasserstrom (ed.), *Morality and the Law,* Belmont, California, Wadsworth (1972), p. 77.

demands of us that we adopt policies, practices and laws which both protect children and their rights. Hence the *via media* I propose.[82]

Thus far this paper has looked at the limits to children's rights as these are expressed in the two paradigmatic orientations of protection and self-determination. But the limits to children's rights can be viewed from a quite different perspective as well.

## Putting Rights into Practice: Surmounting Limits

First, crucial though it is to see children's rights recognised, we must be careful not to mistake the words for the deeds. The passing of laws is only a beginning: it is a signal that must be taken up by society's institutions. That both national laws (albeit patchily) and international conventions recognise the language of rights and concepts inherent in them like dignity as applied to children is important. The case that children have rights has to a large extent been won: the burden now shifts to monitoring how well governments honour the pledges in their national laws and carry out their international obligations.

Take national laws. What impact has the recognition that juveniles deserve 'due process' had on juvenile court practices.[83] The *Gillick* ruling[84] in England that once a child had sufficient intelligence, maturity and understanding and could weigh up the 'pros and cons' of a decision-making process (in this case about contraception, but the ruling may be generalised), she was in a position to make the decision herself. This ruling has influenced, though not consistently, the most recent children's legislation in England (the Children Act 1989),[85] but the extent to which it has influenced practice is debatable. In England too the courts have established that access (visitation, contact) is a child's right,[86] but contact is still forced upon children in unfavourable circumstances, in ways which suggest the honouring of the right in the breach rather than the

82 And see M. D. A. Freeman, *The Rights and Wrongs of Children*, Frances Pinter, London (1983).

83 In the light of which see G. B. Melton 'Taking *Gault* Seriously: Toward a New Juvenile Court', *Nebraska Law Review* 68, 146 (1989).

84 *Gillick* v. *West Norfolk and Wisbech Area Health Authority* (1986) A.C. 112. But see the back-tracking in *Re R* (1991) 4 All E.R. 177.

85 See, for example, section 1, 43, 44.

86 See *M* v. *M* (1973) 2 All E.R. 81 and sections 8 and 34 of the Children Act 1989.

observance.[87] We have to guard against mere tokenism. We must be wary for it is easy to take the words for the act and think that because the words have been enacted the condition of children's lives has changed.

The same point can be made of the International Convention. It is an important achievement, particularly given the cultural diversity and widely different legal systems and traditions of the States represented in the General Assembly of the United Nations. But enacting the Convention is one thing: implementing it in the different countries of the world another. There are clearly difficulties. It is doubtful whether poorer countries can by themselves afford the Convention. They have larger populations and smaller incomes and a higher percentage of their populations tend to be children. And, though it tends to be assumed that the developed world should have no difficulty in complying, that cannot be taken for granted.

The United Kingdom for one will not find it easy to convince its critics, both within and without, that it can comply with a number of the most basic of the protections set out in the Convention. For example, Articles 26 (on social security), 27 (on a standard of living adequate for the child's physical, mental, spiritual, moral and social development) and, in some parts of the country, 28 (on the right to education – there are parts of London, for example, within a couple of kilometres of the Bank of England and the Stock Exchange, where primary education is often not available). Indeed, doubt has been cast upon whether the U.K. collects statistics in sufficient detail to demonstrate whether it can meet the rights or not.[88] But, statistics or not, there is little doubt that it does not comply with Article 10 which commits States to deal with applications by a child or his/her parents to enter or leave for the purpose of family reunification 'in a positive, humane and expeditious manner'. The administration of the immigration laws falls far short of this ideal.[89] Indeed, there are hints that Article 10 may prove the stumbling-block to the U.K. ratifying the Convention. But even if this obstacle is overcome, and the U.K. does ratify the Convention, what impact will this have on poverty, social security standards and education? And, if the U.K. cannot comply, what of the poorer nations?

---

87 There are numerous examples of this until very recently.

88 By Jonathan Bradshaw, *op. cit.*, note 18, pp. 3-4, 14-15, 52.

89 See, further, D. McGoldrick, 'The United Nations Convention on the Rights of The Child', *International Journal of Law and the Family* 5, 132 (1991); B. Walsh, 'The United Nations Convention on the Rights of the Child: A British View', *International Journal of Law and the Family* 5, 170 (1991).

There is a danger, of course, that the Convention may become nothing more than a way of keeping the developed world up to scratch. Much of the world has as much chance of implementing the Convention as sending its citizens to the moon. Unfortunately, most countries would also rather do the latter. Of course, one of the reasons why it is important that we have an international Convention is that the world as a community, having shown a commitment to the rights of children, should now take on international responsibility to ensure that all countries are able to carry out their obligations to children. But international social justice is a pious aspiration and is likely to remain such.

Legislation, national and international, is important as a symbol. This can neither be gainsaid nor underestimated. But the true recognition of children's rights requires implementation in practice. Unimplemented, partially implemented or badly implemented laws (and this applies equally to international legislation) may actually do children more harm than good.

Secondly, the passing of laws can have unfortunate side-effects and unintended consequences. Prohibition in the U.S.A. was not intended to promote the interests of the Mafia. Laws which restrict abortions are not intended, via the crime tariff, to promote the back street abortion. Rights can too easily backfire. Reform movements intended to enhance children's rights and the concomitant development of professional structures to implement such reforms often generate their own sets of problems and these can, not unnaturally, have deleterious effects on children's rights.

The reforms of one era are apt to become the problems of the next. Many examples could be given: the invention of the IQ test,[90] development of the juvenile court,[91] the practice of cautioning juveniles and thus diverting them from formal processes. Looked at in this way, can we be sure that an injection of rights into the juvenile court system (more 'due process') would not at the same time lead to an increase in more informal 'justice without trial',[92] or that more rights for children in the divorce pro-

90 See S. Rose, L.J. Kamin and R. C. Lewontin, *Not In Our Genes*, Harmondsworth, Penguin (1984), ch. 5, where the purposes of Binet in 1905 are described as 'entirely benign' (p. 84).

91 Described as the best plan 'for the conservation of human life and happiness ever conceived by civilized man' (C. W. Hoffman in J. Adams (ed.), *The Child, The Clinic and The Court*, New York, New Republic (1927), p. 266).

92 J. Skolnick, *Justice Without Trial*, Wiley, Chichester (1966).

cess would not be used as a stick to control their mothers?[93] This is not to advocate caution in furthering children's rights, but care in so doing, and to recommend adequate surveillance of the institutional practices of those to whom the task of operationalising children's rights is entrusted. And it may be doubted whether the structure to be established to oversee children's rights within the Convention is adequate within these terms.

Thirdly, rights without services are meaningless. As Monrad Paulsen wrote,[94] in relation to laws regarding the reporting of child abuse, 'no law can be better than its implementation, and implementation can be no better than resources permit'. In many, indeed most, countries children get far too little of the cake that is handed around. In the U.S.A. the phrase the 'feminization of poverty'[95] has been coined and popularised: families headed by women are said to constitute the 'new poor'. The point can be generalised. There is little point creating an improved legal framework, recognising the existence of children's rights and even heightening rights - consciousness, unless resource allocation is addressed and redressed. Ultimately, the question of rights for children dissolves into questions of distributive justice.[96]

## Implementing Rights

Where next? The recognition of children's rights, particularly on the international level, is a major advance. But, as just indicated, rights need implementation. The states, the institutions, must adapt their practices to fit in with the new ideology. On the level of national systems, we need to develop institutions like the Norwegian children's ombudsman[97] to make an ongoing assessment of the impact of policies and practices on children. Independent organisations with power and a commitment to promote the interests of children are vital if noble ideals are not to per-

93 Note the emphasisis on the 'primary caretaker' and its impact on women. See M. Fineman, 'The Politics of Custody and Gender' in C. Smart and S. Sevenhuijsen, *Child Custody and The Politics of Gender*, London, Routledge (1989).

94 'The Law and Abused Children' in R. Heifer and C. Kempe, *The Battered Child*, University of Chicago Press, Chicago (1974).

95 By Diana Pearce, Welfare Is Not *for* Women: Why The War on Poverty Cannot Conquer The Feminization of Poverty ' in L. Gordon (ed.), *Women, The State and Welfare*. University of Wisconsin Press (1990), p. 265.

96 See D. Wikler, 'Paternalism and the Mildly Retarded', *Philosophy and Public Affairs* 8, 377 (1979).

97 See M. G. Flekkoy, *A Voice For Children*, London, Jessica Kingsley (1991).

ish on the altar of political expediency. Within institutions themselves such as welfare agencies, the development of monitoring and complaints agencies[98] and advocacy services along the lines of the 'children's rights officer' pioneered in England by Dr Mike Lindsay in Leicestershire is to be commended.[99]

On the international level, it may be doubted whether the Convention pays enough attention to these problems. The implementation of the Convention is to be governed (as is so much national legislation) by the principle of the 'best interests of the child' (Article 3), though this is not further explained and is, of course, a rather indeterminate notion.[100] When the Convention comes into force, a ten-member committee will supervise the implementation of the Convention by States, which are parties to it. This committee will consist of 'experts of high moral standing and recognised competence in the field': they will serve in their personal capacity (Article 43). State Parties are required to submit written reports to the Committee 'on the measures they have adopted which given effect to the rights recognised herein, and on the progress made on the enjoyment of those rights' (Article 44). It is to be assumed, in line with practice elsewhere, that these reports will be discussed by the General Assembly, though, surprisingly, the Convention is silent as to this. The emphasis in the Convention is on assisting State Parties to meet their obligations rather then on penalising non-compliance. Specific provisions (in Article 45) permit reference of requests for technical assistance directly to UNICEF and specialised agencies. These agencies and bodies are, unusually, given a role in the Committee's monitoring process.

These measures create an innovative structure of enforcement but, I fear, an incomplete one. If the concept of an Ombudsman for children can be operationalised in a national context even in a supposedly third world country like Costa Rica, why not in an international one too?[101] If systems for reviewing child complaints can be advocated within domestic orders, why not a system whereby aggrieved children can complain and seek redress when their State, though a party to the Convention, vio-

98 In England, this process has received an impetus from the Children Act 1989 (s. 26(3)) but see M. Lindsay 'Complaints Procedures and Their Limitations' (1991) *J. S.W.F.L.*, 432.

99 See M. Lindsay, 'The Rights of The Child', Panel News (IRCHIN) 9, 10 (1989).

100 And see R. Mnookin, 'Child-Custody Adjudications: Judicial Functions in the Face of Indeterminacy', *Law and Contemporary Problems* 39(3), 226 (1975).

101 See Flekkoy, *op. cit.*, note 97, p. 197-199.

lates rights contained within it?[102] Perhaps these concepts are too ambitious for a nascent development like international children's rights. But these are directions in which we must ultimately look.

## Conclusion

Children's rights, in a famous aphorism, was once described as a 'slogan in search of a definition'.[103] It has got well beyond that stage now but it has a lot further to go if children's lives are to be measurably improved. It is often said that you can judge a society by its concern and treatment of its less privileged citizens. The same must now be said about the world community.

102 As under the European Convention on Human Rights.

103 By H. Rodham, 'Children Under the Law', *Harvard Educational Review* 43, 487 (1973).

www.ingramcontent.com/pod-product-compliance
Lightning Source LLC
Chambersburg PA
CBHW031321230926
51848CB00001B/38
*9789004219090*